Post-Communist Democracies and Party Organization

Scholars of post-communist politics often argue that parties in new democracies lack strong organizations – sizable membership, local presence, and professional management – because they don't need them to win elections and organizations may hinder a party's flexibility and efficiency in office. *Post-Communist Democracies and Party Organization* explains why some political parties are better able than others to establish themselves in new democracies and excel at staying unified in parliament, whereas others remain dominated by individuals or wither away altogether. Focusing on the democratic transitions in post-communist Europe from 1990 to 2010, Margit Tavits demonstrates that the successful establishment of a political party in a new democracy crucially depends on the strength of its organization. However, not all parties invest in organization development. Tavits finds that when parties recognize the potential of organization building, it is often the result of pragmatic professional leaders and particularly competitive, even hostile, electoral environments. This book uses data from ten post-communist democracies, including detailed analysis of parties in the Czech Republic, Estonia, Hungary, and Poland.

Margit Tavits is an Associate Professor of Political Science at Washington University in St. Louis. She is the author of *Presidents with Prime Ministers: Do Direct Elections Matter?* (2009).

Post-Communist Democracies and Party Organization

MARGIT TAVITS

Washington University, St. Louis, MO

CAMBRIDGE
UNIVERSITY PRESS

CAMBRIDGE UNIVERSITY PRESS
Cambridge, New York, Melbourne, Madrid, Cape Town,
Singapore, São Paulo, Delhi, Mexico City

Cambridge University Press
32 Avenue of the Americas, New York, NY 10013-2473, USA

www.cambridge.org
Information on this title: www.cambridge.org/9781107683358

First published 2013

Printed in the United States of America

A catalog record for this publication is available from the British Library.

Library of Congress Cataloging in Publication Data

Tavits, Margit.
Post-communist democracies and party organization / Margit Tavits, Washington University,
St Louis, MO.
   pages cm
Includes bibliographical references and index.
ISBN 978-1-107-03569-0 (hardback) – ISBN 978-1-107-68335-8 (pbk.)
1. Democratization – Europe.   2. Post-communism – Europe.   3. Political parties – Europe.
4. Europe – Politics and government – 1989–   I. Title.
JN12.T38   2013
324.2094–dc23   2013008967

ISBN 978-1-107-03569-0 Hardback
ISBN 978-1-107-68335-8 Paperback

Contents

Acknowledgments

I have benefited a great deal from the generosity of many people while writing this book.

Many colleagues and friends provided the encouragement to proceed and were generous with their guidance and comments along the way. Specifically, from the earliest stages of the project, discussions with Kevin Deegan-Krause, Anna Grzymala-Busse, and Joshua Tucker provided helpful pointers and much-needed advice. I am also very grateful to those who read and commented on the entire manuscript: Jim Adams and Anna Grzymala-Busse (who not just read the entire manuscript, but helped me with the project through its various stages), André Blais, Ben Bricker, Zsolt Enyedi, Sean Hanley, Tim Haughton, Frances Millard, Bill Mishler, Bing Powell, Guillermo Rosas, Susan Scarrow, Yael Shomer, and Zeynep Somer-Topcu. I am equally indebted to Ken Janda and Scott Morgenstern – who read some chapters of the book, improving them greatly – and to Pradeep Chhibber, Brian Crisp, Kevin Deegan-Krause, Matt Gabel, Herbert Kitschelt, Scott Mainwaring, Bonnie Meguid, and Joshua Potter, who closely read and commented on one or more papers that eventually – and thanks to them in a significantly improved form – became part of the book. Along the way, critical comments from and discussions with Klaus Armingeon, Robin Best, Thomas Bräuninger, José Antonio Cheibub, Thomas Gschwend, Gretchen Helmke, Seth Jolly, and Thomas König on various parts of the book project greatly helped sharpen and clarify my arguments. I was also fortunate to have the opportunity to present portions of this book and receive insightful comments from audiences at Syracuse University, University of Bern, University of Mannheim, and University of Rochester, and at the Annual Meetings of the Midwest Political Science Association (2009) and American Political Science Association (2008, 2009). Because of the suggestions and criticisms from all of these people, the book is much better than it otherwise would have been.

This book has greatly benefited from the diligent work of many research assistants. Paul Bellinger, Ben Bricker, Carlos Costa, Magdalena Drabik, Eve Ilves, Tomáš Lacina, Corinne Mitchell, Santiago Olivella, Michał Pawlak, Joshua Potter, Jan Prouza, Lingling Qi, Aleksandra Sabik, Viktoryia Schnose, Agnes Simon, and Eszter Simon provided invaluable help with collecting, managing, cleaning, and analyzing the data; conducting fieldwork; and proofreading the manuscript. I also could not have done without the kind help of Zsolt Enyedi, Sylwia Gołaszewska, Pavel Kuklík, Natalia Letki, Lukáš Linek, Jan Outlý, Václav Sklenář, and Zuzana Špolcová, who were instrumental in locating and accessing some of the data for this project. The many party officials in the Czech Republic, Estonia, Hungary, and Poland who I met or corresponded with were extremely generous with their time and support in helping me understand their party organizations. I am very grateful for having had the opportunity to meet and learn from these wonderful people, and for the informative and fun time during my fieldwork in these countries.

Thank you also to Robert Dreesen, my editor at Cambridge University Press, for his advice and help along the way. Abigail Zorbaugh and Shana Meyer managed the production process and kept everything in order and everyone on schedule.

Financial support from the Weidenbaum Center of Washington University in St. Louis made completing this project possible. Preliminary research also greatly benefited from a University of Missouri Research Board grant. Research leave granted by Washington University in St. Louis allowed me to finish the book on schedule.

Parts of Chapter 2 have been published in "Organizing for Success: Party Organizational Strength and Electoral Performance in Postcommunist Europe," *Journal of Politics* 74(1): pp. 83–97, 2012 (Copyright © 2012 Southern Political Science Association), and parts of Chapter 4 appeared in "Party Organizational Strength and Party Unity in Post-Communist Europe," *European Political Science Review* 4(3): pp. 409–431, 2012 (Copyright © 2011 European Consortium for Political Research). Sections from both articles are reprinted here with the permission of Cambridge University Press. Parts of Chapter 5 appeared earlier in "Power within Parties: The Strength of the Local Party and MP Independence in Postcommunist Europe," *American Journal of Political Science* 55(4): 923–936, 2011 (Copyright © 2011 Midwest Political Science Association), and are reprinted with the permission of Wiley-Blackwell.

My greatest thanks go to my husband, Taavi, for his endless encouragement and support; detailed, honest, and most helpful criticism; and devotion to helping me follow through with this project as he has done with all the other ones before. I was in the middle of writing the case studies in Chapter 3 when we rushed to the hospital to welcome our little daughter Rita Maria; and in the process of choosing the cover design for the book when our second little sunshine – Linda Karolina – arrived. I want to thank them, too, for the deep sense of contentment and joy that they continue to provide.

1

Introduction

Why are some parties better able than others to establish themselves in new democracies? Specifically, why do some parties succeed electorally and survive and others die? Why are some parties better at becoming unified and cohesive in parliament while others remain dominated by individuals and are less successful in forming "responsible parties"? These questions are critical for understanding democratic consolidation. Numerous studies draw a direct link between party institutionalization and democratic consolidation (Bielasiak 1997, 2002; Birch 2003; Diamond and Linz 1989; Dix 1992; Elster, Offe, and Preuss 1998; Kitschelt et al. 1999; Kostelecky 2002; Kuenzi and Lambright 2005; Levitsky and Cameron 2003; P. Lewis 2000, 2001; Mainwaring 1999; McGuire 1997; Mozafar and Scarritt 2005; Olson 1998; Pridham 1995; Roberts and Wibbels 1999; Stoner-Weiss 2001; Tworzecki 2003). Stable parties generate clear expectations about the political actors, their behavior, and the overall structure and rules of party competition. Because of the stability and predictability, institutionalized parties can perform the fundamental functions of representation more effectively and have less incentive to break the democratic rules of the game. Innes (2002, 85) notes that if parties fail to provide a stable linkage between state and society, democracies will be vulnerable to instability and takeover regardless of "how efficient other institutions of state may have become." Understanding what determines this institutionalization is therefore directly related to the deeper concern over the quality and survival of democracy.

Parties that are able to successfully establish themselves (or institutionalize) – that is, succeed and survive electorally and become cohesive entities in office – form the basis of the new democratic party systems.[1] It is these parties that are

---

[1] This definition of party institutionalization or stability builds directly on the existing literature, which considers coherence (unity) and stable roots in society (electoral support) as the central

responsible for setting up and consolidating the new regime. They become the primary vehicles for integrating diverse interests, formulating policy, and holding officials accountable. These parties also determine which of the preexisting cleavages become politicized and thereby define the bases for future political competition (Zielinski 2002). As the world continues to witness democratic transitions, understanding which of the initial scores of electoral formations remain viable political forces determining the direction of the new regime is ever more relevant. In addition to the broader theoretical and practical significance, the elites in democratizing countries themselves are likely to be interested in the strategies of building viable and unified parties.

Answers to these questions are anything but straightforward as several expectations about party competition, developed on the basis of the experience of advanced democracies, are not likely to hold in newly democratized countries. For example, authoritarian regimes often attempt to level social stratification and other types of cleavages, hindering or entirely preventing the classical cleavage-based party competition from automatically forming after democratization. Similarly, voters in post-authoritarian regimes lack experience with multiparty competition, may have poor understanding of the democratic process, and may not be able to articulate their own (ideological) interests, thus posing a challenge to interest-based representation. Uncertain about voter preferences, lacking identity, facing the initial problem of legitimacy, and dealing with uncommitted elites, how can parties establish themselves in post-authoritarian multiparty democracies?

Focusing on the democratic transitions in post-communist Europe during the period of 1990–2010, this study provides a fresh perspective to understanding the development of parties in new democracies. It demonstrates that the successful establishment of a party in a new democracy crucially depends on the strength of its organization. Specifically, I argue that political parties that invest in strong party organizations (including cultivating a large membership, developing an extensive network of visible local branch offices, and building professional, specialized, and permanent central office staff) are more likely to succeed electorally, survive as significant players in the electoral arena, and behave cohesively in the parliament. That is, they are more likely to establish themselves as the basis of the new party system than those parties whose organizations are weak.

The study takes a step further and addresses a puzzle emerging from these findings: Given the positive effects of party organizational strength, why do only some parties build strong organizations? The evidence suggests that parties with pragmatically oriented professional leaders and those that have faced particularly competitive, even hostile, electoral environments are more likely to invest in strong organizations than those that are led by intellectually and

---

dimensions of the concept (Basedau and Stroh 2008; Dix 1992; Kuenzi and Lambright 2001; Mainwaring 1998).

ideologically oriented amateur leaders and those that have initially experienced easy electoral victories. I also find that uneven distribution of organizational strength within a party, with some local party branches being stronger than others, influences intraorganizational power distribution. Organizationally strong branches are powerful and influential within parties. This may pose an additional obstacle for building party organizations in new democracies because by strengthening the organization, the leadership may be weakening its own power. Although not all parties may build strong organizations because of environmental disincentives, leadership style, or concerns over power distribution, party competition in the critical years after transition is likely to be dominated by those that do.

That party organizations matter goes against the conventional wisdom according to which parties in new democracies do not need and are not likely to build organizations (Agh 1997; Kopecky 1995; Lewis 1996; Mair 1997; Olson 1998; Perkins 1996; Szczerbiak 1999a; Toole 2003; Van Biezen 2003). At the same time, the focus on party structures is in line with the general organizational theory in sociology, economics, and management, which has long recognized that internal organizational factors play at least an equal if not a more important role than environmental constraints in determining organizational success (Lenz 1980; Pfeffer 1997; Scott 2004). Political parties are similarly not simply at the mercy of institutional and social conditions; rather, they can be considered as active agents capable of navigating environmental constraints and influencing their performance through their internal structures (see also Grzymala-Busse 2002a; Panebianco 1988). The goal of this study is to understand whether and how this happens.

Instability of Parties in New Democracies: The Practical Relevance of the Study

Which parties are able to succeed, survive, and unify is not just an interesting theoretical puzzle, but has also been one of the central practical concerns of post-communist democratic transition. As multiple studies document, parties in new democracies often experience large-scale redistribution of votes, and this volatility is related to frequent deaths of existing parties and births of new ones (Birch 2003; Epperly 2011; Innes 2002; Olson 1998; Tavits 2005, 2008a). Such instability of party systems has remained a source of puzzlement and concern. Similarly, studies document the low levels of party discipline in the new parliaments – a phenomenon that further hampered the development of nascent parties in the new regimes (McMenamin and Gwiazda 2011; Montgomery 1996, 1999; Shabad and Slomczynski 2004; Zielinski, Slomczynski, and Shabad 2005).

Although the electoral arena has remained highly unpredictable overall, there are also important differences both across countries and between different parties in the same country in terms of their ability to establish themselves in the new regime. Some parties are systematically better able to cope with the uncertainty than others. What separates these parties from the rest? For example, Rose and Munro (2003) report that, on average, twenty-five parties have won more than 1 percent of votes at least once in any given Central and Eastern European (CEE) country, but only four out of those twenty-five have contested all democratic elections. The survival rate was lowest in Latvia, where only two out of twenty-nine parties contested all elections, and highest in Hungary, where six out of fifteen stayed in the game. Similarly, some parties continued to function as a collection of individuals rather than a unified entity, whereas others were able to adhere to collective accountability and representation. For example, Tavits (2012) reports a fourfold difference in the voting unity of the most and the least unified party in the Czech Republic (0.20 versus 0.96 on a weighted agreement index, where $0 =$ perfect disunity and $1 =$ perfect unity) and a little less than a threefold difference in Poland (0.38 versus 0.98).

The following examples illustrate the significant variance in party instability in post-communist democracies. In Poland, twenty-nine parties and electoral formations were elected into the Sejm in 1991. Only five of those survived through the next election and only two parties – the Polish Peasant Party (PSL) and Democratic Left Alliance (SLD) – were still present in the political scene in some form in 2010. What is different about those two compared to the other twenty-seven original contestants that did not make it? More specifically, Solidarity Electoral Alliance (AWS) ran the first time in 1997 and went on to win about 34 percent of the vote and form a government. In the next election in 2001, however, it received only 5.6 percent of the vote – a result that left AWS without a seat. On the other hand, during the twenty years under consideration, PSL continued to receive at least 7–9 percent of the vote (with a maximum of 15.4 percent in 1993) regardless of whether they were involved in scandals while a governing partner or sat quietly on the opposition bench.

In Estonia, the Coalition Party (KE) won an impressive 32 percent of the vote in 1995, but was able to get only about 7 percent of the vote in the next election and then disintegrated. Similarly, Res Publica (RP) arrived like a meteor (Taagepera 2006) in 2003, receiving about 25 percent of the vote, but ceased to exist four years later when its only viable survival strategy was to merge with another party. At the same time, the Center Party (K) has lived through scandals, which included the resignation, and a temporary absence from politics, of its long-term chairman, with a stable 23–26 percent electoral support.

In Hungary, the Hungarian Democratic Forum (MDF), initially the largest party in parliament, was struggling only a few years later to clear the electoral threshold and faced the threat of being subsumed by another party – the Alliance of Young Democrats (Fidesz). Similarly, the Independent Party of Smallholders (FKgP), which was still the third-largest party in parliament in 1998, was left without a seat four years later and practically ceased to exist as a serious political player. At the same time, the Hungarian Socialist Party

(MSzP) continued to consolidate its support throughout most of the period under study.

Parties in post-communist countries also tended to lack party unity as witnessed in the following cases. Montgomery (1999) reports that in Hungary, MDF fared the worst in this regard as well: together with the Alliance of Free Democrats (SzDSz) these two leading parties emerging from the democratic opposition movement suffered the greatest number of "deserters" and the lowest level of party discipline. The study further argues that only two factions emerged as disciplined: those of MSzP and Fidesz.

For the Czech Republic, according to Kopecky (2000), the Civic Democratic Alliance (ODA) – a party with dissident roots but a short life cycle – was reluctant to impose party discipline and remained dominated by individuals. The Republicans (SPR-RSČ) – another party dominated by individuals – also suffered significant defections and was swept off the political map. R. Zubek (2008) describes that in Poland, too, some parties (SLD and PSL) followed strict intra-party rules for discipline in parliament (see also Grzymala-Busse 2002a); others (notably AWS) lacked such rules. Indeed, several AWS MPs were being noncooperative toward their own party's bills because they did not want to be the rubber stamps of the party (R. Zubek 2008).

These examples illustrate a nontrivial puzzle: Why do some parties succeed, prosper, and unify while others remain fragile and wither? This question remains a serious concern both for voters and parties in new democracies. For this reason, there is potentially a high payoff for research that helps us better understand factors that contribute systematically to the institutionalization of individual parties.

The Theoretical Relevance of the Study

In addition to practical relevance, this study also helps address significant gaps in the scholarly literature. This study, with an explicit focus on the level of the party, is unlike most research on new democracies, which has taken a system-level approach. Several variables have been linked to the stability of *party systems* in new democracies, including the permissiveness of electoral and other political institutions (Birch 2003; Duverger 1954; Elster et al. 1998; Kostelecky 2002; Tavits 2005), the emergence and strength of social cleavages (Bielasiak 1997; Evans and Whitefield 1993; Roberts and Wibbels 1999; Tworzecki 2003), legacies of the previous regime (Kitschelt et al. 1999), and economic conditions (Nooruddin and Chhibber 2008; Pacek 1994; Tucker 2006). Although greatly informative of the cross-national variance, these explanations are not able (and are not meant) to fully account for the variance in the success, survival, and unity of parties *within* countries. Some parties are clearly better at coping with these environmental constraints than others. The current study, therefore, provides a much-needed addition to the study of parties and party systems in new democracies.

By focusing on an organizational explanation of party formation and stabilization, the current study also represents a direct response to the calls for developing an explanatory theory of party organizations (see Janda 1993; Meleshevich 2007; Montero and Gunther 2002; Sartori 1976). Whereas the early theoretical work by Duverger, Michels, and Ostrogorski followed a sociological perspective and an explicitly organizational approach, the recent literature has been criticized for avoiding the subject of party organizations (Gibson, Cotter, and Bibby 1983; Janda 1993). Indeed, the literature is relatively scarce on organizational explanations of party electoral performance. The explanatory (and especially quantitative) analysis of party organizations has largely been limited to the U.S. context (Coleman 1996; Cotter et al. 1984; Crotty 1971; Pomper 1990). An exception to this is a comparative study by Janda and Colman (1998), but it relies on data collected in the 1950s and is by now outdated. In the post-communist context, a few studies have provided organizational explanations of specific, mostly former communist, parties (Grzymala-Busse 2002a; Ishiyama 2001; see also Golosov 1998). However, we lack an explanation of organizational effects more broadly – that is, how they apply to all parties, not just the successors to the communist party.

Literature that considers party unity in parliament – another indicator of the extent to which a party has been able to establish itself – is also devoid of organizational explanations. Rather, the focus is on political institutions, including electoral systems, presidentialism, and federalism, as they influence party unity (Carey 2007; Diermeier and Feddersen 1998; Hix, Noury, and Roland 2005; Mainwaring 1999; Morgenstern 2004; Owens 2003; Sieberer 2006). This research rarely examines party influence on legislative individualism directly. Parties are not conceived of as active agents and party influence is assumed to result from specific institutional structures. At the same time, recent research has shown that legislators can behave rather differently under the same institutional arrangements (Desposato 2006; Herron 2002; Morgenstern and Swindle 2005; Thames 2005). Haspel, Remington, and Smith (1998) and Kunicova and Remington (2008), for example, find no significant difference in the discipline of Russian Duma members elected from single-member districts as opposed to those elected on the basis of party lists. However, they do find significant differences in voting unity across parties, suggesting that party-level factors are likely to have a direct effect on parliamentary behavior.

By providing and analyzing systematic cross-national data on party organizational strength and party institutionalization in the electorate and in parliament, the current study directly addresses these gaps in the existing literature. It not only attempts to demonstrate the relevance or irrelevance of party organizations in the process of democratic development, but also contributes to understanding the broader theoretical questions about party behavior in different arenas and about the consequences of party organizational strength.

Last but not least, one of the most understudied aspects of party literature that this study contributes to concerns the origins of party organizational strength. As is evident in the discussion that follows, there is minimal

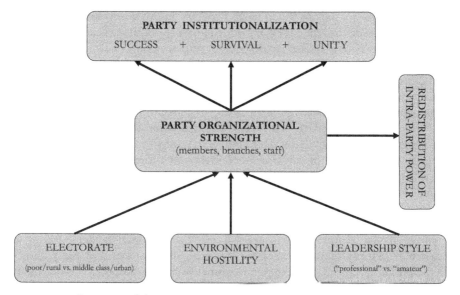

FIGURE 1.1. Summary of the argument.

theoretical guidance to help the empirical exploration of this question. Although the analysis here is understandably exploratory in nature and the conclusions remain tentative, the potential contribution to helping advance future research on the question of why some parties have strong and others weak organizations is significant.

The Causes and Effects of Strong Organizations: Summary of the Main Arguments

Party organizational strength indicates the extensiveness, professionalization, and reach of a party. Specifically, organizational strength is defined here as (1) organizational extensiveness, (2) membership size and activism, and (3) professionalization of the central organization. The establishment or institutionalization of a party involves continued electoral success, long-term survival, and unified behavior in office. Figure 1.1 provides a summary and illustration of the main arguments explaining the causes and effects of party organizational strength.

One of the central arguments of this book is that parties with strong organizations are more likely to be electorally successful and survive as significant players because such parties are able to attract and mobilize voters more effectively than parties with weak organizations. The micro-foundations of this argument are motivated by insights from the cognitive-psychological scholarship on voting behavior and the theory of bounded rationality. These theories suggest that voters rely on information shortcuts when making voting decisions because obtaining detailed information on all parties is too costly (see Brooks

2006 for a review). I argue that a party with strong organization can more easily provide voters with the necessary information shortcuts. These "heuristics," in turn, shape voters' biases in the party's favor for two interrelated reasons. First, because of membership size, extensive local presence, and professional staff, strong parties can have more immediate and frequent contact with more members of the electorate in a more organized manner than parties with weak organizations. Second, parties with strong organizations can be more persuasive than their counterparts with weak organizations. They are more likely to act competently, reliably, and accountably. Thanks to their permanent structures and personnel, they can also more effectively formulate policy, cope with environmental challenges, and take responsibility for their actions. Parties with strong organizations can more credibly claim that they are a stable entity and not just a temporary electoral alliance.

I argue that these effects are likely to be especially pronounced in the context of new democracies in general and post-communist democracies in particular. Simply put, despite some evidence of social bases of party choice in the region (Evans 2006), the party competition in these systems is not likely to be structured to the same extent and in the same manner as in advanced democracies, which makes information shortcuts and credibility especially relevant. Specifically, in newly democratized regimes, voters lack experience with how the democratic elections function (Tavits and Annus 2006), are less likely to have significant (positive) party identification (Rose 1995; Wyman et al. 1995), and are more likely to be confused about the ideological differences between parties (Grzymala-Busse 2002b; Rose 1995) than voters in established democracies, and they may even be hostile toward parties (Mair 1997; Rose and Mishler 1998; Wyman et al. 1995). The voter-level confusion is magnified by erratic elite behavior: in the post-communist context, political elites were not necessarily committed and loyal to their parties and often solved conflicts by creating new parties with little ideological identification (Tavits 2008a, 2008b). Moreover, expressed ideology may not be a very clear indication of behavior, considering that left-wing parties often pursued right-wing economic policies (Tavits and Letki 2009). Additionally, especially in the post-communist context, but possibly also in other new democracies, societies did not have many pronounced cleavages under the previous regime (Lipset 1994). Societies were leveled in terms of social class, church and the role of religion were marginalized, urban-rural differences were largely eliminated, and ethnic differences were suppressed (Ost 1995; Van Biezen 2003). This undermined any cleavage-based party competition. The relative voter availability and ignorance, the weakness of ideological, interest-based, and cleavage-based voting, and the problems with party legitimacy make direct contacts and face-to-face mobilization efforts, made possible by strong organizations, especially crucial. Organization allows more direct (and effective) means of communication with voters than abstract media campaigns, and sizeable membership, local presence, and professional management help signal legitimacy of the party. In a context where little else is available to structure voters' choices and party competition, parties can use their organizations to introduce some structure and predictability to their own short-term support. They can also build a long-term advantage over newcomers with less organizational resources.

This argument and the overall thesis that party organizations matter in new democracies go against the conventional wisdom in the post-communist party literature. In the post-communist context, there were several reasons why parties were not expected to build extensive organizations to win elections: (1) party formation was driven largely by elite behavior and did not follow the classical cleavage theory, (2) antiparty sentiment was high, and (3) partisan loyalties among voters and elites were low (Agh 1997; Kopecky 1995; Lewis 1996; Mair 1997; Olson 1998; Perkins 1996; Szczerbiak 1999a; Toole 2003; Van Biezen 2003). Rather, an expensive media campaign, a visible leader, the use of patronage, and/or populist ideologies were seen as more relevant for party's electoral success (Kopecky 1995; Lewis 2000; Perkins 1996; Römmele 1999). This argument has been often backed up by examples of "flash" parties – those that suddenly emerge and do well in an election – and the fact that party organizations were weaker and less developed in CEE than in the advanced democracies of Western Europe. However, inferring from a generally low level of party organizational strength (as compared to Western Europe) that such organizations are not necessary or beneficial for success assumes away what essentially is an empirical question that needs to be tested. Furthermore, contrary to seeing the peculiarities of the post-communist electoral context as *precluding* the development of strong party organizations, as this literature does, I argue that it is because of these conditions that it is especially advantageous for vote-maximizing parties to build organizations.

In sum, (1) immediate, frequent, and organized contacts with the electorate, and (2) competence, reliability, and accountability – made possible by a strong party's grassroots presence, permanent structures, and professional management – can help parties with strong organizations shape voters' biases in the party's favor and thereby mobilize support for the party. Strong organizations are likely to matter not only at the party level; a similar argument can also explain the variance in the performance of the same party across different districts. That is, parties are likely to do better in districts where their district-level party organization is stronger as manifested in the extensiveness of local structures and membership in that district.

I further argue that organizational strength helps parties establish themselves not only by enhancing their chances of electoral success and survival but also by enhancing elite commitment and unity in office. That is, holding institutional factors constant, the strength of political party organization directly and independently influences the level of party unity. Following from the arguments made previously, I argue that party organizational strength influences party unity because the stronger the party organization the more valuable an electoral asset the party is to individual legislators, an argument in line with recent research on pork-barrel politics (Keefer and Khemani 2009; Lyne 2008; Primo and Snyder 2010). This effect works through two mechanisms. First, if a legislator can rely on party reputation and resources to get reelected, he or she may feel less need to sway voters by building personal reputations in office. Second, and more importantly, the more valuable the party is to the legislator (i.e., the stronger the party), the more credible and effective is its threat to withdraw the electoral benefits (i.e., expel or demote the legislator) if a legislator undermines party unity.

Specifically, in line with the existing literature, I assume that legislators are reelection oriented. In order to get reelected, they can use their personal resources, party resources, or both. The more votes a candidate gets because they belong to a given party list, the more valuable the party is to that person. Parties with stronger organizations are likely to receive more votes, and are more valuable to their legislators. Accordingly, the threat of losing the valuable resource – for example, if the party denies renomination, lowers the list place, or expels the person from the party – is likely to induce compliance. Suffering these punishments is likely to be more consequential to a legislator in a party with a strong rather than a weak organization because the latter is less likely to provide many collective benefits (i.e., party votes) to its legislators. For the relationship between organizational strength and voting unity to emerge, the actual punishment does not have to occur – the threat of punishment is enough to induce compliance. In sum, party organizational strength is positively related to party unity in parliamentary voting.

Which parties, then, are more likely to build strong organizations in new democracies? To put it differently, if a strong organization is beneficial for establishing a party in the new regime, why do all parties not build equally strong organizations? I approach this question from two different angles. First, I argue that the effects of a strong party organization are not necessarily all positive from the point of view of the party. Rather, borrowing insights from organizational theory, I argue that it may bring along a redistribution of power within the party from the leadership to organizationally strong subunits. Specifically, literature on organizational sociology suggests that power within organizations is asymmetrically distributed between different subunits, with more powerful subunits being those that are better able to provide resources critical to the functioning of the organization that cannot be obtained by any other means (Emerson 1962; see also Cook and Emerson 1978; Cook et al. 1983; Fligstein 1987; Pfeffer 1994, 1997; Pfeffer and Salancik 2003). Within political parties, such powerful subunits are likely to be local branches with strong organizations (those with visible and active presence in local life via participating in local politics, being associated with locally known leaders and activists, and having local structures and membership) because these branches are able to help party leadership obtain its central goals – electoral and policy success. Such redistribution of power is likely to be especially concerning to leaders of post-communist parties that are largely elite creations where leaders are used to commanding a high degree of power compared to rank and file (Szczerbiak

2001d). Building an organization, therefore, poses a nontrivial dilemma to new party elites despite the potential positive effects of strong organizations on electoral performance both across and within parties.

Second, I explore what factors external and internal to the parties are more likely to make them inclined to build stronger organizations despite the relative redistribution of power. I argue that a strong party organization is more likely to emerge when a party has an extra incentive to build such an organization and is capable of acting on this incentive. The extra incentive is likely to be present for parties that (a) experience hostile electoral environments and cannot as easily rely on other (less costly) vote-getting strategies, or (b) have chosen to target an electorate (e.g., poor and rural voters) that is hard to reach by other means. Capacity to follow through with organization building, in turn, is likely to depend on whether or not the parties have professional leaders with the necessary skills and motivations.

The argument about the relevance of extra incentives rests on the assumption that building a strong organization is costly not just because of the redistribution of power but also because it takes resources and requires long-term and continuous commitment. Therefore, parties would prefer to avoid building such an organization if elections could be won some other way. Environmental factors, in turn, at least partially influence whether a less costly strategy would work for a given party. Specifically, the electoral environment surrounding the party's first election is likely to be especially relevant for determining the general trajectory of its organizational strength. Parties suffering from environmental hostility may be more inclined to build strong organizations as a way to actively cultivate grassroots support because their electoral prospects are much more uncertain compared to those of their competitors enjoying a friendly electoral environment.

Environmental hostility can originate from partisan competitors, voters, or the media and includes perceived lack of legitimacy, pariah status, media attacks, hostile public opinion, and entry into an already-saturated electoral market. Such hostility indicates that strategies other than building an extensive organization are either not available or have not been effective. Existing studies argue that questions about legitimacy are fueled by lack of information about the internal life of democratic parties (Kopecky 1995; Mair 1997). Expanding membership base and local presence allow close interactions between the party and its voters, helping dispel such perceptions. Similarly, attacks by other parties and the media are difficult to fend off by abstract media campaigns; and such an option may not even be available for pariahs. Organization then becomes pariahs' first resort for maintaining and building voters' support. Finally, for late entrants trying to establish themselves in an already-saturated electoral market, other options are also scarce. They are at a disadvantage compared to the parties that have already contested multiple elections in terms of name recognition and expectations of viability (Boix 2007; Cox 1997). Building a strong party organization can help compensate for these disadvantages and differentiate these late entrants from the existing contestants.

The nature of the party's primary electorate is another environmental factor potentially influencing the extent to which non-organizational vote-getting strategies will work. Parties that are primarily targeting urban voters and wealthy citizens are able to reach their target audience without an extensive organization. They simply need presence in larger cities, resources to communicate their message by posters and media ads, and nationally known public figures to attract voters. No large organization is necessary to achieve that. However, parties that aspire to represent rural electorates and poorer citizens may find that they need to extend their organizations across the country and focus on face-to-face interactions to reach their voters. These segments of society may simply have less access to media and need to be contacted directly in order to be mobilized. They may also be less persuaded by a distant – even if nationally known – candidate than by their friends or neighbors or locally known candidates that a strong organization allows a party to recruit.

In addition to incentives, opportunities or capacities also matter. Specifically, the preferences, priorities, and background of the party leader may influence the organization-building strategies of political parties. Unlike the environmental factors discussed, a leader-based explanation offers a dynamic argument of party organizational strength and is thereby better able to account for why the same party may exhibit different levels of organizational strength at different times. Building on the literature on the state and local party organizations in the United States, management and organizational sociology, and the survival of former regime parties, I argue that parties are likely to have stronger or weaker organizations depending on whether their leaders follow a "professional" or "amateur" leadership style. The former are pragmatists who see the party as an instrument for gaining other goals – such as office and policy – value loyalty to the party, stress the collective over individual achievement, and are less concerned about ideological debates (Cotter et al. 1984). They have background in administration, management, business, or other fields that have provided them with skills at organization. The latter, on the other hand, emphasize the role of ideas and principles, are ideological purists, have little loyalty to party as an organization, and are ready to abandon the organization for the sake of ideas (Gibson, Frendreis, and Vertz 1989). With prior careers in intellectual and cultural spheres, they are more likely to focus on personal rather than collective achievement and lack both the interest in and the necessary skills to build strong organizations.

In sum, party organizational strength is positively associated with electoral performance and overall party unity. However, building organizations is costly. Furthermore, although strong local party branches provide more votes for the party than weak ones, these strong branches are also more likely to challenge the leadership in a struggle for intra-party power. This provides an additional reason for party elites to shy away from building and strengthening their party organizations. Therefore, parties require additional incentives to build organizations as well as capacity to do so. Hostile electoral environment and hard-to-reach electorate can provide the former and professional leaders the latter (in terms of the necessary foresight and skills).

Case Selection and Methods

In order to empirically investigate the causes and consequences of party organizational strength, this book examines four post-communist CEE countries – the Czech Republic, Estonia, Hungary, and Poland – over the period of twenty years (1990–2010). Depending on the specific analysis, I have included either all parliamentary parties (Chapters 4 and 5) or all parties that made it into parliament at least once or contested at least two consecutive parliamentary elections (Chapters 2 and 6), subject to data availability.

The case selection is restricted to these four countries for theoretical and practical reasons. First, data availability is a serious concern. Studying party organizations is notoriously challenging (which probably explains the dearth of empirical studies on this topic, even in advanced democracies). There are no datasets of party organizational strength that could be downloaded easily. Parties themselves are relatively secretive and closed organizations, which only adds to the difficulty of studying them. For each of the four countries it took about a year of intensive work with the literature, archival material, Web sites, and newspapers; the help of multiple research assistants; several field trips and interviews; and endless phone calls and e-mails (not to mention the energy spent on keeping up the spirits of my assistants and myself, on staying calm and patient, and on simple creativity) to compile information about party organizations. Secondary literature, archives, and Web sites provided some useful information. Newspaper research implied browsing through more than 10,000 articles per country from the archives of the major dailies (including, but not limited to, *Lidové noviny*, *Právo*, and *CTK National News Wire* from the Czech Republic; *Eesti Päevaleht* and *Postimees* from Estonia; *HVG*, *MTI*, and *Népszabadság* from Hungary; and *Gazeta Prawna*, *Gazeta Wyborcza*, *PAP News Wire*, and *Rzeczpospolita* from Poland) and sources available in Lexis Nexis for the period 1990–2010. This exercise helped to fill additional gaps in the quantitative data and provided a wealth of information for the qualitative analysis. Finally, it was necessary to contact the primary data source – the parties themselves – to complete the data gathering. This was probably the most challenging part of the project because even basic measures such as membership figures often required multiple return visits, phone calls, and e-mail reminders before they were reluctantly released (even in cases such as Estonia, where parties were required by law to publicize this information).

Although practical reasons set the limit of the number of countries that could be included in the study, theoretical reasons guided the actual country selection. The goal was to select a diverse set of countries (from the universe of CEE democracies) in order to enhance the generalizability and robustness of the findings, and be able to draw firm theoretical conclusions. The four countries differ on several characteristics that could potentially contaminate the relationships under study. Specifically, organizational strength may be electorally less valuable: (1) in more stable party systems – such as the Czech Republic or Hungary – than in less stable ones – such as Estonia and Poland;[2] (2) in countries with stronger cleavages – such as the deep cultural cleavage between urbanists and populists in Hungary or the ethnic cleavage between Estonians and Russians in Estonia – than in countries with less strong cleavages – such as the Czech Republic and Poland; and (3) in countries with more party-centered electoral rules, including closed-list proportional representation (PR) with high district magnitudes – such as the PR tier in Hungary or open-list PR with low district magnitudes in Poland – than in countries with relatively more personalistic rules – such as the Czech Republic and Estonia. The differences between countries help rule out some alternative explanations. If a similar relationship between party organizational strength and party success, survival, and unity emerges in all countries despite these and other system-level differences between them, then we can be more confident that it is a true relationship. These (and other, including historical legacies, level of economic development, ethnic heterogeneity, population size, culture, etc.) differences between the four countries also help to enhance the generalizability of the findings with regard to the origins of party organizational strength. The CEE countries left out of the study – Bulgaria, Latvia, Lithuania, Romania, Slovakia, and Slovenia – do not appear to be systematically different from the ones included, which further suggests that the findings are not likely to be unique to the four countries under study. In fact, I originally attempted to also cover these six additional countries. However, the data that I was able to gather for them were too sporadic to be usable in most analyses. I include these data in the robustness tests of some of the analyses reported in Chapter 2 and find no substantive change in results.

This book relies on a combination of quantitative and qualitative methods. Both methods are used to explore each of the more specific research questions. The quantitative analysis focuses on two different levels of aggregation: (1) party-level analyses pool cases across countries and years; and (2) district-level analyses, performed for each country separately, pool across the electoral districts, parties, and years. Note that the latter strategy considerably increases the number of observations, which allows drawing firmer theoretical conclusions.

Although the main goal of the quantitative statistical analysis is to uncover systematic, generalizable effects, the purpose of the qualitative case studies is twofold: they (1) provide (additional) tests with more detailed and multifaceted data – as will be described – of the relationships under study; and (2) help illustrate and assess causal mechanisms producing the hypothesized relationships, especially with regard to sequencing and timing. Such additional tests and

[2] Since 2010, the party systems of the Czech Republic and Hungary have also experienced increasing instability.

illustrations are employed throughout this book. There are, however, also two central research questions that are examined mostly with the help of process tracing and the comparative case study method. These include the analysis of the effect of party organizational strength on the survival of parties and that of the effects of leadership style on the level of organizational strength.

The intra-country comparison allows minimizing extraneous variance (Peters 1998). Several environmental and institutional factors, similar for all parties, can be held constant. The differences between parties can then be examined to determine whether and how these relate to the dependent variable. I use such explicit intra-country comparison in order to determine whether and how differences in the level of parties' organizational development are associated with their different experiences in the electoral arena, both in terms of success and survival. This complements the quantitative analysis of electoral success and also provides a way to examine whether organizations matter for party survival rather than just success. These case studies consist of (1) focused comparisons of otherwise similar parties with opposing electoral trajectories, and (2) process-tracing narratives of the electoral trajectories of individual parties. The former strategy allows for even more control over possible sources of extraneous variance and helps isolate the effects of the organization. Process tracing, in turn, not only considers the co-variation between variables of interest, but investigates the process by which the independent variable is supposed to bring about the outcome variable (George and McKeown 1985). It therefore allows studying path-dependent developments, which is especially important when trying to establish a causal order between electoral performance and organizational strength.

The case studies examining the effects of leadership style on organizational strength have a descriptive (or measurement) and analytical component. First, using information about all major parliamentary parties during the period under study, I establish the leadership style of the party leaders. I then use nominal comparisons of different party leaders within the same party as well as across different parties – a method that allows eliminating some causal variables. More importantly, I use process tracing to pursue chains of causality and trace how leaders have followed the leadership styles in practice and how this, in turn, has influenced the development of party organizations.

Overall, the analysis in this book uses a combined most similar and most different systems design and a mixture of quantitative and qualitative research methods. This case-selection strategy helps to control for extraneous variance, and simultaneously allows for considerable experimental variance. The mixed methods, in turn, allow for both generalizability and detail by combining systematic quantitative data with a rich pool of information, including qualitative data from party literature and archives, newspapers, secondary studies, and interviews with party officials, staff, and activists. The relationships uncovered in the course of this analysis should, therefore, be both detailed and specific enough to be useful for theory and policy, but generalizable to a broader set of new democracies.

The Concept and Measures of Party Organizational Strength

The conceptualization and measurement of party organizational strength is a central challenge of this study. Not surprisingly, no consensus exists about what aspects of party organizations are most important and what indicators constitute measures of organizational strength.[3] For the purposes of the current study, I have defined the concept of party organizational strength on the basis of three attributes: (1) membership size and activism; (2) organizational extensiveness; and (3) professionalization of the central organization. Organizational strength indicates the extensiveness, professionalization, and reach of a party. This definition is derived from the indicators of party organizational strength used in the existing literature, bearing in mind the theoretical purposes of the current study.

Table 1.1 lists the different ways party organizational strength has been conceptualized in a diverse set of studies. This list does not aspire to be complete, but should be representative of the different conceptualizations used. I have combined conceptually similar or overlapping definitions of strong organizations under the same heading or attribute. Different studies use different degrees of precision in defining their concepts – the empirical studies are usually more precise and provide a list of operational indicators; theoretical studies are less precise and provide broad definitions that may cover several of the attributes listed.

Most existing definitions can be classified relatively easily under one of the first six attributes: professionalization of the central organization; organizational extensiveness; membership size and activism; party performance; issue orientation; and lack of personalization. The relevance and position of the next two attributes – centralization and autonomy – is contested in the literature. Although several scholars agree that these characteristics could be part of the concept, there is no agreement over whether these are attributes of strong or weak parties. This lack of evidence makes it difficult to integrate these aspects of party organization into the concept of party organizational strength.[4]

---

[3] As Janda (1993, 171) notes, "the comparative parties literature has paid relatively little attention to conceptualizing and even less to measurement issues." The existing literature – both quantitative large-N studies of various parties and qualitative case studies of specific parties – provides a bewildering array of indicators of party organization and its strength. Many of the definitions proposed are idiosyncratic to certain regions, countries, or even parties, which is why researchers often develop their own indicators when studying a case.

[4] Similarly, several authors have proposed additional potential attributes of party organizational strength that are not necessarily easily classified under any attribute. These include, for example, party age (Bartolini 2000; Dix 1992), control over party rules, rules and numbers for the representation of women, head office income and expenditure, campaign expenditure (Katz and Mair 1994), and correspondence between a party's statutory norms and actual power structures (Panebianco 1988). Although these indicators capture different aspects of party organizations and may be useful for describing them, it is not clear how they capture organizational strengths or weaknesses or relate to the other attributes listed in Table 1.1.

TABLE 1.1. *Attributes of Party Organizational Strength*

Professionalization of the central organization

- Existence of an extra-parliamentary central organization (Gunther and Hopkin 2002; Ishiyama 2001; Mudde 2007; Panebianco 1988; Van Biezen 2003)
- Existence of organizational structure and procedures (Kostelecky 2002; Mainwaring 1999)
- Organizational continuity (Janda 1980)
- Financial resources (Gibson et al. 1983; Janda 1980; Katz and Mair 1994; Mainwaring 1999; Panebianco 1988; Szczerbiak 1999a)
- Permanent staff, skilled organizers, specialization of staff (Gibson et al. 1983; Janda 1980; Katz and Mair 1994; Mudde 2007)
- Means of communication with the electorate, party newspaper (Katz and Mair 1994)
- Communication and coherence between different levels of party organization (Chhibber 1999; Panebianco 1988)
- Official means of conflict resolution (Gunther and Hopkin 2002; Keck 1992; LeBas 2011; Mudde 2007; Panebianco 1988)

Organizational extensiveness

- Localization of organization; party presence at grassroots; extensive network of local branches (Cotter et al. 1984; Frendreis, Gibson, and Vertz 1990; Golosov 2004; Janda 1980; Levitsky 2003; Mudde 2007; Panebianco 1988; Saiz and Geser 1999; Szczerbiak 1999a; Van Biezen 2003; Wellhofer 1979)
- Formal structures and procedures to convey information across levels of organization (Kostelecky 2002; LeBas 2011)
- The extent of partisan control over access to office (Golosov 2004; Moser 2001)
- Having strong roots in society (Mainwaring 1999)

Membership size and activism

- Membership size (Bartolini 2000; Coppedge 1994; Ishiyama 2001; Janda 1980; Katz and Mair 1994; Levitsky 2003; Van Biezen 2003)
- Frequency of meetings; maintenance of records; means of effective internal communication (Janda 1980; LeBas 2011)
- Institutional support activity: electoral mobilization programs; public opinion polling; etc. (Cotter et al. 1984; Cutright 1963; Frendreis et al. 1990; Gibson et al. 1983; Gibson et al. 1985; Katz and Eldersveld 1961)
- Candidate-directed activity: provision of services to candidates; recruitment of candidates (Gibson et al. 1983; Katz and Mair 1994)
- Membership involvement: extent of membership requirements; incentives (Janda 1980; Katz and Mair 1994)

(*continued*)

TABLE 1.1 *(continued)*

Party performance

- Legislative cohesion; lack of factionalism and splits (Janda 1980)
- Electoral stability (Janda 1980; Mainwaring 1999; Meleshevich 2007)
- Electoral and legislative strength (Janda 1980; Meleshevich 2007)
- Cabinet participation (Janda 1980)
- Diffuse organizational loyalties (Panebianco 1988)
- Lack of antiparty sentiment in the electorate (Kostelecky 2002; Mainwaring 1999)
- Survival and adaptability (Dix 1992; Levitsky 2003)
- Ability to prevent protests by associated groups (Coppedge 1994)

Issue orientation

- Ideological coherence (Janda 1980; Tworzecki 2003)
- Stable issue positions on the left-right scale (Janda 1980)
- Broad ideological appeal (Chandra 2004; Innes 2002; Kitschelt and McGann 1995)

Lack of personalization

- Authority resides in party rather than leader; loyalty to party rather than leader (Panebianco 1988)
- Programmatic rather than clientelistic or charismatic linkage (Kitschelt and McGann 1995; Lawson, Römmele, and Karasimeonov 1999)

Centralization vs. decentralization

- Internal democracy (Keck 1992; Panebianco 1988; Szczerbiak 1999a; Van Biezen 2003)
- Lack of centralized structure (Levitsky 2003)

versus

- Centralization of power and resulting strategic flexibility (Janda 1980; Kitschelt et al. 1999)

Autonomy vs. linkage to other organizations

- Linkage between party and other societal organizations; party penetration to civic associations (Bartolini 2000; Coppedge 1994; Janda 1980; Van Biezen 2003)

versus

- Autonomy from other societal organizations (Kalyvas 1998; Panebianco 1988)

Of the six attributes, the first three deal directly with aspects of organization. They are also all relatively closely linked and interdependent: several indicators under one attribute assume the presence of some indicators under another attribute. For example, "Existence of organizational structure and procedures" under the attribute "Professionalization of the central organization" is closely linked to "extensive network of local branches" and "Formal structures and procedures to convey information across levels of organization" under "Organizational extensiveness" and to "means of effective internal communication" under "Membership size and activism." Such obvious interrelatedness suggests that the attributes ultimately refer to the same concept. Furthermore, notwithstanding the great diversity of indicators of party organizations and their strength in the existing literature, these three attributes attract perhaps the highest level of agreement as valid indicators of strong party organizations across both empirical and theoretical studies conducted in a variety of contexts. The current study takes this rare consensus as a point of departure.

The remaining three attributes are not suitable as part of the concept of party organizational strength if the latter is to be used to predict party success, survival, and unity. This is obvious for the indicators of party performance. Issue orientation is also not necessarily an organizational characteristic, and serves a better purpose as alternative explanations to party establishment/ institutionalization than as part of the concept of party organizational strength. The same is true about the lack of personalization (see Kitschelt 2000; Mudde 2007; Römmele 1999; Van der Brug and Mughan 2007).

To reiterate, a party has a strong organization if it has structures, personnel, and activities beyond public office. Organizational strength indicates the extensiveness, professionalization, and reach of a party. Specifically, for current purposes, the concept of party organizational strength corresponds to the first three attributes listed above and consists of (1) membership size and activism, (2) organizational extensiveness, and (3) professionalization of the central organization.

Measuring this concept of party organizational strength poses an additional challenge. Studies have used a variety of information collection methods to overcome this difficulty. Cross-national studies have used secondary literature, including party statutes, to code information about party organizations (Appleton and Ward 1994; Janda 1980; Katz and Mair 1994). This is a logical and useful approach, but limits the study to variables that are codified in party statutes, which may not (1) reflect the practice, and (2) measure party organizational strength. Furthermore, secondary literature rarely systematically covers the same indicators. Even membership figures can differ drastically between different sources (Mudde 2007), as data collection for this book revealed.

An alternative approach is to use surveys, for example, to ask party staff to fill in a standardized questionnaire about the organizational extensiveness and programmatic capacity of their party (Cotter et al. 1984). A similar data collection procedure is not feasible in post-communist Europe for two reasons.

Compared to the one country and two parties included in Cotter et al. (1984), the current study is much larger in scope and includes four countries and more than thirty parties over twenty years. The resources required to implement a similar data collection procedure in post-communist Europe are enormous and unrealistic to obtain. Furthermore, even if resources were available, the effort would most likely not succeed. I attempted to conduct a pilot study modeled after Cotter et al. (1984) in three post-communist countries (Estonia, Hungary, and Poland) and found that (1) several parties were reluctant to cooperate, (2) the response rate from local leaders of those parties that did cooperate was very low, and (3) the responses given were often unrealistic (i.e., the claims about organizational extensiveness and functions were clearly exaggerated, so that much of the data obtained was unreliable). This pilot experience convinced me not to pursue this strategy any further and to find alternative ways – preferably ones that do not rely on largely unverifiable information only obtainable from parties – to measure party organizational strength. Other authors have been equally frustrated with survey measures and called for the use of "harder" data (Pomper 1990). Pomper even reports how the survey respondents themselves (county-level party chairs) suggested using the percent of precincts with party presence as a measure of party organizational strength instead of the unreliable responses to the questionnaire. Furthermore, even if survey information was perfect, it still only provides us with a snapshot of internal party life. There is no possibility to look at across-time trends or to go back in time to consider parties who did not succeed in the electoral arena, which would create a serious selection bias.

Still another method that researchers have used is to rely on their own or somebody else's (expert) judgment in measuring party organizational strength (Dix 1992). This method, however, is not easily replicable and even expert judgments are relatively problematic. Because very little reliable information is available about the internal structure and functioning of political parties in CEE, there are no or few experts who can place parties across a variety of countries and time on a comparable scale of organizational strength (see Mudde 2007 for a similar criticism).

These challenges motivated me to use objective, hard data that are likely to be available for most parties under study and that can be measured at the national as well as district level, given the two levels of analyses employed in some of the quantitative tests. Specifically, party organizational strength was defined as a unitary concept capturing the level of organizational extensiveness and professionalization. I use four different indicators to measure this concept. First, "Membership" measures the number of party members as the percent of total national (district) electorate. An alternative measure – "Branches" – indicates the number of municipal-level party branches divided by the total number of municipalities in a given country (district). Professionalization is measured by the size of the central-office paid staff. The variable "Staff," measured as a percent of the electorate (in hundred thousands), does not vary across districts and is therefore only included in the cross-national analyses.[5]

Although these measures are straightforward, they are hard or sometimes impossible to obtain. Parties are reluctant to give out information about their organization,[6] and the numbers reported in secondary literature are often inaccurate. Because of these concerns, I will also use an alternative measure of party organizational strength that considers the ability of a party to contest local government (municipal) elections (Deegan-Krause 2006; Mudde 2007). "Participation in local elections" is measured by the share of municipalities, in which a given party runs its candidates in a local-government council election.[7]

In addition to these quantitative indicators, the qualitative analysis allows using a variety of and more detailed information to evaluate the level of party organizational strength. Multiple measures have the same advantage as multiple methods: the results on the basis of using multiple measures are more reliable because the likelihood that the findings are only attributable to measurement bias is lower. The material for the case studies originates from secondary literature, archival material, media monitoring, and surveys of and interviews with party officials.

A Roadmap

The next two chapters focus on the relationship between party organizational strength and electoral performance. Chapter 2 elaborates on the theoretical arguments linking the two phenomena and presents quantitative tests exploring their empirical validity. The focus will mostly be on short-term electoral success. I show that organizational strength matters not only across parties but also within parties. That is, not only are parties with stronger organizations likely to perform better than those with weaker organizations, but also, for any given party, electoral returns are likely to be higher in districts where the party has stronger organizational presence. Chapter 3 complements this analysis with in-depth case studies making use of focused comparison of similar parties that differ on electoral outcome, and process tracing that allows determining the extent to which electoral success follows from rather than causes organizational strength. The case studies also explicitly explore the effect of

---

[5] Information on these indicators was collected using multiple sources including interviews and other correspondence with party officials, party documents (such as financial reports), official records (as collected, for example, by the Estonian Central Commercial Register), newspaper articles, archival materials, and secondary literature.

[6] In Poland and Hungary, party officials claimed that they did not collect information on membership and branch offices on the subnational level. Many parties had no reliable information on even national-level membership size. In the Czech Republic, district-level information on branches is also virtually lacking and membership information is available only for some parties and some elections.

[7] Chapter 2 provides a longer discussion about the validity of this measure.

party organizational strength on the long-term survival of parties and their ability to cope with environmental shocks. Chapter 4 details the argument that connects organizational strength with party unity and provides a systematic quantitative test of this argument. The chapter further explores the plausibility of the causal mechanisms using qualitative analysis. It also provides preliminary tests of an additional observable implication following from this argument (i.e., that parties with strong organizations are more likely to punish their legislators for defecting against the party, by expelling them or lowering their position on the party list). Chapter 5 focuses on the power distribution within parties, arguing that organizationally stronger local party branches are likely to be more powerful than their organizationally weak counterparts. I argue that the asymmetric power distribution is likely to be manifested in the parliamentary behavior and positions of legislators and show that legislators from districts with organizationally strong party branches are (1) less likely to toe the party line set by leaders and more likely to break party unity in legislative voting, and (2) more likely to hold leadership positions in parliamentary committees than legislators that represent districts with weaker party subunits. Chapter 6 presents the argument about the effect of environmental factors and leadership style on party organizational strength. The empirical analysis concerning the effect of the environmental factors uses quantitative data. It examines both the direct effect of environmental hostility and the nature of the electorate as well as the interactive effect of these variables on the organizational strength of post-communist parties. The second part of Chapter 6 focuses on the leadership effect. It documents the leadership style of all major parties in the four post-communist countries under study, and provides an assessment, using qualitative comparative case study method and process tracing, of the extent to which the level of a party's organizational strength can be attributed to its leadership style. The final chapter highlights the contribution of the findings to our understanding of not only the various aspects of party politics but also other phenomena such as elite learning, and assesses the generalizability of the results to contexts beyond post-communist Europe.

2

Organizing for Success

Party Organizational Strength and
Electoral Performance

Succeeding and surviving in the electoral arena is the first crucial obstacle that parties need to clear in order to become institutionalized and participate in the political process. Not surprisingly, then, why some political parties succeed in elections and others do not is one of the most pressing questions in electoral politics in any democracy, regardless of its age or level of development. Office-seeking parties care about the answer because they want to enter and return to office. Policy-seeking parties care about it because they, too, want to gain and keep a position in which they can exercise their policy influence.[1] The extant media coverage of elections and the endless popular discussions and speculations about who is likely to do well and why indicates that voters, too, want to be able to predict who succeeds in the electoral game. This interest is not surprising given how important the winners are in democratic regimes. In advanced democracies, changes in party performance from one election to the next are usually relatively small. However, even these changes generate excitement among the political actors, the public, and the scholarly community because they influence government composition and policy outcomes. As argued in Chapter 1, this concern over the predictability of party performance becomes magnified in the context of new democracies, where the stakes are usually much more substantial. It is, therefore, natural to begin the analysis of whether party organizations matter by looking at their effects on party electoral performance.

---

[1] My definition of party refers only to those parties that contest elections with a goal to win or get into office for office-seeking and/or policy-seeking reasons (Schlesinger 1984; Duverger 1954; Janda 1980). Parties may have other goals, but electoral competition is what makes them interesting, attracts attention, and is most consequential to the functioning of the regime and government performance.

Specifically, this chapter considers whether and to what extent parties themselves can guide their electoral fate by developing and strengthening their organizations. The focus will be on uncovering general patterns of organizational effects on electoral performance using statistical analysis. Recognizing that other factors also matter, the central hypothesis to be tested is that political parties that invest in building professional, specialized, and permanent central office staff; cultivating a large membership; and developing an extensive network of visible local branch offices are better able to increase their support base over time and thereby remain significant players in the electoral arena.

Admittedly, parsing out the (possibly reciprocal) effects of party organizational strength and electoral performance is extremely difficult, so that any single argument or statistical analysis or qualitative case study alone is unlikely to convince a skeptical reader that organizational strength causes (or is prior to) electoral success. This is why I spend two chapters – Chapters 2 and 3 – on evaluating this relationship. The two chapters provide a variety of reasons, which, cumulatively, provide strong grounds for accepting this proposition. Specifically, first, there are good theoretical reasons to believe that organizational strength enhances electoral support in post-communist party systems. These arguments are reviewed in the first part of this chapter. Second, empirical analyses of all relevant cases from not only the four countries under review (the Czech Republic, Estonia, Hungary, and Poland) but also from the entire post-communist Europe document a very strong, positive, statistically and substantively significant relationship between party organizational strength and electoral support. These analyses are presented in the second part of this chapter. Indeed, this relationship is so strong that even if we discount the estimates somewhat to account for the possibility that party organizational strength both influences and is influenced by electoral support, the estimated causal effect of organizational strength on party support would still be large and substantively significant. Third, case studies with process tracing and focused comparisons, reported in Chapter 3, also support the conclusion that organizational strength enhances electoral support. Taken together, I believe that the weight of the evidence as summarized in the three points above strongly supports the proposition that organizational strength enhances electoral performance in post-communist party systems. Although one can criticize any one of the three points on various grounds, the fact that the theoretical arguments, statistical analyses (including a large number of robustness tests and extensions to the main analyses), and case studies all point in the same direction makes this conclusion difficult to refute.

Organizational Strength and Electoral Success: Theoretical Argument

As discussed in Chapter 1, for the purposes of the current study, the concept of party organizational strength consists of the following three attributes: (1) membership size and activism; (2) organizational extensiveness; and

(3) professionalization of the central organization. The central argument of this chapter is that parties with strong organizations are able to attract and mobilize voters more effectively than parties with weak organizations. The micro-foundations of this argument are motivated by insights from the cognitive-psychological scholarship on voting behavior and the theory of bounded rationality. On the basis of these theories, I assume that voters face significant information constraints when making voting decisions (especially in new democracies where long-term voter attachments have not necessarily been developed). Because obtaining information on different parties and candidates is costly, voters rely on heuristics and information shortcuts when making voting decisions (see Brooks 2006 for a review).

A party with a strong organization can more easily provide voters with information shortcuts that shape voters' biases in the party's favor for two interrelated reasons. First, organizationally strong parties are more effective in reaching voters: they can have more immediate and frequent contact with more members of the electorate in a more organized manner than parties with weak organizations. Literature on collective action and canvassing provides robust evidence that immediate contacts are more effective than other forms of contact in persuading voters (Gerber and Green 2000; see also Jason et al. 1984; Reams and Ray 1993).[2]

Second, parties with strong organizations are able to be more persuasive: such parties are more likely to be seen as competent, reliable, and accountable than parties with a weak organization. They can more credibly claim that they are stable entities whose existence is not threatened by environmental shocks. Organizational strength signals a party's ability to effectively formulate policy, cope with environmental challenges, and account rationally for its actions. Sociological literature on business organizations argues that such reliable and accountable organizations are more successful: they are more attractive to potential clients and investors because they can reduce the level of environmental uncertainty for them (Hannan and Freeman 1984). Similarly, strong parties can reduce the level of uncertainty about the future for voters, which is likely to increase the attractiveness of such parties. In sum, (1) immediate, frequent, and organized contacts with the electorate, and (2) competence, reliability, and accountability – made possible by grassroots presence, permanent structures, and professional management – can help parties with strong organizations shape voters' biases (i.e., the information shortcuts that voters use) in the party's favor and thereby mobilize support for the party.[3]

---

[2] Studies showing significant positive effects of local party activity and membership on the electoral success in Britain, Canada, and the United States also support this conclusion (see, for example, Carty and Eagels 1999; Crotty 1971; Pattie and Johnston 2003; Pomper 1990; Whiteley and Seyd 1994).

[3] These arguments are also in line with studies showing that party competition depends significantly on nonideological factors including attachment to the party, communication with the electorate (Adams, Merrill, and Grofman 2005), and competence (Schofield and Sened 2006).

With these theoretical insights in mind, the rest of this section elaborates on exactly how the three attributes of party organizational strength help parties mobilize voters. As stated, the different attributes of party organizational strength are not necessarily always clearly distinguishable, and the causal mechanisms linking each to party performance are also overlapping and mutually reinforcing. I have discussed the effects of each attribute separately for the sake of clarity of presentation. Theoretically and empirically, however, the effects of these three attributes remain interrelated.

Membership

Other things equal, parties with more members are likely to be electorally more successful for three related reasons. First, members are loyal voters (Scarrow 2000). In its extreme (and ideal) form (see Duverger 1954; Sartori 1976), members become "communities of fate" (Wellhofer 1979, 171) or "electorates of belonging" (Panebianco 1988, 267) – they are so attached to the party that they are unlikely to withdraw their support even in the face of major party failures. Even in less extreme form, however, being a member signals deeper identification and commitment to the party and increased threshold, that is, the accumulation of disagreeable developments with party ideological change or behavior in office, on which an individual is likely to abandon the party (Levitsky 2003). Membership, thus, creates a valuable "electoral cushion that enables parties to make strategic changes – or mistakes – without suffering substantial short-term losses" (Levitsky 2003, 13–14) and benefits party survival in the long-term (Ware 1992; Wolinetz 1990). For example, Poguntke (2002) shows that in Western Europe, membership size is significantly related to parties' electoral stability and argues that this alone should create powerful incentives for party leaders to build and maintain a strong membership organization.

Second, a large membership allows the party to make more attractive appeals to its potential electorate. Members are important resources for keeping a party in touch with public opinion at the grassroots level (Scarrow 1994). The wider the membership, the more accurately it represents public opinion and the easier it is for the party to respond to a broader electorate. A party with sizeable membership can simply more credibly claim to appeal to the society as a whole rather than just a specific group (Scarrow 1996; see also Duverger 1954). If a party has only negligible membership with narrow interests, it necessarily remains restricted and selective in the kinds of appeals it is able to make. Furthermore, membership size in itself may send a positive signal to potential voters about the breadth of party appeal: parties with more members are more credible in selling the message that they are more accommodative. Broad appeals, in turn, are likely to attract more voters. For example, research on the success of ethnic parties in divided societies has argued that organizational structures that help ethnic parties make broad electoral appeals significantly account for why they do or do not succeed (Chandra 2004).

Third, membership is an important asset when conducting campaigns. Party members can multiply the party's electoral base through their contacts (Scarrow 1994), which can be at least as effective as centralized media campaigns, offering attractive labels, or presenting a charismatic leader when cultivating support for the party (Scarrow 2000; see also Grzymala-Busse 2002a; Whiteley and Seyd 1994). Members' personal contacts help convey the impression among nonmembers and potential voters that the party is not just an elite-level creation serving the interests of the leadership. Rather, such contacts are likely to encourage beliefs among the electorate that the party knows the concerns of the real people, that they can offer real solutions and are serious about carrying out their commitments (Coleman 1996). Members can be effective in translating abstract political ideologies into specific tangible issues relevant to their contacts (Geser 1999). Therefore, members and their extra-party social networks become an important basis for cultivating and sustaining support for the party. Members can help with fundraising, either by making monetary contributions or other types of aid to help campaign or raise money for the party (Scarrow 1994; Ware 1992). Not less importantly, members can also help compensate for lack of funding by donating their time through voluntary work (Buch Jensen 1999; Levitsky 2003; Ware 1992). Such volunteering during campaigns can be beneficial for both the electoral success of the party and socializing and tying members more closely to the party. In sum, membership is a significant short- and long-term electoral asset for parties.

Network of Branch Offices

Related to the benefits of membership, a wide network of local branches is electorally beneficial to parties because local party organizations provide the necessary structures to mobilize voters during elections and sustain mobilization over time (Bartolini 2000; Clark 2004; Coleman 1996; Cutright 1963; Katz and Eldersveld 1961; LeBas 2011; see also Carty and Eagels 1999; Pattie and Johnston 2003; Wellhofer 1979; Whiteley and Seyd 1994). These structures are seen as especially effective in mobilizing "the faithful," which in turn sends a positive signal to the rest of the electorate about the competitiveness of the party (Huckfeldt and Sprague 1992). Even relatively inactive branches are helpful because the mere presence of a local office increases the local visibility of the party, and sends a message to the local electorate that the party cares about them. The local party office can also become the center for spontaneous mobilization without any significant organizational initiative and activism. It creates an opportunity for local voters to approach the party (given that it is a public institution whose role is to address economic, social, and political issues) with their problems or ideas and participate in political discussions. For example, Shin (2001) demonstrates that in the case of the Democratic Party of the Left (PDS) in Italy, survey respondents drawn from the electorate were considerably more likely to report having frequent political discussions in localities where the party was present compared to those where it was not. The study argues that the local presence of parties provides the missing link or causal mechanism for the often-cited relationship between the geographic place and voting behavior. The presence of a local party branch simply provides the reason or impetus as well as the opportunity for members and supporters to interact and gather, which is likely to translate into heightened electoral activism, as well.[4]

Whereas even the mere presence on the local level can be electorally beneficial for the party, it is quite unlikely for local branches to physically exist and be entirely inactive. In their more likely form as coordinators of local partisan activities, these branches become especially effective tools for cultivating and sustaining party support. During electoral campaigns, local branches serve as effective communicators of the party's central organization's campaign message (Denver and Hands 1997; Ward 2003). Because the local party organization is likely to be acquainted with local problems and needs, it becomes an essential marketing tool for the party's program and ideology. It can sell the party to local voters better than a national campaign, because the local knowledge allows local organizers to translate abstract ideologies into potential solutions to local problems (Geser 1999). This familiarity with the local situation generates a clear advantage for the local party organization over a national party in identifying, targeting, and keeping a record of potential local supporters and using not just passive, but the more effective face-to-face campaign tactics such as social events, rallies, and door-to-door canvassing. Eldersveld (1986), for example, has found that in the United States, local party activists were able to increase the votes given to a specific candidate by 5%–10%. Similarly, Ward (2003) documents an increased local campaign activity in Australia and argues that such a campaign is electorally more beneficial than just a countrywide media campaign, which explains the increasing popularity of this tactic among Australian parties. Rosenstone and Hansen (1993) further illustrate the mobilization capacity of local party organization by suggesting that the absence and inactivity of local party organizations is one of the strongest contributors to the overall turnout decline in the United States.

Other research has shown that local party activity is important not just for mobilizing supporters but also for sustaining the support, as well. The presence of local party structures provides the necessary infrastructure for the party to stay in touch with their supporters during inter-election periods. Shin (2001) reports that the continued success of the PDS in certain regions of Italy is owing to such active and close contacts maintained by the local organizations not just with their supporters and voters but with the entire community. Local organizations can do so through issuing and distributing a local newsletter, by allowing access to local party organizers to discuss one's ideas and concerns, by establishing opening hours for the party office, and by

---

[4] For similar arguments, see the review of literature on the relevance of local parties for success in national elections provided by Clark (2004).

organizing social activities in the community. Geser (1999) argues that local organizations are likely to attract members and activists not necessarily on the basis of their ideological commitment but on the basis of social motivations – getting to know others, having fun, or to better one's reputation (Eldersveld 1986; Marvick 1986). As I argued in the discussion about the effects of membership, members and activists not motivated by ideological reasons are likely to stay party supporters even if the party needs to undertake unpopular but strategic ideological movements. Local branches, thus, play a crucial role in maintaining and mobilizing loyal membership.

Furthermore, local activities are essential not only for voter mobilization but also for potentially converting non-supporters into party supporters. Local party activities and accessibility between elections is likely to cultivate a strong positive image of the party at the local level (regardless of its performance on the national level) as one that cares about real people and real issues. Local parties and their activities are, thus, essential in lowering the information cost for voters (Geser 1999). Lack of information about what a given party stands for may, in turn, prevent people from developing loyalties to a party and being consistent in their vote choice. If costs of gathering information about parties and candidates are too high, some voters will stay away from the polls altogether. Coleman (1996) has shown that in the United States, parties' local presence and activism are significantly increasing electorates' supportive attitudes toward parties. Similarly, Frendreis et al. (1990) envision a potential strategy of party success in overcoming its low support base in a given area by "establishing a token presence, developing a cadre of loyal activists, and gradually recruiting (or converting) credible party candidates" (227). This suggests that parties can use local branches not just for mobilizing their existing voters; building networks of local branches can also become an effective strategy for converting new voters and other parties' supporters into one's own party voters.

Local branches also make it possible for the party to get involved in local politics, which can benefit the party in two interrelated ways. First, local party politics gives the central party a good opportunity to test out new campaign tactics and policy ideas, train new candidates for national elections (Buch Jensen 1999; Geser 1999; Norris and Lovenduski 1995; Seyd and Whiteley 1992), and try out working with different coalition partners (Scarrow 1999; Whiteley, Seyd, and Richardson 1994). Without local presence, parties have to experiment in high-stake national politics where incompetent candidates, policy failures, and coalition debacles are much more costly.

Specifically, ambitious political beginners can test their abilities and motivations to do a political job and can learn the basic things about the political process and institutions on the local level. This experience becomes invaluable for the party once these local politicians advance to the national level. The local training grounds provide the party a wider pool of competent candidates to run on national elections – a clear advantage over parties without local presence.

Shugart, Valdini, and Suominen (2005) argue that prior experience in lower elective office provides voters with substantive cues about politicians' knowledge of the local issues and interests (see also Gallagher 1985; Putnam 1976). It also indicates that such candidates are not just knowledgeable about local issues but that they are also willing and able to tackle them (Marsh 1987). Political experience acts as a heuristic or information shortcut for voters in order to decide which party and candidate to support (Shugart et al. 2005). Given the multitude of candidates on offer, personal attributes that act as information shortcuts make voters' decision making easier.

Research has shown that candidates with prior local-level political experience are likely to significantly improve their party's performance in the national elections. Marsh (1987), for example, finds that in Ireland candidates with local-level political experience are significantly more likely to be elected to the parliament than candidates without such experience. Local-level political experience has also been argued to be an electoral asset in Italy (Katz and Bardi 1980), Finland (Raunio 2005), and Canada (Blais et al. 2003). Tavits (2010) shows with data from Estonia that local-level political experience significantly influences candidate's electoral success compared to his or her co-partisans, and that parties that have more local politicians among their candidates are likely to be electorally more successful.

In addition to training candidates, local presence and involvement in local politics provide a party invaluable experience in campaigning, policy making, and coalition politics. Local parties can try out new campaign tactics. By handling local problems, these branches may be able to develop effective and electorally popular policy initiatives (see Clark 2004). They can also try out working with different coalition partners on the local level. Furthermore, they can do all this within a small, clearly defined territory without affecting the larger party organization at the time of experimentation. Geser (1999), for example, argues that the local sections of the German Social Democratic Party (SDP) were the first to experiment coalitions with the Greens before the national- and state-level parties dared to cooperate with these newcomers. Geser also cites examples of effective national-level SDP policies, such as fighting drug addiction and integrating multicultural populations, that originated from addressing specific problems in specific localities.

In the context of young democracies, where the political elite in general is relatively inexperienced and learning often occurs through trial and error, participating in local politics multiplies the party's opportunities for trial and speeds up the learning process. Furthermore, mistakes made on the local level, because of inexperienced party candidates, incompetent campaigning, unsuccessful (or unrealistic) policy proposals, or failed coalition partnerships, are not as costly as similar mistakes made in the national arena. Parties without local presence and no involvement in local politics necessarily remain less experienced because their learning opportunities are limited and the odds of them making strategic mistakes are increased.

Second, local presence and involvement in local politics helps keep the party afloat even if on the national level the party is experiencing difficult times. Local politics tends to be more pragmatic – citizens are interested in getting solutions to very specific local problems and issues and care less about abstract ideological stances or national-level scandals that the party may be drawn into (Geser 1999). Local parties may, therefore, still attract support and members despite unfavorable macroeconomic or macropolitical conditions or change in the ideological course of the party. This, in turn, creates an opportunity for parties who experience losses on the national level to recuperate and prepare for future opportunities in national politics through their involvement in local affairs. As argued, members' commitment to local parties tends to be less ideological and driven mostly by social gratification (Geser 1999). Studies have shown that such an incentive keeps activists working and local candidates running even if the party on the national level is losing support and members (Eldersveld 1986). Local parties can continue educating the local electorate about party stances and intentions long before the next national campaign. This gives parties with local presence a head start over those parties with no local presence. As previously argued, candidates with local political experience are partisan vote getters. Given this, using their locally experienced and well-known candidates to contest the national elections can overcome temporary setbacks in a way national media campaigns cannot. In short, unlike parties with no local presence, those with a solid network of local branches are not necessarily wiped off of the political map owing to national-level troubles. A network of local branches is a considerable asset for a party's success and long-term survival even in the face of unfavorable environmental conditions.

Existing literature provides several examples of the relevance of a broad network of local branches for parties' electoral success. Early studies in select U.S. cities and counties showed a strong relationship between local party activism and electoral success (Crotty 1971; Cutright 1963; Katz and Eldersveld 1961). On the national level, congressional candidates considered party organizations on local and state level to be important sources of assistance (Herrnson 1986). Similarly, Gibson et al. (1983, 1985, 1989; see also Cotter et al. 1984) document a general strengthening of local organizations of both the Democratic and Republican parties, and argue that a goal of such strengthening was better electoral performance. Given the generally relatively candidate-centered elections in the United States, these findings highlight the relevance of local party organizations and suggest that the effect is likely to be even stronger in more party-centered polities. Indeed, in an early study, Wellhofer (1979) documents that for socialist parties in Argentina, Britain, Norway, and Sweden membership size and extensiveness of local presence increase vote totals. In a similar vein, Bartolini (2000) shows that in Western Europe, organizational density – widespread local presence – is the best predictor of left-party success in the long-term. Several studies have underlined the electoral benefits of local party members and campaigning in Canada and the UK (Black 1984; Carty and

Eagels 1999; Denver and Hands 1997; Johnston and Pattie 2006; Whiteley and Seyd 1994; Whiteley et al. 1994; Widfeldt 1999). Carty (1991) notes that in Canada, a great majority of local party organizations considered local canvassing "important" or "very important" for the party. Pattie et al. (1994, 479) note that in the UK, "an effective and energetic local campaign can make the difference between winning and losing. Political parties ignore their local members at their own peril." More generally, Clark (2004) provides an extensive discussion about the relevance of the local party to electoral performance, reiterating several of the points made here.

In new democracies, too, an extensive network of local branches has been argued to explain the success and failure of parties. Golosov (1998; 2004) provides a convincing account for the argument that in Russia the extensiveness of regional networks of party organizations significantly influenced those parties that survived beyond the first elections and those that did not. Specifically, Golosov showed that by the second democratic Duma election, organizational strength in terms of widespread local presence was the best predictor of the election results, even in terms of the ranking of parties: Communists, with the widest network of local offices, finished first; Liberal Democrats, with the second-widest network, finished second. The study also shows how Communists were in 1995 able to attract a large portion of the 1993 Liberal Democratic electorate with the help of their superior organization. The Liberal Democrats' organizational strength, in turn, accounted for the fact that the party was able to defeat its two ideological rivals and seize the nationalist ideological position all to itself. Golosov (1998, 540) concludes, "This analysis suggests that party organization matters in Russia."

Similarly, LeBas (2011) attributes the initial electoral success of the opposition party Movement for Democratic Change (MDC) in Zimbabwe to the wide and geographically dispersed network of associations that the party possessed. The mobilization of the electorate conducted with the help of these structures led to the MDC's electoral victory despite extremely non-conducive environmental conditions including extensive political violence, the large-scale displacement of party members and supporters, and the creation of areas where it was impossible for the MDC to campaign. Furthermore, as LeBas argues, the electoral strength and internal cohesion of the party was sustained over time partially owing to the effective central organization and partially because that national-level executive devoted a lot of effort in maintaining the network of local party organizations both during and between elections.

Professional Staff
Parties with professional, permanent, and specialized staff at the central level are more likely to succeed in the elections for three interrelated reasons. First, a professional staff is more competent than a pool of volunteers or public office holders to run the administrative affairs of a party. Party-member volunteers

are invaluable for performing short-term non-specialized tasks but not likely to be effective managers of the party. Public office holders (e.g., members of parliament, government, and other elected bodies) simply have no time and often also no skills to run the day-to-day business of a party. Mudde (2007) points out that incompetent personnel is a root cause of a party's disorganized behavior and inability to translate short-term electoral success into long-term political influence. For professional staff, working for the party is not a hobby but a full-time job. Their level of commitment and motivation does not depend on how many other obligations they have or how much they care about some specific issue, as is often the case with volunteers motivated by solidary incentives (Clark and Wilson 1961).

Second, such staff is also more committed to organizing party affairs. Monetary compensation gives party leaders an effective way to motivate their staff and hold them accountable. Third, people employed by the party develop vested interests in the party's survival as an organization (Panebianco 1988); for them, the party is important in itself, not just as a tool for pursuing higher office or policy goals. It is, therefore, in the interests of this bureaucratic structure to keep the party unified and organized, and to help generate party support in the electorate by mediating communication within the organization, with other actors, and the public.

A nonprofessional organization, dependent on the work of volunteers or partisan public office holders, is bound to be less organized and more informal. Furthermore, voluntary work is temporary – it is unlikely that the same people can keep volunteering over long periods of time. The composition of the central office staff consisting of volunteers is therefore likely to change frequently. This also works against developing solid and clear standard operating procedures and rules, keeping records, and successfully managing conflicts. There are no easy tools for party leaders to motivate volunteers, who may quit at any time and are especially likely to quit when the party is experiencing hard times that generate a high workload but little returns in terms of electoral success. Volunteers and partisan elected office holders, who are more likely to be motivated by using party as a tool to meet their goals of office or policy (see Geser 1999) are also more likely to abandon the party during those hard times, when they see that the party no longer serves their purpose. Professional staff, on the other hand, introduces an element of continuity into the organization and makes the survival of this organization as an end goal in its own right.

In accord with these arguments, Mudde (2007) argues that the implosions and unintended splits of the populist radical right parties leading to their demise often result from the weakness of the central organization. Similarly, Gunther and Hopkin (2002) document that the Union of the Democratic Center (UDC) in Spain collapsed in 1982 because of "the highly visible internal struggles and schisms" (191) made possible by the lack of strong central organization and official means of conflict resolution. The UDC case is especially interesting because the party possessed an elaborate network of local branches and a size-able membership – the other two attributes of strong organizations as defined here. This underlines the interdependence of the three attributes, rather than the primacy of any single attribute, in determining party success and survival. Other parties have clearly recognized the importance of a strong and professional central organization. For example, Sorauf and Wilson (1990) argue that the Republican Party in the United States strengthened its central organization with the specific goal of doing better in elections.

Another important function of the central party bureaucracy underlining its interconnectedness with other attributes in determining party success is in mediating communication within the organization and with other actors and the public outside the party. The central organization has an important role in collecting and storing information, and disseminating it down the party structure. The central office staff also manage the party's relations with the media and public and thereby, in a way, conduct an ongoing campaign by publicizing party stances on topical issues. Considering the case of the opposition party MDC in Zimbabwe, LeBas (2011) argues that their initial electoral success and subsequent survival was made possible in large part because the party's central organization was able to both quickly develop means of conflict resolution, and generate and sustain effective channels of communication with the local party branches (which themselves contributed to the party's success, as previously discussed). In the context of CEE, Grzymala-Busse (2002a) provides a well-argued account of the relevance of professional staff for the electoral success of ex-communist parties. In sum, the existence of a central, professional party organization responsible for generating and sustaining procedures to resolve conflict and communicate within the party are crucial for the party's electoral success and survival.

Although I have discussed the role of each attribute of party organizational strength separately, as I stressed earlier, these attributes are mutually interdependent and their effect on party success and survival mutually reinforcing. To reiterate, active and extensive membership and a wide network of branch offices can be of effective service to the party in enhancing their performance only if their activities are successfully coordinated and organized from the center. Huckshorn et al. (1986), for example, show that the development of the local party directly depends on the efforts of the party's central office. At the same time, a professional central office alone remains incapacitated if there is no membership and there are no branches to implement party strategies. Similarly, members and local branches are also interchangeably linked (Clark 2004): the creation of local branches requires the existence of a countrywide membership, because a branch office can only be created in a locality where the party has, or can find, some members. Each branch, in turn, is likely to attract more locals to become party members. Furthermore, members conduct many of their partisan (and electorally beneficial) activities through party units, often at lower than the central level. Therefore, it is reasonable to think of party organizational strength as a unified concept. The attributes have been separated only for the sake of theoretical clarity.

Organizational Strength of the Local Party

So far, the argument relating organizational strength to electoral performance has focused on the national level, with the expectation that organizational strength separates the successful from the unsuccessful parties. However, it is equally interesting to consider how variance in the organizational strength of party subunits affects the electoral performance of the party in different electoral districts. It is possible that a dynamic similar to the one previously described also applies here; that is, a party is more likely to attract votes in districts where it has a stronger organizational presence than in those where its organizational presence is negligible. In fact, considering the variance within parties helps get at the causal mechanisms more directly. For example, if immediate interactions and local presence matter for party success, then we should see organizational strength accounting for at least some of the difference in the level of support for a given party across districts. If, however, organizational strength is important for mobilizing voters only (or mostly) because it helps signal competence, reliability, and accountability of the party at the national arena, then variance in the organizational strength of the local party may be less important for explaining geographical patterns of support for the party. That is, a voter in a given district may be persuaded that a given party is competent and reliable by the fact that the party has, in general, a strong organization, even though its organizational presence in that voter's district is weak. If that is the case, then we might still see that parties with stronger organizations perform better than those with weak organizations, but a party would not necessarily perform better in districts where it has the strongest organizational presence compared to districts where its organization is weak. I will explore these district-level relationships in the second part of the empirical analysis.

Organizational Strength and Electoral Success: Existing Evidence

The discussion previously cited several studies that provided direct or indirect evidence of the relevance of the different aspects of organizational strength on the electoral performance of a party. Existing literature also provides several examples of cases where party organizational strength in general, without being separated into distinct attributes, has been argued to influence party performance. For example, Janda (1983) argues that as much as 30 percent of the electoral success of parties is owing to their organizational strength. When discussing the success of radical right parties, Mudde (2007) argues that their long-term survival depends on organizational factors. In the context of the CEE democracies, Deegan-Krause (2006) argues that in Slovakia parties without strong organizations disappeared throughout the 1990s. Similarly,

Hanley (2003) reports that the two main Czech parties – the Civic Democratic Party (ODS) and the Social Democratic Party (ČSSD) – both succeeded and survived over time because of their organizational strength. Unlike the other studies listed here, Hanley (2003) actually also states the mutually reinforcing elements of organizational strength that the study argued to have led to success – a nationwide network of local branches, professional central staff, and a sizeable number of activists.

Additionally, recent formal theoretical work and its empirical applications increasingly stress the relevance of valence in addition to any substantive issue positions to explain party competition (Ansolabehere and Snyder 2000; Clark 2009; Groseclose 2001; Schofield and Miller 2003; Schofield and Sened 2006). Valence in these studies is interpreted as non–policy-related concerns of voters (see also Stokes 1963, 1992), and it is argued to significantly influence party electoral performance as well as ideological positioning. The substance of the concept of valence has not been clearly specified in the existing literature, but it is often defined as the perceived competence and integrity of a party, that is, the degree to which a party is perceived to be capable of governing effectively (Abney et al. 2013; Adams et al. 2005; Ezrow 2008; Schofield and Miller 2003). Furthermore, a party can increase its valence by cultivating activist resources – money and time – that is used to carry the party's message to the electorate and thereby increase party support among the rank-and-file voters. Note that such description of valence and the interpretation of its role in party competition are very similar to the role of the party organization previously described. It is, therefore, likely that party organizational strength is closely associated with at least some aspects of valence. Such an interpretation of party organizational strength situates the current study at the center of the most recent theoretical work on party competition.

Counterarguments

The proposed relationship between party organizational strength and party performance is not a foregone conclusion. Janda (1993, 178), for example, states that the scholarly community is generally skeptical about the value of party organizational strength in delivering votes, even despite the fact that "practical politicians think otherwise." Studies argue that even if organization mattered, there is not and cannot be one best form of strong party organization because different organizational styles work for different parties (Kitschelt 1994; Luther and Müller-Rommel 2002; Römmele 1999). They therefore conclude that an analysis of the effect of organizational factors becomes almost meaningless (Deschouwer 1994). Others argue that organization does not help but may hurt the party because an extensive organization introduces strategic inflexibility (Kitschelt et al. 1999; Levitsky 2003; Scarrow 1994; Shefter 1994), which may lead to party stagnation and loss of electoral support. Similarly, large organizations may become inefficient and wasteful; they may put the party in a financial strain rather than helping keep down costs (Scarrow 1994).

Money and time "wasted" on developing and maintaining the organization could better be spent on professional media-dependent campaigning that is increasingly argued to be the key to winning elections. Organization is costly in other ways, as well: as the "law of curvilinear disparity" suggests, party activists tend to be more extreme and ideological than either the party leaders or voters (Kitschelt 1989; May 1973). A strong organization may grant too much power to activists and force the leadership to adopt policy positions that are extreme and alienating to voters (see also Schofield and Miller 2003; Schofield and Sened 2006).

The literature on party decline uses the fact that parties in Western Europe have trimmed down their organizations as evidence that such organizations are not needed or wanted to win elections (Harmel and Janda 1994; Katz and Mair 1994, 1995; see also Kitschelt et al. 1999). This is an intuitive argument; it builds on a conventional wisdom that the development of mass media and public opinion polling allows party leaders to communicate with the electorate directly rather than through their party organization. This, in turn, makes party organizations obsolete (Bowler and Farrell 1996; Butler and Kavanagh 1974; Katz and Mair 1995; Webb 1995). The success of Forza Italia is often cited as evidence that strategic media usage, rather than organizational strength, gives a party competitive advantage (Luther and Müller-Rommel 2002).[5] This point is even more strongly echoed by scholars of CEE parties citing instances of a sudden electoral success of parties and candidates without any significant organizational backing.

A number of studies claim that parties in CEE are organizationally weak compared to parties in Western Europe (see, for example, Kopecky 1995; P. Lewis 1996; Perkins 1996; Toole 2003; Van Biezen 2003). In the form of broad generalizations these studies argue that parties in CEE do not prioritize organizationally penetrative strategies, partisan linkages with society are weak, membership is of little importance, territorial presence of parties is limited, and so forth. It is common to conclude, in line with the scholars of party decline, that such organizational weakness means that parties in the region do not need organizations (Kitschelt et al. 1999; Kopecky 1995; P. Lewis 2000; Mickiewicz and Richter 1996; Perkins 1996). There are no strong organizations because electoral campaigns are media based and personality centered rather than ideological. So convicted, these studies did not see organizational weakness as a short-term phenomenon. Rather, they predicted that elitist and slim party organizations will remain the norm in the region (Kopecky 1995; Mair 1997; Szczerbiak 1999a). Other studies, however, used the same general conclusion about the overall weakness of party organizations in CEE to explain why elections were media based and leader-centered (P. Lewis 2000; Tworzecki 2003), assuming that perhaps the situation may change. What characterizes all of these studies, however, is the lack of systematic evidence

---

[5] However, as Seisselberg (1996) notes, even the quintessential media party Forza Italia has been compelled to build a network of local organizations.

about whether or not party organization influences party performance, which is why the predictions and explanations remain mostly speculative.

The criticism of speculative arguments aside, there is some empirical evidence that party organization does not matter or that it inhibits rather than helps electoral success, although the evidence is often on the basis of a limited number of parties or elections only (see also Spirova 2007). For example, Pomper (1990) studies the effect of party organizational strength in one county in the United States and finds that it has almost no effect on party votes in state assembly elections. Similarly, Cotter et al. (1984) report, also in the U.S. context, that organizational factors have only a modest effect on gubernatorial election results. Chhibber (1999) studies the split of the Indian Congress Party into one that consisted mostly of Congress Party Members of Parliament (MPs) (the Ruling Congress Party) and another that maintained control over the party's extensive organization (the Congress Party Organization). The former – the new party without any organization – won the subsequent 1971 elections. Chhibber (1999, 91) concludes, "[E]lections can be won without the benefit of an elaborate party organization to serve as an instrument of electoral mobilization and a mechanism of screening candidates." The Congress Party example also shows that having such an organization is not a guarantee of electoral success. In the context of CEE, P. Lewis (2000) cites the example of the Polish presidential elections in 1990, where Stanisław Tymiński – a candidate with no organizational support – did considerably better than candidates of organizationally well-developed parties.

There are other, more inclusive, studies that also suggest organizations, or some aspects of them, may not matter for electoral success and survival in the new democracies of CEE. Specifically, Grzymala-Busse (2002a) and Ishiyama (2001) argue that those former communist parties who were able to considerably slim down their organizations succeeded and survived in the newly democratized regimes and those that kept their extensive organization failed. Spirova (2007) considers the performance of three Bulgarian and three Hungarian parties and concludes that the effect of organizational factors – membership size, local presence, and professionalization – is inconclusive, with some of the six parties under study confirming and others providing contradictory evidence.

In sum, reasonable doubts have been raised questioning the hypothesized relationship between party organizational strength and electoral performance. This underscores the need to provide systematic empirical evidence of the relationship – a task that has remained challenging, not least because of the difficulties of data collection.

Data, Measures, and Models

The main tests of the hypothesized effect of party organizational strength on electoral success focuses on data from four post-communist democracies – the Czech Republic, Estonia, Hungary, and Poland. I use a party-level dataset for pooling information across all democratic elections in the four countries to test the hypothesis with four different measures of party organizational strength. As part of the robustness tests of the party-level analysis, I extend the sample of countries to include all ten post-communist members of the European Union, that is, I add information from Bulgaria, Latvia, Lithuania, Romania, Slovakia, and Slovenia. Data for the additional countries are sparse and for some variables not available at all, which is why this analysis is part of the additional tests rather than the main test. However, it still helps to establish the generalizability of the findings. The following discussion about measurement refers to the main four countries under study. The extended sample is described under "Robustness tests and additional analyses."

In addition to the cross-national party-level analysis, a separate analysis, focusing on the within-party dynamics on the district level, uses electoral district-level datasets pooling across districts, parties, and election years for each of the four countries separately. The Estonian district-level analysis uses three, the Czech two, and the Hungarian and Polish analyses use one indicator of organizational strength.[6]

For all countries, I have included those parties that have gotten into the parliament at least once or contested at least two parliamentary elections during the period under study.[7] The dependent variable – party success – is measured by a party's national- (or district-)[8] level "Vote share" in lower house parliamentary elections. Appendix 2.1 lists the data sources for all measures.

Measures of Party Organizational Strength

I use four different indicators to measure party organizational strength as explained in Chapter 1. First, "Membership" measures the number of party members as the percent of total national (district) electorate. An alternative measure – "Branches" – indicates the number of municipal-level party branches divided by the total number of municipalities in a given country (district).

---

[6] "District" refers to the electoral districts used in the national parliamentary elections; for Hungary, it refers to the twenty counties serving as regional PR districts. For the Czech Republic, I used the pre-2002 districts for all years to ensure cross-temporal comparability. The Polish dataset effectively excludes elections before 1997 because district-level data on organizational strength are not available for those years; I use the post-2001 districts for all years to ensure cross-temporal comparability.

[7] In most cases, this selection was made for me by virtue of the unavailability of organizational data. However, excluding these cases is not likely to be problematic because, if anything, the remaining sample is biased *against* finding support for the hypothesized effect. A party that only exists for one election and disappears without getting into parliament is unlikely to have an extensive professional organization. Therefore, if data for these cases existed and they were included in the analysis, the results of the hypothesized effect would be even stronger than the ones reported here.

[8] If different from the measure in the cross-national dataset, the measurement for the district-level datasets is indicated in the parentheses.

Professionalization is measured by the size of the central-office paid staff. The variable "Staff," measured as a percent of the electorate (in hundred thousands), does not vary across districts and is therefore only included in the cross-national dataset. Finally, "Participation in local elections" measures the share of municipalities nationwide (within a district), in which a given party runs its candidates in a local-government council election.[9]

The inclusion of the last indicator may require some further elaboration. In essence, this indicator captures all of the different aspects of party organizational strength as defined in this study. Theoretically, a party that is able to run candidates in all (or most) local governments is (1) likely to have organizational presence in these localities in order to be able to nominate local candidates, (2) likely to have membership in these localities from which to draw nominees and which is likely to add up to a sizeable nationwide membership, and (3) likely to have strong and professional central office staff to be able to manage and coordinate the widespread local presence of the party. Whereas even weak parties can manage to find candidates to run full lists in all districts in national elections, being able to do so in local elections truly requires organizational strength in terms of large membership, a wide network of branches, and efficient management. In all four countries, local elections are mostly contested by independent candidates or local candidate lists, and a national party can credibly enter local contests only if it has local presence.

In addition to the face validity and theoretical justification of this measure, existing literature has also referred to it as a potential measure of party strength. When discussing populist radical right parties in Europe, Mudde (2007, 266) argues that parties' organizational weaknesses can be inferred from "their inability to contest the same districts over sustained periods of time." He cites empirical evidence from Germany, Britain, and Belgium to illustrate the validity of this argument. As already mentioned, Pomper (1990) ended up using the share of local precincts where the party had a precinct leader (primary candidate), even if that candidate did not really do any party work, as one of the measures of party organizational strength in the United States. This indicator was recommended by Democratic and Republican county chairs as "harder data on party organization than the unreliable responses to a mail questionnaire" that the study was originally planned to rely on (Pomper 1990, 202). Both Moser (2001) and Golosov (2004, see also 1998) implicitly use the share of partisan versus non-partisan candidates at the district level as a measure of party strength in the context of new democracies of Eastern Europe. More directly related to party presence in local governments, John and Saiz (1999)

---

[9] With a few exceptions, the first three indicators were measured prior to the election year but as close to it as possible (most often the year before the election) to minimize the possible endogeneity problem. Participation in local elections was measured using data from the local election that immediately preceded or occurred in the same year as the national election.

use party membership of mayors as an indicator of party strength. Deegan-Krause (2006, 261) argues that in the Czech Republic and Slovakia "the ability of parties to field candidates in local elections" offers evidence of "the levels of organizational intensiveness," which "correspond closely to parties' claims about their organizational intensiveness." Similarly, Kopecky (2006) shows that in the Czech Republic, parties with a small membership were unable to field candidates in local elections outside the major cities. Furthermore, parties themselves and the media in the region use this indicator to compare the organizational strength of parties in different regions and nationwide (Ideon 2009a; Kalmre 1996; Savisaar 2002; Tammer 1997).

Additionally, Table 2.1 presents (1) pair-wise correlation coefficients between participation in local elections and other measures of party organizational strength using the national and district-level datasets, and (2) the results of a factor analysis. All correlation coefficients are statistically significant at the 1 percent level, and all variables also load on a single factor. This further suggests that participation in local elections is a valid measure of party organizational strength. Finally, this measure also offers practical advantages. Information about candidates in local elections is more likely to be available (if not always easy to locate or access) for all parties – including those that went extinct without leaving a traceable documentation about their organization – across time from national election officials or national archives.

A few additional notes are in order about the specifics of measuring participation in local elections. First, the measure does not include any information on party performance in local elections, which is likely to be significantly related to performance in national elections because of the ideological or partisan affinities of voters. The measure here only considers whether the party participated. Furthermore, as participation in local elections is measured (in some cases several years) prior to when the national election is held, it is unlikely that a party name in the local election ballot directly influences national election results. Rather, it is more likely that the way participation in local elections influences national election results is via party organizational strength: the ability to run candidates in local elections presumes that the party has local organizational presence and membership that it is using for electoral purposes also in national elections.[10]

---

[10] As stated previously, parties may sponsor some of the independent candidates. However, not only is it impossible to get this information, but I also think that it has no significant confounding effect on the measure as it is used here – to capture party organizational strength. If a candidate is unable or unwilling to run under a party label in a given municipality, then it is quite likely that the party has no significant organizational presence there and has just struck a short-term bargain with the candidate. Party leaders and the media in the region echoed this sentiment (Paet 1998c, 1998d; Savisaar 2002), arguing that running in a local electoral coalition indicates the organizational weakness of the party (Tammer 1997). One might also argue that being able to run in local elections simply indicates that the party is attractive to local candidates. However, before joining, these candidates need to also consider whether that party is attractive to the local

TABLE 2.1. *Relationships Between the Different Measures of Party Organizational Strength*

	Correlation w/Participation in Local Elections			Factor Loading		
Variable Label	Estonia (district-level data)	Czech R. (district-level data)	Pooled Cross-National Data	Estonia (district-level data)	Czech R. (district-level data)	Pooled Cross-National Data
Participation in local elections				0.78	0.93	0.77
Membership	0.36*** N = 230	0.41*** N = 86	0.53*** N = 117	0.52	0.76	0.83
Branches	0.79*** N = 288	0.86*** N = 21	0.61*** N = 86	0.80	0.87	0.77
Staff			0.36*** N = 72			0.42

Note: Reliable district-level information on organizational variables other than "Participation in local elections" is not available for Hungary and Poland. Pooled cross-national data includes national-level data for all four countries: the Czech Republic, Estonia, Hungary, and Poland.

*** $p \leq 0.01$

Second, parties can contest local elections alone or in an electoral coalition with other parties or both. In some cases, especially in Hungary and Poland, the coalitions are relatively large and consist of a list of four or five parties. In such cases, party labels do not carry much weight locally, which further suggests that none of the individual parties has a significant actual grassroots presence. A party with a strong local organization would not want to dilute its label by attaching its name to a string of other names. I therefore dismissed participation in coalitions larger than two parties for the purposes of this measure. The order in which parties in such coalitions are listed on the ballot differs in different municipalities, reflecting the relative strength and level of name recognition (i.e., presumably the relative organizational strength) of each partner in a given district. Because of this, I only consider the first listed party in any two-party coalition.

The average number of municipalities in each country was as follows: 6,222 in the Czech Republic; 237 in Estonia; 3,131 in Hungary; and 2,448 in Poland, with an average population per municipality of 1,685; 5,655; 3,200; and 15,584 in each of the four countries, respectively. The exact number of local government units varies somewhat over the years for some countries owing to municipal mergers and splits. In order to get some sense of the extent to which municipal elections are a partisan affair in each of these countries, one could look at the share of municipalities that are not contested by any national party. Considering the latest municipal elections included in this study, these shares are as follows: the Czech Republic 49 percent; Estonia 5 percent; Hungary 62 percent; and Poland 15 percent. One has to bear in mind, however, that according to this measure, it only takes one party to run in a given municipality to count that election as partisan, even if all other candidates or lists are non-partisan. That said, the shares still reflect the presence of some cross-national variance in the extent to which parties contest local elections. In the cross-national analysis, country dummies are employed to control for this variance in the empirical analysis.

In the country-specific district-level datasets, the number of municipalities in each district varies across countries and also somewhat for different years for the same country, owing to municipal mergers and splits. Excluding the capital cities, that tend to contain fewer municipalities, the average number of municipalities per district is as follows: 484 in the Czech Republic; 30 in Estonia; 165 in Hungary; and 60 in Poland. I have excluded those districts that contain only one municipality: Prague in the Czech Republic (except in 2002 and 2006 when Prague contains 58 municipalities), and Tallinn and Tartu in Estonia. With only one municipality, the share of local governments contested

---

electorate – a condition that is more likely to be met by a party with local presence. Another common phenomenon in the region is that governing parties can attract candidates (often with patronage) without significant organizational presence. I will account for this possible confounding effect in the analysis by controlling for governing parties.

TABLE 2.2. *Pair-Wise Correlation Coefficients Between Vote Share and Party Organizational Strength*

Measure of Organizational Strength	Pair-Wise Correlation Coefficient	N
Participation in local elections	0.42***	104
Branches	0.27***	84
Membership	0.16*	104
Staff	0.43***	63

Note: $^*p \leq 0.1$, $^{***}p \leq 0.01$

can only take one of the extreme values – 1 (if contested) or 0 (if did not contest). This would not accurately capture organizational strength and may bias the results. In the reported results, I have also excluded Warsaw in Poland. Warsaw does not include separate municipalities; however, it is divided into separate districts for the municipal elections. The results do not change when the value of participation in local elections for Warsaw is calculated using these districts (the number of which varies from ten to twenty-two depending on the year).

Appendix 2.2 presents descriptive statistics for the measures of party organizational strength. These are calculated after list-wise deletion of cases with missing data to accurately represent the descriptives for the regression results reported. Using the cross-national dataset, Table 2.2 reports pair-wise correlation coefficients between logged vote share and the various measures of organizational strength. All correlation coefficients are positive and statistically significant as expected. Additionally, for each country, Table 2.3 lists the five parties (and corresponding election years) with the strongest organization according to each of the four indicators of organizational strength. Although informative, this is a very crude classification of parties and one should keep in mind that all measures may not be available for all parties, which is likely to influence this ranking. Still, we see many of the same parties appear as the strongest on different measures of organizational strength. Table 2.4 complements this with similar rankings of the weakest parties. There is more variation across the different measures as to the identity of the weakest parties because the missing data has a greater effect on the lower end of the distribution. Overall, not much can be read into the rankings in Tables 2.3 and 2.4. However, they do provide the reader with some information about the measure of the independent variable and identity of the cases included in the analysis.

Other Explanatory Variables

Parties may succeed for other than organizational reasons. First, a charismatic or strong leader may be responsible for party performance in elections. The widespread claim previously discussed about the lack of party organizations

TABLE 2.3. *The Parties with the Strongest Organization by Country and Indicator*

Country	Participation in Local Elections	Membership	Branches	Staff
Czech Republic	KSČM 2002	KSČM 1992	KSČM 1996	ČSSD 2002
	KSČM 1996	KSČM 1996	KSČM 2002	ČSSD 1996
	KDU-ČSL 2002	KSČM 1998	KSČM 1998	ČSSD 1992
	KDU-ČSL 1996	KSČM 2002	KSČM 2006	ČSSD 1998
	KSČM 1998	KDU-ČSL 1992	KDU-ČSL 1996–1998	ČSSD 2006
Estonia	ERL 2007	ERL 2007	K 2007	RP 2003
	K 2007	K 2007	ERL 2003	RE 2007
	ERL 2003	ERL 2003	ERL 2007	IL 2007
	K 2003	K 2003	IL 2007	RE 2003
	RE 2007	RE 2007	RP 2003	K 2007
Hungary	MSzP 1994	KDNP 2002	FKgP 1998	MSzP 1990–1994
	Fidesz 2006	FKgP 1998	MSzP 1994	MSzP 1990–1994
	FKgP 1998	FKgP 1994	KDNP 2002	MSzP 1998
	MSzP 2002	MSzP 1990	MSzP 1990	MSzP 2002
	MSzP 2006	FKgP 1990	FKgP 1994	MSzP 2006
Poland	SLD 2005	PSL 1993	SLD 1997	PiS 2007
	PSL 1997	PSL 1991	SLD 1993	PSL 1997
	PSL 2005	PSL 1997	SLD 2001	PO 2007
	PSL 2001	PSL 2007	SLD 2005	KPN 1997
	PSL 2007	SLD 2001	PSL 1991–2005	PSL 2007

Party abbreviations: ČSSD = Czech Social Democratic Party; ERL = Estonian Peoples' Party; Fidesz = Alliance of Young Democrats; FKgP = Independent Smallholders' Party; IL = Pro Patria; K = Estonian Center Party; KDU-ČSL = Christian Democratic Union – Czechoslovak Peoples' Party; KDNP = Christian Democratic Peoples' Party; KPN = Confederation of Independent Poland; KSČM = Communist Party of Bohemia and Moravia; MSzP = Hungarian Socialist Party; PiS = Law and Justice; PO = Civic Platform; PSL = Polish Peasant Party; RE = Estonian Reform Party; RP = Res Publica; SLD = Democratic Left Alliance.

in CEE was often accompanied by the argument that party politics in the region is strongly personalistic. Noninstitutionalized party systems are almost automatically considered to be driven by ambitious leaders (Mainwaring and Scully 1995). Descriptive accounts were made to back up this argument, with several studies attributing the dominant role in CEE party politics to party leaders (Kopecky 1995; Van Biezen 2003). Furthermore, such leadership was seen as instrumental for gaining votes – having a strong and well-known party leader and other famous personalities as part of the list of candidates was considered a must to successfully contest elections. That is, new parties were expected to provide charismatic linkages to voters (Römmele 1999). Toka (1998), for

TABLE 2.4. *The Parties with the Weakest Organization by Country and Indicator*

Country	Participation in Local Elections	Membership	Branches	Staff
Czech Republic	Moravne 1996	ODA 1992	ODA 1992	Moravne 2006
	ODA 2006	SZ 2002	Moravane 2006	US-DEU 2006
	SPR-RSČ 2006	Moravane 2006	US-DEU 2002	ODA 2006
	US-DEU 2006	SZ 2006	DEU 1996	SZ 2006
	ODA 2002	SPR-RSČ 2006	ODA 2002	ODA 2002
Estonia	KE 2003	PK 1992	SDE 1995	SDE 2003
	PK 1992–2003	Sinine 1995	ROH 2007	ERL 1999
	ROH 2007	PK 1995	RE 1995	SDE 1995
	Sinine 1995–2003	K 1992	K 1995	RE 1995
	VEE 1999 +10 other parties	SDE 1992	RE 1999	IL 1995
Hungary	VP 1998	KDNP 1990	Fidesz 1990	MIÉP 1998
	VP 2002	Fidesz 1990	MIÉP 1998	KDNP 2006
	FKgP 2006	MIÉP 1998	SzDSz 1990	MDF 2002
	ASz 2006	MDF 2006	FKgP 2002	Fidesz 2002
	MIÉP 1994	FKgP 2002	MDF 1990	SzDSz 2006
Poland	PD 2005	PD 2007	UP 2007	UP 2007
	PPPP 1997	KdR 1993	UP 2005	UP 2005
	KdR 1997	UP 1993	PiS 2007	AWS 2001
	BdP 1997	UPR 1993	SRP 2005–2007	UP 2001
	KLD 1997	PiS 2001	SRP 2005–2007	PO 2001

Party abbreviations: ASz = Agrarian Alliance; AWS = Solidarity Election Action; BdP = Bloc for Poland; DEU = Democratic Union; ERL = Estonian Peoples' Party; Fidesz = Alliance of Young Democrats; FKgP = Independent Smallholders' Party; IL = Pro Patria; K = Estonian Center Party; KDNP = Christian Democratic Peoples' Party; KdR = Coalition for the Republic; KE = Coalition Party; KLD = Liberal Democratic Congress; MDF = Hungarian Democratic Forum; MIÉP = Hungarian Justice and Life Party; Moravane = Moravians (formerly HSMS and MDS); ODA = Civic Democratic Alliance; PD = Democratic Party (formerly UD and UW); PiS = Law and Justice; PK = Agrarian Union; PPPP = Polish Beer-Lovers' Party; PO = Civic Platform; RE = Estonian Reform Party; ROH = Estonian Green Party; SDE = Social Democratic Party (formerly Moderates); Sinine = Blue Party; SPR-RSČ = Republican Party of Czechoslovakia; SRP = Self-Defense; SZ = Green Party; SzDSz = Alliance of Free Democrats; UP = Labor Union; UPR = Real Politics Union; US-DEU = Freedom Union – Democratic Union; VEE = Russian Party in Estonia; VP = Party of Entrepreneurs.

example, argued that given the limited information available about the parties, voters frequently relied on the information embedded in leaders' biographies. The leader effect may be even more fundamental, that is, not constrained to new democracies and new parties. Research on advanced democracies has also shown that leaders attract support for the party by personal charisma (Nicholson 1972; Van der Brug and Mughan 2007).

Other studies are more skeptical. Studying the success of populist radical right parties in the case of which charismatic leadership is almost universally claimed to influence electoral success, Mudde (2007) argues that a charismatic leader matters only for a party's initial or occasional success. However, for long-term sustained electoral performance, leaders become much less important. Furthermore, Mudde underlines a major problem with the variable charismatic leader – it is a notoriously vague concept. Overall, however, a leadership effect cannot fully be denied and remains a plausible rival hypothesis for the organization-based argument proposed here.

Given that the Czech, Estonian, and Polish electoral systems allow voters to cast personal votes, the variable "Leader-centeredness" can be measured in a systematic way using these votes. Specifically, for the district-level datasets, I consider the share of district votes for the party leader compared to those for the second–most-popular candidate from the same party (see also Mikkel 1999). The greater this difference, the more leader-centered the party. Unfortunately, a similar measurement technique does not work for Hungary because of the different electoral system. Therefore, I have used expert assessment of whether the party leadership is personalized or not. This assessment is available for all parties, all years since 1990 from Enyedi (2008). The cross-national dataset requires a single measure for all countries. In order to obtain this, I kept the binary coding for the Hungarian parties. For other countries, I classified parties as leader-centered for those election years where their leader's district vote share was at least two times higher than that of his or her second–most-popular co-partisan.

In addition to the charismatic linkage, parties can rely on clientelism to gain votes. This type of linkage is argued to be especially prevalent in newer, less developed democracies and is therefore appropriate to discuss in the current context as a potential rival explanation.[11] The argument about patronage politics and electoral success is not always clear, however. Patronage or clientelism can be conceptualized in two ways. First, it refers to "party colonization of the state" (Kopecky 2008, 8) – the allocation of government administrative jobs in exchange for party loyalty (Perkins 1996). Such an activity can create

---

[11] Of course, one might also argue that clientelistic linkage is not an alternative to party organizational strength, but that such strength makes some forms of clientelism possible in the first place because it may help parties tap into local clientelistic structures. Whether and how party organizational strength is related to clientelism is an interesting topic that future studies may want to explore.

selective incentives only for party elites and activists rather than for members and voters. Therefore, the effect of this type of clientelism on party vote is not straightforward. Another way in which patronage can be defined is in terms of pork-barrel politics, which is directly targeted toward selected segments of society (Crisp et al. 2004; Ferejohn 1974). In this case, the potential electoral linkage is easier to understand.

Regardless of the conceptualization, however, clientelism is almost impossible to capture empirically because parties themselves have an incentive to disguise it, and there are no obvious observable indicators that could be used as hard evidence of clientelism (Kitschelt 2000; Kopecky 2008). Furthermore, instances of clientelism that are publicized or can be tracked suggest that this linkage strategy is not necessarily intrinsic to specific parties, but depends on system characteristics and opportunities (Kitschelt 2000). In a parliamentary system, both types of patronage politics can be exercised only by governing parties, that is, parties that have access to policy making and administrative appointments (see also Dahlberg and Johansson 2002; Tavits 2009c). "Government membership" can serve as a rough indicator of whether clientelism effects may be present, and is measured by whether or not a given party was in government before the election. Note that the possible positive effect of pork and patronage on vote share may be canceled out by an opposite effect that government membership may produce: literature on advanced democracies documents a systematic vote loss ("the cost of ruling") commonly suffered by governing parties (Nannestad and Paldam 2002).

Funding is another major factor determining party success. In addition to influencing electoral success directly, funding determines the extent to which a party can rely on media to run its campaigns. Many studies on party politics in the region argue that campaigns in CEE are almost entirely media driven (Kitschelt et al. 1999; P. Lewis 2000; Mickiewicz and Richter 1996; Perkins 1996), suggesting that parties' ability to run nationwide media campaigns becomes the measure of their success (Römmele 1999). Investing in a nationwide media campaign is seen as a clear alternative for "the arduous task of party organizational development" (P. Lewis 2000, 113), and therefore a path that parties are more likely to follow. After all, an established media network ready to be used for influencing public opinion already exists even in these new democracies. However, access to media has often been related to (or even equated with) access to money, which makes the financial resources an important part of this rival hypothesis. I have used the size of a party's budget in local currency (in millions) as the measure of funding (variable name "Budget").[12] For the sake of comparability, in the cross-national dataset, the budget is measured as a percent of national GDP.

---

[12] In post-communist Europe, parties rely heavily on public funding that is often tied to electoral performance in previous elections. Because I will be controlling for parties' previous vote share in the empirical analysis, the effect of budget may remain underestimated. Another possibility is to

Economic performance (measured by national- [district] level unemployment rate; variable name "Unemployment rate") may also influence the electoral success of parties (Tucker 2006). Following the economic voting literature, I have included an interaction term between government membership and economic performance. Finally, I control for the "Number of lists" competing nationwide (in a district).

One might argue that ideological appeals also influence what parties win or lose votes. The modeling techniques described, including controlling for party effects by clustering the standard errors on party or including party dummies, and controlling for the lagged dependent variable, are expected to control for party ideology, among other things. It is difficult, if not impossible, to account for the role of party ideology more directly. For example, it is not clear that leftist or rightist parties are more likely to be electorally successful. It is also not clear that parties close to the center are necessarily more successful. One could argue that taking into account party placement relative to voter preferences might be appropriate. However, this approach has two possible problems. First, information on the distribution of voter preferences and party positions on the same scale are not available. The national election studies, if available at all, cover only a few elections included in this study. The same is true about the European election studies. Even if the data existed, it is not clear how these could be taken into account in a model predicting party vote share. The ongoing debate over directional versus proximity voting simply does not offer clear answers on how ideological placement might advance a party's electoral performance (Iversen 1994; Lewis and King 1999; see also Fowler and Laver 2008; Kedar 2005). Given this, controlling for party effects is the most direct way these ideological effects can be controlled for. Case studies in Chapter 3 will follow a similar strategy: party ideology is held constant by comparing the electoral success of ideologically very similar parties.

Results of the Cross-Country Analysis

The first analysis focuses on across-party dynamics: Are parties with stronger organizations more likely to succeed electorally than their organizationally weak counterparts? The dependent variable – vote share – is a proportion ranging from 0 to 1. I have log transformed the dependent variable in order to obtain a more or less normal distribution and use ordinary least squares (OLS) regression to estimate the models.[13] All datasets are also pooled

---

look at the size of party campaign expenditure. The budget information is more complete, which is why I have used this measure in the analyses presented. However, if campaign expenditure is used, the substantive results are very similar.

[13] The vote-share data are generally considered to be compositional in nature in that proportions for all parties must sum to one. This poses a potential problem for using OLS regression, which treats vote share for each party independently. Several methods have been proposed for analyzing compositional data (Katz and King 1999; Tomz, Tucker, and Wittenberg 2002).

cross-section time series in nature. However, not all information is available for all parties and years because not all parties contested all elections and because of unavailability of data for some that did. This makes the party-year and party–district-year panels unbalanced. Furthermore, the number of time points is considerably smaller than the number of cross-sectional units. Therefore, I have not used any panel data techniques. Instead, I have used OLS with robust standard errors clustered on party. Such an error estimator remains valid in the presence of any types of correlations among errors within parties, including correlation owing to any party-specific factors or serial correlation (Rogers 1993), both of which are likely to be present here.[14] I also include country dummies in order to control for country-level factors. Additionally, one might argue that it is not strong organizations that bring success, but that only parties that are successful (i.e., have a larger support base) can build stronger organizations. Therefore, I estimate dynamic models of party success by accounting for a party's previous vote share. The lagged dependent variable and standard errors clustered on party also help control for any party-specific factors that cannot directly be measured, including their ideological positioning relative to voter preferences.

The cross-national dataset contains eighty-two parties in four countries across up to six elections. The exact number of cases included in the different models depends on the availability of data. Table 2.5 presents the results of four models: one for each of the four different measures of party organizational strength.[15] As the results show, each of the measures is positively and significantly associated with electoral success. In order to get some sense of the substantive effects of these findings, I have simulated expected vote shares for different values of the party organizational strength variables holding all other variables at their mean. Consider, first, the effect of participating in local elections: the expected vote share of a party that contests no local elections is about 10 percent, as opposed to 13 percent for the one that competes in about 20 percent of all municipalities (mean value) and 16 percent for a party that contests in about 39 percent of all municipalities (one standard deviation [SD]

However, these methods are not applicable or remain impractical for current purposes because my sample does not include all parties (owing to case-selection criteria and missing information on independent variables). The Katz and King (1999) method does not account for partial competition, and Tomz, Tucker, and Wittenberg (2002) state that their method "does not work well for complex patterns of partial contestation" (70), which is the case here. However, the fact that the vote shares do not add up to one and the use of logged rather than raw vote share are likely to make the electoral data less problematic. In alternative analyses, I also used logit transformation of the dependent variable, which did not change the substantive results.

[14] Additionally controlling for election-year dummies does not change the results.

[15] Tests for multicollinearity indicate that variance inflation factor (VIF) is high for the interaction term and for some of the country dummies. Standard errors for these coefficients are likely to be inflated. In bivariate correlations, past vote is significantly correlated with government membership ($r = 0.45$) and budget ($r = 0.48$), and turnout with unemployment ($r = -0.67$), but the VIFs for these variables remain low, indicating that multicollinearity is not likely to be a problem.

TABLE 2.5. *Regression Analysis of Party Organizational Strength and Electoral Success, Pooled Cross-Country Data*

Variables	Local Elections	Branches	Members	Staff
Participation in local elections	1.264** (0.575)			
Branches		0.870*** (0.303)		
Membership			41.058** (22.405)	
Staff				0.693*** (0.170)
Lagged vote share	7.199*** (0.873)	7.015*** (0.931)	7.245*** (0.915)	4.940*** (1.088)
Budget	0.004 (0.003)	0.003 (0.003)	0.005* (0.003)	0.004* (0.002)
Leader-centeredness	0.106 (0.239)	0.172 (0.222)	0.330 (0.226)	0.916*** (0.346)
Government membership	0.961** (0.434)	0.772* (0.458)	0.721* (0.448)	0.205 (0.680)
Unemployment	0.054 (0.058)	0.047 (0.063)	0.018 (0.049)	0.026 (0.056)
Unemployment*Govt. membership	−0.140*** (0.035)	−0.112*** (0.040)	−0.102*** (0.035)	−0.057 (0.061)
Number of lists	−0.012 (0.021)	−0.015 (0.016)	0.007 (0.015)	0.001 (0.023)
Constant	−3.868*** (0.828)	−3.769*** (1.001)	−3.541*** (0.803)	−3.059*** (0.900)
R^2	0.53	0.53	0.51	0.62
N	104	84	104	63

Note: Dependent variable is "Vote share" (logged). Table entries are unstandardized regression coefficients with robust standard errors clustered on party in parentheses. Country dummies are included in the models but not reported. *$p \leq 0.1$, **$p \leq 0.05$, ***$p \leq 0.01$

above the mean). The effect of local branches is comparable: having branches in 33 percent of the municipalities (mean) as opposed to in none increases the expected vote share from 11 percent to 15 percent, and having branches in about 62 percent of the municipalities (one SD above the mean) to 19 percent. The expected vote share for parties with no members is about 11 percent and increases to 13 percent for an average-sized party (sample mean membership size = 0.3 percent of the electorate) and to 16 percent for those parties whose membership is about 0.7 percent of the electorate (one SD above the mean).[16]

---

[16] The differences in the expected vote shares between the minimum and maximum values of each of these variables are sizeable: eighteen percentage points for the participation in local elections and branches, and twenty-four for membership.

The interpretation of the effect of the size of staff is less straightforward because the measure was standardized by the size of the electorate in 100,000s. The expected vote share for parties with no central office staff is about 9 percent. This increases to 15 percent for parties with an average-sized (sample mean) staff, that is, 0.8 staff members for every 100,000 voters. This amounts to about 65 paid staff members for parties in the Czech Republic, 6 in Estonia, 63 in Hungary, and 230 in Poland.

These are substantively significant results that emerge at the presence of several powerful control variables. Abundance of financial resources – often assumed as the single most important factor for party success in CEE – has a positive effect on vote shares in all models, although it falls short of conventional levels of statistical significance in two of them. However, including this variable does not render the effect of organizational variables insignificant. The same is true for the variable measuring leader effects and the conditional effect of economic performance and government membership on electoral success. These variables largely work in the expected manner, but leave the hypothesized effect intact. Most importantly, the relationship between party organizational strength and electoral success remains significant when parties' past performances are controlled for. Although it is certainly likely that there is a reciprocal relationship between these variables, this suggests that organizational strength is not simply endogenous to electoral success.

Robustness Tests and Additional Analyses

The results presented in Table 2.5 are robust to various different model specifications mentioned: using logit rather than log transformed dependent variable (fn. 13); using campaign expenditure instead of party budget as the measure of party resources (fn. 12); and controlling for election-year dummies (fn. 14). I also performed additional robustness tests and explored various extensions of the main analysis, as I will now explain.

Extending the Sample
In order to test the generalizability of the relationship between party organizational strength and electoral performance, I have assembled data about party organizations in six additional post-communist countries: Bulgaria, Latvia, Lithuania, Romania, Slovakia, and Slovenia. Reflecting the difficulties of gathering the kinds of data that are necessary to perform the analysis (as discussed in Chapter 1), several caveats are in order about the additional data. First, the data were mostly gathered on the basis of information reported in newspapers and secondary academic literature, and only in very rare instances on parties' own records. The response rates to my direct inquiries to party managers were admittedly low. This means that the quality of the additional data is lower and the missingness is (considerably) higher than in the case of the original four countries. Second, essentially no information was available about the size

TABLE 2.6. *Regression Analysis of Party Organizational Strength and Electoral Success, Extended Dataset*

Variables	Local Elections	Branches	Members
Participation in local elections	1.324**		
	(0.545)		
Branches		0.840***	
		(0.266)	
Membership			38.950**
			(17.418)
Lagged vote share	6.381***	7.059***	6.077***
	(0.739)	(0.846)	(0.943)
Budget	0.004*	0.002	0.002
	(0.002)	(0.002)	(0.002)
Government membership	1.349***	1.029**	0.912**
	(0.447)	(0.438)	(0.419)
Unemployment	0.038	0.077*	0.019
	(0.047)	(0.048)	(0.037)
Unemployment*Govt. membership	−0.155***	−0.133***	−0.095***
	(0.038)	(0.037)	(0.035)
Number of lists	−0.008	−0.019	0.007
	(0.021)	(0.016)	(0.014)
Constant	−4.279***	−4.360***	−3.757***
	(0.567)	(0.702)	(0.548)
R^2	0.47	0.48	0.41
N	137	95	140

Note: Dependent variable is "Vote share" (logged). Table entries are unstandardized regression coefficients with robust standard errors clustered on party in parentheses. Country dummies are included in the models but not reported. $*p \leq 0.1$, $**p \leq 0.05$, $***p \leq 0.01$

of staff, which is why organizational strength here is only measured by membership, branches, and participation in local elections. Third, I was not able to gather comparable information about the leader-centeredness of parties in these additional countries. The analyses, therefore, omit this variable. Apart from these differences, the selection of cases (i.e., parties), measurement, and modeling techniques remain the same.

Table 2.6 presents the results of the three analyses using the extended sample. In all cases, party organizational strength is positively and significantly related to electoral performance: the stronger the party organization, the more votes a party is likely to get, other things equal. Adding new cases left not only the nature, but also the magnitude of the relationship intact. The control variables also perform in a very similar manner as in Table 2.5. Overall, these findings suggest that the positive effect of party organizational strength on electoral performance is not confined only to a few post-communist democracies, but represents a general phenomenon, one that is relevant in the entire region. Rather than being unique, the four countries under closer scrutiny are likely to be representative of the general trends in the post-communist context.

Dealing with Missingness

The dataset includes a nontrivial degree of missing data. The N reported in Table 2.5 ranges from 63 to 104, whereas without missingness, the analysis could include 135 observations. At such levels of missingness, selection bias generated by missing data becomes a reasonable concern (King et al. 2001). That is, it is possible that the results will change if full information for each case could be used. Getting rid of missingness would not just help test the robustness of the results, but would also allow performing additional analyses of substantive interest that the high level of missingness prevents. For example, obtaining full datasets would allow estimating fully differenced models to better get at the temporal order between organizational strength and success. Such models would provide information about whether and how change in the organizational variables from one election to the next translates into change in the electoral performance. Having full information on all organizational strength variables also allows creating, with the help of factor analysis, a combined index of party organizational strength that would have values for more than just half of the cases in the dataset.

I used multiple imputations to replace missing observations. Imputations were obtained using the MICE software in R (Van Buuren and Groothuis-Oudshoorn 2011). The software uses information from all of the variables included in the models plus additional variables in the dataset that are expected to be correlated with missingness in order to generate values for missing observations. The software generates five imputations – five different complete datasets with no missing data. I then ran the same regressions on each dataset and combined the results by using the Clarify software in Stata (King et al. 2001).

As a first test with the imputed data, I reran the models presented in Table 2.5. As the results presented in the first four columns of Table 2.7 show, the coefficients for the organizational strength variables were all positive and statistically significant. The size of these coefficients is considerably larger than those reported in Table 2.5 in all cases except for the size of staff. The other variables in Table 2.7 behave in a more consistent manner than in Table 2.5: the interaction effect between participation in government and unemployment rate performed in the expected manner and the effect of the party budget was also positive and statistically significant in all models. The other variables remain statistically insignificant. These consistent results suggest that the imputed data are likely to be reliable. The results also suggest that the findings obtained from the analysis of the original data are, if anything, biased downward, that is, they may underestimate but are not likely to overestimate the true effect.

TABLE 2.7. *Regression Analysis of Party Organizational Strength and Electoral Success, Pooled and Multiple Imputed Cross-Country Data*

Variables	Local Elections	Branches	Members	Staff	Combined Index
Participation in local elections	1.966*** (0.575)				
Branches		1.148** (0.463)			
Membership			63.710** (27.595)		
Staff				0.400** (0.189)	
Party organizational strength (factor score)					0.386** (0.105)
Lagged vote share	8.031*** (1.050)	8.887*** (1.127)	9.144*** (1.015)	8.188*** (1.136)	8.340*** (1.032)
Budget	0.006* (0.003)	0.006* (0.004)	0.007** (0.003)	0.006* (0.003)	0.005 (0.003)
Leader-centeredness	−0.179 (0.340)	−0.035 (0.320)	−0.073 (0.330)	0.069 (0.395)	−0.062 (0.336)
Government membership	1.111** (0.543)	1.238** (0.542)	1.026** (0.514)	1.180** (0.554)	1.192** (0.537)
Unemployment	0.003 (0.051)	0.066 (0.057)	0.047 (0.053)	0.056 (0.053)	0.057 (0.052)
Unemp.* Govt. membership	−0.129*** (0.048)	−0.136*** (0.047)	−0.113*** (0.045)	−0.118** (0.049)	−0.133*** (0.047)
Number of lists	0.001 (0.017)	−0.015 (0.017)	−0.006 (0.017)	−0.007 (0.017)	−0.006 (0.017)
Constant	−4.725*** (0.550)	−4.728*** (0.584)	−4.804*** (0.627)	−4.951*** (0.611)	−4.569*** (0.542)
N	135	135	135	135	135

Note: Dependent variable is "Vote share" (logged). Table entries are unstandardized regression coefficients with robust standard errors clustered on party in parentheses. Country dummies are included in the models but not reported. $*p \leq 0.1$, $**p \leq 0.05$, $***p \leq 0.01$

Using the imputed data also allows creating a combined index of party organizational strength by using principal component factor analysis without losing cases: if the original data were used, about half of the cases would be lost because the missingness in the different measures is not necessarily overlapping. The last column in Table 2.7 presents results with the combined index of party organizational strength. In line with the results reported so far, the coefficient for the combined measure is positive and statistically significant, confirming the robustness of the results.

The Immediate Effects of Strengthening Party Organization

Using the multiple imputed datasets, I further estimated a model examining how change in the organizational strength variables related to change in electoral performance.[17] If organizational strength affects electoral performance, one would expect that an increase (decrease) in party organizational strength is associated with a subsequent increase (decrease) in party vote share. Recall that the organizational strength variables were measured one year prior to the election whenever possible. Change in this variable refers to difference in the organizational strength one year before the current election compared to one year before the previous election. Change in vote share simply refers to difference in party vote between election t and $t - 1$. All other time-variant independent variables are differenced in a similar manner. The analyses also include country dummies, and standard errors are clustered on party.

The results of these analyses are presented in Table 2.8. In four out of the five models presented, increasing party organizational strength is associated with a significant increase in party vote share. The effects are also significant in substantive terms: a change of one SD below to one SD above the mean on the organizational strength variables is associated with a 4–percentage-point increase in vote share in the case of participation in local elections and membership, and with a 5–percentage-point increase in the case of branches. More specifically, to use participation in local elections as an example: participating in local elections in about 12 percent more municipalities than previously (a one–SD change) is associated with a 3.5–percentage-point increase in vote share; decreasing party's participation in local elections by the same rate is associated with about 1–percentage-point decrease in its vote share. The effect of size of staff is not statistically significant, that is, increase or decrease in staff size is not associated with an immediate electoral response. This result is not surprising given that the effect of professional staff on electoral performance was argued to mostly work through helping manage the party rather than through direct contact with voters. Increasing membership and local presence is likely to increase the visibility of the party and can thereby have an immediate effect on its electoral success, as confirmed. Increasing party staff may remain invisible to the voter, and whereas improved management of the party will likely help its long-term success and survival, the immediate effect of this change may remain modest. Overall, however, the results from the models using first differences strongly suggest that strengthening party organization increases the vote share for the party.

The Role of Party Type

All subsequent analyses return to using the original dataset. The main findings so far suggest that party organizational strength is associated with electoral

---

[17] Using the imputed datasets is preferable because, owing to missingness, too many additional cases would be lost as a result of differencing if the original data were used.

TABLE 2.8. *Immediate Effects of Strengthening Party Organization, Pooled, Multiple Imputed, and First Differenced Cross-Country Data*

Variables	Local Elections	Branches	Members	Staff	Combined Index
Δ Participation in local elections	0.117* (0.068)				
Δ Branches		0.090*** (0.030)			
Δ Membership			3.918* (2.337)		
Δ Staff				0.009 (0.012)	
Δ Party organizational strength (factor score)					0.034*** (0.011)
Δ Budget	0.000 (0.000)	0.000 (0.000)	0.000 (0.000)	0.000 (0.000)	0.000 (0.000)
Δ Leader-centeredness	0.026 (0.023)	0.018 (0.023)	0.017 (0.024)	0.030 (0.025)	0.019 (0.022)
Government membership	−0.057*** (0.017)	−0.56*** (0.018)	−0.56*** (0.018)	−0.050*** (0.017)	−0.060*** (0.016)
Δ Unemployment	−0.001 (0.002)	−0.001 (0.002)	−0.001 (0.002)	0.000 (0.002)	−0.002 (0.002)
Δ Unemp.* Govt. membership	−0.002 (0.003)	−0.001 (0.004)	−0.002 (0.003)	−0.002 (0.003)	−0.001 (0.003)
Δ Number of lists	0.000 (0.000)	0.000 (0.000)	0.000 (0.000)	0.000 (0.000)	0.000 (0.000)
Constant	0.021* (0.014)	0.022* (0.014)	0.026* (0.015)	0.021 (0.014)	0.017** (0.014)
N	135	135	135	135	135

Note: Dependent variable is "Change in vote share." Table entries are unstandardized regression coefficients with robust standard errors clustered on party in parentheses. Country dummies are included in the models but not reported. *$p \leq 0.1$, **$p \leq 0.05$, ***$p \leq 0.01$

success, holding other variables, including party effects, constant. It is, however, possible that the effect of organizational strength on success varies for different types of parties. For example, parties representing rural and/or poorer segments of society may have more to gain electorally from strengthening their organizations. Using the Comparative Manifesto Project (Klingemann et al. 2006) classification of parties, I created a binary variable coded "1" when a given party is a communist, social-democratic, agrarian, or Christian democratic one, that is, a type of party expected to represent poorer and/or rural voters. I then estimated interaction effects between the organizational-strength variables and the type of party. The coefficient for the interaction term was insignificant in all models. The effect of organizational strength on success remained positive and significant for both types of parties in the case of branches and staff. In the case of participation in local elections, it was also positive for both types but fell short of statistical significance for the parties representing poorer/rural voters, which is contrary to what one would expect if ideology biased the results. In the case of membership size, the effect was insignificant for both types of parties, most likely owing to the high level of multicollinearity introduced by the additional interaction term.[18] Overall, these results suggest that the organizational effects are likely to be similar regardless of the type of constituency the parties are representing.

One might also argue that the results are simply driven by the ex-communist parties that tended to have stronger organizations and were also electorally successful during the time period under consideration. In order to check for such a possibility, I estimated another set of interaction models to consider whether the organizational effect differed for parties created during or after the regime change as opposed to those that had roots in the former regime. The following were identified as ex-communist parties: the Communist Party of Bohemia and Moravia (KSČM), MSzP, PSL and SLD.[19] One may question the inclusion of the PSL because of its status as a satellite rather than an ex-communist party. The substantive results are very similar when PSL is not classified as a former regime party. All organizational variables, except for membership, were positively and significantly associated with electoral success for the new parties. This indicates that organizational strength significantly influences which of these newly created parties is likely to be more successful. It is not the case that organizational strength only or mostly explains the different levels of electoral success between the former regime parties and the newly created ones.

For ex-communist parties, the effect of all organizational variables was insignificant, indicating that these variables are not likely to matter in determining which former regime parties are more likely to succeed electorally. This is not surprising given the small number of ex-communist parties and their relatively similar values on the dependent and independent variables. One additional interesting observation emerges from the comparison of the two groups of parties. Recall that the effect of members was insignificant for both groups. This may suggest one of the following: (a) there is simply too much multicollinearity for any interaction effects to show up; or (b) membership size may explain the difference in the electoral performance between the former regime parties and new parties, but not within either set of parties. In other words, the effect of membership may, indeed, be mostly driven by the

---

[18] The substantive results are similar when Christian democratic parties are not classified as representing rural and/or poorer voters.

[19] Munkaspart was also identified as a former communist party, but it was dropped from the analysis because of missing data.

differences on this variable between the former regime parties and the new ones.

Overall, organization matters for both those parties that represent poorer and rural segments of society and those that do not. Furthermore, the organizational effect is not simply driven by differences between the ex-communist parties and the ones created during or after the regime change. Although ex-communist parties may be more successful than some of the newly created parties because of their superior organization, organizational strength also helps to differentiate – within the group of newly created parties – which one of them is more or less likely to succeed.

The Role of Time

Another interesting extension of the main result is to consider whether and how the effect of organizational strength varies across time. It is, for example, possible that organizational strength mattered less, if at all, in the very first elections where the main goal for most voters was to establish democratic rule. It is also possible that the organizational effect wears off over time as parties learn from their own experience and that of others the necessity to build organizations. When most parties build strong organizations then organizational strength may cease to give any one of them a significant competitive advantage. This would explain the skepticism about the relevance of party organizations in determining the electoral success of parties in advanced democracies.

In order to test for the time effects, I generated a variable called "Election number," coded "1" for the first election, "2" for the second, and so on, and interacted this variable with each of the organizational strength measures. The interactive effects are plotted in Figure 2.1. The solid lines indicate the size of the coefficient for a given organizational strength variable at different times (first through the sixth election). The dashed lines indicate the corresponding 90 percent confidence intervals. All four graphs indicate the presence of some time dependence in the effect of organizational strength on electoral success, although the effects remain positive for the entire time period. The effect of branches and participating in local elections decreases over time, although decrease in the former is only marginal. The effect of both variables is not significant in the first election, and the effect again becomes insignificant for the sixth election in the case of participation in local elections and for the fifth election in the case of branches. For the effect of membership and staff, the trend is somewhat different: these effects are also not significant for the first election (and in the case of membership, also for the second election), but the effect strengthens rather than weakens over time. Both effects remain significant and positive through the sixth election – the maximum number of elections included in the analysis.

Overall, there seems to be support for the argument that the first elections are exceptional: symbolic and emotional factors are likely to trump other

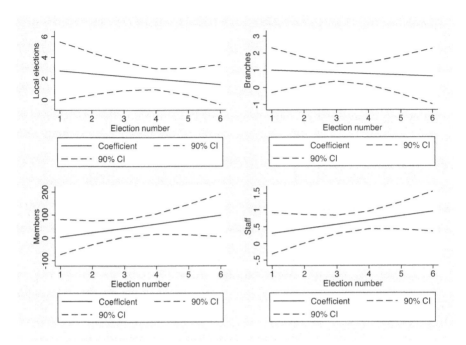

FIGURE 2.1. The effect of party organizational strength on electoral success at different time points.

considerations and organizational strength of parties is not likely to matter for their electoral success. This is in line with findings reported by Golosov (1998) about the 1993 and 1995 Russian Duma elections. The study concludes that in the first democratic elections in 1993 party organization indeed did not matter, "while strong personalities, attractive ideologies, the use of media, and power bases in the state apparatus" were decisive (Golosov 1998, 534). However, the picture had completely changed by 1995, when the network of local organizations was crucial but all of the other variables proved to be insufficient for explaining who won and who lost.

Here, too, for the bulk of the twenty years after the fall of communism, organizational strength significantly and positively affects a party's electoral performance in post-communist countries. This effect wears off in the case of some, but not all organizational-strength variables. One reason for this might be that organization building in terms of participation in local elections and establishing party branches in municipalities may more easily reach their limits. When a party already contests in local government elections in most or all municipalities, there is little that can be improved on this dimension. On the other hand, there is no comparable, easily met limit to professionalizing party staff and increasing the number of members.

TABLE 2.9. *The Average Party Organizational Strength for Parties in and out of Parliament*

	Local Elections	Branches	Members	Staff
Parties in parliament	0.218	0.353	0.004	0.976
	(N = 91)	(N = 84)	(N = 108)	(N = 68)
Parties out of parliament	0.028	0.131	0.001	0.122
	(N = 95)	(N = 23)	(N = 64)	(N = 18)
Difference of means	0.190***	0.222***	0.002***	0.854***

Note: Table entries are mean levels of party organizational strength. ***$p \leq 0.01$

Organizational Strength and Survival

The analysis so far has focused on electoral success rather than survival. Of course, insofar as success is a precondition of survival, the results can speak to expectations about which parties are more likely to survive. Chapter 3 will consider party survival more directly, making use of case studies and process tracing. Studying survival quantitatively is quite challenging, not least because measuring party survival is not straightforward. One could measure it by looking at whether a given party is registered in a given year. However, many marginalized parties remain registered for long after they are no longer active. An alternative is to look at whether or not a given party got into parliament at a given time. This, however, is not, strictly speaking, a measure of survival because a party can remain out of the parliament for one election, but then reenter in a subsequent election. Another problem is that when a party is about to become inactive, information about its organization is less likely to be available, and the case is likely to "exit" the dataset owing to missing data before it becomes extinct (or loses parliamentary representation). Still, with these caveats in mind and considering the setup of the data (i.e., election year rather than annual data), the best definition of survival that can be used is whether or not a given party enters parliament in the given election year. Variable "Outsider" is coded "1" if a party is not represented in parliament and "0" if it is. Rather than being pronounced dead after the first exit from parliament, in this setting a party can move from an "insider" to "outsider" status and back multiple times.

Before getting into any complicated modeling of survival, it is informative to look at the extent to which the organizational strength of parties differs according to their parliamentary status. Table 2.9 lists the mean level of organizational strength for the different groups. By all measures, the organizations of parties out of parliament are significantly weaker (at the 1 percent level) than those of parties in parliament. This, of course, does not directly tell us whether organizational strength helps a party survive as a parliamentary party. Therefore, I also performed binary cross-section time-series analyses using Outsider as the

TABLE 2.10. *Binary Cross-Section Time-Series Analysis of Party Organizational Strength and Party Survival in Parliament, Pooled Cross-Country Data*

Variables	Local Elections	Branches	Members	Staff	Local Elections
Participation in local elections	−13.447*** (5.306)				−9.213** (4.779)
Branches		−5.480** (2.698)			
Membership			−179.014 (133.261)		
Staff				−3.370** (1.499)	
Budget					−0.129** (0.054)
Leader-centeredness					−0.053 (0.683)
Government membership					−3.158* (2.152)
Unemployment					−0.071 (0.161)
Unemp.* Govt. membership					0.424* (0.235)
Number of lists					−0.010 (0.164)
Constant	2.690*** (0.508)	1.372** (0.626)	0.664** (0.331)	−0.480 (0.986)	2.436 (2.731)
Pseudo-R²	0.40	0.28	0.18	0.34	0.56
N	186	87	172	64	116

Note: Dependent variable is "Outsider." Table entries are unstandardized logit coefficients with robust standard errors clustered on party in parentheses. The models also include a counter, three cubic splines, and country dummies, which are not reported. *$p \leq 0.1$, **$p \leq 0.05$, ***$p \leq 0.01$

dependent variable. This method is similar to event-history analysis. It uses a logit regression and employs a variable that counts the number of time periods (elections) since the last event (failure to enter parliament). Such a variable provides the information needed to represent the temporal component of the data. Because the counting variable will be uneven and rough, Beck, Katz and Tucker (1998) suggest a natural cubic spline to smooth it. Including these time variables – a counter and cubic splines – in an ordinary logit (or probit) model makes the estimates robust. In order to account for cross-sectional dependence and heteroskedasticity, I have also used robust standard errors clustered on party and country fixed effects.

The first four columns of Table 2.10 present the results of the analysis including only the respective organizational-strength variable as a predictor (in addition to the variables included as part of the modeling technique). As the results indicate, the likelihood of becoming an outsider decreases as the organizational strength increases for all measures of organizational strength. This effect is significant at least at the 10 percent level in all cases except for membership, where the *p*-value reaches 0.18. I obtained very similar results when the Outsider variable was recoded such that a party could remain an outsider for only one time period and was subsequently coded as missing. For the sake of comparison, the last column in Table 2.10 presents the results of a model that includes the same full set of control variables as the analyses in Table 2.5, and participation in local elections as the measure of organizational strength. As before, organizational strength is still significantly and negatively related to outsider status. Overall, as far as survival is defined in terms of being able to maintain parliamentary representation, the evidence presented here suggests that organizational strength significantly enhances parties' survival chances.

To sum up the cross-national findings, I have demonstrated that parties with stronger organizations are more likely to succeed electorally. This finding is robust regardless of which of the alternative measures of party organizational strength – members, branches, staff, or participation in local elections – is used. The result is general and not driven by missing data, ex-communist parties, or those parties that represent poor and/or rural electorates. The organizational effects are less relevant in first democratic elections, but their effect strengthens over time, especially for membership and staff. Increasing party organizational strength has an immediate positive effect on party vote share, and organizational strength not only helps parties succeed electorally, but also survive as significant players on the political arena. In sum, organizational strength matters for which parties win and lose in the new democracies of CEE.

Results of the District-Level Analysis

The analysis now proceeds to consider whether and how the variance in the organizational strength of different subunits of the same party helps us understand the geographical patterns of support for the party. Is the party electorally more successful in districts where its local organization is stronger, that is, where it has more members and local offices? As I explained previously, this analysis helps to not only determine whether a similar dynamic between organizational strength and success also holds within parties, but also provides an opportunity to evaluate the validity of the proposed causal mechanisms producing this relationship. Specifically, the relationship between district-level electoral success and district-level members and branches is likely to mostly work through the direct contacts with voters and local-level visibility and activism that these aspects of organizational strength allow. Given this, if the relationship holds on the district level, then this suggests that the direct contacts enabled by local-level organizational strength are important for mobilizing voters in addition to any signals of competence, reliability, and accountability that the overall national-level organizational strength provides.

The district-level analyses include the same parties and election years as the cross-national dataset, and all electoral districts in each country. I have created separate datasets for each country. The dependent variable is the district-level vote share (logged), and the models include the same set of explanatory variables as the cross-national analysis, but measured at the district level (when applicable) as described. As was the case with the national-level analysis, I have used different measures of party organizational strength, if available. The size of the national office staff cannot, by definition, be measured on the district level and is, therefore, not included. The other three indicators are measureable on the district level: (1) participation in local elections is measured as a share of municipalities in a given electoral district where the party contests local elections; (2) membership is measured as the number of members per district voter; and (3) branches is measured as the share of municipalities in a given district where the party has a local office. The first measure is available for a large number of cases in each country. Unfortunately, district-level information on members is only available for most parties in Estonia, some parties in the Czech Republic, and branches only for parties in Estonia.

I follow modeling techniques similar to the ones used in the national-level analyses. Specifically, I use OLS with robust standard errors clustered on electoral districts and include party dummies as well as the lagged dependent variable (previous vote share). As in previous analyses, using logit rather than log transformation of the dependent variable does not change the substantive results. The same is true for using a multilevel model with random intercepts for district and party instead of the OLS. Using multiple imputations to get rid of missingness and analyzing the resulting full datasets also produces similar but statistically and substantively even stronger results.

The results for each of the four countries, presented in Table 2.11, provide considerable support for the hypothesized relationship, with all analyses producing a positive and statistically significant effect of party organizational strength on electoral performance.[20] A party is electorally more successful in districts where its organizational presence is stronger than in districts where its organization is weak, other things, including prior electoral performance in a given district, being equal. The relationship holds when controlling for the party dummies, indicating that regardless of the overall level of party organizational strength, the geographic distribution of support for the party is significantly

---

[20] VIF is high for government membership and its interaction term with unemployment in the Estonian and Polish analyses, for party leader and party dummies in the Hungarian analysis, and for some party dummies, government membership, interaction term, and lagged dependent variable for the Czech analysis with members. The respective standard errors are likely to be inflated.

TABLE 2.11. *Regression Analysis of Party Organizational Strength and Electoral Success, District-Level Data*

Variables	Estonia			Hungary		Czech Republic		Poland
	Local el.	Branches	Members	Local el., PR Sample	Local el., SMD Sample	Local el.	Members	Local el.
Participation in local elections	1.069** (0.318)			1.249*** (0.406)	1.083** (0.510)	0.950** (0.324)		0.593*** (0.097)
Branches		0.996*** (0.251)						
Membership			38.071*** (8.179)				31.554*** (6.789)	
Lagged vote share	3.265*** (1.322)	4.043*** (0.485)	2.946*** (0.542)	4.699*** (0.212)	3.134*** (0.447)	1.718* (0.854)	3.695*** (0.831)	1.964*** (0.188)
Budget	0.002 (0.009)	-0.041** (0.013)	-0.039*** (0.007)	-0.005*** (0.0006)	0.001 (0.001)	0.003*** (0.0007)	-0.0004*** (0.0009)	0.011*** (0.001)
Leader-centeredness	-0.036 (0.097)	0.189* (0.098)	0.164 (0.100)	0.006 (0.058)	-0.210*** (0.042)	-0.135** (0.047)	0.048 (0.060)	-1.097*** (0.035)
Government membership	-0.389 (0.247)	-0.214 (0.292)	-0.539* (0.265)	-0.239* (0.143)	0.090 (0.156)	0.279* (0.128)	-0.559** (0.181)	-0.182** (0.079)
Unemployment	0.067*** (0.013)	0.038 (0.031)	-0.022 (0.019)	-0.018** (0.007)	0.003 (0.009)	-0.026* (0.015)	-0.010* (0.007)	0.0008 (0.004)
Unemp. * Govt. membership	-0.059** (0.021)	-0.055 (0.036)	-0.008 (0.032)	0.023* (0.012)	0.003 (0.012)	-0.042** (0.016)	0.006 (0.027)	-0.028*** (0.005)
Number of lists	0.033 (0.035)	-0.107** (0.036)	-0.139** (0.032)	0.117*** (0.013)	0.069*** (0.008)	-0.055*** (0.007)	0.008 (0.009)	-0.005 (0.005)
Constant	-3.767*** (0.798)	-2.171*** (0.399)	-1.133 (0.454)	-4.166*** (0.294)	-3.476*** (0.210)	-1.989*** (0.122)	-5.325*** (0.242)	-1.214*** (0.093)
R^2	0.78	0.85	0.72	0.71	0.69	0.88	0.97	0.81
N	184	154	136	451	455	222	83	835

Note: Dependent variable is "Vote share" (logged). Table entries are unstandardized regression coefficients with robust standard errors clustered on electoral district in parentheses. Party dummies are included in the models but not reported. * $p \leq 0.1$, ** $p \leq 0.05$, *** $p \leq 0.01$

related to its organizational strength on the ground. That is, organizationally strong parties attract more support in districts where they have more members and local structures, and the same is true for organizationally weak parties. Local-level organizational strength matters for electoral support.

It is also worth stressing that the hypothesized effect not only survives the robustness tests described but also holds with different measures of organizational strength and in all four countries – factors that further underscore the robustness and generalizability of the findings. For substantive interpretation, I used simulations as described previously to calculate the difference in the expected vote share between the minimum organizational strength and one SD above the mean. In terms of percentage-point difference in expected vote share, this amounted to 6, 4, and 6 percentage points for Estonia (participation in local elections, branches, and membership, respectively); 3 and 4 percentage points for the Czech Republic (participation in local elections and membership, respectively); 6 and 5 percentage points for Hungary (PR and SMD elections, respectively); and 4–percentage-point difference for Poland.[21] The size of the effect is expectedly larger when similar differences are calculated for changes from the minimum to maximum organizational strength and amount to 6–27 percentage points, depending on the model.

As was the case previously, I also estimated models using first differences of the dependent variable and all independent variables that varied over time to better get at the temporal (if not causal) order between organizational strength and electoral performance. The variables measuring organizational strength also performed in the expected manner in most of those models.[22] That is, increase in local-party organizational strength in a given district is associated with subsequent increase in the vote share for the party in this district. As previously, this result suggests that investing in building a strong party organization has an immediate payoff in terms of increased vote share, and

---

[21] Because district-level information on membership was available only for Estonia and the Czech Republic, and on branches only for Estonia, one might question whether the results concerning these variables are generalizable. This concern is, to an extent, alleviated by the fact that: (1) the different measures of organizational strength produced similar results in the cross-national analysis, where all countries were included; and (2) both district-level membership and branches are highly correlated with the district-level measure of participation in local elections. That parties in these two countries collect organizational data on district level is, in itself, interesting, and may indicate a higher level of organizational capacity and perhaps tendency to rely on members and branches for electoral success.

[22] For Estonia, the effect was not statistically significant when "Members" was used as the measure of organizational strength. For Poland, the hypothesized effect held when campaign expenditure rather than the size of budget was used to control for financial resources. This may be because even though the budget data has better party coverage, the campaign expenditure data are more reliable, as most were coded from the official financial reports submitted by parties to the National Election Commission. For all other countries and models, either measure of financial resources produced the expected effect.

that organizational strength is likely to precede rather than follow electoral success.

Overall, the district-level findings suggest that parties may be able to influence the geographical pattern of their support by targeted organization building. They also suggest that organizational strength matters not only because it helps parties signal their competence and professionalism, but also owing to the direct contacts with voters that local presence and members permit.

Conclusion

The stronger the party organization – that is, the more sizeable its membership, extensive its local presence, and professional its staff – the more successful is the party electorally. Increasing (or avoiding losing) votes in the short run, in turn, contributes to party success (and possibly survival) in the long run. Organization matters regardless of the wealth of the party, the leader's popularity, or access to pork and patronage. The effect remains robust against various different measures of organizational strength and different datasets used. Organizational strength is relevant both in the national and district competition for votes in countries with quite different electoral systems, social cleavages, levels of party system stability, economic development, and political histories. All this strongly suggests that party politics in CEE is not only about money, media access, patronage, and personalities. Parties in the region need organizations if they care about electoral success. Note, however, that although highlighting the organizational effect is the specific contribution of this chapter, I do not claim that party organizational strength is the sole or even the most important contributor to electoral success. I only argue that it makes a discernible difference, other things equal.

The findings in this chapter contribute directly to the literature on party organizations – a topic that is frequently addressed but rarely systematically analyzed in the context of post-communist democracies. These findings help clarify the relationship between organizational strength and electoral success and undermine the arguments about the irrelevance of organizations. The results also contribute to the literature on party system stabilization by drawing attention to parties' own actions and decisions as opposed to exogenous (environmental or institutional) explanations of why some parties succeed and others do not. Furthermore, specifically in the context of post-communist democracies, previous literature suggests that surviving parties are responsible for politicizing cleavages and thereby crafting the ideological space for party competition (Zielinski 2002). However, this literature leaves a critical question unanswered: Which parties are more likely to survive? The findings reported here provide one possible answer: those that invest in building strong organizations.

In addition to substantive contributions, this chapter also develops and establishes the reliability and validity of an indicator of party organizational strength – the capacity of a party to run candidates in local elections. This indicator covers all attributes of the concept reasonably well; can travel across parties, countries, and time; and is, for the most part, publicly available. All these characteristics are crucial because the systematic study of party organizations, at least outside advanced democracies, has been hampered by the unavailability of more direct measures – even as straightforward as membership figures.

3

Organizations at Work

Assessing the Causal Mechanisms

Parties with stronger organizations are electorally more successful. The goal of this chapter is to complement the statistical results in support of this conclusion with an in-depth investigation of specific cases. The case studies enhance the analysis in several distinct ways by helping answer questions that the statistical analysis left open. First, by providing detailed contextual information about causal processes within cases, the qualitative narratives can be used to verify that the relationship between organizational strength and electoral performance is not spurious. Specifically, the case studies help assess whether the proposed causal mechanisms actually work in the expected manner and the theoretical argument is compelling.

Second, process tracing within cases also allows assessing the nature of the causal order between organizational strength and electoral performance. Third, the within-case analysis entails the examination of a diverse set of materials and allows more fine-grained measurement of the key variables. For example, the qualitative analysis can supplement the electoral returns used in Chapter 2 with parties' own assessments of their performance as well as those reported in the media. The case studies can also take into account the long-term survival of the party. Fourth, the narratives provide another opportunity to assess the strength of the rival hypotheses including party ideology, leader effects, and patronage. The qualitative analysis also helps evaluate party performance in the context of environmental hostility, external shocks, and crises.

I use two main methodological tools to conduct the case studies: process tracing and controlled (or focused) comparison. The latter is especially useful for dealing with the possible confounding effects of rival hypotheses and establishing the independent effect of organizational strength on electoral success and survival. It requires comparing parties that differ significantly in terms of their organizational strength but are very similar on a number of potentially relevant explanatory variables. By virtue of case selection, these explanatory variables are held constant because they cannot account for any variance in the dependent variable. The analysis can then focus on determining whether and how organizational strength can explain differences in the electoral performance of the two parties.

This chapter is organized by country, with each providing a number of cases (parties) for closer analysis. The case selection in this chapter is not random but deliberate, given the goal of carrying out a "model-testing small-N analysis" (see Lieberman 2005 for a detailed discussion of the appropriate case-selection strategies for such analysis). Whenever possible, two (or more) cases are used for controlled comparison, selected according to the rules described. These are supplemented by a selection of parties with strong and weak organizations from among those that are generally well predicted by the statistical model, following the case-selection advice in Lieberman (2005).

The Czech Republic

The Czech party system has been relatively stable, especially if one focuses on parliamentary parties since Czech independence.[1] Still, there are some parties – notably the ČSSD, KSČM, and ODS – that were more successful in becoming the core players in the Czech political arena in the 1990s and 2000s despite at times facing significant crises and environmental hostility. The latter is especially true for the KSČM, which has suffered adverse environment at a greater scale than its ex-communist counterparts in other CEE countries because of its choice not to reform itself programmatically. Nonetheless, all predictions about the imminent death of this party have proven wrong – for more than twenty years it has enjoyed a relatively stable support base and at times been the most successful party of the left. At the same time there have been parties in the Czech political arena – such as the ODA, the SPR-RSČ, and the Freedom Union (US) – that have seen their star shine for only one election or two and then withered into oblivion. The narratives confirm that the main difference between the successful and unsuccessful parties is their level of organizational strength, and illustrate how organizations have helped parties succeed or contributed to their failure.

Communist Party of Bohemia and Moravia

KSČM is probably not the first party that comes to mind when one thinks of successful parties in the Czech Republic. However, a closer look reveals several indicators according to which the party has clearly been successful: (1) it has always been represented in the Czech Chamber of Deputies since the regime change; (2) it has received at least 10 percent of the vote in every national

---

[1] The analysis includes the period when the Czech Republic was part of Czechoslovakia (1990–1992). Vote shares for that period refer to the results of the elections to the Czech National Council.

parliamentary election, with a record 18.5 percent in the 2002 election;[2] and (3) it has been the second-largest party in parliament twice and third largest four times. In sum, its support base is stable and so is its presence on the Czech political map. These results are all the more remarkable given the overt environmental hostility the party has faced throughout the post-communist period and the almost unanimous verdict by domestic and international analysts about its imminent death. Why has the party been successful?

KSČM was considered a sore thumb and failure not only in the Czech political scene but also in the entire post-communist region. Unlike ex-communists in neighboring countries, KSČM chose not to part with the past by keeping much of its former ideology and name. The party faced complete isolation by other parties and hostility from media and the public. Grzymala-Busse (2002a) reports that after the regime change, a majority of the voting-age population did not want to see the party in parliament; KSČM was seen as not fully committed to democracy and not capable of governing. KSČM MPs complained about ostracism, "deliberate abuse, and personal isolation" in parliament (Grzymala-Busse 2002a, 238). The party was called a "criminal organization" and attempts were made to ban it (Vachudová 1993). In the early 1990s, rotten eggs were thrown at the attendants of the KSČM party conference (CTK 1993e), and party leader Jiří Svoboda was stabbed in his apartment (CTK 1992d). Although other ex-communist parties in the region also suffered environmental hostility, it is because of its failure to reform that analysts considered KSČM to be a lost cause, a party in decline and about to go extinct (Evans and Whitefield 1995; Grzymala-Busse 2002a; Kopeček 2005; Mahr and Nagle 1995). It was considered a "real 'dinosaur' of Leninism which has no future" (Nagle and Mahr 1999, 179), a party that was "staring defeat in the face" (Advertiser 1990).

KSČM's response to hostilities was to focus on its internal organization. Maintaining and mobilizing members and strengthening its network of local branches became its survival strategy. "Party membership was seen as the one reliable source of votes and support" and mass membership was in general considered to be necessary for the party to be influential (Grzymala-Busse 2002a, 54). Because of this, party leadership did everything to keep their members. They especially made sure that no members were lost when the former workplace-based branches were transformed into local KSČM branches.

KSČM built its electoral strategy on the active involvement of local branches and members. It remained the party with the largest organization in the Czech Republic throughout the 1990s and 2000s despite a steady decline in membership because of deaths. The party valued face-to-face interactions between members and leadership as well as members and voters, and made use of its

---

[2] In 1992, it ran as part of an electoral alliance called Left Bloc together with two very small leftist parties.

daily and weekly newspapers as a means of communication within the organization. Beginning in 1992, the party sought to organize locally based social
movements and engage in activating civil society by using its members and
organizational network (Hanley 2001). It sought to establish links between the
party and civic initiatives and organize a range of nonpolitical activities and
services of practical interest to its constituencies. The party was essentially built
on the demand for an active membership base: members were expected to be
actively involved in party activities on the local level, to win other supporters
for the party, and to promote the party program and leftist ideas (Linek and
Pecháček 2007). Organization was thus not only used for election campaigns
but for ongoing contacts with the potential electorate.

In the 1990 Czech legislative elections, the party received 13.2 percent of
the vote – a result second only to the expected favorite anticommunist social
movement Civic Forum. After the election, party leader Jiří Machalík said,
"[T]he elections had shown that the Communist Party was a viable political
force in Czechoslovakia and the strongest left-wing one" (BBC Summary of
World Broadcasts 1990). At the same time, the party was discriminated against
and kept out of the media. The only resource it could use to attract voters was
its organization, and the party was convinced that using this resource would
pay off. Indeed, after seeing the party's election posters destroyed, Machalík
simply noted, "[P]osters won't decide the outcome" (Advertiser, 1990), and as
far as KSČM was concerned, he was largely right.

KSČM continued to be the second-largest party in parliament after the 1992
election. The results further convinced leaders that their strategies were cor-
rect: what mattered was keeping the membership (Grzymala-Busse 2002a).
The party also did very well in local elections, and although their rivals
mocked that the KSČM was only successful because there was no other choice
in some districts, their criticism actually underlined the importance of party
organization: people will not, and often cannot, vote for parties that are not
present on the ground (BBC Summary of World Broadcasts 1994a). As Hanley (2001) claims, local presence made KSČM popular in local and regional
elections.

KSČM continued to use public meetings (CTK 1995c) and canvassing as
proven methods of campaign strategy (CTK 1995d) in subsequent elections.
Its members, the largest in number, and more experienced in political activism
than members of any other party in the Czech Republic (Handl 2005a), were
engaged in door-to-door campaigning, held demonstrations, and prepared campaign materials (Grzymala-Busse 2002a). The leadership was proud of the mass
character and organizational structure of the party (CTK 1996a). KSČM continued to be rewarded with stable support, and by the end of 1999 even saw
its poll numbers increase to more than 20 percent. Organizational strength
also increased voter commitment: 80–85 percent of KSČM voters remained
loyal to the party (CTK 1999a; Hanley 2001). Only once, in the 2006 election,

did the party change its main campaign strategy, because of insistence by its new leader, and used "billboards and posters featuring its leaders for the first time in history" (Czech News Agency 2005c). After the election, however, the leadership agreed that this had been a bad campaign idea (Czech News Agency 2006a). This experimentation further showed the benefit of staying with their proven method of organizational campaign.

The continued electoral presence and success of KSČM led analysts to change their initial evaluations of the future of the party.[3] An article published in May 1998 claimed that KSČM was "one of the most stable Czech parties" (CTK 1998c). Its voters were most likely to turn out (CTK 1999a). In 2003–2004, the media in the Czech Republic began discussing KSČM as a potential leading leftist force (Czech News Agency 2004a). Whereas other parties still openly shunned KSČM, it became increasingly difficult to ignore it, so they covertly cooperated with it: KSČM was accepted as a coalition partner in subnational governments (Handl 2005a; Šaradín 2007); ODS used its help to have Klaus elected president (CTK 2003c); and ČSSD used its help to govern (Kopeček and Pšeja 2008). Therefore, even according to this measure of success (i.e., being accepted by other parties), KSČM could no longer be considered as a complete failure, contrary to what early studies argued. Indeed, scholarly work now focuses not on explaining the failure of KSČM but rather on its continued endurance and success (Stegmaier and Vlachová 2009). Furthermore, in accord with the claims made here, Handl (2005a) argues that KSČM's electoral success in recent years shows that its strategy of banking on its organization has clearly worked. Hanley (2001) agrees that what made the party successful was giving priority to its loyal mass membership.

Comparing the fate of KSČM to that of its splinters provides additional evidence in support of the argument that organizational strength helped the party survive and succeed. In 1993, a group left KSČM and created their own Czech Party of the Democratic Left and another group created the Left Bloc Party. Both of these shared with KSČM the origins and left-leaning ideology (although they were less "radical" and more liberal than KSČM), but neither commanded its organizational strength; indeed, their membership and local organizations remained marginal (Grzymala-Busse 2002a). Neither of these parties cleared the electoral threshold or became politically significant in any way (CTK 2002a). Although, certainly, other factors might have been at play, organizational strength remains the most glaring difference between KSČM and its splinters, and at least suggests an explanation for KSČM electoral advantage.

---

[3] Depending on the specific goal of their study, authors have used different definitions of success than employed here, which may have led to different conclusions about success. For example, Grzymala-Busse (2002a), although also considering other indicators, focuses strongly on ideological reconstruction – a criterion according to which the KSČM has still not been successful.

Czech Social Democratic Party

ČSSD is a historical party that existed in Czech politics prior to the communist period and operated in exile during communism. Its comeback, however, was not smooth. The party did not get into parliament in 1990 and had only marginal presence in the legislature after the 1992 election. ČSSD's electoral fortunes turned after 1993, and in 1996 it was already the second-largest party in the Chamber of Deputies; in 1998 and 2002 it was the party with the most seats and became the senior governing party. By that time, the party had become a permanent part of the Czech political landscape. It suffered setbacks in opinion polls and non-parliamentary elections, especially during its second term in government, but remained the second-largest party in parliament after the 2006 election. By 2009, the party witnessed another revival, and won the 2010 parliamentary election.

These dynamics in electoral performance can largely be traced back to changes in the organizational strength and development. Before the 1990 election, the party had minimal organizational presence; major party development took place during the first half of the 1990s. Active membership recruitment and the building of structures led to a membership of more than 10,000 and a professional apparatus of about 2,000 staff before the 1992 election (Hanley 2003). After moderate success in that election, the party continued conscious organizational development by extending the organization at the local level, and aspired to increase the membership fourfold (Hanley 2003). It pursued a conscious strategy of "the cadre expansion" (Kopeček and Pšeja 2008, 324), that is, the active recruitment of new members, especially from other small left-wing formations. Rank-and-file members saw the only hope for ČSSD in building local organizations and engaging the experience of individual members to promote and further the party (CTK 1993b). Indeed, grassroots presence and their engagement increased considerably from the early to mid-1990s. For example, in 1990 local government elections, ČSSD ran 3,200 candidates; by the 1994 local contests this number had increased almost threefold, to 9,500 (CTK 1994b). Furthermore, during the 1996 election campaign, the party made use of its presence on the ground and ran a relatively active grassroots campaign; party leader Milos Zeman personally traveled across the country in an old bus, as the party strategy was to get close to the voters in small- and medium-sized towns (Kopeček and Pšeja 2008). This organizational approach "was accompanied by an upturn in the polls" (Kopeček and Pšeja 2008, 326) after 1993, and brought the ČSSD previously unattainable electoral success (Hanley 2003). By the 1996 parliamentary election, the party had moved from the fringes to the center of the political arena, increasing its support from 6 percent to 26 percent.

The success of the ČSSD in becoming the principal party of the left is often attributed to the fact that KSČM refused to reform itself (see Hanley 2001 for examples). However, this explanation is likely to be incomplete because it leaves two central questions unanswered. First, it is unable to explain why it was specifically ČSSD rather than any other of the numerous left-wing formations that succeeded. Second, it cannot account for the timing of ČSSD success: Why did ČSSD become successful only in the mid-1990s when it was clear from the start that KSČM was not reforming itself? Although not denying that the actions and decisions of KSČM may have played a role, the dynamics of organization building can provide a plausible answer to these questions. As explained, ČSSD became successful after meticulous organization building. Furthermore, the other left-wing formations failed to pursue a similar strategy. Kopeček and Pšeja (2008) specifically note that the two KSČM splinter parties – the Left Bloc and the Party of the Democratic Left – failed to pose a significant challenge to both KSČM and ČSSD at least partly because they lacked a "sophisticated organizational [. . .] background" (326).

The electoral success of ČSSD in 1996 did not stop the party from prioritizing and further strengthening their organization. Party leadership considered members the energy and engine of the party, and rather than being self-satisfied with the development of organizational structures, they pointed out the shortage of local branches and personnel in those branches (CTK 1997b). One of the primary goals that the party had for 1997 was to once again considerably increase the membership base because this was considered the key to party success (CTK 1997d). For example, party leader Zeman stated that district organizations with less than 100 members were "a disgrace of the Social Democrats," also suggesting the promotion of those local branch leaders whose branches did well or better than expected in local elections (CTK 1998h).

Continuous investment in organizational development allowed ČSSD to weather political crisis and scandals. Although not comparable to the environmental hostility suffered by KSČM, ČSSD experienced several scandals regarding its finances and the behavior of its candidates and MPs both times the party was in government. For example, in 1999 the scandals included unlawful business activities of the local development minister, Petr Lachnit, suspicious contacts of ČSSD official Jaromír Kuča, opaque activities of Miroslav Šlouf, and party leader Zeman's campaign aimed at discrediting the deputy parliamentary speaker, Petra Buzková (CTK 2000). Additional financial and business scandals flared up in 2005, involving the prime minister and then-party leader Stanislav Gross. Support for the party plummeted to only 10 percent of the electorate at one point before the 2006 parliamentary election (Kopeček and Pšeja 2008).

The party's strategy to get out of this electoral low was again organizational, that is, turning to invigorating and developing its organization. What is more, the party recognized that this was a long-term strategy that might lead to the party being in opposition for some time, however, accepting that organizational strengthening was more important than trying to get to power at any cost (Czech News Agency 2006d). The focus was once again on increasing and strengthening party membership, although the party's new strategy also emphasized developing "cooperation with civic associations, foundations, as well as sport and hobby clubs in towns and villages" (Czech News Agency 2006c). More emphasis was also put on strengthening party management by modernizing it (Czech News Agency 2006c) and making communication with voters and members more effective and regular. For example, the party organized discussions on the regional and local levels during inter-election periods (Czech News Agency 2006c; 2006e). This strategy, once again, helped lift the party up from its electoral low: the ČSSD landslide victories in the 2008 regional and Senate elections were mostly credited to its organizational revitalization (Czech News Agency 2009b).

In sum, the over-time trend in ČSSD electoral fate seems to be closely associated with the dynamics in party organizational strength and development. The party became a significant player in the electoral arena only after it had built up a strong organization. It sustained its position, despite competition from the KSČM on the left and numerous scandals by following a conscious strategy of organizational revitalization. Additionally, organizational strengthening and using the structures for building electoral success occurred at different times in party development under different leaders, which helps rule out the argument that organizational strength simply captures the effect of a popular leader.

Focused Comparison: The Civic Democratic Party and Its Ideological Rivals

The ODS and ODA were similar in many respects potentially relevant for electoral performance. Both emerged from the anticommunist social movement Civic Forum (OF), were ideologically center-right, served together in government between 1993 and 1998, and were involved in major financial scandals, which hit both parties equally hard (Hanley 2008). The major scandals involving ODS concerned party financing, although there was also circumstantial evidence about party corruption during the privatization process. Klaus and his party were expected to be down and out as a result of these scandals (Stroehlein 1998). ODA was in the same situation: as Saxonberg (1999, 415) notes, "[T]he mass media disclosed financial scandals that hit the ODA as hard as the ODS" (see also Hanley 2008; CTK 1998a). However, although both suffered defections as a result, ODA began to disintegrate and ultimately disappeared, but ODS revived and has remained the most successful rightwing party in the Czech Republic.

Despite being similar, the parties differed significantly in their strategies of organization building, which has figured prominently as one of the main priorities of the ODS since its creation. Václav Klaus, the party's first leader, insisted on having an organizationally well-defined party; he referred to the experience of Polish Solidarity and its breakup as evidence that organization was necessary to survive and be successful (Hanley 2004). In fact, Klaus was advocating stronger organizational development and professionalization of the OF even before the movement split and ODS was formed (Hadjiiski 2001). This was in great contrast to the original dissident leaders of OF, who did not realize the importance of building a political organization and "quickly lost contact with the grass roots movement" (Hadjiiski 2001, 54). Klaus was elected the head of the movement in 1990 on a promise to build a strong party organization from bottom up – an idea that the rank and file supported but the former dissidents did not. It is, therefore, not surprising that when OF eventually split, much of the professionalized and strengthened organization joined Klaus in the ODS.

The leadership of the ODS continued in the spirit of organization building. They believed that organization with hierarchy, structures, and formal membership, and not merely some loose movement, was the only possible tool for electoral success (Linek and Pecháček 2007). ODS established a coordinating center in Prague and branch offices across the country (Blahoz 1994). Already in the early 1990s, the party was able to build up an organization that rivaled that of KSČM, including a nationwide network of local groups, well-resourced headquarters, and professional regional structures. As Hadjiiski (2001, 56) notes, Klaus and his team "gave special attention to the professionalization of paid staff." ODS's other explicit strategy was to create mass citizen participation (Hanley 2003). Direct contacts with voters constituted the party's main campaign strategy. Klaus claimed, "I personally have met in the American style of campaigning more citizens of Czechoslovakia than anyone else. I have worked hard. And this is very much different from some other politicians" (quoted in Battiata 1991). Klaus understood the need to reward and stay in touch with the organization the party had built, and on many occasions toured the country (Saxonberg 1999).

Organizational development continued throughout the post-communist era, and did not stop with Klaus becoming prime minister in 1992. In the 1994 party congress, Klaus again stressed the need to build the party organization, despite the fact that they had already done very well in the local elections. Just managing to mobilize their membership base was not enough: the party aspired to actively recruit new members and posed this as one of the main strategic goals in 1995 (BBC Summary of World Broadcasts 1994b). The party continuously recruited new members and effective technocrats to staff its offices (Blahoz 1994).

ODA, on the other hand, was one of the organizationally weakest parties to emerge from OF: in 1990, the party had only 70 members and in the following year only 150 (Hanley 2008). It was a formation that mainly consisted of parliamentary elites, valued low membership (Hanley 2003), maintained a weak organizational structure and negligible degree of direct contact with voters (Klima 1998). Comparing the organizational characteristics of the Czech parliamentary parties in the mid 1990s, Deegan-Krause (2006, 80–83) also reported that ODA (together with SPR-RSČ) had the weakest organization on all dimensions considered, including "territorial extensiveness" and local presence, membership activism, and "permanent party apparatus." More specifically, ODS's membership was about 0.27 percent of the electorate throughout the 1990s, and increased to 0.31 percent by 2006. ODA's membership peaked at the end of the 1990s at 0.03 percent of the electorate and decreased rapidly after that. In terms of local branches, in 1992, ODS had branch offices in 13 percent of all municipalities compared to ODA's 0.5 percent; by 2002, ODS had increased its share to 26 percent, but ODA's decreased to 0.02 percent. ODA and ODS started out on almost equal footing in terms of participation in local elections: in the 1994 local elections, ODS contested in 1.4 percent and ODA in 2.9 percent of all municipalities. By 1998, the differences had become significant – ODA contested in only 1.7 percent of municipalities compared to 21 percent contested by ODS – and remained so for the subsequent election, as well.

The different electoral fates of ODS and ODA may, at least partially, be attributed to these differences in organizational strength. ODS built its organization with the specific purpose of using it for electoral campaigning and a guarantee of party survival. As Hanley (2003) argues, without the quick organization building, it is unlikely that the party would have remained as a viable political player. Evans and Whitefield (1998, 128) further add: "There are no significant ideological differences between the supporters of the Civic Democratic Party and the Civic Democratic Alliance, which is consistent with the argument that their different fortunes are accounted for by organizational factors" (see also Lewis, Lomax, and Wightman 1994). The fact that ODS managed to bounce back from even the most serious financial scandals is credited to their powerful and well-disciplined local organizations (Stroehlein 1998). As Stroehlein (1998) put it, "[W]ith a well disciplined organization behind him, [Klaus] will, like Communists, keep getting the Party faithful to the ballot boxes at the key elections."

As for ODA, Hanley (2008) reports that the party suffered disloyalty before it was engaged in major scandals: many of its members left the party for ODS because there were no local branches in their areas that they could join. Although the party leadership recognized after their failure in the 1994 local elections that "the ODA succeeded everywhere where it was physically present," and acknowledged that the lesson from it was that ODA needed to be present everywhere, they never implemented that lesson, claiming that elite performance is more relevant for electoral success than the number of members (CTK 1995a). Lack of organization made the party dependent on "floating voters," which made it extremely vulnerable to changes in the electoral environment and other events. It is not surprising then that scandals of the same nature and similar magnitude to those that ODS had suffered equaled a death sentence for the organizationally less-endowed ODA.

Although the differences in the organizational strength of ODA and ODS were stark, the extent to which organization has an effect on performance independent of ideology can further be gauged by comparing ODS to its other ideological rivals that emerged either from OF or split off from the ODS later. Specifically, the OF split into two in the very beginning: in addition to ODS, Jiří Dienstbier created another group at first called the Civic Forum, then renamed Civic Movement, and in 1993 renamed again as Free Democrats. Unlike ODS, their survival strategy did not include organizational development but relied on well-known personalities. In the 1992 election, the then-Civic Movement did not clear the 5 percent electoral threshold, even though Dienstbier was one of the most popular politicians in the country and many party members were government ministers at the time. From then on, the party was marginal. ODS, on the other hand, one year after being established and as a result of painstaking organizational development, became the strongest party in the Czech Republic (CTK 1992b).

Divisions among high-ranking ODS members over the direction and management of the party led to a significant split and the foundation of the US in 1998.[4] Because their split had not been because of ideological disagreement, the party remained similar to ODS in terms of its "programs and philosophies" (Jakl 1998; see also CTK 1998d). After creation, the party quickly faced political and organizational difficulties, and appeared vague to voters (Hanley 2004). Hanley further claims that their first electoral trial – regional elections in 1998 – suffered from organizational weakness. In fact, Stroehlein (1998) argues that the anti-Klaus rebels within ODS never wanted to create a new party, but because Klaus was reelected as a leader, they had no other option. Thus, US sort of happened, with the creators not really sure what they wanted from it. The hope was that it would overtake ODS, but as explained, by the time of elections six months later, ODS had totally redeemed itself and proved victorious. At the same time, the US was headed in the other direction (Jakl 1998). Observers explained US's poor electoral performance by lack of a firm organization: "[T]he ODS has a paid manager and party headquarters in every district, the Freedom Union has a total of 20 full-time employees" (CTK 1998e). Whereas the party remained in the parliamentary arena after the 1998 election and managed to get some seats as part of an electoral coalition in 2002, it was in serious decline from the beginning. Members started to leave the party out of frustration (CTK 2002b), and leadership remained more concerned about issues such as whether to cooperate with the ČSSD than

---

[4] Before the creation of the US, a group of radical anticommunists, who had originally supported Klaus, founded the Democratic Union (DEU) in 1994 (Hanley 2004). The party did not manage to get registered at first because it failed to get the necessary 1,000 signatures to do so (CTK 1994a). This suggests that organizational development was not a priority for DEU. The party remained marginal from its inception, and merged with the US in 2001.

building the party (CTK 2003a). The party support plummeted, and US became "clinically dead" in the early 2000s (CTK 2005).

Finally, in 2002, the European Democrats led by the ODS mayor of Prague, Jan Kasl, broke away and formed their own party (Hanley 2004). The party remained centered in Prague, never established an organization of any significance, and after a dismal result in the 2006 parliamentary election (2.1 percent) it became essentially extinct.

Hanley (2008) – the most extensive study of right-wing parties in the Czech Republic – sums up the different fate of ODS compared to its right-wing rivals by stating that other parties of the (dissident) right lacked the organizational resources ODS possessed, and were therefore not competitive. He argues that most viable parties have developed strong organizations and thereby "choked off" their ideological rivals "by effectively monopolizing most organizational 'start-up capital'" (Hanley 2003, 163). Indeed, all of the described examples illustrate how the lack of organization not only hinders a party's ability to build a consolidated support base and therefore maintain support over several consecutive elections, but also exacerbates the effect of any environmental challenges or scandals that the party experiences.

One might argue that the organizational effects uncovered are simply leadership effects, because of ODS's charismatic first leader, Václav Klaus. Considering party performance and organizational development after Klaus stepped down, however, shows otherwise. Klaus left the leadership in 2002 and was replaced by Mirek Topolánek. As Enyedi and Linek (2008) argue, with the new head, rather than witnessing declining organizational activism and development, the party actually started to cultivate relations with civic organizations more actively. They further claim that the party also started providing educational facilities for its candidates, an infrastructure for public lectures, and discussions with its supporters. For example, the party started its own training center to educate its local and regional councilors and MPs on matters of politics and governance. Similar to Klaus, Topolánek announced plans to open ODS local branches to new members to avoid stagnation and power concentration (Linek and Pecháček 2007). Similar to the Klaus era during the early 1990s, the party under Topolánek used grassroots campaigning in regional elections in 2004 (CTK 2004c) and won in twelve out of thirteen regions. Indeed, after the leadership change, several branch organizations actually claimed that the communication within the party had improved, they had become more active, and consequently their membership had grown significantly and voter support for the party had increased, as well (CTK 2003b). Under Topolánek's leadership the party excelled not only in regional but also in Senate and European parliamentary elections. Furthermore, following a slight downturn in the 2002 parliamentary elections, the party excelled again in 2006 after seeing another record growth in its membership in 2005 (Czech News Agency 2006f). All of this indicates that the party success was not dependent on Klaus, but occurred largely because of its organizational strength under different leaders.

Estonia

The Estonian narratives include one case study and one focused comparison. The case of RP demonstrates how investing in building a strong organization leads to subsequent electoral success, but abandoning organizational development can prove fatal. The focused comparison considers two very similar parties – K and KE. The former succeeded in consolidating its support base; the latter has disappeared from the political scene. The comparison suggests that their divergent attitude toward strengthening party organizations was most likely responsible for the dramatically different electoral performance of these parties.

Res Publica

Res Publica – a genuinely new party (Sikk 2005) – was created in 2001. It became the party of the prime minister after the first parliamentary election that it contested in 2003, but then disappeared as a party three years later. RP's quick rise was unprecedented, but so were their organization-building strategies. When the plans to establish a party first surfaced in July 2001, RP was a debating club of about 300 members. The period from mid-2001 to mid-2002 was characterized by intense efforts to build an internal organization, recruit new members, and establish viable local branch offices (Taagepera 2006). This emphasis on building a strong organization before the party was even officially registered was novel in Estonian party politics. Indeed, the party emerged with no philosophy or a new ideological niche; their novelty was their organization: a mass party organization as opposed to the existing parties that the founders of RP described as small and elite centered (Ideon 2001; Postimees 2001b; Sildam 2001; Vaher 2001). RP, for the first time in Estonia, used mass mailings and text messaging for recruiting purposes, and they were very successful. By the end of 2001, the party membership had increased to more than 1,000 and by 2003, the year of the victorious parliamentary election, the membership reached almost 3,700, making it the third-largest party.[5]

Membership proved crucial for building strong local offices. By the time of the local election in October 2002, the party had its network of local offices in place and fully staffed. The fact that party leaders and activists at the central level were personally traveling from one locality to the next in order to introduce the party, recruit more members, and find suitable staff for branch offices demonstrates the high importance of organization building to party activities.

---

[5] Although RP entered the electoral arena with a relatively large membership, it is clear that the membership base was built deliberately in preparation for launching the party. In that sense, it was not a resource that the nascent party "inherited" or "possessed" but one that it had purposefully accumulated to gain electoral advantage in the 2002 local and 2003 national contests. Note, however, that for my argument to hold it does not really matter whether a party inherits or cultivates a membership. What does matter is that the party uses its membership to gain electoral advantage.

Hiring a professional staff both to work in the central and local offices was another clear priority to the party leadership, who considered volunteers to be too unreliable in the long-term (see also EPL 2001c). "You cannot build a party with a group of fanatics, you need professionals," explained a former general secretary.[6] The network of branches, professional staff, and ever-increasing membership were fully utilized to run the party's campaign in the 2002 local elections.[7] Widespread local presence allowed RP to contest elections in 117 out of 241 (49 percent) localities. Only two other parties were able to contest more localities. RP won the second-highest vote share nationwide in that local election.

Investing in organization remained the prominent strategy until the national election six months later – in March 2003. The party leaders and activists again made extensive use of the well-functioning party structure to conduct an electoral campaign across the country. Through local branches, party members and activists as well as leaders themselves were in direct contact with potential voters. The professional staff coordinated leadership visits to localities and searched as well as trained new candidates. Local activists initiated get-out-the-vote drives – again something rather unprecedented in Estonia. These efforts of investing in and maintaining a strong organization paid off – RP obtained the second-largest vote share in the 2003 parliamentary election and tied for first place with the K in terms of seat share. Because K was unable to find coalition partners, RP got the opportunity to form the government and became the party of the prime minister. The party leadership and outside observers have attributed this success directly to RP's strong organization: its professional staff, widespread local presence, and sizeable membership[8] (see also Taagepera 2006). That RP's organization brought votes is also suggested by the fact that the main campaign attraction of the party was essentially its organization, more so than any ideology or policies. Furthermore, when RP emerged, there were other parties that tried to enter the electoral arena, including the Estonian Democratic Party and "With Reason and Heart" (Mõistuse ja südamega; formed by several former leaders of KE), neither of which had built an organization of any significance and neither made any electoral gains.

When RP became a governing party, emphasis on building and maintaining organization disappeared and shifted to governing. The founders and leaders of the party were no longer interested in keeping strong ties with branch organizations, local members, and supporters. "It is clear that after RP became a governing party, less attention was paid to the party organization," claimed a former general secretary.[9] The party elite was now in government and parliament, but still doubled as party officials, as well. This effectively meant that there was no

[6] RP Respondent 1, personal communication, August 6, 2007.
[7] RP Respondent 1, personal communication, August 6, 2007.
[8] RP Respondent 1, personal communication, August 6, 2007.
[9] RP Respondent 1, personal communication, August 6, 2007.

leadership left to direct organizational development and maintenance. Indeed, the first party leader, Rein Taagepera, had predicted that winning more than fifteen seats in parliament would "choke" the party, that is, the party would not be able to build and sustain the organization any longer (Raun 2001). That serving in the government undermined organization development was echoed by other analysts who agreed that after major electoral success, the party no longer had time for internal maturation and growth (Kagge 2005; Postimees 2002b).

Abandoning the organization, in turn, proved to be fatal to the party: among other things, many branch offices lost their professional staff.[10] Several regular as well as prominent members (including Rein Taagepera) became disillusioned and left the party (Ernits 2004a). The party was also no longer able to manage internal conflicts, which were fought out publicly and covered extensively in the media (Ernits 2004b). The party's parliamentary group started to disintegrate, as well, with MPs switching to other parties or leaving the parliament altogether (Koch 2006). The consequences of abandoning the organizational development became especially visible in the 2004 European Parliament election, where RP did not win any seats despite running the second-most expensive campaign. By the beginning of 2006, it was clear to the party leaders and outside observers that the party was unable to recover and that the only viable strategy was to merge with another right-wing party – Pro Patria (IL) (Reinap and Koch 2006) – which happened in 2006.

The rise and fall of RP is attributable to the highs and lows of their organizational strength. This case illustrates well how investing in building a strong party organization can have an almost immediate payoff in terms of electoral success. However, it also shows that inability to maintain its organizational strength risks a party's long-term survival. This can happen regardless of how favorable the other factors, such as financial resources, access to pork and patronage, and beneficial environmental conditions. After all, RP was a governing party until 2005, never lost the support of its main sponsors, and was never involved in major political scandals or crises.

Focused Comparison: Center Party and Coalition Party

K and KE were similar in virtually all respects. Both parties originated in the beginning of the 1990s from the Popular Front movement and both consisted, in large part, of people connected to the previous regime. Both parties were considered to be heavily dependent on their charismatic leader and both had connections to wealthy sponsors, with the KE having a slight edge in financial matters. The members of both parties had served together in the transitional government of 1990–1992 and again in 1995. As governing parties, both had had access to, and made use of, patronage and pork. Both parties were also involved in major scandals – the K leader for secretly taping conversations

---

[10] RP Respondent 1, personal communication, August 6, 2007.

with representatives from other parties, and the KE leader for allegedly corrupt privatization deals. Both parties were Populist in their appeal and classified as center-right in their ideology (Toomla 1999; Villem 1996).

Despite the similarity between these parties, their electoral fate differed dramatically. K did not start out as the most successful party, but steadily increased its vote share with each election and was the biggest or the second-biggest parliamentary party following the 1999, 2003, and 2007 elections, commanding consistently about 25–30 percent of the vote. KE emerged as the biggest party after the 1995 elections, holding an unprecedented 41 percent of seats in parliament together with a few small rural parties that had formed a joint list with KE. Four years later, this had shrunk to only 7 percent, and two years into the parliamentary term the party no longer existed. Why did these parties have such dramatically different electoral trajectories?

There was one crucial difference between the parties – their approach to organization building. K started gradually, building up its organizational network right after the party was created (Kalmre 1996). It invested in professional staff right from the start, and ended up with the most well-functioning central office (Jarne 1996b). The party also prioritized increasing its membership by tracking their supporters and asking current members to recruit new members and supporters (Ideon 1999b). Such recruitment remained a constant priority for the party, and local branches served a crucial role in this effort (Ideon 2000c). The K membership drives were strategic. They tried to lure local elites on the basis of whom they could build a viable pool of local and national candidates in each district. Establishing a countrywide local presence was a conscious strategy of the leadership to increase and consolidate the party's support base (Tootsen 1998). The party had one of the largest membership sizes and most widespread local presence.

The party leadership acknowledged that they invested in conscious organizational development because of the expectation that it would pay off in votes: "[M]oney is important, but even more important are people and time, having access to these is the key," said a member of the party leadership when explaining the party's 2003 national election strategy (Ideon 2002). General Secretary Kadri Must echoed this position, stating that local organizations are the prerequisite to a maximum result at different elections (PM Online 2003). "An attractive leader with a good team can bring short-term electoral success, but for a long-term success the party needs active membership and extensive network of local branches," claimed a member of the party leadership.[11]

The party, indeed, made extensive use of its organizational network during electoral campaigns to different levels of government (see, for example, Postimees 2009a). According to a local leader, local branches saw their main role as preparing for and conducting campaigns during as well as between elections.[12]

[11] K Respondent 1, personal communication, August 7, 2007.
[12] K Respondent 2, personal communication, August 6, 2007.

He was quite certain that the electoral success of the party depended on local activists. Similarly, a prominent MP of K, Ain Seppik, claimed, "Our experience tells us that door-to-door campaigning becomes increasingly more important especially in rural but increasingly also in urban areas [. . .] large billboards and TV ads no longer help" (Ruusing 2007).

Furthermore, the party used the organization as a "safety net" that allowed it to concentrate on and succeed in municipal politics as well as extend its voter base when the party was out of power on the national level (Ideon 2009b). In 2006, the general secretary of the party claimed, "We have proven ourselves to be viable even when power positions slip out of hand; [and] we have remained strong even while being in government" (Postimees 2006b). This organizational strategy and resulting organizational capacity allowed the party to speak and appeal to "the common people," as opposed to – and to the great anguish of – so many of its opponents, who were explicitly or implicitly the "elite" parties with only rudimentary organizations and with no equal understanding of the necessity to build one (Postimees 2009b; Tallo 1996; Turay 2009).

In contrast, the KE was an elite party, sometimes mockingly referred to as a project party or party that exists only on paper (Ülavere 2007; Vöörmann 2001), a party that was created only for its leaders to get to power (EPL 2001b, Postimees 2000). KE never prioritized building an organization (Paet 1998b). Despite having the largest seat share in parliament, it was the only party whose membership remained below 1,000 until 1998, when they needed to cobble together the 1,000 members in order to operate as a legally registered political party. Even many of its parliamentary candidates were not party members (Tarand 1997). Indeed, the leaders of the KE considered the 1,000-member requirement for registering a party to be unnecessarily high (Kubo 1997).[13]

Its local presence was equally nonexistent: in 1996 local elections the party was able to run candidates in only 2 out of 253 municipalities (0.8 percent). Compare that to 65 out of 253 (26 percent) by K. The weakness of the organization eventually led to a situation where the party was in great difficulty to find candidates for the 1999 parliamentary elections (Villem 1998). Because of a lack of candidates, the party had to participate in a variety of local electoral alliances in 1996, and had its ministers run for municipal councils (Ottas 1996). Strategic membership recruitment and local presence, which partially served the purpose of building a candidate pool in K, was simply lacking in KE.

---

[13] In order to gather the necessary 1,000 members, the party leader, Mart Siimann, asked all existing members to actively recruit new ones. One existing member, Ülo Nugis, was most active in doing so and recruited about 500 members, all of whom were loyal personally to him rather than the party. When Nugis left the party because of disagreements with the leadership, he took his followers with him, threatening the extinction of the KE because the membership was about to fall below the legal requirement again (Koni 2000). This is a telling example of the organizational weakness and vulnerability of the KE.

In 1999, the KE conducted the third-most-expensive national election campaign, but they only received seven seats. By that time, most of the small membership had left the party, and soon after the new parliamentary session started, the seven KE MPs also switched allegiance and abandoned the party (Vöörmann 2001). The party officially ceased to exist in November 2001, one and a half years into the parliamentary term. The general verdict from observers was that KE was a party of power, not a party in the electorate; it concentrated on governing and did not pay attention to organization building, which led to its demise (EPL 2001b; Saarts 2004).

Given that practically the only relevant characteristic on which K and KE differed was their organizational strength, there is at least some reason to believe that this is a significant factor explaining their divergent electoral performance. Furthermore, the narratives of both parties illustrate how organizational strength and the use of party organization in an election campaign was associated with subsequent and sustained electoral success, and the lack of organization can be at least partially responsible for the demise of a party.[14]

Hungary

During the time period under consideration, Hungary had one of the most stable party systems in the region: more or less the same parties made it to parliament in all elections. Hidden behind this surface of relative stability, however, were great differences across parties in terms of who succeeded and survived, especially in the long-term. The parties in the first post-communist government, that is, the successful ones in the first election – the MDF, FKgP, and the Christian Democratic Peoples' Party (KDNP) – all experienced major splits and were effectively absorbed by the largest right-wing nationalist party in the early 2000s, Fidesz. However, Fidesz, together with the MSzP – the two relatively mediocre performers in the early 1990s – managed to consolidate and increase their support bases over the years and became the two major political forces. The differences in the performance of MSzP and the four right-wing conservative parties are largely because of organizational factors.

---

[14] In addition to comparing K to KE, comparing the former to parties that have split from it is also informative about the relative importance of ideology versus organization on party success and survival, because the splinter parties are generally ideologically close to the party of their origin. K experienced two major splits: one in 1996 after a leadership struggle, and another in 2004 over a disagreement about opposing the referendum to join the European Union. In both cases, the party organization remained loyal to K. Indeed, the local branches despised the intrigues that played out in the central office, stood for the status quo, and opposed the rebels (PM Online 2004a; Tammer 1996a) – confirming the idea that organization helps a party maintain stability despite internal crisis. In both cases, the splinter parties (the Development Party [Arengupartei] in 1996, and Social Liberals in 2004) did not attract many rebels from K, remained organizationally weak, and did not survive.

Hungarian Socialist Party

In terms of the electoral performance, MSzP got only a modest vote share of 11 percent in 1990 and was the fourth-largest party (out of six) in parliament. However, the party steadily improved its performance and was the one with the highest vote share in the 1994 election, when it got an absolute majority in parliament. MSzP was the senior coalition partner in three out of five post-communist governments before 2010, and was reelected as an incumbent in 2006 – an unusual result in the region. In general, MSzP was able to consolidate its support base and succeeded against the odds.

However, MSzP has not always been successful. In fact, as a "successor party" it suffered considerable environmental hostility. The party was created in 1989 after the Communist Party was disbanded. MSzP claimed not to be an ideological successor, and stressed its institutional discontinuity by not automatically carrying over any old members (Morlang 2003). However, the party was the legal successor and remained one in the eyes of the public and its competitors (Ágh 1991; Bihari 1991). Indeed, MSzP "was constantly rejected, often with hostility, by other parliamentary forces, as 'crypto communist'" (Racz 1993, 657). Therefore, it is not accurate to assume that MSzP enjoyed a comparative advantage over its competitors because of its successor status. Rather, the party was seriously disadvantaged because of the stigma as one local leader and a long-time MP claimed[15] (see also Ágh 2000). Furthermore, the organization that the party maintained was not in great shape or fully functional (Racz 1993). Although MSzP inherited the Communist Party infrastructure, under the threat of public criticism, the party gave 90 percent of its assets to the state (Waller 1995). In sum, thus, MSzP had no electoral success, was politically marginalized, and faced environmental hostility. However, it was able to break out of that situation. As Ágh (2000) argues, the party committed to developing its organization, which eventually led to its success (see also Grzymala-Busse 2002a).

Socialists pursued two strategies of organizational development: (1) acting as a modern, professional party, which mostly entailed strengthening the central office and keeping the party unified; and (2) strengthening the party on the ground (Ágh 2002; Machos 2000; Morlang 2003; Stark and Bruszt 1998). MSzP was successful at both, and developed a reputation of expertise and professionalism. This was greatly helped by the fact that the party office was mainly staffed with experienced professionals. Their technocratic pragmatism made the organization very efficient, facilitated effective campaigning, and helped keep close links between the central and local levels (Lengyel 2004; Racz 2000). Because of these links, local leaders saw themselves foremost as representatives of the national party, and urged their candidates to follow the

---

[15] MSzP Respondent 1, personal communication, June 14, 2007.

party line even if it contradicted the narrow local concerns (Morlang 2003).[16] Local party organizers did not need to "fight" with the center, and felt that their opinion counted, which increased their loyalty to the central office, as a local leader claimed[17] (see also Morlang 2003). This, in turn, helped MSzP avoid splits and defections – common in other parties – despite the diversity of opinions and platforms that the party represented (Morlang 2003, 71).[18] It also helped the party appeal to voters and overcome its pariah status – the contrast in their level of professionalism compared to the other parties was very obvious and visible, (Grzymala-Busse 2002a) as will be described.

Socialists also invested heavily in strengthening the nationwide structures of the party and its membership. They had the widest network of local branches (Morlang 2003) and intensively fostered activism of these branches, especially outside Budapest. Socialist party members were the most active and well-integrated of all Hungarian parties as a result, which, in turn, paid off in maintaining their loyalty to the party (Ilonszki 1999). MSzP also encouraged the participation of their local branches and members in neighborhood and youth organizations that were open to non-partisans (Morlang 2003). This outreach to communities was unprecedented. It gave the party an opportunity to have direct contacts with citizens and promote constituency contacts, which considerably helped the party improve its image and electability.

Local branches also "provided the party with a loyal and politically involved pool of members from which to draw future candidates" (Morlang 2003, 70). The strong network of local branches itself helped maintain party unity because it served as a training ground, instilling loyalty and accumulating political experience and expertise in members – the future candidates and leaders.[19] Morlang (2003) argues that MSzP leaders often linked local presence and activism with party discipline and loyalty.

Not less importantly, local members were valuable assets during election campaigns. In great contrast to other parties, MSzP capitalized on its organization and membership rather than public relations campaigns to get out the vote as early as the 1994 election. Local campaigns helped draw close links between MSzP candidates and local voters, and the well-integrated local branches helped make sure that the party still presented a unified rather than fragmented image to voters (Szekeres 1995; Szekeres and Szeredi 1999). Socialist leaders specifically attributed the unprecedented success of the party in 1994

---

[16] The relationship between locals and the center had not always been good. Szekeres and Szeredi (1999) argue that prior to the 1998 election, the parochial concerns of many local leaders cost MSzP the elections in the SMD tier.

[17] MSzP Respondent 1, personal communication, June 14, 2007.

[18] It should be noted that despite high levels of unity displayed to the public, the party actually experienced serious internal political conflicts, sometimes attributed to its extreme internal democracy (Machos 2000). The fact that the party stayed unified in the eyes of the public despite the actual internal rifts is a further testimony to its professional management.

[19] MSzP Respondent 1, personal communication, June 14, 2007.

(an absolute majority of seats in parliament) and beyond to the work done by local members (Morlang 2003; Szekeres 1995).

The party maintained a strong organization, and professional and integrative practices when in government. Indeed, an extensive network of branches, loyal membership, and professional management allowed the party to not only shed its pariah status, but also successfully undertake difficult ideological and programmatic changes. One of the greatest challenges that MSzP faced was to reconcile the two competing policy directions within the party: market reform on the one hand and protection of traditional working class interests on the other (Morlang 2003; see also Tavits and Letki 2009). Its first time in government, the party implemented economic shock therapy that went seriously against the traditional leftist values (Racz 2000), and did so without losing the backing of its core supporters and members. Indeed, MSzP won the same share of votes in 1998 as it had in 1994. There were no serious defections and no splits. At the same time, ideological and personal disagreements, often much smaller in magnitude, were the primary reason for splits and the demise of various right-wing parties, as will be discussed.

Comparing the Conservatives: Fidesz versus MDF, KDNP, and FKgP

In addition to the case of MSzP, considering Fidesz and its right-wing conservative rivals FKgP, KDNP, and MDF provides another opportunity to probe the plausibility of causal mechanisms and the relevance of alternative explanations. Although not providing the same degree of control as the comparisons in the previous sections because of differences between these parties, this comparison does allow holding constant one of the critical alternative explanations – ideology. Importantly, these parties exhibit a significant contrast on the dependent variable – electoral performance. FKgP, KDNP, and MDF – the original winners and parties that formed the first post-communist government – have effectively disappeared as significant players. Failure to maintain organizational strength and thereby organizational unity was the primary reason for the collapse or near collapse of these parties (Csizmadia 2005). Fidesz, on the other hand, systematically "poached" the voters, candidates, and organizations of these parties. As the analysis will show, it was because of the organizational weakness of the original winners and the simultaneous steady strengthening of Fidesz's organization that allowed the latter to feast on the remains of the original winning parties.

MDF was the winner of the first post-communist election with about 25 percent of the vote and twice as many seats as its closest rival, SzDSz. The success, however, did not last very long. The party assumed office as the senior coalition partner. Two years into its term in office, the party was experiencing major internal frictions because of ideological and personal disagreements. By 1994, the MDF vote share decreased by about half, and seat share even more drastically. MDF has remained a minor party ever since. Fowler (2004) claims that MDF survived as a parliamentary party for a while after 1998 only through being co-opted by Fidesz.

In terms of party organizational extensiveness, MDF started out with a relatively impressive record. Toole (2003) reports that the MDF leadership remained convinced of the electoral benefits of building a membership and local presence. The party noted that their 1994 result was in direct correlation with the strength of their local organization. However, realizing the importance of organization is different than actually being able to implement it. The party had a relatively large membership and network of local offices, but it lacked the professional leadership capacity to manage it (Bakke and Sitter 2005; Toole 2003). The organization was large but weak, and the party leadership remained alienated from the grassroots members (Bozóki and Lomax 1996). The party was generally considered extremely elite-centered, even aristocratic (MTI 1994a), rather than the kind of catch-all people's party that it claimed to be (MTI 1995). In fact, the leadership did not really even care who joined the party (Horn 1999), and did not prioritize developing and maintaining the organization, including holding on to members and local branches. As one of the MPs of the party said, "[M]embership is not important in the modern age."[20] The party also did not care about members and local branches as potential campaign assets, leading to chaotic and uncoordinated electoral campaigns (Szabó 1995). Elite- and leader-centeredness and neglect of the organization further contributed to the fact that MDF lacked mid-level managers (Ágh 1991) and means of training and socializing its candidates (Morlang 2003). It also explains why there was little loyalty among party members – between 1988 and 1996 the membership of the party declined by 18,000 members (MTI 1996). Although the number of its local organizations did not decline drastically (from 575 in 1995 to 540 in 2005) (Enyedi and Linek 2008), Waterbury (2006) claims that, by the mid-1990s, MDF no longer had an effective party organization.

It was not only organizational extensiveness but also the diversity within the organization that the party failed to effectively manage (Bozóki and Lomax 1996). As a result, its MPs, as well as certain groups, abandoned the party. Already in 1993, a populist-nationalist group split off under the leadership of István Csurka and founded the Party of Hungarian Justice and Life (MIÉP), and three MPs joined Fidesz (Fowler 2004). These splits, however, did not resolve the underlying ideological and personal differences, which further suggests a deeper, organizational reason for disunity (Bakke and Sitter 2005). Indeed, the party experienced further splits (in 1996 a group of dissatisfied MDF members created the Hungarian Democratic Peoples' Party [MDNP]) (Markus 1999)[21] and large-scale defections, mostly to Fidesz. Defections by the elite and rank-and-file members, due, at least in part, to weak managerial capacity undermined

---

[20] MDF Respondent 1, personal communication, June 13, 2007.
[21] MDF and MDNP merged again in 2006 (Löffler 2006).

MDF's organizational strength on other dimensions, as well. It is not surprising, then, that this cumulative organizational failure was followed by the electoral demise of the party.

The organizations of FKgP and KDNP were also relatively weak, especially as far as professional management was concerned. Their organizational structures and decision-making procedures dated back to their historical roots in the prewar era, and proved inefficient in modern politics (Machos 2000). The management failures were more immediately visible in KDNP. According to a long-time leader of the Budapest branch, the party experienced similar internal frictions over ideology and personalities as MDF with similar or even more serious consequences: the party effectively ceased to exist.[22] The conflict lasted for about two and a half years, from 1995 to 1997, with one group splitting off and joining Fidesz (Fowler 2004). Within the group that remained in KDNP, internal warfare continued, and the leadership style became increasingly dictatorial (Machos 2000), culminating in the disintegration of the party in the summer of 1997. Some of its members, including its former leader, László Surján, joined Fidesz; the more radical ones preferred FKgP.

FKgP managed to stay in the electoral game as a serious contender for a little longer than MDF and KDNP. Even in 1998 it still attracted about 13 percent of the vote, only slightly less than in the first election. In addition to being in the first post-communist government, the party also served in government together with Fidesz after the 1998 election. However, in 2002 the party received less than 1 percent of the vote and in 2006 they no longer contested the elections.

FKgP was actually seriously fragmented and already experienced its first split in 1991 over the land reform issue (Bozóki and Lomax 1996). Whereas most of the MPs left the party, the more radical wing remained and the party became dominated by its leader, József Torgyán (Lomax 1999). The dominance of its leader hampered organizational development, especially in terms of creating an efficient and professional central office, claimed one of the subsequent leaders of the party[23] (see also Bélafi 2003). He further argued that the party was managed ad hoc with no clear rules, even about how to conduct a meeting. The strength of the other attributes of the FKgP organization was also debatable. The party claimed to have a large membership and widespread local presence (Toole 2003), but these figures were most likely inflated. This is especially true after 1998: Benkő (2002) reports that if we believe the membership figures, then in 2002 FKgP got fewer votes than it had members. Furthermore, members and structures that did exist were never put into effective use – the campaign manager of the party never mentioned local branches as significant campaign assets (Nagyné and Maczó 1995). The situation was not helped by Torgyán's choice to reward and dismiss local leaders at will and exercise

---

[22] FKgP Respondent 1, personal communication, June 19, 2007.
[23] FKgP Respondent 2, personal communication, June 15, 2007.

dictatorial governing style – factors that further worked against integrating the local organizations of the party (Bélafi 2003; Benkő 2002).

The fragmentation and internal conflicts in FKgP escalated after 1998 (Spirova 2007). Without an effective organization, the FKgP depended heavily on its leader's reputation and credibility. The latter was destroyed in 2000 as a result of a series of corruption scandals. Decline in public opinion and internal defections quickly ensued (Fowler 2004): the party suffered multiple splits and formations of nonviable mini-parties, members left the party in large numbers, and local branches ceased to function.[24] The remaining party activists blamed the failure directly on the lack of professional administration and resulting organizational weakness.[25]

In sum, the original group of right-wing parties that formed the first post-communist government all failed to survive as significant players in the electoral arena (Csizmadia 2005). This failure was mostly because of their inability to build strong and functional organizations to manage the diversity of platforms and the larger organization and membership of the party. This inability, in turn, was manifested in continuous splits and infighting – developments that undermined public support for these parties and led to their marginalization.

The failure of the original winners contrasts starkly with the rise and consolidation of Fidesz. The party started out with a relatively modest result – it was one of the two smallest parties in the first post-communist parliament, commanding only 9 percent of the PR vote. Fidesz became very popular in 1991 and 1992: opinion polls showed about 33 percent support for the party (Enyedi 2005). However, its support plummeted by the time of the 1994 elections to only 7 percent. The party lost about 80 percent of its potential voters and barely managed to enter the parliament (ibid.). After the 1994 defeat and its near extinction, the party's fortunes turned. Since 1998, it has been one of the largest parties in parliament and the biggest right-wing force. Its PR vote grew to 29 percent in 1998, 41 percent in 2002 and 2006, and culminated with winning an absolute majority in 2010. As the biggest party in parliament, Fidesz became the senior coalition partner in 1998 and the sole governing party in 2010.

Fidesz started out as a liberal party (i.e., economically centrist party with a primary focus on promoting liberty and equal rights), ideologically rather close to SzDSz. In the early 1990s, these two parties formed a sizeable liberal force that stood in opposition to the (nationalist) conservative right parties of the first post-communist government. It was widely expected at first that liberal-conservative divide would be the primary defining feature of Hungarian party politics, and former communists (MSzP) were counted out almost completely (Kiss 2002). Even in its most successful times in the early 1990s, when opinion polls showed 33 percent support for the party, Fidesz realized that they would

---

[24] FKgP Respondent 2, personal communication, June 15, 2007.
[25] FKgP Respondent 2, personal communication, June 15, 2007.

need to build a coalition in order to govern (Enyedi 2005). By that time, Fidesz's closest ideological ally, SzDSz, had already sided with MSzP. Working with SzDSz and MSzP would have meant aligning with the left and suspending Fidesz's anticommunist rhetoric. Trying to find allies in the right meant that the party needed to tone down its liberal rhetoric, but Fidesz saw that as a lesser evil because the party could be more influential in coalition with the right, who were becoming increasingly unpopular (Deutsch and Gyarmati 1999). Concerns over coalition potential and survival prompted ideological movement from liberalism to conservatism. The ideological turn occurred in 1993, but instead of the desired success, the party suffered a defeat in 1994 elections. Thus, the ideological change alone did not bring success, at least not in the short-term. Rather, Fidesz implemented an additional change to secure long-term performance – it strengthened the party organization.

In the early 1990s, Fidesz disregarded the importance of a strong organization (Toole 2003). It was a party with collective leadership, a loose and lean organizational structure, and low membership (Balázs and Enyedi 1996; Waterbury 2006). Its local branches were unstaffed and not functional, explained a former member of the leadership and MP of Fidesz.[26] The party considered organizational linkages to be superfluous in a modern democracy (Enyedi 2005) and believed that elections can be won without a strong membership base, a network of branches, or efficient management (Toole 2003; Bozóki 1992). Fidesz's electoral campaigns were media-centered and made use of modern marketing techniques (Waterbury 2006).

The ideological change did not bring about organizational change automatically. Only after the 1994 defeat did Fidesz change its organizational strategy. The relatively stable high-level support for MSzP made the party leaders realize that links to social networks were necessary for electoral success (Waterbury 2006), and they blamed their own electoral failure on the weak party organization (Balázs and Enyedi 1996). Furthermore, the media-centered strategy paid off only as far as Fidesz was successful in avoiding conflicts with journalists and opinion leaders. Once such conflicts occurred, the lack of committed activists and organizational network became a considerable liability (Balázs and Enyedi 1996). The impetus for organization building was the fear of electoral marginalization – a similar factor that had motivated the organizational strengthening of MSzP.

The party first streamlined its inner administration (Enyedi 2005), and was unified under the strong leadership of Viktor Orbán. Although he was a charismatic leader, it is generally recognized that Fidesz was not a personality-centered party. Key decisions were made by a core leadership group rather than by Orbán himself (Fowler 2004). After streamlining the central office management, the leadership then spent considerable effort on building the party's organizational network and establishing ties with civic organizations

---

[26] Fidesz Respondent 1, personal communication, June 12, 2007.

(Enyedi 2005). The party started mobilizing potential voters not simply by extending its membership, but by organizing mass rallies and establishing Civic Circles. The latter attracted a membership of 100,000, increasing the party's support base tenfold. Local branches were encouraged to open their doors to these Civic Circle members – a move that increased party membership to 30,000 by 2005 (Enyedi 2005, 2006). This growth in membership was accompanied by similar growth in the number of local branches (Enyedi 2006), which had increased to 1,050 in 2005 from 400 in 2001 (Enyedi and Linek 2008). Building organizational structures and attracting membership became even more active after losing to MSzP in 2002 (Navracsics 2005; Spirova 2007).

Furthermore, this structure and membership were well managed and guided. Local branches and members were expected to remain active during and between elections (Enyedi 2006). The central office measured "all potential outputs of local organizations, such as the number of new members, number of organized events, local turnout at elections and referendums, the number of signatures collected, etc." (Enyedi and Linek 2008, 464). Organizations that did not perform well were reorganized or dissolved from above (Enyedi 2006). As a result, Fidesz is argued to have sustained more committed activists than other parties (Enyedi 2005). In general, the central office maintained an effective nationally coordinated and well-organized system (T. Lánczi 2005).

The strong and effective organization, especially compared to the organizational weakness of other right-wing groups, allowed Fidesz to attract and integrate elites from failing parties (Fowler 2004). Furthermore, Fidesz continued organizational development regardless of whether it was in government or in opposition. By the end of its governing term in 2002, it had effectively absorbed KDNP, FKgP, and MDF. It was only because of its strong organization that Fidesz was able to manage such diversity within the party (Csizmadia 2005; Fowler 2004; Giró-Szász, Héjj, and Kisgyőri 2007; Giró-Szász et al. 2008; Navracsics 2005). Efficient organization allowed overcoming leaders' and activists' personal considerations in the pursuit of votes and office and helped preserve a high level of party unity (Fowler 2004). The organizational strength not only allowed the party to become the major right-wing force but also a formidable opponent to the increasingly successful MSzP by making it attractive to a broad electorate (T. Lánczi 2005).[27]

---

[27] Fidesz's initial ideological rival, SzDSz, also possessed only weak organization and, in the end, shared the fate of the original winners. It was the second-largest party in the first post-communist parliament but has seen its vote and seat share decrease consistently and considerably since then. In 2009, it effectively ceased to exist as a significant player. Balázs and Enyedi (1996) argue that SzDSz leadership initially recognized the importance of building an extensive organization, and had already started broadening their membership and establishing local presence in 1989. Other sources disagree and claim that the party saw membership and local branches as superfluous to win votes in the modern era (Spirova 2007). In any event, their network of branches remained loose and was hard to control and manage. Local branches were not well integrated into a unified party organization and lacked a voice in party leadership, which made them ineffective

Poland

The Polish case study will primarily focus on two relatively successful parties with strong organizations during the period under consideration: PSL and SLD, and a failing case of AWS. I will also briefly describe smaller parties in comparison to these big ones. The Polish party scene has simply been too diverse to be able to analyze each small entity at length. As previously, the goal of these case studies is to illustrate whether and how party organizational strength influences its electoral success. The analysis will also address the main alternative arguments – the charismatic leader, appealing ideology, and patronage politics – and assess their explanatory power compared to that of party organizational strength.

Polish Peasant Party

PSL was established in 1990 on the basis of the United Peasant Party (ZSL) and former exiled peasants (Dudek 2008). ZSL was a former communist satellite party representing the large farming sector. The newly created PSL, however, by incorporating exiled peasants and selecting their representative, Roman Bartoszcze, as the party leader, sought to establish continuity with pre-communist peasant parties instead (Sabbat-Swidlicka 1990). PSL was considered to be the party with the most stable support base (P. Lewis 1994). Unlike any other Polish party, PSL was represented in every parliament since 1991, it experienced no major splits despite being involved in various scandals, and it commanded a predictable core vote of 7–8 percent. A closer examination of this case suggests that this stability and success in terms of electoral performance can most directly be accredited to the extraordinary organizational strength of the party.

PSL has the most extensive organization of all Polish parties. Although exact membership figures (and other numerical measures of organizational structure) are hard to come by for any Polish party, the estimated PSL membership at various times exceeds that of all other parties – even the communist successor party. The average PSL membership during the period under consideration was about 160,000 compared to the average membership of 72,000 in the SLD, the second-largest party in terms of membership. PSL is also the only Polish

within the organization (Bozóki 1992). Much of the originally built organization was therefore effectively abandoned rather than made into an electoral asset, leading to a steady decline in the number of members and local branches (SzDSz Respondent 1, personal communication, June 13, 2007). In hindsight, party leaders actually acknowledged that organizational factors played a major role in SzDSz's poor performance (SzDSz Respondent 1, personal communication, June 13, 2007). However, ideological factors cannot entirely be ruled out either. After 1993, SzDSz remained the only liberal party in Hungary. It is possible that its ideological position was simply not viable and the party would have withered regardless of whether or not they had a strong organization. Another possibility, however, is that MSzP, appealing to liberal voters, has robbed SzDSz of its supporters. If this is true, it still underlines the importance of organizational superiority to fend off competitors and consolidate support.

party with a significant local presence. Szczerbiak (1999a) reports that in 1997, PSL had local branches in 79 percent of communities compared to 65 percent for the former communist SLD and 13 percent and 8 percent for the post-Solidarity parties Freedom Union (UW) and Labor Party (UP), respectively. PSL routinely contested local government elections in more than 50 percent of municipalities – more than any other party.

Throughout the 1990s, PSL was also the most professional party, with twenty full-time staff employed in party headquarters. This was about the same as all other major parties combined (Szczerbiak 2001c).[28] Such level of professionalization helped keep the party running smoothly even in the face of major internal divisions and provided the necessary machinery to manage a large and widespread structure.

PSL was not just locally present but also locally active, providing social functions to members and anchoring their support. Even the party program reflected a commitment to supporting peasant movements and activities in line with the historical tradition of the party.[29] PSL had developed links with a sizeable network of various social and cultural organizations in the country-side including voluntary firefighters, women's clubs, agricultural organizations, and others. Many members of these civic organizations are also members and supporters of PSL.[30] Szczerbiak (2001b) reports that in 1997, PSL set up a National Organization of Village Administrators with a membership of more than 37,000, all of whom were a natural support group of PSL. The party did not simply want to represent rural interests but be part of local life.

Large direct membership in the party and a support base through these ancillary organizations provided PSL with loyal voters and an experienced, locally known and respected candidate pool.[31] Membership, local presence, and social activism helped the party root itself firmly within its electorate and guaranteed steady support regardless of any national-level crisis the party experienced. In many respects, PSL acquired a life and identity that was independent of it as a political party or electoral alliance. Perhaps paradoxically, this made the party especially resilient and electorally stable.

Although much of PSL organizational strength stemmed from the fact that it was a successor party and could rely on at least some members and structures being carried over, it is equally important that the new leaders and activists pursued restoring and maintaining the organization after the regime change. PSL leadership and activists shared a clear understanding of the need for organization building and maintenance, and of the importance of members and

---

[28] Additionally, the PSL operated two nationwide weeklies, *Zielony Sztandar* (Green Banner) and *Dziennik Ludowy* (Rural Daily), and two regional weeklies, *Wiesci* (News) published in Cracow and *Tygodnik Ludowy* (Rural Weekly) published in Poznan (Kurski, Nowakowska, and Wielowieyska 1993).

[29] PSL Respondent 2, personal communication, May 30, 2007.

[30] PSL Respondent 1, personal communication, May 29, 2007.

[31] PSL Respondent 2, personal communication, May 30, 2007.

branches for winning votes and stabilizing support (Szczerbiak 2001b). This realization was present from very early on, even in the midst of severe resource constraints all parties faced in the first free elections. For example, the party used its 1993 campaign refund not to prepare for an even more expensive media campaign in the next election, but to purchase office space for local branches (Szczerbiak 2001b). In its 1995 program resolution, the party claimed that it was and wished to remain a mass party because this was the principal source of its strength. On the basis of his interviews, Szczerbiak (2001d) reports that PSL organizers always saw membership growth and local branches as an asset, never a liability; it was considered a proven way to increase the electoral potential of the party. The party's regional leaders prioritized setting up offices in communities that still lacked a PSL branch. They attributed PSL strength directly to a network of organizational structures in local areas.

After the first post-communist election in 1991, PSL was the fourth-largest party in parliament and commanded about 9 percent of the vote. Considering that PSL was still somewhat tainted by its ex-communist ties, the result was perceived as a great success.[32] This first election also established a measure of the "normal vote" for the party – party support remained at about that level for the rest of the period under consideration.

PSL was not the only party trying to capture the rural electorate. There were a number of parties within the Solidarity camp that had similar goals. For the 1991 election, these united under the Polish Peasant Party – Peasant Alliance (PSL-PL). However, like most post-Solidarity parties, it only had a residual organization: even the party itself did not know how many members it had, and there were practically no regional (*voivodship*) or local (*gmina*) structures (Kurski et al. 1993). Because of a lack of an organization that would have helped keep the party unified and support base stable, PSL-PL split almost immediately after the election in 1991 and ceased to be a significant player (Szczerbiak 2001b). By the 1993 election, PSL had gained credibility because of its coherence and unity. As a result, it finished with the second-best result in that election and the best result ever achieved by any farmers' party in Polish history – 15.4 percent of the vote. At the same time, several new post-Solidarity agrarian parties again failed to get into parliament. As P. Lewis (1994, 785) notes, the organizational weakness of post-Solidarity parties, including those that targeted farmers, was deliberate: "[T]he Solidarity ethic, particularly during the early stages, appeared to speak directly against the very concept of party and undermined the whole idea of party formation." Thus, it was not ideological monopoly or easily identifiable and narrow constituency that produced PSL victory. Rather, it was the organizational advantage that was crucial in allowing PSL to emerge with stronger support and a more convincing case to represent peasantry (Szczerbiak 2001b).

[32] PSL Respondent 2, personal communication, May 30, 2007.

Before the 1997 Sejm election, PSL was a governing party together with SLD, and was the target of much of the blame directed toward the government, but not getting much credit for positive developments.[33] Furthermore, at that time, PSL was bitterly divided internally between those who supported the leader (Waldemar Pawlak) and those who opposed him. Pawlak himself had a public image of a frightened, incompetent, and unfriendly politician, which is why his leadership hurt more than helped the party image (Szczerbiak 2001b). Indeed, the preelection polls in 1997 predicted that the party was going to suffer a great loss. However, PSL got its core vote – 7.31 percent – and remained a key third force in a Polish party system that was becoming increasingly polarized between the post-Solidarity and post-communist camps.

PSL survived despite the hostile environment and internal conflicts. Furthermore, in a year, the party was already fully recovered and received about 12 percent of the vote in the 1998 local elections (Szczerbiak 1999b). Party organizers accredited this recovery directly to the strong organization of the party.[34] PSL also remained in a strong position after the 2001 election, with the support of 9 percent of voters and government membership. The party was largely perceived as stable, reliable, and predictable – in great contrast to the fragmentation, fluidity, and conflict characterizing the post-Solidarity right.

However, after two years in office, PSL suffered several major crises. First, in 2003, the party was removed from the governing coalition, reintroducing internal divisions. Many blamed Jarosław Kalinowski – the PSL leader at the time – for the party's failure in government. Kalinowski's opponents gathered behind Janusz Wojciechowski, who wanted the party to be more right-wing and broader in its appeal. Furthermore, in 2003, the party was in financial difficulty because the Electoral Commission rejected its financial report and denied funding for the next three years. One of the party organizers commented that if the party had had a weaker organization, this financial crisis would have given it a death blow.[35] Indeed, polls showed very little support for the party and predicted that it would not win any seats in the 2004 European Parliament election. However, the party ended up winning four out of the fifty-two seats allocated to Poland.

The financial difficulties and internal conflicts haunted the party until 2005. By this time, PSL was also facing a new serious challenger claiming the rural vote – the populist and leader-centered Samoobrona of the Polish Republic (SRP). Nevertheless, PSL did not suffer electorally. Despite the fact that the polls predicted its demise – only 1 percent of voters were expected to vote for them – the PSL actually received 7 percent of the vote. A party organizer commented, "No matter what the polls say, even if we ourselves doubt that we will receive much support, there are still always these one million voters

---

[33] PSL Respondent 2, personal communication, May 30, 2007.
[34] PSL Respondent 2, personal communication, May 30, 2007.
[35] PSL Respondent 2, personal communication, May 30, 2007.

who keep voting for us."[36] These votes remained loyal not as a result of expensive media campaign, but as a result of hard work on the ground, using the party organization. The party organizers in central office and regional branches claimed that the 1 million votes directly reflected their organizational capacity; extra votes the party earned were because of favorable environmental factors.[37]

In contrast to the survival of PSL, SRP followed the path of the post-Solidarity PSL challengers: it lost the battle for rural votes and failed to gain parliamentary representation in 2007. Unlike PSL, SRP placed little value in building party membership and structures, and in using these as part of their electoral strategy. Rather, they considered structures to hamper the party's flexibility, which they thought was imperative for operating in a volatile electoral arena.[38] Thus, once again, PSL's superior organization served the party well in eliminating ideological rivals.

The case of PSL illustrates well how strong organization helps a party establish itself as a significant player, overcome negative image, and weather both internal crises and external hostility. It also shows the primacy of organizational factors over the alternative explanations including ideology, leader charisma (which PSL leaders almost uniformly lacked), and party finances.

Democratic Left Alliance

SLD was able to establish itself as a major political force from the status of a pariah party in an extremely hostile environment. The party steadily increased its support base throughout the 1990s and early 2000s. It became the party with the biggest support base and the only one that was able to govern two consecutive terms. SLD was caught in major corruption scandals after 2003 and, therefore, lost much of its support gained. However, despite scandals of the greatest magnitude that post-communist Poland had ever experienced, the party survived and still had a respectable representation in different levels of government. As the analysis will show, organizational strength accounts for much of this success and resilience.

SLD was, at first, not a single party but an electoral alliance of about thirty political formations (Dudek 2008). The alliance, however, was very stable, acted as if it was a unified party, and was dominated by the Social Democracy of Polish Republic (SdRP). The latter emerged in 1990 mostly on the basis of the remnants of the communist Polish United Workers' Party (PZPR) after its dissolution. Because the alliance was unified and dominated by SdRP, for the sake of clarity of presentation, I will refer to SLD as a single party with post-communist ties.

---

[36] PSL Respondent 2, personal communication, May 30, 2007.
[37] PSL Respondent 1, personal communication, May 29, 2007; PSL Respondent 2, personal communication, May 30, 2007.
[38] SO Respondent 1, personal communication, June 1, 2007.

At its inception, the party was immediately rendered a pariah status because of its association with the previous regime. Compared to other parties formed after the regime change, this posed an extra challenge to the SLD when trying to establish itself as a political force. People associated with SLD were discredited, local party offices were robbed or attacked, and local members assaulted (J. Curry 2003). In the post-1989 pluralist Sejm, no party wanted to cooperate with SLD, and individual politicians from the party were shunned and ignored by others (J. Curry 2003; Grzymala-Busse 2002a). The media were also filled with criticism of the former communists. The party was highly stigmatized and widely rejected as a legitimate political force. It was treated as "a bunch of Polish People's Republic [. . .] orphans with no future" (Kubiak 2007), and stripped of any resources it previously commanded. It seemed that the party was "clearly on its way to oblivion" (V. Zubek 1995, 281). Contrary to a widespread assumption that successor parties had an edge over new parties because they inherited a lot of resources from the former regime, for SLD the heritage was markedly negative and put it at a serious disadvantage compared to other parties.

Despite this explicit hostility, SLD was the second-largest party in the first fully democratically elected and extremely fragmented Sejm. It had the support of 12 percent of voters, only 0.3 percent less than the biggest post-Solidarity party, Democratic Union (UD). This initial success, bringing the party out of a near-certain defeat, was possible mostly because of pragmatic choices by the party leadership to focus on organizational development and unity (Grzymala-Busse 2002a).

Perhaps paradoxically, it was largely because of SLD's pariah status that the party was able to stay unified and focused despite the fact that it did not have any formal means of holding onto its members or controlling the party (Buras 2005; J. Curry 2003). Being socially rejected, the members of SLD, many of whom were former members of PZPR, remained loyal to the new party (Grzymala-Busse 2002a). This, coupled with having experience in organizing, creating, and maintaining party structure became the support-building strategy for SLD. The party's Sejm deputies were forced to work almost exclusively with each other, which tightened their unity and increased the sense of the importance of the party structures and membership as a necessary support organization (J. Curry 2003; Szczerbiak 2001d). This, in turn, led to an explicit focus on building party infrastructure. The SLD used their parliamentary deputies' resources, allocated to all parties by the state, to build up party branches in districts. Because of such strategic use of resources, the SLD ended up with a better infrastructure than its competitors, although it did not command significantly more assets. As J. Curry (2003, 37) notes, "SdRP leaders, from their training in the Communist Party, saw infrastructure as crucial and made the choice to invest in it as a first priority." Furthermore, the party also made use of old PZPR membership lists to try to find and establish contacts with people potentially interested in the party and willing to work for its local offices (J. Curry 2003).

By the 1991 election, SLD had already assembled a membership of 60,000, second only in size to the membership of PSL. Although the reliability of the reported membership figures is not always clear, these figures show a steady increase over time, reaching, by some accounts (Grzymala-Busse 2007), to PSL levels by 2003 (150,000 SLD members). As for local presence, SLD had the highest number of local offices – about 400 more than PSL (Grzymala-Busse 2007). Compared to PSL, however, SLD was less implanted in civil society via associations with civic groups. Still, it had close ties with the All-Poland Alliance of Trade Unions – the most important post-communist trade union in Poland. This organization was a great resource during campaigns and elections because it was able to mobilize its members for party rallies and other activities (J. Curry 2003), and provided a pool of supporters.

Local structures and membership served as the primary vehicle for conducting campaign activities (Grzymala-Busse 2002a; Szczerbiak 2001d). Indeed, SLD was exceptional in the Polish electoral scene in that it used canvassing and local electoral activities as part of its campaign. As J. Curry (2003, 36) notes, what separated SLD from its competitors (with the exception of PSL), was "a cost-free cadre of people to do the legwork of putting leaflets under doors, organizing voter meetings, and marching for candidates." SLD organizers echo this argument by stating that "the best programs, the strongest slogans, the best advisors are of no use unless you can implement them. Someone has to go out and put that poster on that lamppost, organize that meeting, bring the sound equipment, put up the lectern, rustle up some sausages and beer. Someone has to do this! Physically!" (quoted in Szczerbiak 2001d, 189). That membership and local presence were likely playing a significant role in the party's electoral support is further suggested by the fact that the territorial distribution of SLD members is highly correlated with the vote share for the party (Kubiak 2007). Grzymala-Busse (2002a, 206) reports that "local mobilization was effective where it was used – the [SLD's] strongest organizations, such as Katowice, Bydgoszcz, and Włocławek, saw the best electoral returns as well."

This was a completely different strategy than that pursued by post-Solidarity parties, who were convinced that media campaigns guarantee electoral success. The two biggest competitors of SLD were a leftist Labor Party (UP) and centrist Democratic Party (PD) (formerly Democratic Union [UD], 1990–1994, and Freedom Union [UW], 1994–2005).[39] Both of these had their origins in the Solidarity movement, and both placed the greatest emphasis on mass media to run their campaigns. A PD spokesman, for example, claimed in 1997: "Eighty percent of [the party's] success was based in the mass media and maybe

---

[39] Although the genealogy of parties in the region is not always very clear, the PD is generally considered a direct successor of UW (Millard 2007; Gazeta.pl 2011).

20 percent on local activities" (quoted in Szczerbiak 2001d, 192). UP leadership was similarly dismissive of the relevance of organization. Szczerbiak (2001a) argued that compared to other parties in Poland, UP was probably most extreme in rejecting the relevance of members[40] and what they called "setting up fictional structures." The party organizers argued that members and structures were relevant only in the context of mass parties – which clearly did not exist in Poland – and that these indicators were in no way related to the party's electoral capacity because, after all, the party still attracted support although it lacked any significant organization. J. Curry (2003) notes that by the time the post-Solidarity parties realized the importance of organizational development, the costs of setting up a party infrastructure had already increased dramatically. This, together with an explicit antiparty sentiment, effectively locked the new parties into an organizational disadvantage despite all the positive media coverage they were getting (Kurski et al. 1993). Indeed, the UP was effectively absorbed by SLD by 1997 (Smolar 1998).

In addition to membership and local structures, SLD also maintained a high-capacity central office, which helped keep the alliance and party disciplined and pragmatic rather than ideological (Kubiak 2007). Although its professional staff was not very large – fewer than twenty staff in central and regional levels combined, Szczerbiak (2001c, 82) argues that the party headquarters had a unique capacity to turn itself into "the organizational backbone for professionally organized and well-financed elections campaigns."

Organizational strength helped SLD not only survive and succeed in 1991, but also build a loyal core support base. Ninety percent of its supporters in 1991 voted again for SLD in 1993 and subsequent elections (Raciborski 1999). Furthermore, organizational strength was at least partially responsible for improving the party position in subsequent elections. The early emphasis on management tasks, insistence on party unity, and avoidance of ideological and personal attacks helped the party create a public image of a professional and pragmatic political organization (Grzymala-Busse 2002a). The contrast was especially stark with other parties whose prestige was seriously damaged by their mutual attacks and internal bickering, which received extensive media coverage (J. Curry 2003). Thus, the extensive and active organization was necessary to mobilize the core vote, and organizational strength helped create an image of the party that was attractive to the wider audience.

It was therefore not surprising that in the 1993 Sejm elections, SLD almost doubled its vote share and tripled its seat share.[41] The party went on to form a government with PSL. Because of its recent pariah status, SLD kept a low profile

---

[40] A review of membership of different parties in Poland in 1992 had the following entry about UP: "It is difficult to provide any figures, but party membership does not exceed several hundred" (Polish News Bulletin 1992b).
[41] The larger increase in seat share was because of the electoral system that overcompensated parties with greater vote shares.

despite its senior status in terms of size, and left the position of prime minister to their smaller coalition partner. They also gave PSL a disproportionally higher share of cabinet posts (Grzymala-Busse 2002a).

While in government, the party maintained its unity and professional style and continued to develop the party organization in the main office and on the ground. Holding the party together and keeping its public image as a rational, predictable, and stable party remained the priority of the leadership. Together with building the party on the ground, SLD invested in professionalizing the party: they explicitly acknowledged that volunteering alone would not be able to sustain the organization (Szczerbiak 2001d).

In 1997, the party lost its governing status, although it made gains in terms of vote share. Regardless of whether the party was in or out of government, it maintained an image of a professional and pragmatic party. Its voter base kept increasing beyond its one-time core voters to include a cross section of social strata. Despite the broadening of the party constituency, SLD strategies remained stable: it was the same party ideologically and in terms of structural goals, "leadership, and strategy of electioneering" (J. Curry 2003, 42; see also Millard 2003). SLD was also successful in consolidating the electoral alliance into a unified party – SLD registered as a single party in 1999. This was in great contrast to post-Solidarity parties whose attempts to cooperate in an electoral alliance – AWS – was short-lived and disastrous, as will be described.

SLD maintained its image as a reliable and stable party until 2003. Now operating for almost a decade in an increasingly friendly and supportive environment, SLD was elected back to government in 2001 with the biggest seat share for any party since the regime change: 41 percent.[42] This election victory was largely credited to the party's organizational strength and efficiency (Majcherek 2000). It was during the tenure of this government that the environment again turned negative for the party. Two developments contributed to the hostility of the environment. First, since 2003, several corruption scandals had been revealed that included prominent figures of the SLD (Mrozinski 2004; Olczyk 2003b). The number and the severity of these scandals were unprecedented and underlined SLD's attempts to take advantage of state resources (Grzymala-Busse 2007; see also Olczyk 2003a; Mrozinski 2004). A scandal about SLD became virtually a permanent section of daily news. Perhaps the most damaging scandal was Rywingate, referred to as the biggest corruption scandal in Polish history (Dudek 2008; Skórzyński 2003). Lew Rywin – claiming that he represented the group wielding power – was seeking $ 17.5 billion in bribes from a media company in exchange for favorable legislation (Jędrzejczyk 2003). This scandal gave the biggest blow to SLD popularity (Dudek 2008; Skórzyński 2003). Others include the Starachowice scandal concerning a leakage of information from the Ministry of Interior (Drabikowska 2003). Whereas

[42] In 2001, SLD ran together with UP – a post-Solidarity leftist party – that it essentially absorbed. Their combined seat share was 47 percent.

several SLD functionaries were convicted in relation to this incident, the situation was made worse by president Kwasniewski (SLD), who decided to pardon Zbigniew Sobotka, one of the main actors in the scandal (Rzeczpospolita 2005). The Orlengate scandal involved a questionable arrest of the chairman of the largest Polish oil company, ordered by Prime Minister Miller (Rzeczpospolita 2004; Gazeta Wyborcza 2004). The Pęczak's corruption scandal concerned SLD member Andrzej Pęczak, who was accused of embezzlement twice (Patora and Stelmasiak 2004). There were also corruption scandals in local administration in Opole and Bydgoszcz districts, and incidents elsewhere (Kubiak 2007). In addition to these scandals, SLD was also suffering its first major internal conflict between personalities, most notably between Prime Minister Miller and the ex-party leader Jósef Oleksy (Polish News Bulletin 2001b, 2001e), as well as between Miller and Kwasniewski (Kubiak 2007).

Given the extremely hostile environment created by these developments, it is not surprising that SLD vote share plummeted in the 2005 Sejm election to only 11%. As some observers noted: the accumulation of scandals that SLD faced would have tumbled any party (Polish News Bulletin 2004a). However, given the circumstances, the party perceived this as a success. After all, although it experienced large-scale defections of MPs and members, the party did not disintegrate and die, as had happened to AWS. Furthermore, the SLD vote share was reduced to about the same level where it started in 1991 – also at the time of an extremely hostile environment on the electoral arena. This suggests that 11–12 percent may directly reflect the organizational capacity of the party, the part of the electorate that SLD has locked in because of its organizational strength. Furthermore, in addition to the scandals, the party organization itself had been considerably weakened by the time of these elections. This was partially because the fear of decommunization was no longer present and the party felt less pressure to stay unified, disciplined, and focused on developing the party organization (Polish News Bulletin 2004c) and partially because the corruption scandals led to a large-scale "house-cleaning" and membership purges, in the course of which the party lost about half its members (Mrozinski 2004).

In sum, the SLD example shows that strong organization can help a party win votes and consolidate as well as increase its support base in the short-term. More importantly, strong organization helped the party survive against extremely unfavorable odds. The primacy of organizational strength in explaining SLD success in good and bad fortune is further underlined by considering alternative explanations. The fact that SLD did not have an advantage over other parties resource-wise was already mentioned. Given this, resource-based arguments cannot explain the discrepancy between SLD and post-Solidarity parties' electoral performances. In terms of leader charisma, SLD, again, had little advantage. None of the leaders of SLD have been considered particularly charismatic, and SLD has never been particularly leader-centered (P. Lewis 1994). In 2001, when party support was at its all-time high – some 48 percent of voters said that they would support SLD – the analysts argued that this support did not come from leader Leszek Miller's personal charisma but from the strong political backup provided the party organization (Polish News Bulletin 2001b). A nice contrast to this is the situation with the then-newly created Law and Justice whose leader enjoyed 53 percent support, although his party – organizationless at the time – was only supported by 8 percent of the voters (Polish News Bulletin 2001b).

Ideology as an explanation of electoral success remains equally inadequate and is best refuted by the fact that there were several other parties claiming the same ideological positioning as SLD. However, all those attempts were organizationally inferior and therefore either lost to SLD or were absorbed by it. Specifically, before the creation of SdRP, a group of former PZPR representatives formed Polish Social Democratic Union (PUS). The party ignored local organizations and did not attempt to build membership (J. Curry 2003). Less than four years after its creation, PUS was dead. In addition to PUS, orthodox communists, former members of PZPR, formed another party to rival SdRP in 1990 – the Union of Polish Communists (ZKP). This party lacked any significant organization, failed to receive any support, and did not even contest the 1991 election (Grzymala-Busse 2002a).

Similarly, SLD was more resilient than any of the post-Solidarity leftist parties because the latter remained inferior in terms of their organization. The greatest competition was at first offered by UP, but even this party was never a serious competitor – the best result UP ever got was 7 percent of the votes. As described, UP lacked the kind of local presence and membership that SLD commanded (Szczerbiak 1999a). This organizational superiority eventually led to UP signing a coalition agreement with SLD prior to the 2001 elections, which for all practical purposes represented the absorption of UP into SLD (Olczyk 2003c). Another party that was ideologically and programmatically relatively close to SLD was the centrist UW (formerly UD). The organizational weakness of that party has also been discussed. In terms of electoral performance, UW emerged as the party with the greatest support in 1991, although SLD was a close second. The party kept a steady performance of about 10–13 percent of votes until 2001, when it was not elected to parliament. In 2005, the party (now called the Democratic Party and established as a "new" party) also did not make it to parliament, and in 2007 its only strategy of survival was to form an electoral alliance with SLD.

SLD faced its latest challenge when it was already suffering the consequences of post-2003 scandals. During that time, many SLD MPs and prominent members left the party and created a new party – Polish Social Democracy (SdPL). The new party claimed a membership of 4,000. Even if true, it is considerably less than the 80,000 confirmed members that SLD still had. Furthermore, the new party lacked any infrastructure and party organization. Although the initial expectations were that SdPL might overtake its predecessor, this failed to materialize (Kubiak 2007). In the 2007 Sejm elections, the new party was back where it came from: it formed an electoral alliance with SLD. Indeed, in

2007, SLD was still the only leftist party with stable funding and voter support (Polish News Bulletin 2007a).

Post-Solidarity Parties

The relevance of strong organization in producing the success of PSL and SLD and helping them survive political crises becomes more evident when their fate is compared to that of post-Solidarity parties. I will concentrate on post-Solidarity right, as post-Solidarity left was already briefly discussed and because it was relatively small, whereas the great majority of post-Solidarity parties were right-wing in their ideological appeal. A striking difference between PSL and SLD on the one hand and the post-Solidarity right on the other was the extreme fragmentation and fluidity of the latter's electoral performance and its inability to weather political crises, which usually constituted a death blow to the party (or parties) involved. The analysis suggests that this difference in outcomes is most convincingly accounted for by the great discrepancy in the level of organizational strength between PSL/SLD and the post-Solidarity right.

As mentioned previously, the legacy of Solidarity trade unions as a social movement made it explicitly antiparty and undermined party formation (Smolar 1998). Solidarity relied on social unity and post-communist opposition as its political strategy, with no attempt to create party structures. Because no organization was developed, the movement lacked a training ground for candidates and leaders, and provided almost no opportunities for elite circulation. Low levels of party development and no outlets for ambitious younger generations, in turn, led to a situation where personality clashes and individual rivalry ruled the post-Solidarity political scene, which became inundated with a large number of proto-parties (Szczerbiak 2004).

None of these post-Solidarity groups favored growth through increased membership and geographical diffusion. Similar to their predecessor social movement, they showed no interest in organizational development (P. Lewis 1994). Some of the biggest vote getters in 1991 – Center Agreement (PC) and Christian National Union (ZChN) – were explicitly not concerned with recruiting members because they believed they did not need them: they believed that the mass party era was over (P. Lewis 1994). PC actually claimed a membership of 40,000 in 1991, but reduced these numbers to 15,000 by early 1993 (P. Lewis 1994). By that time, the party had split and become virtually extinct. ZChN was also a purely electoral formation, claiming a membership of only 6,000. Neither party made it to parliament in 1993. Indeed, almost no right-wing parties made it to parliament that year. The two exceptions were Confederation of Independent Poland (KPN) and Non-Party Bloc of Cooperation with the Government (BBWR), but even these "proceeded to disintegrate rapidly" (Szczerbiak 2004, 59). Although KPN claimed a membership of 20,000–30,000, its local presence remains undocumented, and BBWR had hardly any organizational existence at all. Millard (2009, 789–790) writes, "[T]he BBWR was little more than a collection of individuals united by their pro-presidential stance," and "it hardly warranted the party label, given its amorphous nature and ephemeral existence."

Comparing the average membership and local presence of the post-Solidarity parties to those of PSL and SLD best illustrates their organizational inferiority. As stated, the average membership of the former during the period under consideration was about 160,000 and that of SLD was about 72,000. Compare this to an average of about 12,000 members for post-Solidarity parties. Even AWS itself had only about 30,000 members at its peak. A majority of parties had only virtual existence, and this made even elite-level loyalty difficult to achieve. A routine behavior by right-wing politicians was to create a new party label if their previous party failed to deliver the votes (Kubiak 2007). Many also simply jumped ship, shopping for a more viable party label among the existing ones (Matraszek 2005).

The right made a final push toward consolidation by creating an electoral alliance of thirty-nine organizations called AWS in 1996. This mimicked the strategy of SLD, which was also an electoral alliance, as discussed previously. Contrary to SLD, however, AWS failed to consolidate the coalition into a single party. The leading party among the AWS coalition was the Solidarity trade union's political representation RS AWS. However, unlike SdRP's role in SLD, Solidarity's leader position within AWS was much less readily accepted. Furthermore, neither Solidarity, nor any other party within AWS, made attempts to build a unified and strong organization. As one commentary noted, "A large number of right-wing politicians behave as if the political market was the realm of producers, not customers. [AWS] lacks an attractive election campaign idea, and moreover, does not have a political apparatus efficient enough to put ideas into practice" (Polish News Bulletin 2001b). P. Lewis (2000) agrees, stating that AWS was a great idea, but not an organization.

AWS succeeded in winning the 1997 election and forming a government together with UW (the former UD, later PD). The coalition partners were in constant conflict and mutually distrustful. Because of this, the government became very unpopular very quickly. The UW left the coalition in 2000. Additionally, when in government, AWS faced a wave of protests and labor disputes, was associated with unpopular reforms, and got involved in a variety of corruption scandals (Dudek 2008). The party environment was turning increasingly hostile; the coalition was internally unstable and ridden with personal conflict. By the 2001 elections, AWS virtually no longer existed as an idea, much less as a viable coalition.

What explains the demise of AWS? Scandals alone do not provide a sufficient explanation. After all, SLD was facing a significantly more hostile environment in 1991 and 2005, but survived both times. It is generally argued that structural weakness rather than scandals, ideological diversity, or weak performance of the AWS government led to the disintegration of the alliance. AWS did not overcome, but simply combined the organizational weakness of its constituent parts – low membership, lack of local structures, poor management of resources, and lack of enforced self-discipline. Szczerbiak (2004, 56) argues, "Solidarity Electoral Action's key structural weakness was its failure to develop a strong institutional centre combined with (and caused by) the lack of organizational self-discipline among its leading elite. These leaders failed to fashion a structure and ideological profile that could hold together a fractious and eclectic grouping in the long term" (see also Matraszek 2005).

Conclusion

This chapter served three main goals: to assess (1) the plausibility of the proposed causal mechanisms and causal order, (2) the effect of party organizational strength not simply on electoral success but also on a party's longer-term performance, and (3) the strength of the rival hypotheses, especially that of party ideology. The narratives from different countries provided ample illustrations and examples in support of the proposed causal mechanisms relating party organizational strength with electoral success and survival.

In the Czech Republic, building a strong organization helped ČSSD emerge from a marginal party to a significant player and allowed it to revive from crisis. It helped ODS emerge and remain the strongest right-wing party by providing stable and loyal support as well as undermining the success of ideological rivals. It also helped KSČM survive in the extremely hostile environment. Indeed, all of the parties that invested in building and maintaining strong organizations have been the major players in post-communist Czech politics, whereas none of those parties that disregarded the relevance of organization building proved viable (Deegan-Krause 2006; Hanley 2003).

The Estonian case studies of RP and K similarly illustrated that building a strong organization can have an almost immediate payoff. Dismissing the importance of organization, or neglecting organizational development, however, can quickly become fatal, as the RP and KE cases showed. Additionally, in Hungary, Fidesz and MSzP prioritized organization building in terms of membership, local branches, and professional staff, and used this organization to establish ties with their voters. This not only helped them succeed electorally in the short-term but also survive long-term as significant players, and – especially in the case of MSzP – overcome environmental hostility and implement programmatic changes. Lack of professional management and neglect of organization building in FKgP, KDNP, and MDF was largely responsible for the implosion and electoral marginalization of these parties. These conclusions were also confirmed by the Polish case studies: the one factor on which the failing post-Solidarity parties most distinctly differed from the succeeding PSL and SLD was their level of organizational strength.

The case studies further suggested the relevance of all three attributes of party organizational strength, although some attributes may have been more relevant than others for explaining any specific case. Overall, however, parties that consciously built party membership, branch offices, and employed professional staff, and used these resources strategically to gain and maintain electoral prominence, succeeded and survived electorally. On the other hand, those parties that failed to invest in organizations and/or use them for electoral purposes did not succeed, and often disintegrated. Specifically, the narratives demonstrated that members proved loyal voters, helped parties stay in touch with the grassroots voters and make broader appeals, and provided valuable campaign assistance. Branches, in turn, served as structures and venues for member activities that parties used to become involved in local life and politics. This involvement allowed parties not only to cultivate and sustain support but also to train candidates and recuperate at times of crisis. Last, but not least, professional staff benefited party success and survival because of their high level of commitment to the party and incentives as well as ability to keep the party unified and well managed.

Tracing the processes of parties' electoral performance and organizational development over time, the narratives provide uniform evidence that organizational strength precedes electoral success rather than vice versa. Those parties that invested in and used their organizations for electoral mobilization subsequently saw their vote shares increase or stabilize and survival chances strengthen. This was especially evident in the cases of MSzP and SLD, that used their organizational strength to break with the stigma of the past. It was also evident in the case of the Czech KSČM, that survived and became increasingly more accepted by other parties despite not breaking with the past, and in the case of Fidesz, that explicitly responded to each perceived electoral failure with subsequent strengthening of the organization.

On the other hand, parties that failed to build a strong organization or neglected their organizations consequently suffered electoral demise even if their original performance had been outstanding. Consider, for example, the fate of FKgP, KDNP, and MDF in Hungary, and the post-Solidarity parties in Poland, all of which neglected their organizations before becoming electorally marginal. Other "failing" parties, such as KE in Estonia and ODA and US in the Czech Republic, did not even start building their organizations despite initial electoral success. It is, therefore, not possible that their electoral performance hindered organization-building efforts. Furthermore, as the case of RP in Estonia suggested, the same party can either prosper or suffer electorally at different times depending on the direction it takes with regard to its organizational development.

Finally, the (controlled) comparisons offered the best evidence that party organizational strength has independent effect on electoral performance by demonstrating the alternative explanations remained inadequate. For example, parties may be successful because of their leader rather than their organization: a strong, visible, popular leader may be better at attracting votes than having a strong organization. This alternative did not find support. Specifically, the success of ODS in the Czech Republic continued after its charismatic leader

Klaus left the party, and the other successful parties considered – ČSSD and KSČM – had not been particularly leader-centered or relied on popular figures for their electoral success. At the same time, some of the leader-centered right-wing competitors of ODS failed as parties. The case of RP in Estonia also strongly suggests that the leader may be less relevant for electoral performance at least in the short-term because the party was successful before it had identified a single leader. The Hungarian and Polish case studies also supported the lack of relevance of leaders. None of the Polish parties considered had a charismatic or particularly strong leader. In Hungary, although Fidesz had a strong leader, he did not dominate the party. At the same time, the only really leader-centered mainstream party in Hungary – FKgP – failed to succeed and was forced to disintegrate. Similarly, KDNP also disintegrated during the period that the party had become increasingly leader-centered. Rather than being an electoral asset, especially in the long-term, the problem of leader-centered parties is that the survival of the party is entirely dependent on the leader and his or her performance. As the FKgP case aptly illustrated, if there is no party structure independent of the leader to fall back to during times of crisis, the party is likely to fail.

Second, patronage politics, assumed to be available for governing parties, may help attract and keep voters. This, again, did not find strong support as a viable alternative explanation. In the Czech Republic, several of the ODS's ideological rivals – including ODA and US – served in government, but were not able to use it to maintain a support base. KSČM had never served in government, but commanded stable support. Similarly, all of the three major Polish parties considered as well as the Estonian K and KE had been in government, and all of them should have had similar access to patronage, but their outcomes on electoral performance are very different. In Hungary, the first governing parties all failed in the long-term. At the same time, those parties that had no access to government and faced threat of marginalization (MSzP) or extinction (Fidesz) were the ones that survived and succeeded. In general, successful parties had their organizations built and functioning before they made significant electoral gains. For example, Enyedi and Linek (2008) note that during the main periods of organizational growth, the Czech ODS was in opposition, indicating that growth was not because of institutionalizing clientelistic structures but reflected a genuine mobilization breakthrough.

Finally, some parties may be more successful because they offer more attractive ideological programs than others. However, the analysis showed that when party ideology was held constant, that is, when comparing ideologically similar parties, the ones with stronger organizations were always more successful electorally and more likely to survive than those whose organizations were weak. This, of course, does not suggest that ideology does not matter for electoral performance. It does mean, however, that party organizational strength has significant independent explanatory power, other things equal.

In sum, organizational strength significantly accounts for electoral success in all four countries. The case studies confirmed that all three attributes of party organizational strength – members, branches, and professional staff – can be used to achieve electoral success and survival. Furthermore, the uncovered organizational effects are genuine and cannot simply be explained away by other factors.

4

Organizing for Unity

Organizational Strength and Parties in Parliament

Institutionalized parties are not only electorally successful but also develop a unified identity and behave in a coordinated and cohesive manner in parliament. The goal of this chapter is to understand why some parties are better at achieving such unity than others. In addition to being an important aspect of party institutionalization, this question is of considerable scholarly and substantive interest because lack of party unity threatens the quality of representation and the efficiency of governing, and thereby undermines the stability of democracy. Examples of serious consequences arising from MP dissent abound. In Estonia in 2002, the failure of two coalition politicians to vote with their party helped derail the budgetary process (Parve 2002). Defections within the ruling party have contributed to several significant policy failures in Slovakia including the failure to elect a president in 1993[1] and the adoption of the opposition proposal for administrative-territorial reform in 2001 (TASR News Agency 2001). The European Union Lisbon Treaty was ratified in Slovakia only with the help of dissenting opposition members (EU Business 2008). In 1993, the Polish government fell after intra-party dissent helped fail a vote on the budget (Perlez 1993). The Czech government fell in March 2009 with the help of four lawmakers breaking ranks with their party and voting with the opposition (Bos 2009). In 2003, the ruling ČSSD in the Czech Republic failed to unite and push through their presidential candidate (CTK 2003d).

A growing literature argues that political institutions influence party unity (Carey 2009; Diermeier and Feddersen 1998; Hix 2004; Hix, Noury, and Roland 2005; Mainwaring 1999; Morgenstern 2004; Owens 2003; Sieberer 2006). These studies assume that legislators are primarily motivated by reelection and that institutional structures constrain their voting behavior in pursuit

---

[1] In 1993, the Slovakian president had to be elected by the parliament. New elections, that managed to produce a president, were held later in the year (Tavits 2009d).

of this goal. If the institutional setting allows attaining the goal only through party leadership, then legislators will adhere to the party line in their voting. However, the institutional setting can create opportunities to achieve the goal by some other way – for example, through a direct relationship with voters. In this case, party loyalty in parliament becomes less important.

Existing research rarely examines party influence on legislative individualism directly. Parties are not active agents in this theory. Instead, party influence is assumed to result from specific institutional structures. At the same time, recent research has shown that legislators can behave rather differently under the same institutional arrangements (Desposato 2006; Herron 2002; Morgenstern and Swindle 2005; Thames 2005). Haspel, Remington, and Smith (1998) and Kunicova and Remington (2008), for example, find no significant difference in the discipline of Russian Duma members elected from single-member districts as opposed to party lists. However, they do find significant differences in voting unity across parties, suggesting that party-level factors are likely to have a direct effect on parliamentary behavior.

This chapter demonstrates that the strength of political party organization directly and independently influences the level of party unity. Building on the results of Chapters 2 and 3, and in line with recent research on pork-barrel politics (Keefer and Khemani 2009; Lyne 2008; Primo and Snyder 2010), I argue that party organizational strength influences party unity because the stronger the party organization the more valuable an electoral asset the party is to individual legislators. This may decrease the need to sway voters by building personal reputations in parliament. More importantly, the more valuable the party is to the legislator (i.e., the stronger the party), the more credible and effective its threat to withdraw the electoral benefits if a legislator undermines party unity.

I test this argument with data on party organizational strength and parliamentary voting from the Czech Republic, Estonia, Hungary, and Poland. Using different measures of party unity and those of party organizational strength (including party membership size, network of branch offices, and local presence), the results provide consistent evidence that parties with stronger organizations are more unified in parliament. I also provide illustrative examples and narratives to further substantiate the plausibility of the proposed causal mechanism.

Party Organizational Strength and Party Unity in Parliament

I argue that party organizational strength influences party unity in parliament via collective electoral benefits it helps to provide. A party represents the collective component in the reelection chances of its members (Cox and McCubbins 1993). The more significant this collective component, that is, the more the party can help maximize the reelection probabilities of its candidates, the more valuable the party is as an electoral resource to the legislator. This is better achieved by parties with strong rather than weak organizations. Being valuable for the legislators gives the party leverage over them to induce unity in parliament. Compliance results from the threat of losing – by being denied nomination or expelled from the party – the electoral benefits that party could otherwise deliver. The threat of punishment is more effective, that is, more likely to induce compliance, when the party can more credibly claim to provide electoral benefits (i.e., the stronger its organization). The rest of this section explains this argument in more detail.

It is in the interest of the party to stay unified in parliament, because unity affects parties' ability to hold onto office, influence policy, and win votes. On the other hand, much of the existing literature argues that individual legislators are first and foremost interested in their own reelection (Cox and McCubbins 1993; Mayhew 1974). In order to maximize their probability of reelection they can take various actions in the legislature that help build personal reputations. An attempt to build such reputations can be manifested, among other things, in individualistic- rather than party-oriented behavior in parliament. Personal reputation serves as an electoral resource for legislators – it signals legislators' ability and preferences to voters (Ashworth and Bueno de Mesquita 2008).

When parties are weak (or absent), personal reputation is the only electoral resource that legislators have. Strong parties are likely to alter this dynamic. A party can function as a substitute for personal reputation if it is capable of delivering votes for its candidates. This capacity is higher for parties with a strong organization than for those with a weak organization. Party organizational strength consists of the extensiveness, professionalization, and reach of a party (Cotter et al. 1984; Janda 1980; Katz and Mair 1994; Mainwaring 1999; Panebianco 1988). A party has a strong organization if it has structures, personnel, and activities beyond public office. This includes extensive membership and widespread local presence.

As Chapters 2 and 3 demonstrated, the stronger the party organization, the more electorally viable the party, which also means the higher the reelection probabilities of each of its candidates. The evidence showed that the extensiveness of party structures outside its function in public office helps parties prosper electorally mostly by providing effective means of communicating party reputation to the electorate and thereby making it easier for voters to base their voting decision on the party brand rather than an individual candidate's ability or personal reputation.

A strong party organization can effectively deliver votes for its candidates. Although this provides legislators with an opportunity to rely on the party rather than personal reputation for the reelection pursuit, it is not sufficient to guarantee that legislators abandon individualism. From the point of view of the legislator, who wants to maximize his or her reelection potential, it would be more beneficial to use personal resources (personal reputation) and electoral benefits accruing from party membership and nomination simultaneously rather than as substitutes. If the strong party's only function is to provide electoral benefits to its candidates, we are not likely to see party unity in parliament – individual legislators have little incentive to adhere to the party line because they can claim the electoral benefit by belonging to the party regardless of whether they contribute to unity.

In order to avoid such free riding, electoral benefits provided by a strong party cannot be unconditional. In order to effectively induce compliance, a party can threaten to withhold electoral benefits from a legislator who does not adhere to the party line by denying that legislator a high position or any position on the party list or expelling him or her from the party altogether. The more electorally beneficial the party organization is to the legislator, the more consequential such a threat to the electoral fate of the legislator. Because parties with strong organizations are more likely to succeed electorally, it follows that parties with strong organizations can more effectively enforce party unity than parties with weak organizations. The weaker the party organization the less consequential that party's threat to withdraw its electoral support from a noncompliant legislator, because the potential electoral benefits that a weak party is able to provide are not likely to be substantial enough to outweigh the benefit of building personal reputation via individualism in parliament. In the case of weak parties, it is the legislator who is likely to earn votes for the party by his or her personal reputation rather than vice versa, and the legislator can easily change parties without losing much electorally.

In sum, parties that are well organized are better able to capture any potential collective electoral benefits than parties whose organizations are weak or nonexistent. Without collective benefits, including strong organizations, individual legislators need to fend for themselves and are therefore likely to behave individualistically in parliament. Party organizational strength, by providing such electoral benefits, gives legislators an alternative way to increase their reelection probabilities: legislators can rely on the party and no longer depend solely on building personal reputations. The fact that a strong party organization is a valuable electoral asset for legislators allows a party with such an organization to effectively enforce compliance with the party line in parliamentary voting. Compliance results from the threat of losing the electoral benefits that party membership and nomination can provide if a legislator breaks party unity.[2]

The proposed argument is in accord with recent research on pork-barrel politics: Keefer and Khemani (2009) show that, in India, legislators are less likely to deliver pork to districts where voter attachment to parties (rather than

---

[2] Put differently, from the point of view of the legislator, party organizational strength changes his or her cost-benefit calculation. The weaker the party organization the less likely the party is to control the reelection chances of the legislator and the less costly it is for him or her to defect. On the contrary, the stronger the party organization, the more likely the party resources benefit the legislator electorally and, hence, the costlier the defection.

individual candidates) is strong. Party organizational strength is likely to be an important source of voter attachment and can therefore at least partially explain the relationship. Similarly, Primo and Snyder (2010) argue, in the context of the United States, that strong party organizations reduce the need for pork-barreling – a form of personal rather than party reputation building. Lyne (2008) argues that although the individualistic electoral system predicts otherwise, party unity in the Brazilian Chamber of Deputies is high because party organizations control legislators' access to important electoral resources. However, the direct effects of party organizations on party unity in the manner hypothesized here have not been established.[3]

Research Design

In order to test this argument, I use information from thirteen legislative terms: the Czech Republic 1996–1998, 1998–2002, 2002–2006, 2006–2009; Estonia 1999–2003, 2003–2007; Hungary 1994–1998, 1998–2002, 2002–2006, 2006–2010; and Poland 1997–2001, 2001–2005, 2005–2007 for all parliamentary parties. MPs' voting records and/or other data were not available for earlier years. The number of parties included in the analysis per country and parliamentary term is presented in Appendix 4.1.

Dependent Variable: Party Unity
There are several different ways of measuring party unity, but all of these measures are based on MPs' voting records. In all of the countries included in the analysis, all votes but a very few exceptional ones (such as votes on some senior personnel appointments) are publicly recorded "roll-call" votes and included in the current study. This eliminates the concern about the bias that haunts roll-call vote analysis if only certain votes are recorded (Carrubba et al. 2006).[4]

---

[3] An alternative argument posits a negative relationship between party organizational strength and party unity in parliament. Strong party organization – especially large membership and widespread local presence – may indicate that the party is very diverse. The more heterogeneous the party, the more likely is it that legislators from the same party adhere to very different policy positions. This may make it more difficult for the party to keep its legislators unified in parliament (Amorim Neto and Santos 2001). However, although diversity directly decreases any unity that results from cohesion, it is less clear that it will affect the ability of the party to enforce discipline. The latter might be a problem if large membership indicates democratized decision-making rules that account for member preferences, which may make it harder for the party to decisively punish legislators. However, as the analyses show, membership size is associated with unity in the same way as the other two measures of organizational strength, which suggests that it is not a worse indicator of organizational strength than the other measures.

[4] The number of votes included in the study by legislature is as follows: 5,000, 14,081, 14,148, and 4,739 for the four terms in Czech Republic; 4,741 and 1,844 for the two terms in Estonia; 6,772, 7,310, 15,682, and 7,573 for the four terms in Hungary; 11,881, 11,490, and 3,480 for the three terms in Poland.

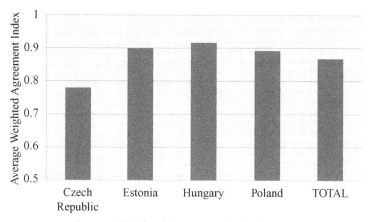

FIGURE 4.1. Average Weighted Agreement Index by country.

For current purposes, I use Weighted Agreement Index as the measure of the dependent variable. This measure indicates the extent to which members of a given party pick the same voting option ("yes," "no," or "abstain"), weighing close votes more heavily. The index simultaneously accounts for two deficiencies of the most common measure of party unity – the regular Rice score (Rice 1925). First, in addition to the two voting options – yes and no – it also accounts for voting abstain. This is a voting option in three out of the four countries included in this analysis, and can be a significant manifestation of disagreement with the party.[5] Second, unlike the regular Rice score, it accounts for the closeness of the vote. Many votes are uncontroversial and therefore the Rice formula overestimates the level of party unity. Existing literature has dealt with each of these concerns separately: Hix et al. (2005) developed an Agreement Index in order to account for the former, and Carey (2009) and Morgenstern (2004) used a Weighted Rice score to address the latter. The formulas for calculating each of these measures are given in Appendix 4.2. As a robustness test, I also performed separate analyses with the Weighted Rice and non-weighted Agreement Index, which are presented in Appendix 4.4.[6]

Figure 4.1 provides the average values of the dependent variable for the entire dataset and for each country separately. The average party unity is lowest in the Czech Republic and highest in Hungary. In general, these values are

[5] No existing measure is able to account for nonvotes (an MP is present but does not cast a vote) and absences, both of which can also be strategic behavior by MPs (Rosas and Shomer 2008). However, these assumptions about potential strategic behavior are not verifiable (because MPs may also have valid reasons for not voting and for being absent), which is why existing studies have ignored nonvotes and absences as missing data – an example followed here.

[6] In an alternative analysis, I used logit transformation of the different measures of the dependent variable because these scores are bound by 0 and 1. The results were similar.

considerably lower than the unity scores reported for advanced West European countries (Bowler, Farrell, and Katz 1999). The scores range from a minimum of 0.2 (US in the Czech Republic in the 1996–1998 parliament) to a maximum of 0.99 (MSzP in Hungary in the 2002–2006 parliament). The wide range of values indicates that there is considerable variance in the dependent variable and allows for a meaningful empirical analysis.

Independent Variable: Party Organizational Strength

Party organizational strength was defined as extensive membership and widespread local presence and is measured in a similar way as in Chapter 2. Specifically, I have used four different measures of party organizational strength: (1) "Members" measured as the number of party members as the percent of total electorate, (2) "Branches," that is, the number of municipal-level party branches divided by the total number of municipalities in a given country,[7] (3) "Staff" measured as a percent of the electorate (in hundred thousands), and (4) "Participation in local elections" measured by the share of local governments nationwide where a given party runs its candidates in a local government election.

All four indicators vary for each term. Membership, local branches, and staff size are measured before or at the start of the parliamentary term. For participation in local elections, I have used data from the local election that immediately preceded or occurred in the same year as the start of a given legislative term. In other words, party organizational strength is measured temporally prior to measuring unity: for example, in the case of the Czech Republic, party organizational strength in 2001 (members, branches, staff) or 2002 (local elections) is used to predict party unity in 2002–2006. This helps alleviate any endogeneity concerns. The relationships of interest also remain intact when a lagged dependent variable is included in the models as an additional attempt to control for endogeneity. I have reported the results without the lagged dependent variable because including it decreases the number of observations by about a half. Instead of combining the measures into a single indicator, I will estimate separate models with each to allow for a better substantive interpretation of the results. The results do not change when a combined index is used.

Other Explanatory Variables

"Centralized candidate selection" is measured by a dummy variable coded "1" when the national-level party leadership has the final say over candidate selection and "0" otherwise.[8] If the central party office is in charge of selecting

---

[7] The maximum value on this variable is 1.1 rather than 1 because some parties (the KSČM in the Czech Republic and SLD in Poland) report having multiple branch offices in the same municipality.

[8] Sources: Deegan-Krause (2006); Enyedi (2008); Kangur (2004); Kowalczyk (2004); Otepalu (2008); Spurek (2002); interviews with party officials.

candidates to run in national elections or can revise and veto lower-level decisions, then the renomination of MPs directly depends on the central party organization. If, however, candidates are selected on the local (district) level, then the renomination of an MP depends on his or her reputation on the local level. In order to maintain a good local reputation, an MP may have an incentive, at least sometimes, to go against the party line in parliament. Therefore, the more centralized this procedure the more unity one should observe (Bowler et al. 1999; Hazan 2003; Sieberer 2006; but see Shomer 2009).

"Party size" is measured in vote share for the party in the election preceding a given parliamentary term,[9] and is included because previous literature has argued that smaller parties tend to be less unified (Desposato 2005; Sieberer 2006).[10] "Governing parties," coded "1" for parties that formed the governing coalition during the given parliamentary term and "0" otherwise, are argued to be more unified given the higher stakes of disunity for governing parties in parliamentary systems (Carey 2009; Sieberer 2006).[11]

The "Size of governing majority" is measured by the difference between half the parliamentary seat share and the seat share of governing parties. The larger the difference the stronger a majority the government commands. For minority governments, this difference is negative. When the governing party or coalition of parties has only a slim majority over the opposition the overall party unity should be greater – every vote becomes more valuable to both sides because a few votes can decide whether the preferences of the governing parties prevail (Sieberer 2006).

"Number of votes" indicates the number of recorded votes in a given parliamentary term (in thousands). There is a great variance in the number of times MPs take the vote even within one country between different terms (see fn 4). It is possible that as the volume of voting increases, the overall unity decreases

---

[9] Source: National Election Commissions.

[10] Sieberer (2006) also suggests that policy extremism increases unity because it makes it less attractive for dissatisfied MPs to go against the party because it is unlikely that there are alternative parties to switch to. I calculated party distance from the center using party placement on the left-right scale as reported in Benoit and Laver (2006). This variable was consistently insignificant in the analysis and did not alter the effect of other variables. Sieberer's (2006) argument may be more relevant for understanding party switching and not necessarily party unity. In an alternative analysis, I also controlled for the communist successor parties that (1) may be more disciplined perhaps because, at least initially, they were more united in their goals, and (2) are also more likely to have stronger organizations. Including this variable did not substantively change the effect of party organizational strength. The variable itself was insignificant in models that used members and branches as indicators of party organizational strength. It was positive and statistically significant at the 10 percent level in the model using participation in local elections as the measure of organizational strength.

[11] Governments can change mid-term – they did so in Estonia and Poland during all terms included in the dataset. In order to avoid coding potentially all parties as governing parties because of the change in government in mid-term, I only accounted for the longest-serving government in any given term. Source: Keesing's World News Archive.

because the significance of any single vote is going to be lower (see also Hix et al. 2005).

"Party budget" measures the size of the party income as a percent of GDP (in thousands).[12] I include this variable because the organizational strength of parties may simply reflect their financial situation.[13]

Country dummies control for any unmeasured country-level effects, including that of the electoral systems – one of the most prominent explanations in the existing literature (Carey 2009). The prediction about the effect of electoral systems for the current cases is not very straightforward. Carey (2009) argues that unity should be lower in systems where co-partisans compete against each other. As noted above, the Czech Republic, Estonia, and Poland use open-list PR where such intra-party competition can take place. Hungary, on the other hand, uses a mixed SMD–closed-list PR electoral system. Although neither of these tiers produces intra-party competition, one could still argue that legislators from SMDs may be more constituency-oriented in their parliamentary behavior and therefore more likely to go against the party than MPs from party lists. Therefore, the mixed system could also decrease rather than increase unity. Because sorting out the electoral system effects is not the goal of the current analysis these concerns are less relevant here. However, any potential electoral system effects justify the inclusion of country dummies for accurate estimation of the effect of party organizational strength.

Results

I estimated the models using OLS regression with robust standard errors to account for potential heteroskedasticity.[14] Appendix 4.3 presents descriptive statistics for the variables included in the models. As the findings reported in Table 4.1 show, three of the four measures of party organizational strength – participation in local elections, members, and branches – are significantly related to the party unity as measured by the Weighted Agreement Index. Appendix 4.4 presents results with the alternative measures of the dependent variable for the sake of testing whether the results are sensitive to the measure used. The results with the raw Agreement Index and Weighted Rice support the hypothesized effect with the same three measures of organizational strength

---

[12] Source: financial reports of parties, party archives, interviews with party officials, the Political Yearbook of Hungary (various issues), Enyedi (2008), G. Juhász (2001), Kopecky (2007).

[13] The organizational strength of parties may also simply reflect their age, with older parties having stronger organizations. In an alternative analysis, I controlled for party age in years. Including this variable did not change the substantive effect of party organizational strength in any of the three alternative models. The variable itself remained statistically insignificant in the model with participation in local elections and branches as measures of party organizational strength. It was negative and statistically significant (at the 10 percent level) in the model with members as the measure of organizational strength.

[14] The main findings also remain robust when time dummies for parliamentary term are included.

TABLE 4.1. *Regression Analysis of Party Organizational Strength and Voting Unity in Parliament*

	Local Elections	Members	Branches	Staff
Participation in local elections	0.152** (0.067)			
Members		5.478*** (1.831)		
Local branches			0.166*** (0.064)	
Staff				−0.011 (0.015)
Centralized candidate selection	0.042 (0.035)	0.007 (0.019)	0.040 (0.032)	0.002 (0.026)
Party size	0.120* (0.071)	0.146** (0.074)	0.130* (0.076)	0.199* (0.112)
Governing party	0.039* (0.023)	0.023 (0.016)	0.058** (0.028)	0.044** (0.020)
Size of governing majority	−0.907*** (0.189)	−0.850*** (0.168)	−1.041*** (0.198)	−0.779*** (0.195)
Number of votes	−0.003 (0.004)	−0.005* (0.003)	−0.003 (0.004)	−0.005 (0.004)
Party budget (% GDP)	0.484* (0.304)	0.398* (0.242)	0.741** (0.350)	0.652*** (0.243)
Czech Republic	−0.184*** (0.045)	−0.186*** (0.030)	−0.176*** (0.051)	−0.193*** (0.061)
Estonia	−0.002 (0.034)	−0.028 (0.029)	0.088* (0.048)	0.035 (0.062)
Hungary	0.062 (0.045)	0.031 (0.037)	0.108* (0.057)	0.061 (0.067)
Constant	0.843*** (0.069)	0.927*** (0.028)	0.767*** (0.085)	0.892*** (0.063)
R^2	0.42	0.41	0.58	0.48
N	73	73	63	50

Note: Dependent variable is the Weighted Agreement Index. Table entries are unstandardized regression coefficients with robust standard errors in parentheses. Poland is the reference category.
*$p \leq 0.1$, **$p \leq 0.05$, ***$p \leq 0.01$

significantly and positively related to party unity in parliament. Overall, the results indicate that parties with stronger organizations are likely to be more unified in parliament as suggested by the theory. The only exception to this robust pattern is the effect of the size of staff, which does not reach the level of statistical significance. This non-finding may be because of collinearity: the variable is highly correlated with vote share and party budget. When the latter two controls are excluded from the model, the effect of the size of staff becomes

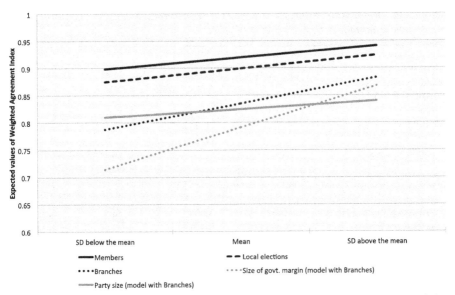

FIGURE 4.2. Expected values of Weighted Agreement Index at different values of the independent variables.

statistically significant and positive. Such sensitivity to model specification does not allow making any strong claims about the insignificance of the size of staff for the level of party unity.

The effects of the participation in local elections, members and branches are not only robust but also substantively significant. I have picked the model that uses local branches as the indicator of organizational strength to illustrate these effects. Figure 4.2 summarizes the expected values of the Weighted Agreement Index for the mean value and one SD below and above the mean; all other variables are held at their median value. The change from one SD below to one SD above the mean on local branches increases party unity from about 0.79 to 0.88. The effect of the other organizational-strength variables is somewhat weaker: a similar change in (1) membership increases the expected value of the weighted agreement index from 0.89 to 0.94, and (2) participation in local elections from 0.87 to 0.92.[15]

---

[15] One might argue that it is not organizational strength because of its vote-getting potential but other factors, such as past governance experience and party reputation, that make a party valuable for an MP. I reestimated the models in Table 4.1, adding a variable that measures for each parliamentary term whether a given party has ever served or is currently serving in government (this is different from "Governing party," which only indicates parties currently in government). The variable was not significant in any of the models and the effect of organizational strength did not change. Party reputation is more difficult to capture, but one might argue that it is reflected in a party's vote share, already controlled for in the models. Additionally, party may be valuable for MPs because of ideological considerations. However, this is an MP-level rather

Two other variables that reach the level of statistical significance in all models are government margin and party size. For the sake of comparison, Figure 4.2 also presents the substantive effects of these variables (marked in gray) using the model with branches as the measure of organizational strength. The effect of the governing margin is very strong: at one SD above the mean, the expected value of the weighted agreement index is only 0.71. In comparison, the expected value of agreement index is 0.87 for governments that control less than a majority of seats (one SD below the mean).[16] The effect of party size is somewhat weaker than that of organizational strength: the expected value of the weighted agreement index is 0.81 for the smallest party in the dataset and 0.84 for the largest.

Interestingly, one of the most prominent explanations of party unity in the existing literature – the candidate selection procedure – does not find strong empirical support. The variable has a positive coefficient, but it does not reach the level of statistical significance in any of the three models. It does become statistically significant, however, under slightly different model specifications – that is, when (1) the lagged dependent variable is included, or (2) vote share and country dummies are excluded. Because of this sensitivity, it is hard to make any strong claims about the non-finding. This is especially true given the small number of countries and relatively low variance in the selection procedures, as most parties in the region favor centralized candidate selection. The finding does, however, suggest that the power to nominate alone may not be a credible threat to induce unity when the party cannot guarantee electoral benefits. Although weak parties may control nominations, they may be reluctant to use this as a disciplinary tool – unlike strong parties where candidates depend on the party for electoral support, weak parties are likely to depend on their candidates if they want to preserve or maximize their presence in parliament. Denying a renomination may mean losing a seat for the party. The effect may appear insignificant also because renomination is not the only disciplinary tool that strong parties can use – they can also threaten to deny other electoral resources to the maverick MPs. Furthermore, even if nomination rights are officially delegated to the local party organization, the local organization may still follow the preferences of the party leadership or the leadership may have informal power to intervene and deny renominating a maverick.

The size of the party budget is significant when branches and members are used as the organizational-strength measures and insignificant in the model with local elections. The effect of organizational strength remains significant in

than party-level factor, that is, it is difficult to see what makes ideological considerations more prominent about some parties than others.

[16] It is also possible that the effect of the size of government majority is curvilinear: a smaller margin should discipline all parties, but when the government has only a minority share of seats, the farther away they are from achieving majority the less reason there is to stay unified. I calculated the absolute government margin, but the effect of this variable remained insignificant in all models.

all models. This suggests that although certainly related, party organizational strength is not simply an indicator of the wealth of the party. Recall that the results in Chapter 2 similarly suggest that although party budget and campaign expenditure may or may not have an effect on the electoral performance of the party, these variables do not eliminate the independent effect that the organizational strength has on the electoral performance.

In sum, the findings suggest that party organizational strength is associated with more party unity in parliament. This result is substantively and statistically significant for most indicators of organizational strength despite the relatively small sample size, and remains robust against the inclusion of powerful controls.

Narratives and Illustrations

The goal of this section is to provide illustrations of the causal mechanism, and examples of other possible empirical manifestations of the theoretical logic linking party organizational strength and party unity. Recall that the theoretical argument proposes the following causal mechanism: strong party organization is associated with successful electoral performance, which makes parties with such organizations more valuable to legislators; the threat of losing such a valuable electoral asset is more likely to induce compliance in parliamentary voting behavior in the case of parties with strong than weak organizations. The empirical analyses presented offer a test of the relationship between organizational strength and compliance, and Chapters 2 and 3 provide evidence that the stronger the party organization the more electorally successful the party. The one link in the causal story that remains untested is that MPs from parties with strong organizations are more likely to consider their parties electorally valuable than legislators from parties with weak organizations. Case studies can probe the plausibility of this theoretical link.

Montgomery (1999) provides a detailed account of the development of party discipline in the Hungarian parliament, and the evidence presented illustrates well the theoretical argument that MPs from organizationally strong parties are more likely to realize the electoral value of their party than their counterparts from weak parties. Montgomery's study describes how all MPs initially struggled to establish personal reputations on the basis of the assumption that building such reputations was necessary for reelection (see also Ágh 1995). The MPs not only were independent in their voting behavior, but also engaged in legislative activism with even the ruling parties' MPs proposing a large percentage of the amendments to government bills – a behavior unheard of in advanced parliamentary systems. Evidence from elite surveys suggested that MPs believed that in order to be reelected they needed to build personal reputations and should not rely on the party as an electoral resource (Ilonszki 1994). Parties at the time were only starting to build organizations, with

MSzP taking the lead and Fidesz following the example. As a result, in subsequent elections it became increasingly clear that "there were no safe seats, only safe parties" (Montgomery 1999, 518), and MPs learned that parties were key to achieving their private goals. The first parties to show stronger discipline were those with stronger organizations – MSzP and Fidesz (Montgomery 1999). It became very obvious to members of these parties that they could get anything they wanted when they cooperated with the party and lose everything if they did not. Fidesz members have explicitly admitted that they follow party line rather than constituency interest because of their reelection incentive (Pogonyi 2002). In sum, the realization that strong parties provided significant electoral benefits and the threat of losing these induced increased discipline among MPs.

Similar differences between strong and weak parties have been pointed out about other countries under study. R. Zubek (2008) describes how parties with a strong organization (SLD and PSL) had strict intra-party rules for discipline, but those with a weak organization (AWS) lacked such rules. There were several AWS MPs who were being noncooperative toward their own party's bills because they thought that they were the decision makers and vote getters and not just rubber stamps of the party. Contrary to strong parties, disagreements within weak parties often led to a series of defections and setting up of new formations (Nalewajko and Wesołowski 2007), indicating that the weak party was electorally valueless for the MPs. Similarly, Kopecky (2000) describes that contrary to the organizationally strong ODS and ČSSD in the Czech parliament, the organizationally weak ODA was reluctant to impose party discipline because the party essentially relied on its MPs – all prominent personalities – for its existence and lacked any significant organization outside parliament. The SPR-RSČ – another party with a weak organization – did impose strict discipline in the beginning, but experienced a party split as a result.

Possible Extensions

Although not directly part of the causal mechanism proposed here, the theory provides other observable implications that could be explored. For example, although it was argued that compliance with party line should result from the mere threat of losing party support rather than the actual use of punishments, one might still expect that if the need to punish emerges then strong parties are more likely to follow through with such punishment than weak parties. The fact that strong parties can rely on their organizations to win votes and seats in parliament makes the individual MPs not as valuable for the party – such a party needs to rely less on the individual reputations of MPs to do well electorally. The situation is different for parties with weak organizations, whose electoral record and parliamentary presence is more likely to depend on the individual reputations of their MPs. Because of this, they may be reluctant to use disciplinary measures against their MPs.

One way parties can withdraw their support from specific MPs is to expel them from the party. There are several examples from the countries in the region on how parties with strong organizations use such punishment. Consider, for example, a controversial vote over the dismissal of the commander of the Estonian Defense Forces in 2000. The coalition and opposition were bitterly divided over the issue, and one vote by a defecting member of the opposition decided it in the coalition's favor. The defector was expelled from K – organizationally one of the strongest parties in Estonia, as discussed in Chapter 3. Defectors themselves can sometimes miscalculate: in 2004, defectors in K claimed, "[T]he party needs us more than we need the party" (Mattheus 2004b). Such a claim might have been true for weak parties, but not for an organizationally strong one. Not surprisingly, the defectors were expelled.

In Hungary, two members of the ruling, organizationally strong MSzP, who voted against the government's health-care bill were expelled (Hungary Around the Clock 2008). In the Czech Republic, the ruling ODS expelled its two members who supported the opposition in a no-confidence vote in 2009 (CTK 2009b). A year earlier, ČSSD expelled an MP who voted for the reelection of the incumbent president and not for the ČSSD candidate (CTK 2008a). Both of these major parties have relatively strong organizations and a long history of expelling rebels.

Weak parties are less likely to punish dissenters. Even local media in the region has pointed out that "only strong parties expel members" (Alaküla 1996). Indeed, rather than the party with a weak organization denying membership to dissenters, those with disagreeing opinions often choose to leave themselves. Ilonszki (2007) describes how in Hungary internal disagreements constantly led to series of defections in the case of parties with weak organizations, such as FKgP, MDF, and KDNP, but not in the case of strong parties. Nalewajko and Wesołowski (2007) provide evidence that leads to a similar conclusion in the case of Polish parties.

To obtain some systematic support for the implication that weak parties are less likely to expel members, I collected information on expulsions of MPs from parties by performing a Lexis-Nexis search of news for a ten-year period (December 1999–December 2009) using the name of the country and "expelled" and "party" as search terms.[17] I filtered out cases where the reported

---

[17] This exercise is meant as an illustration and not as a test: the cases do not represent a universe but include only those covered in the news sources reported in Lexis-Nexis, which may be more likely to report on strong parties or more prominent cases. A more systematic analysis requires an extensive research documenting reasons for an MP leaving a party – a task that is beyond the scope and purpose of this study and poses a considerable challenge given that it is difficult to objectively determine whether somebody was expelled or left the party voluntarily and why.

expulsions were because of reasons other than dissent in parliament.[18] The ratio of the remaining cases by the strength of the party organization (strong vs. weak)[19] and country are as follows: Czech Republic, 11 versus 3; Estonia, 9 versus 3; Hungary, 5 versus 0; Poland, 4 versus 1.[20] In the case of both Hungary and Poland, weak parties (FKgP MDF, SRP, and AWS) did expel MPs, usually en masse, and these expulsions were followed by additional MPs leaving the party voluntarily – developments that essentially amounted to party splits rather than punishments for dissent.

The different strategies of strong and weak parties in dealing with internal dissent can be further illustrated by considering other types of punishments. For example, a party can punish dissenters by lowering their list position and thereby reducing their chances of reelection. As one of the Estonian Center Party MPs commented, "[T]he day when the list places for the Riigikogu elections are announced is like a pay day, when [our] previous work at the Riigikogu gets rated" (Sepp 2011). This same MP saw her list place slide from 12th to 123rd as a result, by at least some accounts, of her "disregard for the party" and unwillingness to be a "team player" (Vahe 2011).

To explore the possibility that strong parties are more likely than weak parties to punish defectors by lowering their list place, I picked the ten most-frequent dissenters from strong parties and ten from weak(er) parties in the 2003–2007 parliamentary term in Estonia. I then considered the positioning of these dissenters in the national party list in the 2003 and 2007 parliamentary elections. The strong parties are those scoring above the country-level average on at least two organizational-strength measures for a given parliamentary term and include K, RP, and Peoples' Party (ERL). RP is excluded because it no longer existed in 2007. The weak parties are the IL, the Reform Party (RE), and the Social Democratic Party (SDE).

The results turned out as expected and are presented in Table 4.2. The table includes two sets of top-ten dissenters: (1) including and (2) excluding those who no longer ran under the same party label in 2007. In some cases, not running may indicate that the dissenters were expelled from the party, but in other cases they may have left voluntarily. Especially in the latter case, knowing

---

[18] For example, MPs were expelled for being involved in a publicized corruption scandal or for improper conduct (e.g., being intoxicated, making racist comments).

[19] Parties that score above the country-level average on at least two organizational-strength measures for the time period 1999–2009 are classified as "strong" and the rest as "weak." The share of strong parties ranges from 30 percent (Hungary) to 53 percent (Czech Republic).

[20] One might argue that the likelihood of using expulsions is related to the margin the party enjoys rather than to organizational strength. One way to explore this possibility is to consider two parties with the exact same seat share but different levels of organizational strength. K and RP in the 2003–2007 legislative term in Estonia fit these criteria: both had twenty-eight seats but the former had a stronger organization (with about twice the number of members and presence in 65 versus 49 percent of the municipalities). During that legislative period, K expelled eight members for indiscipline; RP expelled none.

TABLE 4.2. *The Fate of Top-Ten Defectors, Estonia 2003–2007*

	Including MPs Who Left the Party		*Excluding* MPs Who Left the Party	
	Strong parties (K, ERL)	Weak parties (IL, RE, SDE)	Strong parties (K, ERL)	Weak parties (IL, RE, SDE)
Promoted	1	7	3	8
Demoted	5	2	7	2
Left the party	4	1		

Note: Table entries refer to the number of the ten most frequently defecting MPs from strong and weak parties whose list place was decreased (i.e., who were promoted), increased (demoted), or who left the party between the 2003 and 2007 elections.

that this will be their final term, these legislators might be less worried about reelection, which may explain their maverick behavior. Alternatively, they may be in deep disagreement with their party, a condition that affects both their readiness to leave the party and vote against it in parliament. For these reasons, it is informative to consider the different sets of top dissenters.

Consider first the set of top-ten defectors that includes those MPs who eventually left the party. In the case of strong parties, four defectors left the party, five were demoted in that their list place was lowered, and only one was promoted. Weak parties exhibit the opposite trend: seven of the top-ten defectors were promoted, only two were demoted, and one left the party. The contrast is equally telling when MPs who left the party are not considered: the outcomes for strong and weak parties are almost mirror images of each other. Seven top defectors from strong parties faced demotion, but only two top defectors from weak parties suffered a similar fate. In contrast, eight top defectors from weak parties (compared to only three from strong ones) were promoted.

Conclusion

This chapter provided robust evidence that parties with stronger organizations are more likely to behave in a unified manner in parliament. The narratives and additional qualitative evidence illustrated the plausibility of the proposed causal mechanisms and provided preliminary evidence in support of other observable implications of the argument. In new democracies, party organizational strength matters not just for establishing the party electorally but also for creating a unified and cohesive entity in office. By influencing legislative behavior, party organizational strength also affects policy making. This gives another reason, in addition to vote maximization, for office- and policy-seeking parties in post-communist countries to build organizations: parties with strong organizations can better serve their own policy (and office) goals. Further-more, my results are also important for understanding the role of parties in supporting democratic development in new democracies. Given the extent to which unity contributes to effective governing, public goods provision, and bet-ter representation, parties with strong organizations serve to help democracies consolidate.

The implications of the findings in this chapter extend beyond new democra-cies and contribute to the growing literature on party unity in general. Existing studies usually explain variance in party unity by institutional variables, such as federalism, presidentialism, and the electoral system. At the party level, the most common explanatory variable is the candidate selection procedure; other party effects are generally neglected. This chapter has shown that party orga-nizations can have a more comprehensive and substantial effect on legislator's behavior beyond just candidate selection procedures. Because of the electoral benefits that strong organizations can provide, strong parties alter the incentive structure of MPs and thereby influence their behavior.

Additionally, the findings further the growing body of research that explores the various representational linkages that parties offer – a topic that is, again, relevant both in new as well as more long-standing democracies. Although I am not able to demonstrate exactly the type of representational linkage practiced by strong parties, their tendency to be more unified in parliament suggests a more programmatic rather than clientelistic appeal. Future research could look more directly at whether and to what extent party organizational strength fosters programmatic representation.

Finally, I would like to reiterate that the focus of this chapter is on the party level. It provides a rationale for why some parties are more unified than others. The goal has not been to account for within-party variation. It is likely that within both weak and strong parties some MPs are more or less likely to follow party unity. In fact, as Chapter 5 demonstrates, party organizational strength at other levels – such as the strength of the local party branch in the constituency that an MP is representing – may provide different individual-level incentives to adhere or not adhere to the (national) party line in parliament.

5

Power within Parties

The Consequences of Subunit Organizational Strength

The evidence so far indicates that party organizational strength is positively associated with party institutionalization in new democracies. A strong organization is advantageous both in terms of winning and maintaining electoral support, and disciplining party elites to stay loyal and unified. Given these positive consequences, why do not all parties build strong organizations? This chapter and Chapter 6 present some potential answers to this puzzle. Specifically, in this chapter I consider how organizational strength disaggregated to the party subunit (i.e., branch) level affects the power distribution within parties. If organizational strength pulls power away from the center to certain branches, then party leadership may be reluctant to make organizational investments. In Chapter 6, I will further examine a number of other factors, such as the role of party ideology, environment, and leadership style. These may influence the extent to which the party sees the organization as a benefit or a burden, and thereby determine the level of its organizational strength.

How organizational strength affects power distribution within parties also helps address questions of broader theoretical interest that extend beyond the context of party institutionalization in new democracies: How is power distributed within political parties and what are the effects of the power distribution? The internal life of parties is, in general, relatively unexplored in the otherwise voluminous literature on political parties. It is common to treat parties as unitary actors and ignore their internal diversity despite frequent calls to account for it (Laver 1998; Laver and Schofield 1998; Strom 1990). At the same time, parties' internal power distribution is important for understanding the dynamics of party behavior. Knowing what party subunits or individuals are more influential or independent can help us better understand party policy choices, position taking, electoral campaigns and performance, interparty relations, coalition decisions, representational linkage types, restructuring attempts, and the like – that is, the aspects of party politics that are extensively studied by political scientists but so far mostly from the unitary actor perspective.[1]

This chapter explores the power distribution within political parties by borrowing insights from organizational theory. Literature on organizational sociology suggests that power within organizations is asymmetrically distributed between different subunits, with more powerful subunits being those that are better able to provide resources critical to the functioning of the organization that cannot be obtained by any other means. Within political parties, such powerful subunits are likely to be local branches with strong organizations (those with visible and active presence in local life via participating in local politics, being associated with locally known leaders and activists, and having local structures and membership) because these branches are able to help party leadership obtain its central goals – electoral and policy success. Such power distribution is likely to be manifested in the parliamentary behavior of MPs. I hypothesize that MPs from districts with organizationally strong party branches are (1) less likely to toe the party line set by leaders and more likely to break party unity in legislative voting, and (2) more likely to hold leadership positions in parliamentary committees than MPs that represent districts with weaker party subunits.

The empirical test is performed with MP-level data from thirteen legislatures in the already-familiar four post-communist democracies: the Czech Republic, Estonia, Hungary, and Poland. In a pooled analysis, and taking into account various control variables, MPs from districts with strong party branches are more likely to break party unity and hold leadership positions in parliamentary committees than MPs from districts with weak subunits. When analyzing each legislature separately, I find that both relationships hold in all four countries and in nine out of the thirteen legislative terms. In short, branches with strong organizations are powerful within the party in that they can influence the behavior of their MPs and the central party disproportionately.

These results suggest that increasing the organizational strength of some party subunits may change the power balance within the party away from the center to the organizationally strongest subunits. This provides one potential solution to the lack of uniformly strong party organizations in new democracies: the redistribution of power resulting from organization building may discourage leaders to invest in building any strong branches and instead encourage them to spend resources on national media campaigns. Seeing parties with weak organizations is, therefore, not surprising. Although the effects of unequal power distribution are similar for all parties, leaders of parties with weaker organization may be more conscious and concerned about this loss of power to branches if they strengthened the ground organization any further.

---

[1] However, see Giannetti and Laver (2001), Laver and Shepsle (1990), and Luebbert (1986), who account for preference diversity within parties when explaining coalition politics.

Because one of the variables considered in this chapter is the likelihood of an MP defecting against the party, and Chapter 4 focused on party unity, let me reiterate some points before the reader gets confused. The current chapter is about individual MPs and within-party variation in organizational strength. Chapter 4 was about party-level unity and across-party variation in party organizational strength. These chapters address essentially different research questions. In Chapter 4, I showed that parties with stronger organizations are more unified in parliament. That is, a party is more (less) unified compared to other parties when it has a strong (weak) organization. The current chapter, however, asks – regardless of the overall organizational strength of the party – if defection happens, who (i.e., what kind of an MP) is more likely to be that defector? Parties with strong organizations are generally more unified because they are generally electorally more valuable to MPs than weak parties. However, the rebels that do exist even in these strong parties are more likely to come from districts where the local party organization is strong than from districts where it is weak. Similarly, weak parties are, overall, less unified because they can offer fewer electoral benefits to their MPs. As the current chapter informs, however, the disunity is most likely caused by MPs from districts where the local party is the strongest. The overall party organizational strength can incentivize most MPs to comply with the party most of the time. However, this does not deny the possibility that defections may happen, nor does it contradict the argument that if defections do occur, they are more likely to be because of MPs whose local parties are strong.

Power Distribution within Political Parties

I treat political parties as organizations (Panebianco 1988; Schlesinger 1984) and build on theoretical insights from the literature on organizational behavior to develop an argument about the distribution of power within parties and the manifestation of this power distribution in MP behavior. Parties are likely to be different from business or voluntary organizations in that they operate in a political culture that sets certain expectations to the behavior of their members. However, they also share several characteristics with these types of organizations as well as with public-sector organizations (Schlesinger 1984). Furthermore, organizational theory, which acknowledges that different organizations operate in different environments, defines organizations in general terms as social structures with specific goals, clearly defined boundaries, and formal recognition (Pfeffer 1997), all of which are applicable to parties. Therefore, general ideas from organizational theory can still help us understand intra-party relationships.

Intraorganizational Power Distribution

Literature on organizational sociology suggests that power within an organization is not uniformly distributed. Rather, some subunits are more powerful than others owing to asymmetries in intraorganizational dependency relationships (Emerson 1962; Pfeffer 1994, 1997; Pfeffer and Salancik 2003; Tjosvold and Wisse 2009). Specifically, subunit power originates from its ability to cope with the uncertainty that the organization faces by having access to, and control over, crucial resources (Hickson et al. 1971; Hinings et al. 1974; Pfeffer and Salancik 2003). The general argument runs as follows: organizations require a supply of resources from the environment in order to operate. These resources vary in terms of how difficult they are to obtain or how critical they are to the functioning of the organization. Each subunit extracts some of these resources and provides them to others in exchange for those resources that they need. Because of the dependencies generated, asymmetries emerge: those subunits that are more effective in securing critical and difficult-to-obtain resources acquire more power. Some authors refer to the capacity to cope with uncertainty itself as the most critical resource that any organization needs (Pfeffer 1994, 1997; Pfeffer and Salancik 2003). Subunits possessing such capacity are expected to obtain more power; in that sense, resource dependence and uncertainty coping amount to the same argument (Astley and Sachdeva 1984).

The nature of uncertainty coping and resource dependence can vary over organizations and time. For example, in a study of a university, Salancik and Pfeffer (1974) show that the power of a university department is highly correlated with its ability to obtain outside grants and contracts – critical resources in a university setting. Crozier (1964) shows that the most powerful subunit in a tobacco factory was that of the maintenance engineers: they could manage the only real uncertainty ever faced by the plant – the breakdown of the highly automated cigarette manufacturing equipment.

In sum, subunit power within an organization is enhanced by its ability to effectively control resources that help reduce the uncertainty for the organization. In other words, power is directly proportional to the organizational value of the resource that the subunit provides and inversely proportional to the availability of this resource from other sources (Emerson 1962; see also Cook and Emerson 1978; Cook et al. 1983; Fligstein 1987; Pfeffer 1994, 1997; Pfeffer and Salancik 2003).

Intra-party Power Distribution

This argument can be applied to understanding the distribution of power within political parties. Parties, as other organizations, are not monolithic entities, but consist of various subunits, including party branches. Branches that are better at performing the essential tasks of the party are likely to be more powerful.

In line with the existing literature, I assume that a party's central goals include votes (plus office) and policy (Strom 1990). The essential tasks performed by party branches that help achieve these goals include communication with, and mobilization of, the electorate. Party subunits with strong organizations – those that are more strongly socially rooted with visible and active presence in local life via participating in local government and politics, being associated with locally known leaders and activists, and having local structures and membership – have more control over these sources of power than subunits with weak organizations. Several arguments and evidence presented in Chapters 2 and 3 support this line of reasoning.[2]

First, we saw that parties were more successful in winning votes in those electoral districts where they had stronger organizations. This was likely to occur for different related reasons: a local party branch with a strong local presence has greater expertise in how to present their party's message to the local electorate and how to run successful campaigns for the party in the national elections than a branch with little local-level presence and expertise. Furthermore, a local branch with a stronger organization, given its involvement in and contribution to local affairs, is likely to appear credible in the eyes of the local population. Branches with weak organizations, on the other hand, lack such credibility and are therefore less able to extract the critical resources (i.e., votes from the local electorate). As further argued in Chapter 2 and suggested by narratives in Chapter 3, participation in local politics permitted by strong local organization is especially relevant in helping parties survive. Strong local branches allow parties who experience political crises on the national level to recover and reestablish themselves through their involvement in local affairs. This ability to provide the necessary electoral resources at a particularly critical time, which weak branches lack, further underlines the value of the strong branches to the party.

Second, the functions that strong local organizations perform and that help them win votes also help a party reach its other central goal – success in policy making, both in terms of finding support for their policies and formulating popular new initiatives. Communication with the electorate is a crucial task in achieving this goal. As demonstrated by narratives in Chapter 3, local branches

---

[2] As especially Chapter 3 illustrated, post-communist leaders themselves have pointed out most of these arguments in interviews and opinion articles as reasons why local branches are valuable. To bring additional examples, one of the leaders of K in Estonia, Värner Lootsmann, stated, "It is the work at the local level that brings people to the realization that they need to vote for us" (Ideon 2000c). A leading politician from the Pro Patria party, Tõnis Lukas, wrote:

> "If a party has strong activists and many members in a given community then they can actively participate in the work of various foundations and organizations that help the party meet its programmatic goals, organize educational seminars, write to local newspapers, and otherwise engage in the day-to-day life of the community. All this makes the party visible and accessible to the voter" (Lukas 1995).

The leadership of the ERL stressed, "Only daily, planned activities by the local branches will bring us success" (Porila 1999). The general secretaries of the party acknowledged that active and strong local branches helped the party stay in touch with the opinions of its voters, create a stable electorate, and compensate for the shortage of financial resources (ERL Respondent 1, ERL Respondent 2, personal communication, August 6, 2007). Additionally, a local leader stressed that local presence allows for door-to-door campaigning, which is "the main way to get votes" (ERL Respondent 3, personal communication, August 13, 2007).

and their members help conduct grassroots campaigns for candidates as well as policy proposals, and are important resources for keeping a party in touch with public opinion. Organizationally strong branches that are involved in local politics can also serve as testing grounds for new policy ideas. Alternatively, by handling local problems, party branches may be able to develop effective and electorally popular policy initiatives that the national party can borrow for their national program.

In sum, party branches that have strong organizations should be better able to perform the central tasks of the party and thereby help the party succeed in elections and policy making than branches with weak organizations. Therefore, branches with strong organizations are likely to be more powerful than their organizationally weak counterparts.

Power within Parties and the Behavior of MPs

One observable implication of this theory is that the behavior and status of representatives from powerful subunits is likely to be different than the behavior of representatives from weak subunits. Specifically, the theory implies that MPs from districts with strong party branches are more likely to (1) behave independently in parliament and break party unity, and (2) hold powerful positions – such as leadership positions in parliamentary committees – than MPs from districts with weak party branches.

Parliamentary Voting Behavior

MPs are generally elected from specific electoral districts and are therefore tied, at least to some extent, to a party subunit in that district. Even in countries with one nationwide district, most MPs get their votes in a geographically concentrated manner and are tied to a geographically based party subunit (Crisp and Ingall 2002; Hazan 1999). Representatives are likely to be at least partially focused on issues and preferences of their district, and these preferences may not always be in line with those of the national party leadership. Several studies argue that there is an inherent tension between local- and national-level representation, and that the former is likely to lead to more individualistic behavior in parliament (Ames 2001; Bowler and Farrell 1993; Cain, Ferejohn, and Fiorina 1987; Carey 2009; Crisp et al. 2004; Morgenstern 2004; Sieberer 2006; Stratmann and Baur 2002). The pressure to sometimes prioritize local issues over national party interests, exerted by the local party organization or by voters directly, is likely to be present regardless of the strength of the local organization.[3] Where subunit power is likely to make a difference, however,

---

[3] In fact, MPs may be motivated to vote against the national party for reasons other than local pressures. The motivation is not of direct interest here. The argument here assumes that regardless of the motivation, MPs from strong party branches are more likely to act on this motivation because of the power of their branch within the party.

is in whether or not – and if so, how frequently – an MP chooses to give in to this pressure. MPs from more powerful subunits can pursue local or personal interests more freely, that is, with less fear of punishment by party leadership, than MPs from less powerful branches. Because the central party leadership depends crucially on the powerful subunits, they are more likely to overlook and not punish dissenting behavior by MPs from those subunits. MPs are likely to be prominent and critical actors in their branch; punishing them equals punishing the subunit, and this association is one way they can be shielded from the wrath of the central party. In cases where branches themselves, and not the central party leadership, are in charge of executing any punishments decided on the central level, a branch can protect MPs even more directly by refusing to discipline them. In sum, because subunits with strong local party organization are indispensable for the party leadership, MPs from districts with such subunits are more likely to vote against the party line than their co-partisans from districts with weak party subunits.[4]

An example may help illustrate the theoretical argument. In the Czech Republic, MP Vlasimil Tlusty, who belonged to the ruling ODS, frequently voted against the government's policy proposals throughout the 2006–2009 legislative term and was in general known as a rebel within the party. This led the national-level party leadership to call for the local branch to expel him from the party. The central party also wanted to expel another ODS rebel – Jan Schwippel – after he voted with the opposition to topple the ODS government in the spring of 2009 (CTK 2009d). However, the two MPs fared quite differently. Schwippel's branch was under a serious threat of dissolution if it did not expel the MP (CTK 2009c). The branch was weak: it only had five members, most of whom were Schwippel's own relatives, and doing away with it would not have done much harm to the party. Schwippel resigned on his own initiative to avoid the dissolution of the local organization. Tlusty's branch refused to abide by the leadership's request to expel him despite the potential threat of dissolution (CTK 2008c). This branch was considerably stronger, as indicated by the twenty-nine members who turned out to vote on Tlusty's case. The central office withdrew the calls for dissolving the branch (CTK 2009a). The local organization in question was simply too valuable an asset for the party.[5]

Committee Leadership Positions

Subunit power is manifested not only in voting behavior, but also in the positions MPs hold when in parliament. Some of these positions are more desirable than others because they allow for more resources, visibility, and/or policy influence. A leadership position within a parliamentary committee is an

---

[4] Candidate nomination rules are constant for all local branches of the same party. In the empirical analysis, party fixed effects control for any party-level variance in these rules.

[5] Tlusty left the party voluntarily in spring 2009 because he wanted to run in the election to the European Parliament – an opportunity offered him by another party.

example of such a position. Committee chairs and vice-chairs plan and direct the legislative, oversight, and appointment responsibilities of the committee and thereby potentially exercise more influence in the parliamentary arena than the ordinary members of the assembly. Indeed, literature on parliamentary politics in various contexts, including advanced democracies as well as the post-communist countries, treats committee leadership positions as influential and desirable (see Clark, Verseckaite, and Lukosaitis 2006; Fenno 1973; Holbrook and Tidmarch 1993; Smith and Remington 2001; R. Zubek 2008). Committee membership and leadership positions are generally decided at the party level. It is therefore fair to assume that intra-party power plays a role in who is nominated for a committee leadership position. If subunit strength indicates such power, then MPs from organizationally strong subunits are more likely to obtain leadership positions compared to their co-partisans from weak subunits. Party leadership may want to nominate MPs from powerful branches to influential positions in order to keep the branches motivated – to reward them for good work and give incentives to continue mobilizing and communicating with voters. In addition to the visibility and influence, such positions may also provide MPs better access to electorally valuable distributive goods, which further motivate and help the strong branches in their mobilization efforts.

Contrary to the arguments presented here, the existing literature has largely assumed that power within parties is concentrated in the hands of the leadership who have demonstrated their superiority of expertise or other skills and have therefore become indispensable for members (Michels 1966; Panebianco 1988; Scarrow, Webb, and Farrell 2002). These studies generally disregard party subunits as potential loci of power and therefore provide no prediction about the distribution of power beyond the leadership, or implicitly assume that all subunits possess equally little power because the center has an equal control over party subunits via the allocation of resources such as funding and a party label. For the relationship explored here, this would mean that an MP's branch affiliation plays no role in his or her behavior or position in parliament.[6]

Research Design

In order to test the proposed hypotheses, I have collected information from thirteen legislative terms: the Czech Republic, 1996–1998, 1998–2002, 2002 2006, 2006–2009;[7] Estonia, 1999–2003, 2003–2007; Hungary, 1994–1998,

---

[6] There is also literature on federal regimes, especially in Latin America, that focuses on determining whether party delegations from the same state vote in a similar manner (Cantu and Desposato 2009; Cheibub, Figueiredo, and Limongi 2009; Desposato 2004; Rosas and Langston 2011). However, this literature is mostly concerned with the representation of local versus national interests and does not address asymmetries in intra-party power distribution.

[7] The elections for the Chamber of Deputies were eventually held in May 2010. However, I have included votes only until the incumbent Prime Minister Mirek Topolánek lost a vote of no-confidence in March 2009 and the caretaker government of experts took office shortly after.

1998–2002, 2002–2006, 2006–2010; and Poland 1997–2001, 2001–2005, 2005–2007 for all MPs that belong to a party (i.e., excluding independents).[8] I will first perform the analyses on the pooled dataset, and then reestimate the models on each parliamentary term separately.

Analysis I: Subunit Strength and Voting Behavior

The first hypothesis to be tested is that MPs from districts where their party has a stronger local organization are more likely to vote against the party line than their co-partisans from districts where the local party organization is weak. The dependent variable for this analysis – "Defection rate" or the rate at which an MP has defected from the party line of voting – is measured on the basis of MP voting records in a given legislative term. In all four countries almost all votes, with only a handful of exceptions, are publicly recorded votes. As previously argued, this avoids selection bias in determining MPs' voting behavior (Carrubba et al. 2006). Specifically, the measure identifies the share of recorded votes by a given legislator that deviate from the party line of voting. Following previous research, I infer party line from the behavior of the majority of its members who are present and participate in voting (Carey 2009; Skjæveland 2001). That is, when a majority of party members vote yes, then no and abstain votes are coded as defections.[9] When no majority of party members who are present vote the same way, then there is no party line and no defections are possible. The participation rate can vary significantly and it is fair to assume that votes where very few party members participate are not important to the party and no clear party position exists. Therefore, for measurement purposes, defection is only possible in the case of those votes where the majority (at least 50 percent) of party members were present and voting.[10] The formal presentation of the measurement of this variable is given in Appendix 5.1. The measure ranges from 0 to 1. The values in all countries and parliamentary terms are highly

---

[8] Some MPs switched their party affiliation in the middle of the parliamentary term. If they became independents or switched to a newly created parliamentary party that had no record of organizational strength, then they were excluded from the analysis after the switch. Those switching to an existing party are included both before and after the switch, that is, the same MP is included twice with the same district of origin but different party affiliation. This offers a more difficult test of the hypothesis because the newly switched MPs may feel more pressure to comply with the party leadership in order to be accepted even if they are representing a district with a strong branch. Excluding these MPs from the analysis after they had switched parties does not change the substantive results.

[9] Voting abstain is possible in all countries included in the study but the Czech Republic. Absences are not treated as abstentions. Results are substantively similar when abstentions are excluded.

[10] In an alternative analysis, I used weighted defection, that is, a measure of the dependent variable where each defection was weighted by the share of party members present, in order to further adjust the measure according to the importance of the vote by giving higher significance to better-attended votes. The results of the alternative analyses were similar to the ones presented here.

skewed toward the low end of the scale as most MPs vote with the party most of the time (although the share of zeros per se is less than 1 percent). Therefore, I have log transformed the dependent variable before using it in the analysis.[11]

The independent variable, "Subunit organizational strength" was defined as the extensive local presence of the local party unit and its participation in local affairs. This variable is measured by the district-level indicator of participation in local elections used in Chapter 2, that is, the share of local governments within the MP's electoral district in which a party runs its candidates in the local government election under the MP's party label. The theoretical range of the measure is from 0 to 1.[12] For each parliamentary term, I consider those local elections that immediately preceded or occurred in the same year as the start of that parliamentary term.[13] Therefore, the values of this variable are different for the different parliamentary terms of one country.[14] Descriptive statistics for the dependent and independent variables are available in Appendix 5.2.

Other variables may account for why some MPs are more rebellious than others. I control for seniority, which can be measured in two different ways. First, "Parliamentary term" indicates the length of an MP's political career. It

[11] For all parliamentary terms analyzed, the dependent variable appears normally distributed after the log transformation, suggesting that it is appropriate to use OLS. Logit transformation of the dependent variable does not change the results. The inferences from more complex models meant for analyzing proportions data such as fractional logit (Papke and Wooldridge 1996) and extended beta binomial (Palmquist 1999) are also similar to the ones reported here. The results of these models are presented in Appendix 5.3.

[12] In some cases (the Czech Republic 1996–1998 and 1998–2002, and Estonia all terms) the capital city constitutes a single municipality within a single (or even multiple) electoral district. The measure for the organizational strength of the party subunit in the capital city can then only take one of the extreme values: 0 or 1. In order to avoid potential bias in the estimations that this can cause, I have excluded the local elections in the capital city from those cases. For Warsaw in Poland, I have treated the ten to twenty-two municipal districts of the capital city as separate municipalities for the purposes of calculating the organizational-strength score (see also Chapter 2) to avoid losing additional cases.

[13] In none of the cases were local elections held concurrently with parliamentary elections. Local elections were held in the same year (but not at the same time) as the parliamentary elections in all but five cases: the Czech Republic 1996–1998 (local elections in 1994), Estonia 2003–2007 (local elections in 2002), and Poland all datasets (local elections in 1994, 1998, and 2002). Because the findings for these five parliamentary terms are not systematically different from the rest, the timing of local elections does not seem to affect the results.

[14] Hungary employs a mixed electoral system and therefore has two different kinds of districts: SMD and PR districts. The latter overlap with county borders and the SMDs are embedded in counties. In order to accurately test the theoretical argument, the analysis needs to include information about party subunits at the same hierarchical level. That is why I have measured organizational strength at the county level. This is justified because MPs from SMDs in a given county belong to that county's party branch although they may also belong to a party subunit in a subcounty (i.e., SMD) level. One may still argue that the measure is more appropriate for MPs from the PR districts only. The results of the analyses of the Hungarian cases are similar when the MPs from SMDs are excluded. However, I decided to include all MPs for the sake of generalizability.

is measured by the number of terms (including the current one) that an MP has served in parliament. Second, "National politician" – measured by whether or not a given MP has held or is holding a cabinet position – indicates seniority in terms of one's position in the party. The predictions of the effects of these variables are not straightforward. On the one hand, politicians who have been in parliament longer and have more seniority may be less likely to break party unity (Bowler et al. 1999) because their longevity and position are likely to be due, at least partially, to their loyalty (see Kam 2009). Furthermore, it is likely that such senior members belong to the party leadership and have an active role in designing party policies in the first place. On the other hand, nationally known politicians may have built strong personal reputations, feel less dependent on their party, and be more likely to vote against the party line.

Party dummies are also included in order to accurately capture the intra-party rather than cross-party effects. Parties may differ in their overall level of voting unity. For example, opposition parliamentarians may be more likely to break party unity than coalition politicians, regardless of their local ties, given that they have lower stakes in the policy-making process (Owens 2003). Similarly, other party-specific factors may influence the likelihood of defections. For example, parties with centralized nomination rules may be more coherent (although, see Shomer 2009), and those with no real chance of winning or losing as a result of defections (i.e., very small and very big parties) face no real incentive to preserve unity (Bowler et al. 1999). The analyses of the pooled dataset also control for country dummies, parliamentary-term dummies, and electoral-district dummies, and employ robust standard errors. In the analyses of the separate parliamentary terms, district-level correlation is accounted for by the robust standard errors clustered on electoral district.

Results of Analysis I: MP Voting Behavior

Table 5.1 presents the results of the pooled dataset and the thirteen parliamentary term-level datasets using OLS regression. The table is arranged with independent variables in columns and different analyses in rows. Pooling across all countries and parliamentary terms, the strength of the local party organization is positively and significantly associated with the frequency of defections. MPs from districts where the local party organization has strong grassroots presence behave more independently in parliament than their co-partisans from districts where the local party organization is weak. This effect holds in nine out of thirteen parliamentary terms analyzed. Furthermore, the fact that it holds in all four countries is suggestive of a general effect. Overall, there is a very strong relationship between local subunit strength and the likelihood of MP dissent.

Because the dependent variable is log transformed, the coefficients of the independent variables can be interpreted as the percent change in the dependent variable given one unit change in the independent variable (Wooldridge 2002). One unit increase in the strength of the local party organization implies a

TABLE 5.1. *Regression Analysis of the Effect of Subunit Organizational Strength on Defections*

	Org. Strength	Parl. Term	National Polit.	Constant	R^2	N
Pooled	0.468***	0.090***	0.074**	−4.181***	0.51	3931
	(0.098)	(0.010)	(0.033)	(0.094)		
Czech R.	0.855***	0.022	−0.005	−4.283***	0.59	216
1996–1998	(0.234)	(0.069)	(0.110)	(0.164)		
Czech R.	0.727***	0.005	−0.077	−3.563***	0.38	182
1998–2002	(0.127)	(0.013)	(0.089)	(0.081)		
Czech R.	0.398***	0.110***	0.324**	−5.115***	0.18	235
2002–2006	(0.134)	(0.023)	(0.130)	(0.171)		
Czech R.	−0.170	0.146***	0.316**	−5.055***	0.28	208
2006–2009	(0.165)	(0.048)	(0.149)	(0.396)		
Estonia	0.270***	0.051	0.172	−3.859***	0.12	80
1999–2003	(0.081)	(0.090)	(0.153)	(0.135)		
Estonia	−0.062	0.099	−0.051	−5.482***	0.05	106
2003–2007	(0.524)	(0.132)	(0.188)	(0.872)		
Hungary	−0.100	−0.021	−0.143	−2.852***	0.51	365
1994–1998	(0.084)	(0.104)	(0.065)	(0.142)		
Hungary	0.297*	0.180***	0.014	−3.678***	0.47	324
1998–2002	(0.163)	(0.054)	(0.112)	(0.543)		
Hungary	0.395***	0.050	0.001	−4.525***	0.29	372
2002–2006	(0.117)	(0.042)	(0.086)	(0.198)		
Hungary	0.220***	0.087***	−0.052	−3.937***	0.58	366
2006–2010	(0.062)	(0.020)	(0.088)	(0.110)		
Poland	0.252***	0.180***	−0.020	−3.638***	0.26	481
1997–2001	(0.103)	(0.033)	(0.066)	(0.098)		
Poland	−0.164	0.134***	0.135*	−4.187***	0.50	311
2001–2005	(0.185)	(0.024)	(0.081)	(0.111)		
Poland	0.411***	0.070***	0.251**	−3.886***	0.62	450
2005–2007	(0.113)	(0.021)	(0.107)	(0.127)		

Note: Table entries are unstandardized regression coefficients with robust standard errors in parentheses. Dependent variable is the natural log of "Defection rate." The pooled model includes country, term, party, and district dummies. All other models include party dummies. $*p \leq 0.1$, $**p \leq 0.05$, $***p \leq 0.01$

change from the minimum to the theoretical maximum, because the variable ranges from 0 to 1. The latter may not always be the actual maximum, although in most cases it closely approximates it. With these caveats in mind, the results for the pooled model suggest that one unit increase in subunit organizational strength results in about 49 percent increase in the defection rate. To avoid the extreme values, it is also helpful to consider changes from one SD below to one SD above the mean value of organizational strength. The effect of such a change is comparable and increases the expected defection rate from 0.025 to 0.032.

The substantive effects are also sizable for the nine parliamentary terms with statistically significant results. The results for the Czech Republic show very strong effects: a one-unit increase (i.e., an increase from 0 to 1) in subunit organizational strength results in 86 percent, 73 percent, and 40 percent increase in the defection rate in 1996–1998, 1998–2002, and 2002–2006, respectively. For the other cases, this effect is somewhat lower, ranging from 22 percent and 25 percent in Hungary (2006–2010) and Poland (1997–2001), respectively, to about 30–40 percent in Estonia (1999–2003), Hungary (1998–2002, 2002–2006), and Poland (2005–2007). These results suggest that the intraorganizational power of strong subunits enables MPs from those subunits not to follow the central party line if it contradicts their personal or constituency preferences. Although all MPs may have equally strong incentives to sometimes serve their personal or constituency interests by dissenting from the party line in parliament, those from more powerful branches are more likely to get away with such dissent.

A few words are in order about the datasets where the hypothesis did not find support. Because there was one failing case for all countries, the reasons for finding a null effect are not likely to be country specific but specific to a parliamentary term. A few possible factors separate the failing cases from the rest: the entry of many or large new parties to the parliament, party splits, and a polarized legislature. Estonia and Poland both witnessed the emergence of successful new parties in which the internal organizational-power distribution may not have taken root yet. In Estonia, RP entered parliament for the first time in 2003, tying for the largest number of seats in parliament. In Poland, a total of three new parties entered the 2001 parliament: Law and Justice (PiS), Civic Platform (PO), and League of Polish Families (LPR). It is possible that in new parties and legislatures dominated by these parties, the personal attributes of the MPs have a stronger effect on voting behavior than any organizational factors. Additionally, in Hungary, the right-wing parties of KDNP and FKgP experienced significant splits during the 1994–1998 legislative term. As was the case with new party entry, during the institutional flux created by party splits, the patterns of power distribution may be disrupted. Finally, in the Czech Republic the parliament was significantly polarized during the 2006–2009 legislative term, and the government controlled only a slim (if any) majority. This may also have altered the intra-party power dynamics by making it more costly to defect. Future studies may want to more systematically analyze conditions under which intraorganizational power structure breaks down or changes. The failing cases may be especially informative for this purpose.

Alternative Explanations

The analysis so far provides significant evidence that MPs from districts with weak party branches are more loyal to the party leadership in their parliamentary behavior than MPs from districts with strong party branches. This finding gives some credence to the argument that organizational strength increases the power of the party subunit as suggested by the theory. However, the proposed relationship may emerge for reasons other than the one suggested here.

For example, it is possible that MPs from districts that have strong organizations behave independently not because of the strength of the subunits, but because of their personal characteristics or attributes. It may even be that the local organization, rather than empowering the MP, is strong only because of the strength of their MP. There is some evidence that MPs with local-level representative experience – local politicians – are less dependent on parties for their (political) careers because of their local prominence and therefore more likely to break party unity (Tavits 2009a). This is in line with the theoretical logic about the distribution of power within the organization proposed here, but focuses on the individual rather than organizational attributes, and therefore represents a potential alternative causal mechanism. "Local politician" is measured by a dummy variable coded "1" for those MPs that have had subnational-level representative experience as mayors or local or regional councilors in their electoral district prior to or simultaneously with their current national legislative appointment.[15]

Another alternative interpretation of the relationship proposed here is that MPs from districts with strong party organizations appear more independent not because of the power of their branch but because in such districts the intra-party competition for a seat is more fierce. Strong subunits are more likely to have more members – that is, more potential candidates to choose from – than weak ones. Strong subunits are also more likely than weak subunits to participate in local politics and local affairs in other ways, which helps a greater number of potential candidates obtain local name recognition and gather political experience. Therefore, in districts where the party has a strong as opposed to a weak organization, there are more likely to be a number of well-qualified candidates, and intra-party competition for votes is greater. This incentivizes MPs from that district to differentiate themselves from co-partisans (Carey and Shugart 1995). One way to do so is to behave more independently in parliament. The level of internal competition can be controlled for by the "Number of competitors" – a variable measured for each MP as the number of co-partisan MPs from his or her district. Because district size varies within datasets, this measure, to an extent, also represents district size in addition to competitiveness.[16]

---

[15] The information was obtained from the following sources: Czech Republic: Web sites of political parties, MPs' personal Web sites, Třeštík (2005), and various Web pages containing biographical data for MPs; Estonia: Web site of the parliament at www.riigikogu.ee; Hungary: Web site of the parliament at www.parlament.hu; Poland: Kancelaria Sejmu (1999; 2002; 2006).

[16] In Hungary, because the MPs from SMDs are not competing against the PR MPs from their county, this variable is coded "0" for SMD MPs and the number of county-level PR co-MPs for PR MPs. Such measurement also effectively controls for whether or not an MP is from an SMD or PR list.

Third, I argued that some subunits are more powerful within the party because their organization is stronger at the grassroots level, and therefore better able to perform the tasks central to the party – winning votes and communicating with the electorate. One might argue that the reported finding is not because of any organizational strength, but solely owing to the electoral strength of the party in some districts compared to others. In order to control for such a possibility, I will also include a variable measuring the "Vote share" for each party in each district in the national election that occurred prior to the start of the parliamentary term.

Before presenting the results, it is worth noting that these new variables are, in most of the thirteen datasets, highly correlated with each other and with the measure of organizational strength. Therefore, these additional tests pose an extra challenge for detecting any organizational effects. If these effects still emerge, we can be more confident that the strength of the organizational subunits truly matters for the parliamentary independence of the MPs from those subunits.

Table 5.2 presents the results of the analyses that include these additional controls. I have only included those parliamentary terms from Table 5.1 where the hypothesized relationship found support; the modeling techniques remain the same. In the case of the pooled dataset and nine datasets for different parliamentary terms, the effect of the strength of local party organization is still significantly and positively related to the voting behavior of the MPs from these organizations: the stronger the local organization, the more likely an MP is to dissent from the party line of voting. Because MPs from organizationally stronger subunits are systematically more likely to break party unity in parliament – regardless of any personal-level characteristics that may make some MPs more or less independent – this additional evidence suggests that local organizations have a direct and robust influence on the behavior of their MPs. The hypothesized effect does not occur simply because of the personal attributes of MPs, the level of electoral competitiveness, and the electoral strength of the party.

In sum, MPs from organizationally stronger subunits are systematically more likely to break party unity in parliament than MPs from weak subunits. This implies that stronger subunits are able to provide MPs with something that weak subunits are not: arguably because of the extent of intraorganizational power they command, they enable MPs not to follow the central party line if it contradicts their personal or constituency preferences.

Before proceeding, I would like to, once again, contrast the results presented here with those presented in Chapter 4. Recall that Chapter 4 argued that parties with strong organizations are more likely to be unified because they are electorally more valuable to the MPs and thereby elicit compliance. The findings here show that, regardless of the overall level of party organizational strength, if defection happens, it is more likely to be committed by an MP from an organizationally strong rather than weak party subunit. This does not deny

TABLE 5.2. *Regression Analysis of the Effect of Subunit Organizational Strength on Defections, Additional Variables*

Dataset	Independent Variables						Constant	R²	N
	Org. Strength	Parl. Term	National Polit.	Local Polit.	No. Competitors	Vote Share			
Pooled	0.474***	0.090***	0.072**	-0.022	0.005*	-0.006	-4.055***	0.51	3927
	(0.099)	(0.010)	(0.033)	(0.027)	(0.003)	(0.004)	(0.151)		
Czech R. 1996–1998	0.935**	0.018	-0.016	-0.026	-0.009	0.006	-4.246***	0.59	216
	(0.297)	(0.072)	(0.112)	(0.064)	(0.017)	(0.010)	(0.188)		
Czech R. 1998–2002	0.784***	0.009	-0.078	0.058	0.000	-0.005	-3.528***	0.39	182
	(0.183)	(0.014)	(0.095)	(0.066)	(0.006)	(0.006)	(0.072)		
Czech R. 2002–2006	0.657***	0.105***	0.330**	-0.059	-0.025*	-0.006	-5.010***	0.20	235
	(0.124)	(0.028)	(0.137)	(0.111)	(0.012)	(0.008)	(0.173)		
Estonia 1999–2003	0.382***	0.003	0.191	-0.168	-0.024	-1.603	-3.234***	0.15	80
	(0.101)	(0.115)	(0.131)	(0.266)	(0.042)	(1.068)	(0.448)		
Hungary 1998–2002	0.307*	0.177***	0.029	0.034	-0.009	0.895	-3.709***	0.48	324
	(0.189)	(0.057)	(0.111)	(0.070)	(0.016)	(0.966)	(0.476)		
Hungary 2002–2006	0.274*	0.054	-0.043	0.044	0.001	-1.336*	-4.096***	0.32	368
	(0.163)	(0.041)	(0.102)	(0.068)	(0.006)	(0.736)	(0.161)		
Hungary 2006–2010	0.184***	0.089***	-0.073	-0.037	0.001	-1.029	-3.823***	0.34	366
	(0.065)	(0.020)	(0.099)	(0.062)	(0.001)	(0.743)	(0.141)		
Poland 1997–2001	0.221**	0.181***	-0.007	0.031	-0.010	0.276	-3.664***	0.27	481
	(0.111)	(0.033)	(0.069)	(0.051)	(0.010)	(0.346)	(0.111)		
Poland 2005–2007	0.396***	0.075***	0.276**	0.076	-0.002	0.494	-3.975***	0.62	450
	(0.137)	(0.020)	(0.110)	(0.057)	(0.018)	(0.504)	(0.159)		

Note: Table entries are unstandardized regression coefficients with robust standard errors clustered on electoral district in parentheses. Dependent variable is the natural log of "Defection rate." The pooled model includes country, term, party, and district dummies, all other models include party dummies.
*p ≤ 0.1, **p ≤ 0.05, ***p ≤ 0.01

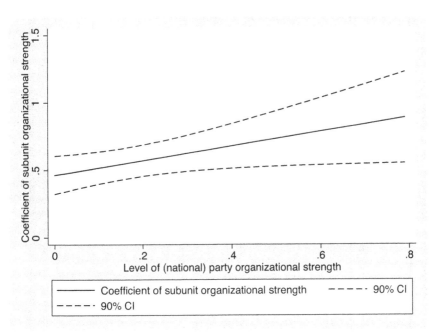

FIGURE 5.1. The effect of subunit organizational strength on the likelihood of defection conditional on party organizational strength at the national level.

the possibility that parties with strong organizations are still, overall, more unified than parties with weak organizations. However, in order to explore in more detail whether and how the effect of subunit strength varies for parties with different (national-level) organizational strength, I used the pooled model presented in Table 5.2 and estimated an interaction effect between the overall (national-level) party organizational strength and subunit organizational strength on the likelihood of defecting against the party. As expected, the effect of party organizational strength was negative and significant, and remained so for all except the most extreme high value of subunit organizational strength: MPs from parties with strong organizations are generally less likely to defect than their counterparts from weak parties. This confirms the results presented in Chapter 4. As also expected, the effect of subunit organizational strength was positive and significant. Calculating the full set of conditional coefficients indicated that this effect remained positive and statistically significant (at the 1 percent level) for all values of the (national-level) party organizational strength (i.e., for all parties regardless of their organizational strength). This finding is presented in Figure 5.1. As is also evident from the figure, however, the effect is considerably stronger – the conditional coefficient of subunit organizational strength is greater – for parties with nationally strong rather than weak organizations. Strong subunits are powerful in every party, but they are especially powerful in organizationally strong parties.

Analysis II: Committee Leadership Positions

In addition to voting behavior, I have also hypothesized that subunit power can be manifested in the committee leadership positions. Specifically, because these positions are desirable and influential within the parliament, the party leadership should fill them with MPs who command more intraorganizational power, that is, those MPs who are associated with strong party branches. In order to test this hypothesis, I have assembled information on committee chairs and vice-chairs in each parliamentary term. In all four countries included in this study, these positions are filled with MPs from both the coalition and opposition parties, and committee membership and nomination for leadership positions are decided at the party level. The variable is labeled "Committee leadership position" and coded "1" if a given MP holds (at least) one such position during a given parliamentary term and "0" otherwise.[17] On average, about 20–30 percent of MPs had held such a position. The average is higher (52 percent) in the Czech Chamber of Deputies in 2006–2009. The descriptive statistics are presented in Appendix 5.2.

Table 5.3 presents the results of probit regressions using committee leadership position, which is a binary measure, as the dependent variable and subunit organizational strength as the independent variable. For the sake of consistency, all control variables and modeling techniques remain the same as in Table 5.2.[18]

As the results show, subunit organizational strength has a positive and significant effect on the probability of holding committee leadership positions. MPs that come from organizationally strong party subunits are more likely to become committee chairs and vice-chairs than their co-partisans from weak subunits. This general pattern supports the substantive conclusion drawn from the analysis of parliamentary voting – organizationally strong subunits are likely to command more intra-party power than weak subunits. The effect holds in nine of the thirteen parliamentary terms analyzed. Furthermore, note that although this effect is not statistically significant in all datasets, there is no dataset where both tests (Tables 5.1/5.2 and Table 5.3) generate insignificant results. At least one of the alternative measures of the dependent variable (i.e., either the defection rate or the committee leadership position) is related to organizational strength in a statistically significant manner in all thirteen cases.

The substantive effects of organizational strength can be gauged by looking at the changes in predicted probabilities of holding a committee leadership

---

[17] Data sources: Czech Republic: Web site of the Chamber of Deputies http://www.psp.cz/sqw/hp.sqw; Estonia: Mõttus (2004) and Sikk (2007); Hungary: Web site of the National Assembly www.parlament.hu; Poland: Web site of Sejm www.sejm.gov.pl.

[18] In some models, some party dummies were dropped and the corresponding observations not used because these predicted success or failure perfectly: ODA in Czech R. (1996–1998), Christian Democratic Union (KDU-ČSL) in Czech R. (2006–2009), KE in Estonia (1999–2003), FKgP in Hungary (1998–2002), KPN in Poland (1997–2001). In the pooled model, several party and district dummies were also dropped for the same reason. Estonia 1999–2003 was estimated with robust, not clustered robust standard errors because of too few cases.

TABLE 5.3. *Probit Regression of the Effect of Subunit Organizational Strength on the Probability of Holding a Committee Leadership Position*

				Independent Variables					
Dataset	Org. Strength b (rob. SE)	Parl. Term b (rob. SE)	National Pol. b (rob. SE)	Local pol. b (rob. SE)	No. competitors b (rob. SE)	Vote Share b (rob. SE)	Constant b (rob. SE)	Pseudo-R²	N
Pooled	0.492*** (0.198)	0.300*** (0.024)	0.045 (0.069)	−0.186*** (0.060)	−0.009* (0.006)	−0.016* (0.009)	−0.260 (0.332)	0.13	3870
Czech R. 1996–1998	2.791* (1.517)	0.656*** (0.163)	−0.645* (0.379)	−0.714*** (0.176)	−0.090* (0.053)	0.046 (0.034)	−1.107*** (0.422)	0.21	196
Czech R. 1998–2002	2.409* (1.392)	0.468*** (0.068)	−0.331 (0.312)	0.303** (0.151)	−0.036** (0.018)	−0.040** (0.019)	−1.419*** (0.449)	0.12	182
Czech R. 2002–2006	0.530** (0.258)	0.305*** (0.044)	−0.081 (0.354)	−0.236 (0.301)	0.083*** (0.030)	−0.075*** (0.020)	0.502 (0.526)	0.11	235
Czech R. 2006–2009	1.011*** (0.322)	0.313*** (0.079)	−0.421* (0.270)	−0.463* (0.316)	−0.006 (0.033)	−0.036** (0.018)	−0.124 (0.662)	0.11	195
Estonia 1999–2003	−0.078 (0.353)	0.320 (0.314)	0.557 (0.319)	0.560 (0.457)	−0.148 (0.190)	−0.271 (1.786)	−5.438*** (0.484)	0.13	80
Estonia 2003–2007	0.859* (0.458)	0.042 (0.246)	−0.117 (0.342)	−0.632** (0.313)	−0.372*** (0.096)	1.328 (2.138)	−0.970 (0.966)	0.10	106

Hungary 1994–1998	0.586* (0.305)	0.636*** (0.242)	0.147 (0.235)	0.053 (0.256)	0.037 (0.026)	2.946 (3.765)	−3.035*** (0.991)	0.09	365
Hungary 1998–2002	0.099 (0.331)	0.272* (0.176)	0.522** (0.235)	−0.038 (0.166)	0.032 (0.025)	0.072 (0.904)	−0.913*** (0.241)	0.06	315
Hungary 2002–2006	0.583** (0.265)	0.195 (0.199)	0.365* (0.261)	−0.183 (0.152)	−0.004 (0.007)	−3.259** (1.585)	−0.540 (0.621)	0.06	368
Hungary 2006–2010	0.194 (0.253)	0.223*** (0.063)	0.078 (0.202)	−0.238 (0.203)	−0.008*** (0.003)	−1.072 (1.318)	−1.252** (0.550)	0.08	366
Poland 1997–2001	0.873** (0.406)	0.361*** (0.071)	−0.192 (0.231)	−0.117 (0.184)	0.061*** (0.019)	−0.752 (0.818)	−1.088*** (0.270)	0.13	474
Poland 2001–2005	0.621* (0.418)	0.327*** (0.079)	−0.197 (0.284)	−0.019 (0.188)	0.041 (0.047)	0.079 (0.888)	−1.253*** (0.357)	0.07	311
Poland 2005–2007	0.023 (0.441)	0.267*** (0.070)	−0.337 (0.436)	−0.284* (0.151)	0.033 (0.060)	0.049 (1.721)	−1.411*** (0.472)	0.06	450

Note: Table entries are unstandardized probit coefficients with robust standard in parentheses. Dependent variable is "Committee leadership position." The pooled model includes country, term, party, and district dummies, and all other models include party dummies. $^* p \leq 0.1$, $^{**} p \leq 0.05$, $^{***} p \leq 0.01$

position when the value of organizational strength is increased from its actual minimum to actual maximum and all other variables are held at their mean (for continuous variables) or median (for categorical variables). This change is quite sizeable in some cases: organizational strength has the strongest effect on the likelihood of holding a committee leadership position in the 1996–1998 Czech assembly (change in predicted probability = 0.54) followed by the 1998–2002 and the 2006–2009 Czech assemblies and the 1997–2001 Polish Sejm (change in predicted probability ≈ 0.35). The effect is somewhat weaker for the other dataset with the change in predicted probabilities ranging from 0.08 (Hungary 1994–1998) to 0.18 (Poland 2001–2005). Furthermore, because the dependent variable represents a binary outcome, one can interpret predicted probabilities above 0.5 as predictions of holding a leadership position and those below 0.5 as predictions of not holding one. In four datasets with significant results in Table 5.3 (the Czech Republic 1998–2002, 2002–2006, 2006–2009, and Poland 1997–2001), the outcome predicted for MPs from the strongest subunits is different from that for MPs from the weakest subunits – the former are likely to hold a committee leadership position; the latter are not. Overall, these results provide further support that organizationally stronger subunits are powerful in that they can influence the central leadership disproportionately.

Conclusion

This chapter explored the internal power distribution within political parties. I argued that those party branches that have a strong organization on the grass-roots level are more likely to be powerful within the party than branches with weak organizations. Organizational strength leads to power because branches with a strong organization are better able to perform the central tasks of the party (communication with and mobilization of the electorate) and thereby decrease uncertainty about achieving the main goals of the party (votes and policy).

I tested this argument by considering the relative independence and visibility of MPs elected from districts where party branches are strong compared to MPs elected from districts with weak branches. Specifically, I considered the likelihood of MPs to vote against the official party line and occupy positions important for the party in public office. The results of the analyses using data from different parliamentary terms in four post-communist countries confirm that MPs from districts where the local party organization is strong are more likely to behave independently in parliament and ignore the party line of voting. This effect is not an artifact of MPs' personal characteristics or party's electoral popularity but is likely to result from a direct influence of the power of local party subunits on the behavior of the MP. That MPs from strong party subunits can ignore the party leadership in voting strongly suggests that such subunits are powerful within the party. Further support for this inference was provided by the result that MPs from organizationally strong subunits are more likely to hold leadership positions within parliamentary committees than their co-partisans from weak subunits.

The findings in this chapter together with those in Chapters 2–4 imply that party leaders face a nontrivial dilemma: by strengthening their party organization on the ground in different electoral districts, they potentially improve its electability, and possibly survival chances. However, they simultaneously risk losing intra-party power to the organizationally strong subunits. The prospects of such power redistribution may make organization building less appealing. The presence of strong branches means that decision making is effectively no longer concentrated in the hands of the leadership, and that the latter will need to negotiate and build coalitions with the organizationally strong branches to get things done. The leadership needs to take into account, if not follow, the interests and preferences of these branches and cannot operate as freely, quickly, and without constraint as they could in the absence of strong branches. Indeed, commentators in the region have pointed out that strong party structure at the local level increases the personal influence of activists from that branch (Polish News Bulletin 2001d), and that the support of such branches is necessary for the party leader to construct a power base within the party (CTK 1994c). Therefore, although the attraction of a strong organization may be significant, its positive consequences may seem less tangible and certain than the fear of losing power – a consequence that is visible not once every few years but on a daily basis in the intra-party interactions.

Of course, strong branches are powerful in (nationally) strong and weak parties alike. However, the results also showed that the power of strong subunits is especially intense in strong as opposed to weak parties. Therefore, the leadership of organizationally weak parties may be especially reluctant to strengthen their party organizations any further, because by strengthening the overall party organization, they are also increasingly empowering stronger subunits. Similarly, for the leadership of a newly created party (as many parties in new democracies are), the relationship uncovered here provides incentives to not even start building a significant ground organization. Given this, especially in the volatile and unpredictable context of new democracies, party leadership may choose to try their electoral luck with the help of national media campaigns if it means that they can maintain centralized control over party affairs. It is, therefore, not surprising that parties do not necessarily have strong organizations.

Before closing, let me highlight some additional contributions of the findings in this chapter. By providing a way to understand power distribution within political parties, the results of this chapter enhance our understanding of the internal life of parties in general. Specifically, the asymmetry in power distribution may have an impact on party behavior in different arenas, which future studies of party politics may want to account for. Additionally, the chapter provides important implications to the literature on representation and party unity in parliament. The existing studies have mainly focused on the incentives provided by electoral systems and other institutional structures to explain why MPs stay loyal to the party and represent national-level issues or become more parochial and ignore the party line in their representational style. The findings here suggest that (1) under similar electoral rules, and (2) within the same party under similar party rules MPs still behave differently. The power distribution within parties itself can determine where MPs' loyalties lie, and these informal ways in which power is accrued may be more difficult to control by electoral or party rules.

6

Environment, Ideology, and Leaders

Why Do Some Parties Have a Strong and Others a Weak Organization?

The previous chapters have shown that parties in new democracies have contradictory incentives with regard to organization building. However, these contradictory incentives are present for all parties and it, therefore, remains unclear why some parties build strong organizations and others do not. The current chapter focuses on this very question – one that has received virtually no attention in the existing literature. A few studies have discussed the origins of organizational models and styles in the case of Western European party systems. However, the explanations provided do not appear to be very generalizable, especially to party systems under consideration here – those of new democracies – and are not necessarily helpful in explaining organizational strength. For example, Duverger (1954) and Panebianco (1988) have argued that the resources available at the time of parties' inceptions and other factors resulting from historical path dependency influence organizational style. This explanation may help understand why, in advanced democracies, parties that were created at different times in history under different circumstances have evolved over the decades or centuries into organizations of diverging strength. However, the argument is not likely to apply in new democracies, where parties emerged relatively simultaneously, with all possessing relatively comparable resources and none being tied to any particular social cleavage. Other explanations refer to contextual factors such as the type of electoral system, party system, population density, and so forth, which operate on the national level (Harmel and Janda 1982; R. Katz 1980; Lowenberg and Patterson 1979; Tan 2000) and are therefore not able to account for differences across parties in the same country.

In this chapter, I argue that a strong party organization is more likely to emerge when a party has an extra incentive to build such an organization and is capable of acting on this incentive. The extra incentive is likely to be present for parties that (1) experience hostile electoral environments and therefore believe that no other vote-getting strategy but building a strong organization will be effective, or (2) have chosen to target an electorate (e.g., poor and rural voters) that is hard to reach by other means. Capacity to follow through with organization building, in turn, is likely to depend on whether or not the parties have professional leaders with the necessary skills and motivations. The following discussion elaborates on this general argument by first examining the role of environmental factors and then focusing on the effect of the leadership style on the level of organizational strength.

Contextual Factors: Environmental Hostility and the Nature of the Electorate

Parties care about winning votes and office. As we saw in Chapter 3, party elites believe that elections can be won in a variety of ways including on the basis of leader charisma, candidate name recognition, attractive programs, and party organization. Building a strong organization is a large-scale commitment that parties would likely prefer to avoid if elections could be won some other way (see also Aldrich 1995). Therefore, it is fair to argue that only those parties whose electoral prospects are otherwise uncertain (i.e., who believe that they do not have other options available or that those options are unlikely to bring them success) will follow this strategy. Such belief, in turn, is likely to be stronger for those parties that experience environmental hostility, especially at the time of the party's inception and its first election.

In general terms, such different incentive structures with regard to building an organization are likely to separate underdogs from the perceived front-runners in any context. For the sake of argument, consider the example of the 2008 U.S. presidential election. The candidate that felt the need to build an extensive and disciplined organization – Barack Obama – was the one who was a newcomer to high-stakes politics. The organizational superiority of his campaign was extensively covered in the media. For example, Obama's victories at the primary stage were credited to his "superb field organization" (T. Curry 2008). In the general election, "McCain and his campaign [...] lagged far behind Obama in every key metric – money, organization, discipline – and failed to embrace Obama's organizational model" (Lister 2008). In a dramatic comparison, Smith and Martin (2008) argued that Obama had the capability of setting up "four times as many campaign offices as Mr. McCain." In fact, in the beginning of his quest for the Democratic Party nomination, Obama controlled very few resources and had almost no name recognition. Such an underdog position may have been the primary motivation behind building an extensive organization on the ground to compensate for the lack of those resources that his rivals had. Obama's rivals, both at the primary stage and in the general election, were party veterans with access to extensive resources and well-established names – Hillary Clinton and John McCain. Perhaps this was the reason they felt that elections could be won without an extensive and committed organization but rather with the existing resources or advantages that they already possessed. Although the actual motivations of each of these candidates remains unknown, the observable outcomes certainly suggest each of the candidates behaved as if the mechanism described was at work.

Environmental hostility can manifest itself in different ways. In the post-communist context, what is likely to matter is the role and status of the party in the process of regime transition as representatives of the former authoritarian regime versus the new democratic opposition. Parties associated with the former regime faced environmental hostility given that the public, media, and other contestants questioned their position as legitimate players. Grzymala-Busse (2002a), for example, argues (and the case studies provided in Chapter 3 support the argument) that the pariah status and environmental hostility that former communist parties in post-communist countries faced prompted them to build organizations as a way to legitimize themselves through close ties with the electorate.

On the other hand, parties emerging from the democratic opposition movements may feel entitled to election victory or be convinced that their path to success is to rely on their policy positions and ideology. They may see themselves as already embodying the will of the people and therefore have no incentive to "earn" public support the hard way – by cultivating ties via an extensive organization. The relatively easy election victories that they experienced in the first democratic elections likely only reinforced the perception that elections can be won without building strong organizations. After all, they now had "the proof" – their election result – that organizations were not necessary. This is likely to have further depressed incentives to invest in building an organization. In line with these arguments and in a more broadly cross-national context, Cross and Blais (2012) have also argued that it is usually after an electoral defeat that parties may decide to expand their organization (i.e., the selectorate for the leader).

Easy election victories (without having to build a strong organization), and especially governing status, that many significant communist opposition movements experienced after the regime transition can not only create disincentives to organization building but also diminish opportunities to do so. The leadership of a governing party may simply face serious time constraints that do not allow it to actively focus on strengthening party organization when its primary job is to govern. Furthermore, governing parties may hope to hold on to their position by using their positions – they may hope to maintain voters by access to pork and patronage – which is the privilege of governing parties over the opposition. The initial underdogs, on the other hand, being left out of government, have more opportunity and stronger motivation to engage in organization development, because they do not face similar time constraints and lack the potential to lure voters by other means. For example, in Estonia, other parties often shunned K as a coalition partner, and because of that it was mostly in opposition. However, the party leader saw that as an opportunity and claimed, "In the end, being in opposition serves us well. One reason why we are such a strong party is that we have had time for ourselves. If some of our opponents had spent less time in power and more time in opposition, they would be stronger too" (Kauba 2001).

The argument about the relevance of environmental hostility is not confined to communist successor parties only. Other parties may also face environmental hostility in the form of a pariah status, media attacks, or hostile public opinion. Such hostility indicates that strategies other than building an extensive organization are either not available or have not been effective for improving the status of the party. For example, K in Estonia has experienced negative media coverage and been excluded from cooperation with other parties throughout most of its existence. Although still using the other vote-gaining tactics, the party has clearly been motivated to establish direct contacts with voters through its strong organization.

Still other kinds of environmental challenge are posed to parties that enter later, into an already-saturated electoral arena. Late entrants may be at a disadvantage compared to the existing parties in terms of financial resources, name recognition, and ideological brand. For them, building a strong party organization can help compensate for these disadvantages and differentiate them from the existing contestants. Boix (2007, 510) argues that new parties form only when they "are able to break the 'expectations' advantage that the existing parties tap into to sustain their leading position." He notes that "[t]his can only happen if the entering parties enjoy sufficient organizational strength to mobilize their electors." For example, as discussed in the case studies in Chapter 3, RP in Estonia engaged in a large-scale organization building effort by recruiting members, setting up local offices, and establishing itself in local politics before entering the national election competition in 2003. Although their ideological competition was stiff, this organization-building effort was new and unprecedented – a strategy that allowed RP to differentiate itself from the established competitors. Parties suffering from these additional types of environmental hostility are likely to have an extra incentive to strengthen themselves organizationally for the same reason as the former communist parties – to increase their electoral appeal by building close links with voters. For these parties, legitimacy cannot be easily established or elections easily won without such links.

In sum, environmental hostility experienced by parties in the electoral arena creates incentives to strengthen party organizations. It is, therefore, likely that parties who have to establish their legitimacy or face other types of environmental hostility but are still office seeking in nature build strong organizations. At the same time, parties that operate in friendly environments (i.e., parties that are not rendered pariah status and are treated neutrally or positively by the media and the public) and that enjoy initial front-runner status have fewer incentives to invest in organization building and are, therefore, more likely to end up with weaker organizations.

Literature on partisan clientelism hints at another factor potentially influencing party leaders' incentives to engage in organization building – the nature of the party's primary electorate. Literature on clientelism argues that parties with poorer and rural voters are more likely to offer clientelist linkages (Brusco, Nazareno, and Stokes 2004; Grzymala-Busse 2007; S. Stokes 2005; Remmer 2007), and that clientelist parties tend to have more extensive organizations (Grzymala-Busse 2007). Parties that primarily target urban voters and wealthy citizens are able to reach their target audience without an extensive organization. They simply need a presence in larger cities and resources to make themselves visible, such as posters and media ads. No large organization is necessary to achieve that (although professional staff is likely still useful). However, parties that aspire to represent rural electorate and poorer citizens may find that they need to extend their organizations across the country and to focus on face-to-face interactions to reach their voters. In line with this argument, literature on the development of parties in Western Europe also argues that leftist parties are more likely to have large membership than centrist and rightist parties (Duverger 1954; Kitschelt 1994).[1]

This explanation, although certainly plausible, is less satisfying because it leaves open the question of why certain parties choose to represent electorates that require building extensive organizations in order to reach them. In the context of post-communist party politics that is characterized by a relatively level playing field for all contestants and an electorate with few preexisting cleavages, this is a relevant question. If parties emerge from grassroots movements, they are created to represent a specific social cleavage. However, in the context of post-communist Europe, parties were created by elites and these elites then had to make a decision as to which segments of society they should target. At least to an extent, parties were free agents choosing whom to represent rather than being assigned to represent certain social groups exogenously. However, given the uncertainty under which this decision had to be made, it is likely that the decision was exogenous to organization building.

Contextual Factors: Analysis and Results

In order to study the effect of contextual factors, I have generated a cross-national party-level dataset, where the organizational-strength measures are calculated as averages for the entire period the party existed between 1990 and 2010, subject to data availability. I have resorted to a cross-sectional analysis because the environmental factors are relatively constant over time: parties either do or do not cater to poorer and/or rural segments of society; similarly,

---

[1] This argument is somewhat contested. For example, in a systematic analysis of the Czech parties, Enyedi and Linek (2008) conclude that the membership size of the party and its social embeddedness do not differ between parties of the left and those of the right (see also, Klima 1998).

they either have or have not experienced significant environmental hostility. Because the availability of data varies considerably across different measures of organizational strength, the final number of cases included in each analysis also varies, ranging from twenty-eight to fifty-five.

The nature of the electorate can be captured by classifying parties according to whether or not they primarily target poor or rural voters. I used the variable "party family" in the Comparative Manifesto Project (CMP) dataset (Klingemann et al. 2006; Volkens et al. 2010) to identify such parties (variable name "Poor/rural voters"), coding "1" those parties that were classified as communist (CMP score 200), socialist, social-democratic (CMP code 300), or agrarian (CMP score 800), and "0" otherwise.[2,3] About 33 percent of the parties included in the dataset are coded as having poorer and/or rural electorates.

Whether or not a party has faced any significant "Environmental hostility" is captured by another indicator variable measured "1" for parties that satisfy at least one of the following conditions: (1) former regime party (i.e., communist or satellite successor party); (2) a party considered a pariah by other parties in the system (i.e., one that all other parties refuse to cooperate with; for example, the SPR-RSČ in the Czech Republic); (3) a party that has received the highest share of votes but not been included in government (for example, K in Estonia); or (4) a party that entered the electoral contest in the fourth or later post-communist election. I chose the fourth election as the cutoff point on the basis of the finding in Tavits (2005) that in the region, electoral volatility starts to decrease and party systems to stabilize after about eleven years from the transition. Given that in most cases elections are held every four years, this amounts to a year less than four election cycles. It is, therefore, fair to assume that by the fourth election the party system has already started to stabilize and new entry becomes more difficult.[4]

---

[2] The CMP does not have information on all parties included in the analysis. The following parties were coded either 1 or 0 using the party name as a cue: Farmers Union (Estonia), Estonian Agrarian People's Party, and Hungarian Communist Workers' Party were coded 1; Estonian Christian Democrats and Entrepreneurs' Party (Hungary) were coded 0. The CMP codes the Czech KDU-ČSL as a Christian democratic party rather than agrarian or rural. The party, although centrist in nature, is generally acknowledged to represent rural voters (Hanley 2008). Coding it either way does not significantly alter the results. For the sake of consistency, I followed the CMP classification for the final analysis.

[3] The other party families that the CMP identifies include ecology parties (code 100), liberal parties (code 400), Christian Democratic and other religious parties (code 500), conservative parties (code 600), national parties (code 700), ethnic and regional parties (code 901), and special interest parties (code 951).

[4] Of course, potential new parties can try to cope with the expected environmental hostility owing to saturated electoral market by other than organizational means (e.g., by introducing new issues). Excluding new entrants from the set of parties coded as experiencing environmental hostility does not change the results significantly.

Former regime stigma, pariah status, and exclusion from government despite best electoral performance directly signal environmental hostility and under-dog status (i.e., the hostility of other parties, the media, and the general public toward these parties). Similarly, parties entering an already-saturated elec-toral market and lacking established reputation or brand name may need to find alternative ways, including building a strong organization, to estab-lish their competitiveness. In terms of descriptive statistics, about 22 percent of the parties in the dataset are classified as suffering from environmental hostility.

These two independent variables can be included in simple OLS models of party organizational strength to determine their relative explanatory power.[5] The models also control for each party's average "Campaign expenditure"[6] as a percent of GDP and country dummies. Campaign expenditure captures the wealth of the party, which may independently affect the strength of the party organization, and therefore needs to be controlled for to accurately estimate the effect of environmental factors. I have performed separate analyses for each measure of the organizational strength: (1) "Participation in local elections" (the average share of municipalities contested in all post-communist local elec-tions); (2) "Membership" (the average annual membership as a percent of the electorate); (3) "Branches" (the average annual number of branches as a share of the number of municipalities); and (4) "Size of staff" (the average annual number of central office staff as a share of 100,000 electorate).

The results of the analyses are presented in Table 6.1. The type of the primary electorate and environmental hostility are positively and significantly related to party organizational strength for the first three measures. Both independent variables remain insignificant for predicting the size of the staff employed in the headquarters. The latter is not surprising given that all types of parties can benefit from this aspect of organizational strength. The overall evidence, thus, suggests that parties representing rural areas (agrarian parties) and/or poorer segments of society (communist, socialist, and social-democratic parties) and those suffering from environmental hostility because of pariah status or late entry are significantly more likely to build extensive organizations than middle-class oriented urban parties operating in relatively friendly and familiar electoral environments. Note that these relationships hold when party wealth is controlled for. That is, although money may be helpful or even necessary for building an organization, it does not appear to be sufficient.

TABLE 6.1. *The Effect of Environmental Factors on Party Organizational Strength*

	Participation in Local Elections	Membership	Branches	Size of Staff	Participation in Local Elections (excludes ex-communist parties)
Poor/rural voters	0.085*** (0.032)	0.003** (0.001)	0.325* (0.203)	0.234 (0.307)	0.056* (0.035)
Environmental hostility	0.133*** (0.040)	0.003* (0.001)	0.431* (0.225)	0.336 (0.324)	0.087* (0.049)
Campaign expenditure	0.003*** (0.001)	0.000 (0.000)	−0.001 (0.006)	−0.002 (0.007)	0.003*** (0.001)
Constant	0.048* (0.030)	−0.0005 (0.001)	0.102 (0.205)	−0.216 (0.321)	0.040 (0.029)
R^2	0.55	0.32	0.35	0.41	0.48
N	55	47	28	31	50

Note: The different dependent variables are noted in column headings. Table entries are unstandardized regression coefficients with standard errors in parentheses. Country dummies are included in the models but not reported. $^*p \leq 0.1$, $^{**}p \leq 0.05$, $^{***}p \leq 0.01$

The substantive effects of these variables are also significant. The leftist and/or agrarian parties are likely to contest 9 percent more municipalities, have branches in 32 percent more municipalities, and a 0.3 percent larger membership than other parties. Similarly, environmental hostility is associated with a 13 percent increase in the municipalities contested, 43 percent increase in the share of branches, and a 0.3 percent increase in the membership share.

One might question to what extent environmental hostility really indicates inherited organization because this variable measures former regime parties that may be argued to have an organizational advantage. In fact, only five[7] out of the thirteen parties coded as having suffered from hostile environment are former regime parties; the others include pariahs and new parties. Additionally, as discussed in the case studies in Chapter 3, it is not clear whether former communist parties really had much of an organizational advantage because they had to give up a lot of their organizational assets after the regime change or did so voluntarily to mitigate environmental hostility. The last column in Table 6.1 presents the results when ex-communist parties are excluded. Although the effect of both environmental variables weakens, it remains positive and statistically significant, indicating that the findings are not entirely driven by the ex-communist parties.

---

[7] According to the classification in Chapter 2, these include KSČM, MSzP, Munkaspart, PSL, and SLD. Excluding the PSL improves the results considerably.

TABLE 6.2. *The Conditional Effects of the Type of Electorate and Environmental Hostility on Party Organizational Strength*

	Participation in Local Elections
The effect of "Poor/rural voters" when "Environmental hostility" = 0	0.055* (0.037)
The effect of "Poor/rural voters" when "Environmental hostility" = 1	0.181*** (0.067)
The effect of "Environmental hostility" when "Poor/rural voters" = 0	0.080* (0.051)
The effect of "Environmental hostility" when "Poor/rural voters" = 1	0.206*** (0.060)

Note: The dependent variable is "Participation in local elections." Table entries are unstandardized regression coefficients with standard errors in parentheses.
$*p \leq 0.1$, $***p \leq 0.01$

These effects can be explored further: the effect of the type of electorate may depend on the level of environmental hostility and vice versa. In order to examine this possibility, I have estimated interaction effects between these variables using participation in local elections as the dependent variable.[8] The other variables in the model remain the same. Table 6.2 presents the conditional coefficients for different scenarios.[9] Both effects are weakly statistically significant (at the 10 percent level) when the other two conditions are absent. However, both of these effects become much stronger when the other condition is present. That is, poor/rural electorate is associated with stronger party organizations for parties experiencing no environmental hostility. However, this effect is considerably stronger – the conditional coefficient increases from 0.05 to 0.18 – for parties that suffer from environmental hostility. This captures well the situation of the communist successor parties that continued subscribing to a leftist ideology and appealing to poorer segments of society, which in itself required a more extensive organizational presence to reach those voters. In addition to that, these parties also experienced significant hostility from their competitors, the media, and the public owing to their communist past – a condition that further strengthened the incentive to look at internal party structures as a possible source for regeneration. The case studies of the Hungarian MSzP, Polish SLD, and Czech KSČM described in Chapter 3 are supportive of this conclusion. Leftist and rural parties that did not suffer from environmental hostility have been less pressed to build strong organizations. For example, SDE in Estonia, although subscribing to social-democratic ideology, has never prioritized organization building. The same was true of the Peasant Alliance in Poland, despite the fact that it represented a rural electorate. Both parties

---

[8] The results are similar when membership or branches is used as the dependent variable.
[9] Full results of these analyses are presented in Appendix 6.1.

initially experienced relatively easy election victories and participated in first governments, which may have created a false sense of security that elections could be won without an organization.

The effect of environmental hostility on party organizational strength is also conditional on the nature of the electorate. The effect is positive and statistically significant for parties that do not target poor/rural electorate; the size of the effect of environmental hostility increases almost threefold (from 0.08 to 0.21) and becomes highly statistically significant for parties that do target such voters. This describes the situation of several later entries to the electoral arena. For example, the Green Party in Estonia did not build a strong party organization despite entering an electoral market saturated with more established parties (and thereby facing environmental hostility). On the contrary, for leftist and/or rural parties such hostility reinforced the incentive to strengthen their organizations. This is also true for the non-communist left. For example, the left-wing K of Estonia has been shunned by most other parties in the system and suffered an effective pariah status despite repeatedly receiving the highest vote share. As the analysis of this case in Chapter 3 showed, this party has very explicitly followed a strategy of strengthening the party internally and reaching the voters through its own organization. The negative attitude of the other parties and the media toward them has likely contributed to focusing on building a strong organization rather than relying on other, less personal means of communicating with voters. In general, the results strongly suggest that the nature of the electorate and environmental conditions reinforce each other's effect on party incentives to build a strong organization.

I have also calculated the expected levels of organizational strength for the different scenarios – quantities that are easier to interpret than conditional coefficients. When both environmental conditions are absent (i.e., for middle-class oriented urban parties operating in a friendly environment), the expected level of organizational strength is 0.07. In other words, they are expected to have organizational presence in about 7 percent of all municipalities. When either of the environmental conditions is present, the expected value of organizational strength increases to about 0.13–0.16. That is, parties with a poorer and/or rural electorate operating in a friendly environment are expected to have organizational presence in approximately 13 percent of all municipalities, and middle-class oriented urban parties operating in hostile environment in approximately 16 percent of municipalities. When both conditions are present, the expected level of organizational strength increases substantially. Specifically, parties representing poorer and/or rural voters in a hostile environment are expected to have organizational presence in about 33 percent of all municipalities, other things equal.

In sum, party organizational strength is influenced by the nature of the electorate and the environmental conditions that the party experiences. Parties with poorer and/or rural electorates are more likely to build extensive organizations. The same is true for parties that have experienced significant hostility from other parties in the system, media, and public. These effects are also mutually reinforcing: both effects are stronger if the other condition is also present. Furthermore, these effects are not simply capturing the extent of resources that a party controls.

The Role of Party Leadership

The nature of the electorate and environmental hostility, although mattering for the strength of the party organizations, are both relatively deterministic and static explanations. Indeed, there are several cases that cannot easily be explained by environmental conditions. For example, neither ODS in the Czech Republic nor Fidesz in Hungary targeted poor and rural voters or had experienced the kind of environmental hostility described. However, their organizations were strong during the time period under consideration. Similarly, the organizations of several parties representing poor and/or rural electorates in Estonia and Poland (e.g., the Farmers' Union and SDE in Estonia, and Peasant Alliance in Poland) were quite weak. This suggests that other, party-specific factors are also likely to influence the level of party organizational strength.

Parties are not just objects at the mercy of environmental conditions, but are composed of purposive actors whose decisions may also affect the organizational direction of the party. Party leaders are likely to be the most influential of these actors. Leadership remains understudied in political science, but the studies that do exist show that leadership matters for a variety of outcomes and that leaders are able to move the preferences of the group in their desired direction (Ahlquist and Levi 2011; Humphreys, Masters, and Sandbu 2006).[10] Investigating whether or not the preferences and predispositions of leaders matter for the organizational strategies of parties allows providing a fuller and more dynamic picture of the development of parties. A systematic study of leadership effects requires identifying the types of leaders that are more likely to invest in building an organization. Different sets of literatures – including literature on (1) U.S. state and local party organizations, (2) management and organizational sociology, and (3) the survival of former regime parties – have discussed the effect of leader characteristics on organization building.

The literature on leadership and party organizations in U.S. politics provides a classification of leader types and relates each with a different level of party organizational strength: "amateur" leaders are more likely to be associated with weak party organizations and "professional" leaders with strong. This relationship emerges either because of the different role perceptions of

---

[10] Another significant line of research on political (including party) leadership has examined the mechanisms of leadership selection, removal, succession, and survival (see, for example, Bueno de Mesquita et al. 2003; Bynander and 't Hart 2007; Courtney 1995; Davis 1998; Kenig 2009; LeDuc 2001; 't Hart and Uhr 2011).

amateurs versus professionals or their different organizational capabilities or both. Specifically, analyzing leadership in the U.S. party politics, Wilson (1962) drew a distinction between the professional and the amateur in politics (see also Aldrich 1995; Fiorina, Abrams, and Pope 2005; Kirkpatrick 1976; Soule and Clarke 1970; Wildavsky 1965). Cotter et al. (1984) and Gibson et al. (1989) adopted this dichotomy and applied it directly to explain party organizational strength.

Amateurs and professionals differ in their values, cognitions, and behavior. The former emphasize the role of ideas and principles; they are policy oriented and ideological purists (Wilson 1962). They may have little or no loyalty to party organization (Stone and Abramowitz 1983) and are likely to eschew party organization for ideology (Gibson et al. 1989). Professionals, on the other hand, are pragmatists. They emphasize "interpersonal relations and the accommodation of interests" (Cotter et al. 1984, 142). They have "high instrumental concern for party as a vehicle for winning office and providing rewards" (Cotter et al. 1984, 142). In general, professionals tend to see politics in terms of winning or losing, and be less concerned about ideological issues. For them, the latter can be compromised, but the organizational coherence and strength of the party has to be maximized (Hoffstetter 1971; Wilson 1962). Because of their antiorganizational values, amateurs are generally associated with negative consequences to the development and functioning of party organizations; the opposite is true of professionals, who should see the building of the party organization as their "core purpose" (Gibson et al. 1989, 71).

Evidence in support of these predictions is somewhat mixed. Although Cotter et al. (1984) find no difference in the organizational strength of local parties according to the role orientation of the leader, in a repeat study a few years later, Gibson et al. (1989) report moderate-to-strong leader effects. Specifically, they find that leaders who (1) think that party organization and unity are more important than issues, (2) value loyalty to the party, and (3) are concerned primarily with the good of the party, not with the ideological purity of candidates and issues, are more likely to head strong party organizations.

Gibson et al. (1989) further speculate that the difference between amateurs and professionals may emerge not simply because of differences in values, but in their capabilities (abilities). That is, amateurs may be more likely to head weak party organizations because they literally are amateurs: "[T]hey are not committed to developing the sort of ongoing, structured party organization that is indicated by party organizational strength" (Gibson et al. 1989, 82). By the same token, professionals need not necessarily abandon all concern for ideology to be successful at building organizations; they simply need to be skilled at organization. To partially support this interpretation, Gibson et al. (1989) report that amateurs indeed spend considerably less time on party affairs than professionals.

The distinction between amateurs and professionals is a helpful way to think about leader effects. However, for better testing, the argument could be specified further by elaborating on what characteristics of leaders – their background, education, experiences, values – make them more or less skilled at developing an organization. This is where the other two sets of literature prove useful. Specifically, Grzymala-Busse (2002a) provides a comprehensive study of the regeneration of former communist parties in post-communist CEE. It explores why some former regime parties are successfully able to regenerate but others are not, and reports that the characteristics of party organizations and leaders play a significant role in the success of regeneration. Specifically, those leaders that are able to build and maintain strong party organizations, and thereby lead the party through a quick and effective transformation, are significantly different from those leaders whose parties are unable to transform. In line with the argument given, the former types of leaders are pragmatic and professional; the latter types are ideological. Grzymala-Busse, however, further argues that the professional leaders possess practical resources that the ideologues lack, such as administrative skills and expertise. Professionals have obtained the resources by being highly educated and experienced in management, governance, policy formulation, and innovation prior to becoming party leaders. That is, prior careers of leaders, their prior experience in leadership, administrative or managerial positions, give the professionals the necessary practical resources that lead them to value building and maintaining party organizations. By the same token, leaders with prior careers in nonmanagerial or administrative positions, such as the intellectual or cultural sphere, are less likely to value building a strong party organization, more likely to be associated with organizational amateurism, and also more likely to focus on ideas, policies, and values.

Literature on organizational sociology and management, although not about political parties, also considers the effect of leaders on building (business) organizations and provides hints about the leader characteristics that are likely to make him or her more oriented toward organization building. Specifically, Collins (2001) has identified several variables that contribute to making "good" organizations "great," with a specific type of leadership being the first necessary condition for a successful breakthrough. These "level five leaders," as Collins calls them, are characterized by being ambitious but humble and modest. That is, they are goal oriented and "fanatically driven," set high standards of building an enduring great organization, and settle for nothing less; organization is their first and foremost priority. At the same time, they are not seeking personal profit or personal greatness; tend to credit others for the success of the organization and blame themselves for its failures; talk about their organization, not about themselves; and use "we" more often than "I" when discussing the accomplishments of the organization. Collins further argues that these characteristics are not present for just any highly capable individual, competent manager, or effective leader, and need to be understood as uniquely contributing to building enduring greatness in organizations. Admittedly, the definition of level-five leader does not offer very concrete behaviors or characteristics

TABLE 6.3. *Amateur/Ideologue vs. Professional/Pragmatist*

Amateur/Ideological Leader	Professional/Pragmatic Leader
Focus on ideas and principles	Focus on pragmatism
Ideological purist	Less concerned about ideology
Lack of administrative skills and expertise	Considerable administrative skills and expertise
No prior experience in management, government, policy formulation, and innovation;	Experience in management, government, policy formulation, and/or innovation
Prior career in intellectual/cultural sphere	
Lacking level-five leader qualities	Level-five leader
• Lack of ambition • Interest in personal greatness • Blame avoidance	• Ambitious, goal oriented, but humble • No interest in personal greatness • Credits others for party success, blames themselves for failures

that could be easily systematically measured (the evidence is presented in the form of narratives). However, together with the desirable leader characteristics identified elsewhere, the general description of effective leaders is still helpful for identifying professionally oriented (as opposed to amateur) leaders.[11]

To summarize, Table 6.3 provides a list of identifiable characteristics and personal resources of the amateur-/ideological-type leaders and the professional-/pragmatic-type leaders. The expectation is that the professional

[11] Literature on organizational behavior, although also addressing the role of leaders, remains less useful for current purposes. The primary focus in this literature is on distinguishing charismatic and noncharismatic or transactional leaders. The former inspire and motivate people in the organization to forgo their own self-interest and follow the collective good; the latter use rewards in exchange for desired behavior (Bass 1985 in Pfeffer 1997). The behavioral manifestations of a charismatic leader include emphasizing values and using moral justification, stressing the collective over individual, setting more distant objectives and greater expectations, and making more positive statements about followers' self-worth (Shamir, House, and Arthur 1993 in Pfeffer 1997). Charismatic leaders are characterized by dominance, self-confidence, need for influence and power, and a strong belief in the righteousness of their ideas (House 1977 in Pfeffer 1997). Unfortunately, the literature is not clear about what to expect in terms of commitment to building an organization from either type of leader. Furthermore, whether their effects are likely to differ is not immediately clear either. A charismatic leader may be more likely to build a strong organization, or at least be able to do so, because he or she may be better able to motivate the members of the organization and count on their loyalty. On the other hand, ability to build an organization is not necessarily a guarantee that one will be built. A charismatic leader may also enjoy more power and dominance if the organization remains small and his or her person more prominent. Overall, the specific arguments provided in the organizational sociology literature are not directly applicable to the empirical study of political parties pursued here.

types are more likely and the amateur types less likely to support and engage in building strong party organizations for the reasons outlined. This provides theoretical guidance for the empirical analysis.

Leaders and Organizations: Analysis

The analysis of the effect of leadership style on organizational strength proceeds in two steps. First, I will provide qualitative narratives of sixteen parties – four from each country – to assess the proposed relationship. I have selected the parties on the basis of their values on the independent variable – leadership style – and include, from each country, two parties dominated by professional and two by amateur leaders. For each party and each leader, the narratives focus on two questions: (1) Is this leader more of an amateur or a professional; and (2) Is there any direct evidence that this particular leader prioritizes and/or directly engages in organization building? The goal is to provide an initial assessment of the proposed relationship and illustrate the causal mechanisms. The second part of the analysis will present a quantitative study to get at the leadership effect in a more systematic and generalizable manner.

In both types of analyses, only those cases could be covered for which sufficient information exists to assess the role of leaders in organization building. Sometimes, only some leaders of a party can be covered because of lack of information for all. Usually, however, information is available on the more influential, long-term leaders, which allows for making some general conclusions about the effect of leadership. In general, in accord with the rest of the book, the time period under consideration spans from the regime change until 2010. Similar to Chapter 3, information for the case studies (and for coding the leader type in the quantitative analysis) was collected from media sources (the main daily newspapers and magazines), interviews with party activists, party documents, speeches and writings by party leaders, and secondary sources describing and analyzing political parties in these countries. Appendix 6.1 summarizes basic information for the leaders of all parties analyzed.

The Czech Republic

Civic Democratic Party (ODS) has had two leaders during the time period under study: Václav Klaus (1991–2002) and Mirek Topolánek (2002–2010). Both leaders are generally characterized as pragmatists and both have valued and heavily invested in building a strong organization for ODS. More specifically, Klaus was known by his forceful and pragmatic leadership style (Hanley 2004). Before becoming the party leader, he served as the finance minister and built a high profile as the architect of successful economic reforms (Hanley 2008). An economist by training, he served as the finance minister before becoming the party leader and acquired a reputation of being very goal oriented, a technocrat, and a pragmatist (CTK 1993f; Saxonberg 1999); he cared less about the means and more about the ends and focused on victory rather than compromise (Stránský 2004). He stood in contrast to many dissident leaders who were primarily ideologues and intellectuals "used to contemplating rather than making decisions" (Saxonberg 1999, 409). Because of his prior experience in governance, he also possessed the necessary skills of using and managing political structures.

Klaus is the primary reason ODS ended up with a strong party organization. It was his conviction that the then OF needed to be developed into an organizationally well-defined party oriented toward electoral competition (Hanley 2004). According to Klaus, ODS needed to be a party "with firm organizational structure and membership" (BBC Summary of World Broadcasts 1990). Many have argued that Klaus was a charismatic leader (Saxonberg 1999), but as Hanley (2004, 47) notes, charisma alone is not the key to success; rather "it seems necessary, [...], that charismatic leaders should be committed to developing party organization." Klaus initiated the organization building and insisted on its continuation (Hanley 2008). Even after electoral victory in the 1994 party congress, Klaus stressed the need to further build the party organization and attract new members. He set organizational development as the primary goal of the party for 1995 (BBC 1994). He personally cultivated close ties with rank-and-file members in branches across the country (Saxonberg 1999). The party was Klaus's mission; as Saxoberg (1999, 406) notes, "[W]ere he only interested in power, he would have tried to keep the [Civic] Forum together once he had secured his leadership position." However, he was less interested in personal reward and more interested in building sustainable electoral success by investing in party organization.

Klaus's successor, Topolánek, has also been characterized as "a practical political manager," capable of bringing the diverse party together into a unified organization (Hanley 2008). With a background in business and local politics, he had gained experience in political leadership before becoming the party leader (Pečinka 2003). Similar to Klaus, he also strongly believed in the need to build and maintain a strong party organization. In his election bid to the party leader position he declared that his goal was to revitalize and reinvigorate ODS's organization (CTK 2003b; World News Connection 2002) and open local branches up to more new members (Linek and Pecháček 2007). Again similar to Klaus, Topolánek kept active contact with the grassroots organization by touring the regions (CTK 2004c).

Czech Social Democratic Party (ČSSD) has been ruled by a number of leaders including Jiří Horák (1990–1993), Miloš Zeman (1993–2001), Vladimír Špidla (2001–2004), Stanislav Gross (2004–2005), and Jiří Paroubek (2006–2010).[12] The leaders with the longest tenure – Zeman and Paroubek – have both been

---

[12] Bohuslav Sobotka was an acting leader in 2005–2006 after Gross resigned and before Paroubek was elected.

characterized as pragmatists, leaders with an authoritative managerial style, and both invested considerably in building the organization. The leadership style of other leaders has been more varied, generally, although not always, reflected in the ups and downs of organizational development across time as discussed in Chapter 3.

The first leader of the ČSSD after the regime change was an American émigré, Jiří Horák. It is difficult to classify Horák as either an amateur or a professional because of a lack of sufficient information about his experience and character. He was a professor at Columbia University, suggesting no managerial-professional background as defined here. However, as a member of the U.S. Democratic Party, he had been active in the U.S. presidential campaigns and therefore possessed political skills. Some authors claim, however, that he was not necessarily capable of translating those skills to the post-communist context (CTK 1993a; Kopeček and Pšeja 2008). Under Horák's leadership, the party was struggling to establish itself, and Horák was not considered to be an effective party leader, felt out of place in the Czech Republic, and moved back to the United States as a result (CTK 1993b). By other accounts, ČSSD gave significant priority to organization building in 1990–1992. The driving force behind this organization building, however, was Jiří Paroubek – the then-general secretary of the party – rather than by the leader, Horák.[13]

Horák's successor was the pragmatic Miloš Zeman – an economist who had worked in research departments of various state companies and at the Czech Academy of Sciences. He was well-connected and had prior work experience with the leaders of the major parties (CTK 1993c). In short, he possessed skills, expertise, and connections necessary for a professional rather than an amateur leader. It is, therefore, not surprising that, as already discussed in Chapter 3, Zeman was the engine behind the continued organization building, insisting on extending the party organization on the local level, increasing membership, and engaging rank and file in election campaigns (CTK 1997b, 1997d; Hanley 2003). As Klaus in ODS, Zeman personally stayed in touch with the party grassroots members and conducted constituency campaigns (Kopeček and Pšeja 2008).

Contrary to Zeman's professionalism, Vladimír Špidla was accused of political clumsiness (CTK 2002c). With a PhD in history and prehistory, Špidla was more of an ideologue and intellectual than a pragmatic manager. He lacked the skills and interests to continue with Zeman's professional style; as an observer notes, Špidla "is totally incapable to manage the party accustomed to the rough grip of Zeman" (Czech News Agency 2003). This was reflected in the fact that important party posts were filled with people that lacked the necessary skills (Czech News Agency 2003). Members also complained, "Špidla does not communicate with deputies and party members, that he does not manage rebelling

---

[13] Sean Hanley, personal communication, October 27, 2011.

groups within the party, that he is unable to comprehensibly present the party program and achievements" (CTK 2004b).

Špidla was briefly succeeded by Stanislav Gross, but the organizational revival of ČSSD was accomplished by Gross's successor, Jiří Paroubek. He was also an economist and had served in several top managerial positions from 1979 to 1990, as well as in leadership positions within the party before becoming the actual leader. This set the stage for his professional, pragmatic, and managerial leadership style (Czech News Agency 2006e; 2009a). Indeed, as noted, Paroubek credits himself with significantly contributing to the creation of the nationwide network of party organization during his tenure as the general secretary in the early 1990s (http://www.paroubek.cz/). After becoming the leader, he set out to modernize the party and use "a managerial method of the party direction" (Czech News Agency 2006d). His goal was to strengthen the membership of the party, professionalize the management of regional-level branches, keep the organization active during inter-election periods, develop cooperation with civic associations in towns and villages, and increase the effectiveness of communication within the party and with voters by making better use of electronic media (Czech News Agency 2006c) as well as organize discussions and meetings in regions and districts (Czech News Agency 2006e).

Civic Democratic Alliance (ODA) has had five different leaders, none of whom served for very long: Pavel Bratinka (1990–1992), Jan Kalvoda (1992–1997), Michael Žantovský (1997), Jiří Skalický (1997–1998), and Daniel Kroupa (1998–2001). The last party leader was again Michael Žantovský (2001–2007). Most of these leaders were part of a group of intellectuals who founded ODA and shared the idea that the party aspired to be an elite formation (Hanley 2003, 2008). The party presented itself as an intellectual club, holding seminars and debating culture, religion, and politics. It was a prime example of ideological purists interested in ideas and principles rather than in sustained work on organization. In an interview in 1992, Daniel Kroupa, for example, argued that ODA was "an electoral type party" and "not trying to get a massive membership base" (CTK 1992c). Kalvoda similarly asserts that even after electoral failure in the 1994 local election and realization that if the party had had a more widespread local presence it would have done better, "the credibility of the party depends on its performance, not on the number of its members" (CTK 1995a). Michael Žantovský, too, had the background of an intellectual (Mainville 2001). Furthermore, he stayed in office for only a very brief period. His successor, Jiří Skalický, argued that the party was already politically dead when he took office (CTK 1998a). The party finally dissolved itself in 2007.

Freedom Union (US) has also been led by a large number of different leaders, all of which have held on to the post for a very short period of time: Jan Ruml (1998–1999), Karel Kühnl (2000–2001), Hana Marvanová (2001–2002), Ivan Pilip (2002–2003), Petr Mareš (2003–2004), Pavel Němec (2004–2006), Jan

Hadrava (2006–2007), and Jan Černý (since 2007). This large number of leaders already indicates that none had a strong commitment to the organization, and even if they possessed the necessary skills, there would be little opportunity to work on developing the organization. The party creation itself is rather telling: the anti-Klaus rebels in ODS who eventually formed US actually did not want to create a party, but because Klaus won the ODS leadership election, they had no other choice (Stroehlein 1998). Rather than resulting from conscious party building, the US sort of just "happened," with the creators not really sure of what they wanted from it. The first leader, Jan Ruml, was more of an ideologue than a pragmatist, as indicated by his nonmanagerial background, and prioritized building a political profile for the party rather than developing its organization (CTK 1998b). His successors followed this amateur style during the short period each was in office. For example, in her election bid, Marvanová stressed the need to stay true to US values and principles (CTK 2001c). She was considered an idealist, too ideological, and even a little naïve (Pitkin 2001). Throughout the existence of the party, the leadership was mostly occupied with ideological debates and issues such as whether or not the party should cooperate with ČSSD rather than being concerned about how to build and strengthen their organization (CTK 2003a). Once Mareš became the leader, the party was already considered to be "clinically dead or in agony" (CTK 2005).

In sum, the Czech case provides general support for the leadership hypothesis. Professional and pragmatic leaders have dominated the ODS and ČSSD and, as the narratives indicate, they have directly contributed to strengthening the party organization. On the contrary, the ODA and US have mostly been led by amateur leaders and, consequently, experienced organizational weakness. In most (although not all) cases, leaders played a significant and direct role in shaping the level of organizational strength. The ČSSD case was especially interesting because its leaders over the years exhibited a mix of leadership styles, with Zeman and Paroubek standing out as pragmatists and Špidla appearing more as an amateur. The former two were both concerned about organization as one of their core purposes, but Špidla was more ideological and, fittingly, less concerned about the organization. Horák's leadership style was hard to define and, therefore, could not effectively be used to confirm or refute the hypothesis that leaders matter. What Horák's case suggests, however, is that it may not always be the leader that matters most, but the party manager or general secretary who was driving the organization building at that time.[14]

---

[14] The role of general secretaries may be more generally relevant here because, in many cases, they are directly responsible for implementing any party strategies concerning organizational development. Studying their role more systematically, however, remains challenging given the scarcity of information about their characteristics and behavior.

Estonia

Center Party (K) has almost exclusively been led by Edgar Savisaar. The only exception is a brief period in 1995 when Savisaar stepped down because of a secret taping scandal and Andra Veidemann became the party leader. Savisaar is often described as an autocratic leader (Made 1996; Mattheus 2004b; Mattson and Sildam 2004; Postimees 2004), but he is also extremely pragmatic and calculating rather than an ideologue. His prior career in leadership positions in the Planning Committee during the Soviet time also gave him the necessary managerial background to be classified as a professional leader.

Savisaar's behavior with regard to the party organization accords well with the expectations of the leadership hypothesis. He quickly realized the importance of party organization for the continued electoral success and survival of the party as well as for building his own support base within the party. With these goals in mind, Savisaar was personally behind much of the organization building and maintenance of organizational loyalty and strength. In all major party meetings he stressed the importance of the organization, praised the party achievements with regard to organizational strengthening, and acknowledged the contributions of organizational structures and members in party success (Kauba 2001; Postimees 2006b; Simson 2002). This is how he motivated members to stay active and loyal during and between elections. He often used the growing membership numbers and increased number of municipalities contested in local elections to illustrate his party's strength (Savisaar 2002; Simson 2002). Savisaar made sure to personally visit local branches and stay in touch with grassroots members – a strategy that guaranteed his success in leadership struggles because his rivals generally ignored the organization and concentrated on building support among the MPs or leadership only (Jarne 1996a; Veidemann 1996). For example, in 2000, during the election of the party leader, different candidates were asked why they were running and what they would change. In his answers, Savisaar did several things that suggested that he was a professional and pragmatic leader who understood the importance of a strong organization and focused on maintaining one: (1) he stressed the unity of the party and talked about himself as part of "us" rather than focusing on his person or personal achievements; (2) he credited others – rival candidates for the leader position and rank-and-file party members – for the success of the party; and (3) he underlined the importance of building and maintaining a strong organization as the main goal of his leadership term (Ideon 2000a). His rival candidates said that they would think about what to do once they were elected or criticized several things about the party rather than offering a positive program – behavior that suggests a clear difference in leadership style.

Reform (RE) has had only two leaders – Siim Kallas (1994–2004) and Andrus Ansip (since 2004). Both leaders have professional backgrounds in business, banking, and public service. Both are also considered pragmatic, ambitious, intelligent, rational, and highly capable individuals (Koch 2008;

Odres 2004; Tänavsuu 2004). They are therefore likely to qualify as professional leaders, and possess the necessary skills for organization building. However, despite this, RE initially attempted to maximize votes by populating their electoral lists with well-known individuals, thinking that this was a proven strategy (Paet 1999), and they also believed that their policies were "self-evidently preferable to those of other parties" (Ideon 1999a). The role of the organization was not recognized, and in the late 1990s the party had barely 1,000 members – the minimum legal requirement. This strategy, however, produced disappointing results in the 1999 election (Ideon 1999a). It is only then that the party leadership realized that well-known personalities alone were no longer able to attract voters and that the party strategy needed to be changed. The new strategy involved organization building: Kallas stressed in his speech to the party congress the need to recruit new members, and in the early 2000s the membership numbers started to increase dramatically (Postimees 2002a; Saarlane 2000). The successful membership recruitment was accompanied by the creation of a wide network of local branches (Postimees 2003). As a result of the active recruitment campaigns, the RE was the fastest-growing party in terms of membership under Ansip's leadership. The recruitment efforts and organization building were part of RE's vote-getting strategy in the 2007 parliamentary election (Postimees 2006a), and one of the goals of the party in 2009 continued to be increasing membership and local presence because this was seen as essential in order to succeed in the upcoming local and European elections (Tamm 2009).

In sum, the impetus for organization building in the RE originated from disappointing election results, which lead the leadership to reconsider their electoral strategies. The backgrounds and attitudes of leaders did not directly lead them to this strategy initially. At the same time, the role of leaders was important for organization building, because leaders with different backgrounds and attitudes might have had a different response to the perceived electoral failure, as the IL and SDE cases to be described suggest. Therefore, although not refuting the proposed relationship between leaders and organizational strength, the RE case implies an intermediary effect for leaders where the leadership is triggered into action by environmental factors.

Pro Patria (IL) (as well as the SDE) has experienced multiple splits and mergers, making their original identities often hard to trace. In fact, IL ceased to exist in 2006 when the party merged with RP. Until then, the party had had six leaders, with Mart Laar – although not the longest-serving leader (1998–2002)[15] – being probably the most prominent member of the party from the time of its foundation. I will, therefore, concentrate on his leadership. In fact, none of the IL leaders have put much effort into developing the party organization. Rather, the survival and growth strategy has been to merge or

---

[15] The other leaders of IL include Lagle Parek (1988–1993), Tunne Kelam (1993–1995, 2002–2005), Toivo Jürgenson (1995–1998), and Tõnis Lukas (2005–2006).

form joint lists or electoral alliances with other parties (Talving 1998a). In the mid 1990s, IL was labeled as a "pocket party," such as the KE discussed in Chapter 3, with no significant organization and no interest in building one (Alaküla 1995). The party leadership claimed that the party was already organizationally strong and needed no additional investment in building its organization: "We are one of the few, if not the only party that has a nationwide structure and about 20–30 members in every branch," claimed then-leader Toivo Jürgenson (Tammer 1995a). Laar was also quite satisfied with the way the party was functioning and thought that it already had a strong network of local branches (Paet 1997). Not only that, but the leadership also did not believe that organization was relevant. Laar, for example, claimed that the success of the party depended on the popularity of the leader (Paet 1997) rather than on the party organization. Other people in the leadership agreed that personalities and attractive media campaigns were more important than the party organization (Talving 1998b). Fitting with this, Laar's leadership style appeared to resemble that of an amateur more than a professional. A historian by training, he had had no managerial or administrative experience before becoming the party leader. As is also characteristic of amateur leaders, Laar often seemed to use the party for personal ambition rather than showing concern for the party as a collective vehicle for public office. The fact that Laar did not seem to be very strategic in planning the electoral strategies of the party and often expressed the opinion that electoral victories (as well as failures) happen by chance rather than result from persistent and meticulous work (Laar 2005) further suggests his amateur rather than professional style of leadership.

Social Democratic Party (SDE) has been very similar to IL with regard to attitudes about organization building and electoral strategies. It, too, has lived through multiple mergers and used electoral alliances and joint lists for electoral survival (Tammer 1996c; Tarand 1999a). The leadership of SDE has changed equally frequently; here the most prominent and longest-serving leaders include Marju Lauristin (1990–1995), Andres Tarand (1996–2001), and Ivari Padar (2002–2009).[16] It was an elite party where leaders were not very interested in or concerned about local issues and grassroots members (Org 1996; Tammer 1995b). In the mid-1990s, the party (or rather, the two parties that merged at the time to form a predecessor of today's SDE) did not even keep track of its membership (Tammer 1996c). This disconnect with grassroots supporters is also exemplified by SDE's 1999 municipal election campaign. Rather than getting to know local problems and campaigning on local issues, the party campaigned under the slogan "Tarand for president!" The rationale for such a slogan was that representatives of local governments belong to the electoral college that elects the president of the republic. However,

[16] The other leaders of SDE include Eiki Nestor (1995–1996), Toomas Hendrik Ilves (2001–2002), Jüri Pihl (2009–2010), and Sven Mikser (since 2010).

seeing this as the most important role that local governments perform shows that the party was out of touch with the concerns of local voters (Huang 1999; Ideon 1999c) – something that strong organization might have helped prevent. Similar ineptitude to engage in local issues persisted in the 2002 local election campaign (Hiiesalu et al. 2002). Not surprisingly, both elections were utter failures for the party.

SDE has relied on intellectuals, such as Lauristin and Tarand, as leaders throughout most of its existence. Lauristin was an academic, an ideas person fixated by culture and literature earlier in her life and sociology and communication later (Lauristin 2010). Working in academia throughout her life, she became politically active as one of the leaders of the Estonian Popular Front participating in the process of restoring Estonian independence from the USSR. Although politically active for some time, she stressed that she had "never felt as a professional politician, but always as a university professor and social scientist" (see also Balbat 2004). In the Popular Front, she focused on the programmatic development and ideas, whereas Edgar Savisaar, the later leader of K – whom Lauristin called "genius at organizing" (Lauristin 2010, 130) – focused on the organization. Lauristin admitted that if the Popular Front did not have another, intellectually oriented center at her university, then it would have been much more organized, membership-based formal institution (Raudvere 2008). She did not have the background of a professional leader, and in her memoirs, Lauristin stressed the importance of ideas, ideology, and world view in motivating her involvement in party politics, when leading the SDE (Lauristin 2010, 152–154). She underscored the importance of "building social democracy" (Lauristin 2010, 152) and spreading social-democratic ideas rather than building the Social Democratic Party as an organization. It is also worth mention, however, that two years (1992–1994) out of the five that Lauristin was the party leader, she also served as the minister of social affairs. Because of the difficult social situation during the early years of transition, her ministry was the target of a lot of public criticism and blame. Not surprisingly, then, she has referred to these years as "the most horrible two years" of her life (Lauristin 2010, 144). Therefore, in addition to her leadership style, her difficult and time-consuming job in government may also have hampered her ability to concentrate on party affairs, including building an organization.

Andres Tarand opposed parties as organizations as a matter of principle (Tammer 1996c) and believed that well-known personalities drive electoral politics; he was convinced that the party needed him more (in order to survive) than he needed the party. Tarand even drew parallels between the party and a religious procession: the latter needs a portrait of a saint for people to carry just like a party needs a portrait of a leader, and he gave his portrait to SDE to carry (Tammer 1996c). The example of the 1999 local election campaign described previously further suggests that Tarand used the party mostly for fulfilling personal ambition (Huang 1999).

Although he had served as the director of the botanical gardens, Tarand, like Lauristin, was primarily an ideas person, an academic. The nonprofessional nature of Tarand's leadership is further exemplified by the fact that he did not like to admit that the party's own mistakes may have explained some of its electoral failures. Rather, Tarand often blamed low turnout, the strategies of other parties, and the modesty of the SDE – which prevented them from boasting about their achievements to voters – as explanations for the disappointing electoral performance (Tarand 1999a; Tarand 1999b; Tarand 2002).[17]

Ivari Padar differed from the previous leaders of the party in that he was personally well-connected at the grassroots level, and he valued these contacts. Under his leadership, the party even started a membership campaign (Šmutov 2006), although it remained relatively inefficient because by that time most of their competitors (most notably the K and ERL) were already far ahead in terms of their organization building. Padar did not make any more persistent effort in strengthening the party organization. Rather, like his predecessors, he was also mostly banking on well-known personalities as the campaign strategy (Valner 2003). Before becoming the party leader, Padar had served in a variety of jobs, including the minister of agricultural affairs, but he generally lacked a longer-term career in management. At the same time, he was generally perceived as a pragmatist and not an ideologue. His leadership style was, therefore, somewhat mixed, fitting the equally mixed outcome in terms of organizational development that occurred under his leadership.

In sum, the evidence from the Estonian cases is more varied than was the case with the Czech parties. However, on balance, there is general support for the leadership hypothesis and the narratives indicate that the different types of leaders played a direct role in influencing the level of party organizational strength. The strongest confirmation comes from the cases of K, IL, and SDE. In the former, a professional leader played a crucial role in building and maintaining party organization. It is likely that under a different leader the party would not have ended up with an equally strong organization as the comparison of Savisaar to his rivals suggests – these rivals simply valued the organization much less. In the latter two, amateur style dominated and organizational weakness ensued. In both parties, with the possible exception of Padar, leaders were more interested in intellectual exchange of ideas and/or fulfilling personal ambitions than developing an effective and strong grassroots presence, and overemphasized the role of individual candidates as opposed to the party in their election campaigns.[18] RE proved an interesting case where the hypothesis found only conditional support: the professional leaders of the party started to

---

[17] Other leaders, such as Toomas Hendrik Ilves and Ivari Padar, shared the latter interpretation (Reinap 2006; Valner 2003).

[18] These different campaign strategies of parties with weak versus strong organization were also reflected in the results of the opinion polls, according to which the organizationally strong K

prioritize organizational development only after perceived electoral failure. In this case, environmental factors played an important intermediary role in the relationship between leadership style and organizational strength.

Hungary

The Hungarian Socialist Party's (MSzP) case requires no lengthy elaboration here because Grzymala-Busse (2002a) eloquently documented that the organizational strength of the MSzP resulted from the choices of its professional leadership, especially during the immediate post-communist era (see also Morlang 2003; Ziblatt 1998). The long-term leaders and those who served during the party's regeneration years – Rezső Nyers (1989–1990), Gyula Horn (1990–1998), and László Kovács (1998–2008) – all had backgrounds in economics or trade and had served in managerial or leadership positions under the previous regime. Nyers's leadership was largely responsible for the regeneration of the party as an efficient and professionally managed organization – he staffed the central office and the leadership with pragmatic experts such as himself (Grzymala-Busse 2002a). Horn followed with an equal level of professionalism: he was generally considered to be a good, skillful, and firm manager (Debreczeni 2006; Index 2004; Körösényi 2006), a pragmatic leader with little interest in ideological debates and intellectual idealism (Ripp 2008). His goal was to continue Nyers's work and rebuild the party to make it competitive. Building the party organization was part of his strategy. He personally traveled across the country visiting small villages and towns to meet people in civic forums, learn about their problems, meet local MSzP leaders, and recruit new members and supporters (Horn 1999). He had regular meetings with local leaders throughout 1990–1994, and if he could not attend personally, he made sure that one of their MPs did (Horn 1999). This behavior indicates that he was personally committed to building ties with grassroots members and cared about the organizational presence and strength of the party.

When Kovács took over MSzP leadership, the party had already established itself as a major player – its organization building and regeneration phase was largely over. Kovács was an elder statesman, often criticized as too "quiet" and noneffective (Morlang 2003). In terms of values, however, he was not interested in ideological debates and, rather, set mainly organizational goals for his leadership: he wanted to democratize the decision-making process and attract more young members to the party (Aczél 2001). In the end, he largely maintained status quo in the party as far as organizational development was concerned, possibly because of the governing responsibilities of the party (Debreczeni 2006; Népszava online 2004).

voters had cast their vote for the party; the SDE and IL voters had voted for an individual (PM Online 2004c).

Of the subsequent leaders, Ferenc Gyurcsány (2007–2009) was probably the most influential. With his prior experience in various managerial roles in public and private sectors, and a practical rather than an ideological orientation, Gyurcsány fits the description of a professional leader. Although he only became leader in 2007, he had a significant impact on the practical leadership of the party from 2001. In fact, he was considered to be more influential than the nominal leader, István Hiller (2004–2007) (Debreczeni 2006; Mohai 2006; Szabados and Krekó 2007). In contrast to all other MSzP leaders, Hiller was an intellectual rather than a professional, lacking the necessary skills and experience to manage and maintain the party (HVG 2004a). He cared more about the image of the party; Gyurcsány cared about the organization. As an indication of his commitment to the party organization, Gyurcsány used the opportunity as a government minister to travel across the country and visit as many places as possible. As part of these visits he always found time to meet and get to know local party activists. In fact, Gyurcsány had a map in his office that he used to track and plan his travels. He also built a database of names and contact information of every local activist he met and could contact in the future (Debreczeni 2006). Additionally, Gyurcsány actively tried to modernize the party by attracting young members and organizing the youth into community networks (Papp 2009). Whatever the failures of Gyurcsány's leadership,[19] he managed to maintain the organizational strength of the party.

Fidesz has basically had only one leader throughout its existence: Viktor Orbán. Even during the three years that he was not formally the party president (2000–2003), he remained the de facto leader of the party (Bozóki and Simon 2006; Sebestyén 2007). Fidesz grew out of a group of university friends, and Orbán was already considered the leader of that group before the party was created (Fowler 2004). The other three leaders were each in office for a maximum of one year – not long enough to have any substantial influence on the organization. Furthermore, they were part of the group of friends who established Fidesz together with Orbán and remained his close associates, with a strong sense of loyalty to Orbán (Fowler 2004). This discussion will therefore concentrate on Orbán only.

Viktor Orbán is generally considered to be a skillful politician (Sebestyén 2007). Trained as a lawyer, he has been in politics since the regime change and has not had any other career. Although he therefore lacked managerial experience before becoming the party leader, he clearly qualifies as a professional leader according to the other characteristics summarized in Table 6.3. As a politician, he is described as a pragmatist, not interested in ideological debates or chained to any ideological position (Földvári 2001; Szobota 2000). It has

---

[19] It is argued that during his actual leadership, Gyurcsány tried to centralize and streamline the party, but found no support for it within the organization, which made him look like an authoritarian figure who attempted to rule with an iron fist (Jakus 2005; Juhász and Krekó 2008; Lengyel 2009).

been argued that Orbán does not think in ideological terms and tries to avoid talking about ideology, which is why Fidesz itself has been described as being in an ideological chaos (A. Lánczi 2002; Szobota 2000). As is characteristic of professional leaders, he and his close associates were clear about their goal of winning votes and office and their willingness to "subordinate personal considerations in pursuit of them" (Fowler 2004, 107). Fowler (2004, 108) further says that Fidesz's leadership had a strong sense of "party-ness," "a powerful sense of group identity," and "intense sense of institutional ownership and loyalty." Additionally, rather than engaging in programmatic debates at the elite level, Orbán enjoyed face-to-face contacts with voters and frequently toured the country (HVG 2005; Juhász and Szabados 2006).

Orbán is also largely responsible for the organization building within Fidesz. However, as we saw in Chapter 3, he was not necessarily convinced of the usefulness of the organization right from the start. Rather, initially, the party was "a loose federation of autonomous groups practicing direct democracy, and operating under collective leadership" (Lomax 1999, 113), and the leadership disregarded the importance of a strong organization (Toole 2003). The change of heart occurred only after the 1994 electoral defeat. Looking at the MSzP example made the party leaders realize that links to social networks were necessary for electoral success and stable support (Balázs and Enyedi 1996; Waterbury 2006). Under Orbán's leadership, the organization was restructured into that of a professional party with a conscious goal of winning the elections. Orbán deliberately studied the organizational structures of West European parties as examples for his own party, and was the first in Hungary to set up a political think tank (Csizmadia 2006b). The success came in 1998, when Fidesz finished with the largest vote and seat share in the parliamentary elections.

After losing the elections in 2002, Orbán decided to rebuild and strengthen the organization again (MTI 2003a). Indeed, he believed that party organizational weakness was the main reason for their defeat (Gavra 2004), and that further party building was necessary to make their mobilization and campaign efforts successful (T. Lánczi 2005). Because of this, Orbán built a new network-like party organization that linked a large number of supporters and voters to the party through Civic Circles. As Enyedi (2005, 13) reported, "Within months more than 10,000 Civic Circles were formed across the country, with more than 100,000 members." Local party branches accepted new members from these circles, and as a result, the party membership grew about two and a half times (Enyedi 2005).

The Hungarian Democratic Forum (MDF) started out as an intellectual movement, which is why it is not surprising that most of its leadership figures were intellectually oriented. This was certainly true of the first leader, Zoltán Bíró (1988–1989): although his idealism made him suitable to lead a social movement, he was generally considered to lack the skills necessary to lead MDF when it became a political party (Debreczeni 1998). Under Bíró, the party remained a loosely organized, bottom-up movement of intellectuals.

Bíró was succeeded by probably the most influential leader of MDF: József Antall (1989–1993). He ruled the party during its formative years and served as the prime minister during his leadership; both of these factors increased his profile within the party and allowed for a great influence. Although Antall was not one of the founding members of MDF, he was still more of an ideologue than pragmatist. His leadership style was authoritarian rather than professional. After the 1990 parliamentary election, MDF essentially became a one-man party, with Antall pushing through a modification of the party constitution to strengthen his powers (Bihari 1991; Bozóki and Simon 2006). He imposed no real organizational structure on the loose conglomerate that MDF had been before 1990. Electorally, Antall envisioned MDF as a catch-all party, and he favored expansion of membership, but with little concern for who joined (Horn 1999) and making no use of members to strengthen the party among the electorate. Antall was not interested in meeting with local party activists or voters (Csizmadia 2006a). Rather, as a prime minister, he was interested in governing (HVG 2004b) and policy making (Debreczeni 1998).

Lajos Für became the party leader after Antall's death in 1993, and remained in office until 1996. A professor of history, he was one of the founding members of MDF and carried their idealistic intellectual spirit. He was not considered to be a good organizer or talented leader (Debreczeni 1998). The media and other politicians characterized both Antall and Für's leadership as "ivory tower arrogance, aristocratism, and lack of expertise" (MTI 1994a). In fact, Für himself became aware of this after the 1994 election debacle when he stated, "We realized too late that it was wrong trying to teach to the majority the language that we speak instead of learning how to speak the language of the majority" (Vidos 1994). Indeed, the leadership had considered opinion polls showing low support for MDF as "liberal-cosmopolitan conspiracy" (Vidos 1994). All of this further speaks to the fact that party leadership was alienated from the members and voters, and made no use of the organization to establish a grassroots connection. Although Für was able to identify the problem, his plans to renew the party still did not involve organization building and strengthening. Rather, under his and Antall's leaderships, the party was poorly managed and the membership of the party declined drastically – by 18,000 people from about 43,000 to about 25,000 (MTI 1996). The renewal was focused on the ideas, "policies, and the image of the party" (MTI 1994b) underlining Für's amateur rather than professional leadership style.

Before the tenures of Antall and Für were over, the party was already relegated to a position of minor player in Hungarian party politics. The leadership of Sándor Lezsák (a teacher-poet) (1996–1999) and Ibolya Dávid (a lawyer) (1999–2010) brought no improvement in terms of organizational development. Both leaders placed more emphasis on elite-level politicking and deal making than on strengthening the party organization, door-to-door campaigning, or local politics.

Christian Democratic Peoples' Party (KDNP) provides another example of a party where organizational weakness coincides with and is exacerbated by non-professional leadership style. The party has had six leaders, but because it basically disintegrated in 1997 and was surviving through the 2000s only thanks to cooperation with Fidesz, I will concentrate on the tenure of the first three of them: Sándor Keresztes (1989–1990), László Surján (1990–1994), and György Giczy (1995–2001). These leaders did not have a professional-managerial background: Keresztes had two PhDs, in law and political science, and had worked as a Catholic journalist and publisher; Giczy was also a religious journalist; and Surján had a medical degree but had mostly engaged in manual labor under the previous regime. These backgrounds suggest an ideational and intellectual rather than pragmatic and professional orientation to party building. Indeed, the first leader, Keresztes, was explicitly cautious about establishing KDNP as a political party after it had functioned as a civic organization since 1988, because of his principled opposition to parties as organizations (Tamási Orosz 2006). He was characterized as honest and faithful but lacking political skills (Tamási Orosz 2006). Under László Surján's leadership, the party remained mostly focused on debates about ideology, program, and image, not on its organization (Kéri 1995; MTI 1992). Because KDNP was a governing party at the time, Surján himself was mostly focused on governing, which helped keep the internal ideological debates under cover (MTI 1992). These debates erupted fully when the party no longer had access to power under Giczy's leadership (Gazsó and Stumpf 1997; Hetek 1998c; Szarvas 1998). Rather than focusing on strengthening the party structures and professionally managing the conflict, Giczy's response was to redirect the party ideologically into more extremist positions (Varga 1996). During his first year as leader, the party started to rapidly disintegrate as a result.

Similar to the conclusions from the Czech and Estonian cases, the Hungarian parties provide general support for the leadership hypothesis. Again, however, some cases fit the hypothesis better than others. Fidesz, MDF, and MSzP appear to confirm the hypothesis most clearly. Orbán's profile fits with the definition of a professional leader: he stressed the primacy of the party over personal gains and instrumental concerns over ideological ones. The analysis also showed that the professional style not only corresponded with efforts to strengthen the party organization, but also that it was specifically Orbán who was behind much of the organization building because of his concern for party success. Of course, environmental factors played an important role too: it is only after electoral defeat that Orbán decided to invest in organization. Contrary to Orbán, the intellectually or personal–gain-oriented leaders of MDF undermined the organizational development. The MSzP case combined both types of leaders, and similarly suggests that leaders with a professional leadership style are markedly more concerned about building and maintaining party organizational strength than amateur leaders, as demonstrated by the leadership of István Hiller compared to the other leaders of MSzP. The case of KDNP, although generally supportive of the hypothesis, is slightly more complicated. Whereas it was the choice of different leaders of KDNP to focus on ideology and not engage in organizational development, this may have been as a result of a combination of leadership style and environmental factors. That is, although Keresztes clearly expressed his anti-party stance, Surján may have focused on governing rather than the organization by necessity and not choice.

Poland

The Polish Peasant Party (PSL) has had four different leaders since its creation: Roman Bartoszcze (1990–1991), Waldemar Pawlak (1991–1997, and since 2005), Jarosław Kalinowski (1997–2001), and Janusz Wojciechowski (2004–2005). Bartoszcze – an ex-Solidarity member – remained the leader for only about a year and then left with discontent to create his own party (Kurski et al. 1993). His main concern in the party was to cleanse it of former communists – a decision that was quite destructive for the party morale and organization (PAP 1991; Polish News Bulletin 1991a). He was clearly more of an ideologue than a party builder, which also determined the shortness of his tenure (Polish News Bulletin 1991b) because the rest of the party leadership generally agreed on the need to build and maintain a strong organization. Szczerbiak (2001b) reports, on the basis of his interviews with the party's vice presidents and parliamentary caucus leaders in the mid-1990s, that the leadership stood firmly behind the idea that the party needed to purposefully develop its organization, be actively involved in local life, encourage and support activists to create ties to other social organizations, and rely on its organization as the main strength of the party. Bartoszcze's successor, Waldemar Pawlak, fit this ethos. Credited as being one of the most skillful rural politicians, he was described as efficient, calm, restrained, detail oriented, always well prepared, and to the point, but also ready to compromise (Polish News Bulletin 1992a). He was neither driven by strong ideas and principles nor interested in ideological purity; rather, he was a pragmatic manager showing instrumental concern for the party as a vehicle for electoral success. He therefore better fits the description of a professional than an amateur leader. Although he was only in his early 30s when he became the party leader, he already had several years of experience as a party activist and representative under the previous regime. He was therefore familiar with and invested in the party organization. He removed the more–strongly-ideological communists and the most ardent ex-Solidarity members from positions of power to unite the party, and concentrated on practical, down-to-earth strategies to get the party elected (Janicki 1994). Pawlak has explicitly said that the real strength and influence of PSL depends on the active participation of all its members and organizational structures on the local level (PAP 1992). He stressed the need to become rooted in society before entering the political game, because only this way had the PSL been able to survive for more than 100 years (PAP 1993a). Janicki (1994) describes PSL under Pawlak leadership as follows: "The Polish Peasant Party's power base, even if not a majority [of the] electorate, is very dependable. The party will never trade it for a broader but more volatile one. The PSL does not buy risk[y] stocks and it firmly believes in investing in itself."

Pawlak's successor – Jarosław Kalinowski – can be classified as a professional rather than an amateur leader: he possessed administrative and political experience by having served as a local mayor and MP for several years before becoming the leader. However, he was not strongly concerned about the party organization, at least not in the beginning. Quite to the contrary of the theoretical prediction, he was more interested in the ideological direction of the party, by seeking cooperation with the left and rejecting any cooperation with the right (Dudek 2008). To reflect this, PSL formed a governing coalition with the SLD for the second time after the 2001 elections. When in government, analysts argued that Kalinowski was mostly driven by his interest in obtaining government posts and appointments, which led his co-partisans to accuse him of being too deferential to SLD, whose decisions were harming peasants (i.e., the PSL electorate) (Polish News Bulletin 2002a). Eventually, the party pulled out of the coalition. It was only then, after a serious internal crisis and declining support in the public opinion polls, that Kalinowski decided to turn to the party organization. He redirected his attention to the local level in an attempt to redeem the party's electoral success and image. Gajewski (2003) writes, "It is among the party's local-government activists that Kalinowski enjoys the highest support. They are his staunchest servicemen. Nine out of the NKW's [party's chief executive committee] 16 members are local-government activists; one in four village administrators in Poland has a PSL badge in his pocket." Using the party organization and building up the party's position in local governments as well as among local small business owners became the survival strategy for Kalinowski (Gajewski 2003). Furthermore, when Kalinowski unexpectedly resigned in 2004 in the midst of unresolved internal conflicts after the party lost state financial support, he explained, "For me, the PSL is the supreme value. I am resigning so that there not be torn hearts among PSL activists, so that there not be a fight that will weaken the party" (BBC Summary of World Broadcasts 2004). All of this indicates that, at the end of his career, Kalinowski behaved as a professional leader who did not seek personal ambition, but saw organizational advancement as his main goal. In sum, although Kalinowski was certainly not opposed to organizational development and possessed the qualities to be a professional rather than an amateur leader, he did not pay active attention to it and started showing instrumental concern for the party only after environmental factors turned negative for the party. Kalinowski and Pawlak remain the central leader figures for PSL. Before Pawlak's return, the party was also briefly led by Janusz Wojciechowski, but this episode lasted less than a year, leaving little opportunity to influence the organization.

The Democratic Left Alliance (SLD) has had six different leaders during the time period under consideration: Aleksander Kwaśniewski (1990–1995), Jósef Oleksy (1996–1997, 2004–2005), Leszek Miller (1997–2004), Krzysztof Janik (2004), Wojciech Olejniczak (2005–2008), and Grzegorz Napieralski (since 2008). The analysis concentrates on Kwaśniewski, Oleksy, and Miller, and as much as available information permits, briefly also considers the younger generation leaders (Olejniczak and Napieralski), although their tenure has been relatively short.

Kwaśniewski, Oleksy, and Miller were all closely engaged in revitalizing the ex-communist party, and all exhibited characteristics of professional leaders. As Grzymala-Busse (2002a) observes, ex-communists, thanks to their past positions, had an edge over their non-communist competitors in terms of administrative knowledge, skills, and personal contacts (see also Smolar 1998). Indeed, portraying themselves as the professionals "who did not debate and fight over procedure or grand issues but, rather, focused on making things work" was one of the explicit revival strategies for the party developed under Kwaśniewski's leadership (J. Curry 2003, 36). The other was to focus on organization and infrastructure. All of these leaders agreed from early on that all activity needed to be aimed at attracting the electorate rather than on ideological debates (Greenhouse 1990).

The first leader, Kwaśniewski, had been active in the Polish Student Association – one of the communist youth organizations, which was "pragmatic by style of its activities" and produced many top managers and high-skilled administrative officers (Kubiak 2007). He had also served as the youth and sports minister during the communist rule (Borger 1993). Both of these positions gave him hands-on administrative experience and skills. His professional style was reflected not only in his background but also his activities: Kwaśniewski was the driving force behind creating an extraordinary sense of party unity and "a clear and visceral sense of the importance of 'party'" among its members (J. Curry 2003, 36). Organization was the core purpose of the party for him.

Similarly to Kwaśniewski, Oleksy had also gained administrative experience under the previous regime, believed in the pragmatic rather than ideological reorientation of the party, and relied on building the party organization and infrastructure as his main leadership strategy (Polish News Bulletin 1995a). He was not concerned with ideological purity but rather with building close ties with members, activists, and voters (Polish News Bulletin 1996a). Oleksy has been characterized as an ambitious but self-critical and pragmatic leader, who approached problem solving by trying to find practical solutions rather than attributing blame (BBC Monitoring Europe 1999).

Contrary to Kwaśniewski and Oleksy, some sources consider Miller an ideologue because of his somewhat different background (Kurski et al. 1993; Polish News Bulletin 1996a). Specifically, like Kwaśniewski, he had also been active in a communist youth organization, but in a different kind: the Polish Socialist Youth Union. Contrary to the Student Association, this was a closed and hierarchical organization focused mostly on ideological disputes rather than developing practical skills (Kubiak 2007). However, when working on regenerating the party and later as the party leader, Miller was a pragmatist to the same extent as Kwaśniewski and Oleksy (J. Curry 2003). For example, after being elected leader in 1997, he stressed the need to make the party more efficient and focus on strengthening the party organization at the local level (Polish News Bulletin 1997d). The party credited Miller for being the true architect of the SLD's success in 1998 local elections (Polish News Bulletin 1998). As an additional characteristic of a professional leader, he (similar to Kwaśniewski and Oleksy) did not seek to lay the blame for party failures on others but instead readily admitted his own mistakes (Polish News Bulletin 1997d). Furthermore, when becoming the party leader, Miller explicitly distanced himself from the ideologues and surrounded himself with pragmatists (Polish News Bulletin 2001a). He followed a professional management style (Osser 2001) without encumbering the party in ideological debates (Matraszek 2002), which helped unite the party, develop and strengthen its organization, and maintain SLD's image as a competent administrator (Andrews 2001), at least until the party was drawn into numerous serious scandals. It was during Miller's time as prime minister that the party reputation was being undermined and organization weakened. This development is partially explained by the shift of leadership's focus on governing and away from the organization and infrastructure – people in high positions within the party were doing double duty by also serving in Miller's government, and the party no longer had an effective and independent administrative apparatus (Olczyk 2003a; Urbanek 2002). On top of that, scandals that the party was drawn into were of a magnitude that would have tumbled any party (Polish News Bulletin 2004a). This illustrates the theoretical argument about the relevance of contextual factors (including government membership and environmental hostility) in directly affecting as well as constraining any positive impact of professional leaders on party organizational strength.

After the crisis-ridden years in government and subsequent electoral losses, party leadership was entrusted to younger leaders: Olejniczak and Napieralski. Both were seen as not really interested in ideological debates about the direction of the party and at least initially portrayed as optimistic pragmatists focusing on the way forward for the party, on uniting and modernizing it. Both reminded the public of Kwaśniewski's style, and both therefore attracted positive media attention as well as new hope for the party (BBC Monitoring Europe 2005). However, these expectations were not necessarily met by their actual performance in office. Although highly regarded as a minister of agriculture (Millard 2007), by some accounts, Olejniczak turned out to be not much of a professional; rather, he was described as a person who was not very engaged, did not pay much attention to the news, and had no ambition or skills (Kalukin 2008). Olejniczak was also accused of neglecting the party organization and not developing or prioritizing relations with party branches – a problem serious enough for the old cadre, such as Leszek Miller, to leave the party (Polish News Bulletin 2007b), and for Olejniczak to lose the support of local structures (Kalukin 2008). It was argued that under Olejniczak's leadership, the organization became less motivated and less active, and therefore less able to deliver subsequent success (Olczyk 2008).

Napieralski became leader in 2008. He is claimed to be more oriented toward engaging local structures (Krysiak 2007). This may be related to his slow and steady move through the party career ladder, and his previous job as the general secretary of the party, as opposed to Olejniczak, who was easily elevated to leadership positions as Kwaśniewski's protégé (BBC Monitoring Europe 2005). As one observer noted, "Napieralski still goes around Poland and meets local activists," he knows how to talk to them and understands them (Kalukin 2008). He realized that organization was necessary for his party to survive on the political scene (Krysiak 2007). Napieralski was determined to achieve success and use the help of his organization and activists to do so (Zaluska 2008).

The Democratic Party (PD; formerly UW and UD) leaders set their party up as an expressly non-organizational entity: it was the party of the "best and the brightest," by and for the intelligentsia (V. Zubek 1995). The main leaders of the party were Tadeusz Mazowiecki (1991–1995), Leszek Balcerowicz (1995–2000), Bronisław Geremek (2000–2001), Wladysław Frasyniuk (2001–2006), and Janusz Onyszkiewicz (2006–2009). The amateur style is best exemplified by the first leader, Mazowiecki, who was an intellectual driven by political idealism and the idea that there is no need to divide the political scene into parties (Smolar 1998). Under Mazowiecki, UD developed an organization that resembled an informal arrangement rather than a political party (Polish News Bulletin 1993c). When Balcerowicz made efforts to strengthen the party organization, Mazowiecki criticized him for taking a pragmatic line and neglecting ideological debates (Polish News Bulletin 1997a).

Balcerowicz, with a background in economics and with prior managerial and policy-making experience, indeed, presented himself as a pragmatist and described his party as follows: "[T]he firm is manufacturing good products but they should be sold more efficiently" (Polish News Bulletin 1995b). "I have always been an advocate of good organization. A professional, modern party must be founded on good organization and discipline," claimed Balcerowicz (Polish News Bulletin 1995e). He also pointed out that SLD success was owing to its large party apparatus: "Modern politics is precisely about apparatus" he stated, and recognized that his own party had a great disadvantage in this regard (Polish News Bulletin 1996b). However, as was the case with the AWS leader Krzaklewski, Balcerowicz's actions did not follow from his stated convictions. Rather than actually building the organization on the ground, by "strong organization" he meant "strategic leaders," disciplined office holders, and programmatic work – that is, he had an elitist view of the party and its organization (Polish News Bulletin 1995c). He was not concerned with groundwork and grassroots members, but considered leaders and the program as vehicles for party success. Additionally, he was also relatively self-satisfied when assessing his party's strength, claiming that "the UW is [...] the strongest single party in Poland" (BBC Monitoring Europe 1998) right before the party suffered a great failure at the local elections. Rather than admitting that the party had failed to build a grassroots organization, Balcerowicz criticized the electoral law that favored bigger parties such as SLD, although he realized that SLD had won precisely because it was able to field more candidates, which indicated its superior organizational strength (BBC Summary of World Broadcasts 1998b).

Bronisław Geremek followed Balcerowicz's style of accusing others for his party's failures – although this time the scapegoat was not SLD but the newly created PO. It is quite ironic, and suggestive of amateur rather than professional leadership style, to accuse PO of posing political competition to UW and thereby undermining the latter's position, as Geremek did (PAP 2001). Geremek launched these accusations without realizing that (1) the leadership style and the organizational status quo of UW might have been responsible for why PO – a party whose several creators had defected from UW – was created in the first place, and (2) by strengthening his own party organization he might have been able to fight off any competition from ideological rivals, as some of the party's local leaders pointed out (PAP 2001). His emphasis on ideas and principles also corresponds with the amateur rather than professional leadership style. Geremek, part of the group of intellectuals to set up the party, claimed in an interview, "If it is worthwhile to take part in politics at all, it is primarily because one can turn it into a sphere for pursuing one's values and ethical principles" (Polish News Bulletin 1993b).

The Labor Union (UP), a labor party with Solidarity roots, was also dominated by ideological rather than pragmatic leaders. The first party leader, Ryszard Bugaj (1992–1997), was an academic, a deeply ideological "ideas person" (Polish News Bulletin 1993b). His amateur style was also reflected in the fact that he did not accept making any mistakes when facing declining public support, claiming that the downfall of the party was not related to the decisions made by the party (PAP 1996). Rather, Bugaj blamed (1) the continued economic growth, which made leftist ideas less appealing, (2) the voters, who had failed to grasp their program, and (3) the dailies for publishing opinion polls that showed support for UP below the 5 percent threshold of parliamentary representation and thereby discouraged people from voting for the party (Polish News Bulletin 1997c). Additionally, party activists complained that Bugaj undermined party unity and organizational strength by initiating conflicts between local branches (Polish News Bulletin 1997b).

Bugaj's successor, Marek Pol (1998–2004), also claimed to be more concerned about preserving the ideology of UP than its organization (BBC Summary of World Broadcasts 1998a). The former is somewhat questionable, the latter appears truer, as illustrated by the fact that under his leadership the party entered into several election coalitions, culminating in the electoral alliance with SLD at the national level (BBC Summary of World Broadcasts 2000; PAP 1998). The choice to closely ally with others rather than develop its own organization led rank-and-file members to fear for the survival of the party and caused further organizational decline, with members leaving and branches ceasing to function (Olczyk 2003b). Poor internal management under Pol was also reflected in the party losing its state financial support because of irregularities in their financial reports – a development that further undermined the organization by threatening the survival of local branches (Olczyk 2003b). In April 2004, the leadership position was taken over by Izabela Jaruga-Nowacka. By that time, UP had ceased to be a political force of much significance.

The Polish cases provide an interesting variation in the leadership style within most of the parties analyzed here. The only exception is UP, which only experienced amateur leadership and ended up with a weak and declining organization as a result. Most PD leaders (with the exception of Balcerowicz) were also intellectuals and amateurs in terms of leadership style, and none of them (including Balcerowicz) fully acknowledged, much less actively invested in, building and strengthening their party organization.

The other cases, although generally supporting the leadership hypothesis, also point at the relevance of environmental factors conditioning the leader effects. Specifically, the SLD party organization was at its strongest during the tenure of professional and organization-minded leaders, and weakened under Olejniczak – a nonprofessional leader. However, as mentioned, the organization was weakened when the leadership lost the pressure inflicted on them throughout the 1990s because of their image as ex-communists, and got tainted by numerous corruption scandals. It is, therefore, less clear to what extent leader effect worked in isolation as opposed to in combination with the environmental factors. Similarly, the effect of Pawlak and Kalinowski's leaderships of PSL offer illustrations of a direct leader effect and a combined effect of leadership and contextual factors. Whereas in Pawlak's case it seems that his professional style directly and positively affected the development of PSL's organizational strength, Kalinowski's leader effect seems to have been mediated by environmental factors: although largely a pragmatist and professional, Kalinowski started showing interest in organizational development only after the external and internal environment had turned hostile.

Qualitative Analysis: Summary

In most cases analyzed, leadership style played a significant role in determining the kind of organization the party would have. Parties with strong organizations were mostly dominated by leaders with professional style – pragmatic rather than ideological, ambitious but not self-centered, experienced in management and administration – who, as expected by the theory, consciously invested in developing the party organization. Those parties with weak organizations, on the other hand, tended to be dominated by leaders whose main attention was on ideas, ideologies, or principles, and who lacked the interest or capability to exercise sustained work on party organization.

In all countries there were parties predominantly led by either professional or amateur leaders, and this difference in the leadership style matched well with the level of organizational strength. For example, parties mainly led by professional leaders and having correspondingly strong party organizations included ČSSD and ODS in the Czech Republic, Fidesz and MSzP in Hungary, and K in Estonia. The narratives suggested that these leaders did not just happen to lead parties with strong organizations, but were personally involved in the organization building, and their decisions and actions had a direct impact on increasing or maintaining the organizational strength of their parties. In contrast, amateur leaders dominated ODA and US in the Czech Republic, KDNP and MDF in Hungary, IL and SDE in Estonia, and PD and UP in Poland, and were largely responsible for the continued organizational weakness of these parties.

Over-time comparison provided further evidence. In some cases, leaders with different leadership styles within the same party paid more or less attention to developing the party organization, which was manifested in fluctuations in the organizational strength. For example, in the ČSSD Zeman and Paroubek stood out as pragmatists and Špidla appeared more as an amateur. The former two were both concerned about organization as one of their core purposes; Špidla was more ideological and, fittingly, less concerned about the organization.

Several cases, although supporting the general logic of the argument, also provided evidence for the theoretical argument that party organizational development is a function of both the leadership effect as well as environmental factors. The Estonian, Hungarian, and Polish case studies provided most examples of the combined and conditional effects of these variables. For example, the case of the RE in Estonia indicated the relevance of the electoral environment in influencing the leadership effect. Looking only at the second half of the period under consideration suggests a robust relationship between leadership effects and organizational strength: by the mid-2000s, RE commanded a strong party organization and had always been led by professional leaders. However, this relationship occurred only after the party experienced unsatisfactory electoral result that prompted the professional leadership to invest in the party organization, suggesting that leadership style alone may not always be sufficient for a party to end up with a strong organization. A similar scenario applied to Fidesz in Hungary. The analysis of Kalinowski's leadership of PSL led to a similar conclusion, and the SLD case, too, suggests the relevance of electoral pressures.

Overall, the analysis suggests that leadership style has considerable explanatory power over party organizational strength. Professional leaders are more likely to prioritize and engage in organizational development and, as a consequence, lead organizationally strong parties; amateur leaders downplay or ignore the relevance of the party organization and therefore end up leading parties that are organizationally weak. I will now explore the extent to which this effect is generalizable and robust.

Quantitative Analysis

The statistical analysis of leader effects relies on the same dataset already used earlier in this chapter. The variable "Leadership style" is measured as follows. First, for each leader I have identified on the basis of information about their backgrounds and attitudes whether they can be classified as professional (coded as "1") or amateur (coded as "0") style leaders. These coding decisions are detailed in Appendix 6.2 which provides summary information for each leader together with the coding decision and a short narrative presenting (1) a description of the information that determined the coding decision, and (2) a short evaluation of that leader's behavior toward organizational development. Note that coding decisions are based only on (1) and not on (2), which would lead to a tautology. Second, for each leader, the appendix also identifies the years that he or she was in power. Finally, in order to obtain the leadership-style score for a party for the entire period under consideration, I summarized the type of leadership of each leader weighted by the fraction of time they were in power. The theoretical range of the variable is, therefore, from 0 to 1; the former indicates that all of the party leaders over the years have followed amateur style and the latter indicates the opposite.[20]

I have reestimated the analyses presented in Table 6.1 by replacing the variables "Environmental hostility" and "Poor/rural electorate" with "Leadership style." The results of these analyses are presented in Table 6.4. As the results show, with the exception of membership size, leadership style is significantly and positively related to party organizational strength. The effect is also positive for membership size, but it falls short of statistical significance on a two-tailed test ($p = 0.15$).[21] Overall, the results confirm the conclusion from the qualitative analysis that leadership style is significantly related to organizational strength: the more dominated the party is by professional leaders, the stronger the party organization. As the last column in Table 6.4 indicates, the leadership effect remains positive and significant when ex-communist parties are excluded from the analysis.

Substantively, a party that has only had amateur-style leaders (e.g., ODA, IL, MDF, LPR) (holding all other variables at their mean or median values)

---

[20] The number of parties included in this analysis is limited because of unavailability of data. Furthermore, as stated, sufficient information may not be available for all leaders, especially those that have served for a short period of time. I have treated these as missing data and not included them in the calculation of the "Leadership style" variable. For parties that effectively ceased to exist as political actors before 2010, I have only considered the period in which they were still active to calculate the fraction of time in office for each leader.

[21] The effect is significant when using a one-tailed test.

TABLE 6.4. *The Effect of Leadership Style on Party Organizational Strength*

	Participation in Local Elections	Membership	Branches	Size of Staff	Participation in Local Elections; Ex-communist Parties Excluded
Leadership	0.213***	0.004#	0.710***	0.892**	0.132*
style	(0.064)	(0.002)	(0.243)	(0.384)	(0.076)
Campaign	0.001	0.000	−0.004	−0.009	0.001
expenditure	(0.001)	(0.000)	(0.005)	(0.008)	(0.001)
Constant	0.181***	0.0004	0.384*	−0.099	0.154***
	(0.050)	(0.002)	(0.189)	(0.313)	(0.051)
R^2	0.50	0.20	0.35	0.53	0.42
N	29	29	25	25	25

Note: The different dependent variables are noted in column headings. Table entries are unstandardized regression coefficients with standard errors in parentheses. Country dummies are included in the models but not reported. $^{#}p = 0.15$, $^{*}p \leq 0.1$, $^{**}p \leq 0.05$, $^{***}p \leq 0.01$

is expected to contest local election in about 20 percent of municipalities, have a membership of 0.05 percent of the electorate, organizational presence in 28 percent of municipalities, and no paid staff. In contrast, a party that has had only professional-style leaders (e.g., Fidesz, K, ODS) is expected to have a significantly stronger organization including contesting local elections in about 42 percent of municipalities, have a membership of 0.4 percent of the electorate, organizational presence in 99 percent of municipalities, and 1 staff member per about every 200,000 voters.

In addition to the individual effect of leadership style on party organizational strength, it is also relevant to study its combined effect with the environmental factors. First, as the theory assigns significance to both the internal (leadership) and external (environmental) factors, it is important to determine whether leadership style still matters when environmental conditions are controlled for and vice versa. In addition to additive effects, however, the case studies suggested that leadership style and environmental factors can also work in combination, with the effect of one influencing that of the other. For example, it is possible that leadership style influences how a given party is likely to react to environmental constraints. Hostile environment, underdog status, and poor/rural electorate may not be enough to trigger organization building in the absence of a professional leader, especially if, as the theory suggests, nonprofessional leaders are less likely to admit mistakes and more likely to blame adverse circumstances for failures. Similarly, professional leaders may have the skills and abilities, but not the incentive, to build party organizations in the absence of environmental hostility and a hard-to-reach electorate.

TABLE 6.5. *The Combined and Conditional Effect of Environment and Leadership on Organizational Strength*

	Additive Model	Interactive Model
Leadership style	0.158**	0.096
	(0.063)	(0.082)
Environmental incentive	0.081**	0.012
	(0.035)	(0.069)
Leadership style*		0.108
Environmental incentive		(0.092)
Campaign expenditure	0.001	0.001
	(0.001)	(0.001)
Constant	0.112	0.157**
	(0.054)	(0.066)
R^2	0.60	0.62
N	29	29

Note: The dependent variable is "Participation in local elections." Table entries are unstandardized regression coefficients with standard errors in parentheses. Country dummies are included in the models but not reported. $^*p \leq 0.1$, $^{**}p \leq 0.05$

In order to test the additive and combined effects, I added the values of the poor/rural electorate and environmental hostility into a single variable called "Environmental incentive," which ranges from 0 to 2. This is preferable to including two environmental variables given the small number of cases and growing number of variables, especially with the interaction effects. The pair-wise correlation coefficient between leadership style and environmental incentive is only 0.28, indicating that professional leaders are likely to emerge and dominate different kinds of parties: those that represent poorer and/or rural electorate as well as those that are oriented toward middle-class urban voters, and those that have experienced environmental hostility as well as those that have not.

The results of the additive model, using participation in local elections as the dependent variable, are presented in Table 6.5. Both the leadership style and environmental incentive are positively and significantly associated with party organizational strength. I also calculated the standardized coefficients to be able to compare their size: the effect of the leadership style is slightly stronger (standardized coefficient = 0.40) than that of environmental incentive (standardized coefficient = 0.36). However, the fact that both effects remain significant in the presence of the other, underlines the importance of both the environmental conditions as well as agency in determining the level of party organizational strength.

I then included in the model an interaction effect between environmental incentive and leadership style. The results of this model are presented in the last column of Table 6.5. Note that the full effects of interaction models are not directly interpretable from the results table. All that these results tell us is that if the value of the leadership variable is 0 (i.e., the party has been lead by amateur leaders only), environmental incentives have no significant effect on organizational strength. Similarly, if the value of environmental incentive is 0 (i.e., the party represents middle-class urban voters and enjoys friendly electoral environment), then leadership style has no discernible effect on organizational strength. When calculating the conditional coefficients, however, it appears that leadership style positively and significantly influences organizational strength for parties that either represent poor/rural electorate or face environmental hostility (i.e., when the value of environmental incentive is at least 1) and the effect strengthens even more when both conditions are present. Similarly, the effect of environmental incentive on organizational strength becomes significant for parties that have been led by professional leaders at least half of the time, and the effect strengthens the more dominated the party is by professional as opposed to amateur leaders.

To get a better substantive sense of these conditionalities, I calculated expected values of organizational strength for different scenarios holding other variables at their mean or median values. The expected number of local governments contested for parties who lack environmental incentive and professional leaders is about 19 percent. This increases to 21 percent for parties that have the environmental incentive but lack professional leadership and to 28 percent for parties that lack the environmental incentive but have professional leaders. When both conditions are at their maximum value, the expected share of local governments contested reaches 50 percent. In sum, these results confirm the conclusions derived from the case studies that environmental conditions and leadership effects reinforce each other in their relationship to party organizational strength.

Conclusion

The goal in this chapter has been to provide a preliminary explanation of the origins of strong party organizations. I focused on three main explanations: the nature of the party's electorate, the level of environmental hostility against the party, and the leadership style of the party.

The analysis suggests that all three factors are likely to matter for whether a party will have a strong or weak organization. Specifically, parties that are mostly targeting poorer or rural voters are more likely to build strong organizations. The same is true of parties suffering from environmental hostility, such as former regime stigma, pariah status, or stiff competition in a saturated arena because of late entry. These factors are especially influential during the initial years after party formation. The environmental conditions further reinforce each other's effects in that parties for which both conditions are present are more likely to have strong organizations.

Leader characteristics also matter for whether or not the party builds a strong organization. Leaders following a professional style were more likely to prioritize organization building and be personally involved with the process than leaders with an amateur style. Indeed, the case studies indicated not only a correlation between leadership style and organizational strength, but also that leaders were directly responsible for organizational development or lack thereof. The quantitative analysis confirmed the generalizability and robustness of the effect of leadership style on organizational strength. It also demonstrated that environmental conditions and leadership style significantly and independently influence the extent to which a party is likely to build a strong organization.

The narratives further illustrated how the contextual factors and leadership style can work in tandem to increase or decrease party organizational strength. Specifically, in several cases, environmental conditions mediated the leadership effect with the (perceived) underdog status augmenting the positive effect of professional leadership or even acting as the necessary condition for the professional leadership style to take effect. The quantitative analysis confirmed this conditional effect. It also demonstrated that this interaction effect works the other way around, as well: environmental incentives alone, in the absence of a professional leader, may not be sufficient to trigger organizational strengthening. After all, most parties with amateur leaders suffered electoral failure, but their organizations still remained weak. As we saw, such leaders were simply much less likely to admit failures.

In sum, it is likely that environmental conditions and leadership style influence party organizational strength not only directly but also condition each other's effect on organization building. The same leader can choose a different course of action with regard to organization building depending on the environmental conditions. Similarly, different leaders may address the same environmental condition – the nature of the electorate or environmental hostility – quite differently. Such conditionality may explain why the same party can take different turns in terms of organization building even if the environmental conditions remain the same, as the ČSSD case exemplified. It also helps understand why leaders may seem to change their minds about organizational development in the course of their careers, as was the case, for example, with Kallas in RE, Orbán in Fidesz, and Kalinowski in PSL.

7

Conclusion

The establishment of stable parties is critical to democratic stabilization. How parties and party systems evolve and stabilize has, therefore, been one of the most important questions in the context of democratic transitions in post-communist Europe. Understanding why some parties succeed in becoming the defining features of the new party systems and others fail is central to answering this question. The results of this study suggest that the electoral success and survival of the party, and its elite cohesion, crucially depend on its organizational strength. The stronger the party organization (the larger its membership, more extensive its local presence, and more professional its staff), the more electorally successful the party. Even within the same party, the organizationally stronger the party branch in a given electoral district, the more electorally successful the party in that district. Organizationally strong parties are also more likely to successfully overcome any crises and survive as significant players than their organizationally weak counterparts. Additionally, such parties are significantly better able to keep their representatives unified and the party cohesive in office.

Party organizational strength positively affects electoral success and survival because a strong grassroots presence, permanent structures, and professional management make it possible for parties to have immediate, frequent, and organized contacts with the electorate, and to credibly portray themselves as competent, reliable, and accountable. This, in turn, allows parties to more effectively shape voters' biases in their favor and thereby mobilize support for the party. This book shows that parties with strong organizations in CEE could and did use their members and local structures for mobilizing voters and creating sustained contacts with them, getting involved in local affairs, training new candidates, and gathering policy ideas. These activities helped generate support for the party and sustain the support even through political crises. Professional staff, on the other hand, was largely responsible for managing diversity and conflict within the party organization, further helping sustain the image of reliability and accountability and, consequently, electability. All these factors in combination significantly increased the survival and success chances of organizationally strong parties over their organizationally weak competitors. The latter did not prioritize organization building and downplayed the importance of members, branches, and professional management in succeeding and surviving electorally. Without organizational support, the emphasis was on short-term factors such as appealing candidates, media-based campaigns, and Populist policies to attract support. Such a strategy did not allow cultivating sustained relationships with voters and supporters and relied on "floating voters" for electoral success. Lack of professional management, in turn, allowed internal conflicts to thrive uncontrolled. The different aspects of organizational weakness worked in combination to undermine the prospects of successfully establishing the party in the new democracy.

The positive effects of strong organizations on electoral success and survival also benefit party unity. Party elites are more willing to remain loyal to the party that is able to better guarantee their reelection. Furthermore, because it is the organization that brings success, parties with strong organizations do not have to rely heavily on candidate personalities and popularity. This makes parties less dependent on their candidates and allows them to more freely use (the threat of) punishment for defection to keep representatives unified. Parties with weak organizations, on the other hand, are less able to guarantee the reelection of their candidates on the basis of party reputation and therefore lack the means to motivate representatives to remain loyal. They are simultaneously more dependent on the reputation of these candidates for electoral success and therefore also lack the motivation to discipline them for undermining party unity. Individualism and defections from the party line during legislative voting ensue.

In the context of new democracies, where parties emerge relatively simultaneously, with all possessing relatively comparable resources and none really tied to any particular social cleavage, it is the strategic choice of building strong party organization that provides the necessary competitive advantage and significantly affects which parties become the basis of the emerging party system. Organizational strength is a key factor in remaining competitive and becoming institutionalized in an otherwise tumultuous and unpredictable electoral environment.

Despite the positive consequences of party organizational strength, not all parties in new democracies choose to invest in organization building, and this poses an interesting puzzle. One possibility, of course, is that in the context of young democracies, where the political elite is relatively inexperienced and learning often occurs through trial and error, these party elites have not realized the benefits of strong organizations. As the case studies in Chapters 3 and 6 showed, in several instances, this realization came only later, after multiple trials to win elections by other methods or after observing the performance trajectories of organizationally well-endowed parties. In other cases, party elites simply refused to acknowledge the relevance of organizations. After all, the scholarly community has also been skeptical about the relevance of organizations and it is, therefore, not surprising that party elites echoed this sentiment. For example, we saw in Chapter 3 how the Czech ODA stubbornly claimed that elite performance is more relevant for electoral success than the number of members, even in the face of contrary evidence from its own election analysis. In Estonia, Hungary, and Poland, too, some of the biggest vote getters in the early 1990s were explicitly not concerned with recruiting members because they believed that the mass party era was over and members were not important in the modern time.

Although lack of knowledge and refusal to update ones' beliefs may be plausible explanations for the persistent organizational weakness of some parties, political scientists generally like to think of politicians as strategic actors. The study, therefore, explored the possibility of strategic reasons for keeping organizations small. Internal party politics provides one such reason. Specifically, building a strong organization may be quite risky for the party leadership because it may undermine their intra-party power. We saw that party subunits that are organizationally strong are also more powerful as reflected in the legislative behavior and positions of representatives from these subunits. This power, again, originates from the ability of organizationally strong subunits to mobilize and communicate with voters; that is, to provide the resources critical for the functioning of the party. Such redistribution of power that organization building necessarily entails may not be very appealing to party leadership concerned with maintaining control over party internal decision making. This argument, therefore, provides a plausible rational explanation for why it should not be surprising to see weak party organizations despite the positive consequences of party organizational strength.

Still, there is variance as to whether parties prioritize the negative or positive consequences of party organizational strength. That is, party organizations in new democracies are not uniformly strong or weak: some parties build strong organizations and others do not. I have argued that at least some of this variance is because of whether or not a party has an extra incentive to build a strong organization and is capable of acting on this incentive. The extra incentive can emerge from the nature of the electoral environment that the party is facing. This extra incentive is more likely to be present for parties that experience environmental hostility in the form of a pariah status or late entry into an already-saturated electoral market. It is easier for parties that have not experienced such underdog status to convince themselves that elections can be won without costly organization building. For underdogs, those parties that are struggling against negative media image, establishing direct contacts with voters by way of party organization building may be the only strategy available. The extra incentive is also more likely to be present for parties that target poorer and/or rural voters than those parties that target middle-class urban voters and operate in a friendly environment. The former are simply harder to reach by abstract media campaigns and effective communication with them requires organizational presence.

Capacity to successfully act on the incentive to build an organization, in turn, depends on the style of the leadership in that the experiences and convictions of party leaders shape their choices with regard to party building. Specifically, we saw that leaders with professional background and pragmatic attitudes were more likely to prioritize organization building than intellectually and ideologically oriented leaders. The latter often lacked the skills of organization building. Not less importantly, their understanding of a party was likely to center on ideas, vision, and ideology; the pragmatic leaders were more likely to see party organization as the core element of a party. In sum, the combination of environmental factors and leadership style significantly influence the extent to which organization building becomes part of a party's strategy.

Broader Implications

The patterns of party development uncovered in this study contribute to several strands of literature. The most direct and substantial contribution is to the literature on party development, institutionalization, and party organization. In short, party organizational strength matters for party institutionalization in new democracies. Scholars of CEE have remained skeptical about this possibility and empirical evidence has largely been lacking. The current study provides the missing comprehensive empirical analysis and confirmatory evidence. It complements a large literature that has identified institutional, sociological, and economic factors influencing the evolution of parties and party systems in new democracies by focusing on the decisions and choices by parties themselves. Whereas institutions and environment matter for the stability and institutionalization of entire party systems, the party-level explanation provided here can account for why certain parties and not others succeed and stabilize in the new regimes. The organizational explanation highlights the relevance of purposive action rather than simply environmental determinism in affecting the nature of party competition and, consequently, democratic development. Furthermore, this book clearly shows that the "old-fashioned" tools of organizational mobilization work, not only in terms of voter mobilization, but also in terms of building real and strong linkages between voters and parties.

The practical implications of these findings are equally significant. By stressing that parties' own decisions with regard to organization building affect their success, survival, and unity, the study offers party leaders as well as international democracy promoters a concrete and manageable tool to help party institutionalization. These domestic and international actors can direct resources to building and strengthening party organizations. This will not only help individual parties succeed and survive in democracy, but also creates better opportunities for democratic consolidation. Indeed, given the positive consequences of party organizational strength to electoral success and party unity, there is a significant motivation for parties to want to build strong organizations, and this bodes well for future prospects of party development and democratic stability in the region. It implies that there are significant incentives for parties to try to avoid cartelization and state colonization at the expense of voter mobilization – trends that are argued to be present especially in long-term European democracies (Katz and Mair 1995, 2009; see also Grzymala-Busse 2007). By pointing at the positive consequences of organization building the study may help advance the literature on cartel parties more generally, especially in terms of when cartelization is more or less likely to occur.

The findings here also directly contribute to the literature on the emergence and stabilization of political cleavages (Lipset and Rokkan 1967) by suggesting one possible explanation for the politicization of certain types of cleavages over others. Specifically in the context of post-communist democracies, previous literature suggests that surviving parties are responsible for politicizing cleavages and thereby crafting the ideological space for party competition (Zielinski 2002). The critical question that this literature has left unanswered is which parties are more likely to survive. The findings reported here provide one possible answer – those that invest in building strong organizations – and thereby help paint a more complete picture of the origins of politically relevant cleavages.

In addition to party institutionalization, the study provides one of the most comprehensive analyses of party organizations in the post-communist region. It uncovers significant diversity in the level of organizational strength across parties and even for the same party across time. This is in great contrast to existing studies that often portray party organizations in the region as uniformly weak, thereby undercutting the possibility that this factor might help us understand party competition. The study not only explores some of the most important consequences of party organizational strength in new democracies but also provides an analysis of its causes. This is a novel contribution to the literature on party organization, which to date has been relatively descriptive in nature. The argument about the combination of environmental and leadership effects on the level of party organizational strength can help explain the diversity in party organizations in any setting, not just in new democracies. Importantly, once again, these results underline the importance of actors, their predispositions, skills, and choices in determining the direction of party building. This complements the existing literature on party organizations with its focus mostly on long-standing democracies and, consequently, on almost immovable social factors and long-term historical path dependency in affecting the nature of parties and their organizations.

This study also makes a significant empirical contribution to the literature on party organizations by developing an indicator of party organizational strength – the capacity of a party to run candidates in local elections. This indicator covers all attributes of the concept as defined here; can travel across parties, countries, and time; and is, for the most part, publicly available, even if not always easy to access. All these properties are important for a consistent, standardized, and generalizable indicator because the systematic study of party organizations, at least outside advanced democracies, has been hampered by the unavailability of such a measure. Information on other indicators – even as straightforward as membership figures – is often unobtainable. Although the number of members, information on the network of local branches, the level of professionalization of staff, and numerous other more qualitative evaluations of party organizational strength are certainly valuable, the capacity to contest local elections nationwide can systematically and reliably capture the different attributes of organizational strength and thereby aid the empirical analysis of the causes and consequences of party organizational strength across space and time.

The implications of this study reach beyond the primary topic of party development, and some extend to areas outside party politics altogether. Specifically, the other sets of literatures that this study contributes to include the analysis of party unity, intra-party distribution of power, and leadership effects. Party unity depends not only on the institutional environment but also on how parties are organized. Additionally, the arguments and evidence in Chapter 5 complement the existing party-unity literature by focusing on the individual rather than the party or country level, and showing that incentives to comply with the party line can vary significantly for different MPs within the same party depending on the relative power of the party branch in their district.

The intra-party power distribution itself has received very little attention in the literature, despite the fact that much of party politics depends on who is influential. It is therefore a crucial area for future research, with this study describing but one way power can be unevenly distributed within parties. Future studies may extend this line of research by conducting large-scale surveys of party members, leaders, local subunit organizers, and MPs in order to measure their perception of the distribution of intra-party power, the sources of power, and the effects of it. It is likely that the unequal distribution of power between subunits affects observable outcomes not examined here, such as the ideological placement of the party, its coalition preferences, and policy choices. In general, research on any aspect of party politics may want to take into account the possible uneven internal power distribution within political parties.

Finally, the study contributes to the literature on leadership effects – an area of renewed interest in political science (Ahlquist and Levi 2011). Comparative studies of party leaders have mostly focused on their role in electoral competition. The evidence here shows that a leader is relevant not just as the face of the party but also as a key actor whose preferences, beliefs, and background influence the nature of the party organization. The difference between professional and amateur leaders – a classification of party leaders and activists developed for the U.S. context – significantly helps in understanding the organization-building trajectories of parties in new democracies, as well. Furthermore, the analysis of leadership effects demonstrated that not only were professional leaders more likely to engage in organizational development, they were also more likely to learn to recognize the importance of organization from their own (and sometimes others') past mistakes and the party's past performance than amateur leaders. This finding adds an important new perspective to the vast and growing literature on policy learning and diffusion (see, e.g., Gilardi 2010; Meseguer 2005; Shippan and Volden 2008), which often refers to the characteristics of a given policy or polity in determining the likelihood of policy learning to occur. The findings in this book, however, highlight the characteristics of the elite that may equally importantly condition the nature and extent of learning that takes place.

Parties in Post-Communist Europe and Beyond

How generalizable are the results presented in this book? Although primarily motivated by the development of parties in new democracies, the theoretical arguments presented here are all relatively general in nature. Questions of party success, survival, and unity and of conditions helping build and maintain strong party organizations are universal to parties in all competitive systems. Of course, in new democracies, the consequences of success, survival, and unity are likely to be more serious given that they may affect not only the nature of the party systems but also the stability of the regime. In advanced democracies, changes in party performance and unity from one election to the next are usually relatively small. However, even these changes generate excitement among the political actors, public, and scholarly community. After all, small changes can influence government composition and policy outcomes. Concern over predictability of party performance is therefore a serious one, and focus on party organization can help us better understand this phenomenon. Furthermore, the argument about the relevance of party organizational strength is in line with more resent research on advanced democracies that is increasingly, and in contrast to much of the earlier literature, relying on non-policy explanations of party performance.

Although generalizable, it is possible that the relationships studied in this book are less pronounced in old democracies than in new. There may simply be less variance in the level of organizational strength between parties in established democracies. As evidence in Chapter 2 demonstrated, the effect of some organizational-strength variables diminishes as the post-communist democracies mature. This mostly reflects the fact that weak organizations tend to die, and some organizational-strength variables may reach their maximum values beyond which strengthening party organization is no longer paying off. This may explain the skepticism of some scholars of West European parties with regard to the competitive advantage of organization building. What the findings in this book do imply, however, is that organizational strength is likely to be a key element for the success and survival of new parties in established democracies. Without a credible organization, the new contestants will very clearly be at a disadvantage compared to the existing parties. Studies of specific types of new parties – the radical right – have, indeed, pointed out organizational weakness as one of the primary reasons for their frequent implosion (Mudde 2007). Even beyond the new parties, the ongoing, intense attention that political candidates in the United States pay to building strong ground organizations, and the increasing recognition of the relevance of local parties for national party performance in other advanced democracies (Carty and Eagels 1999; Johnston and Pattie 2006) suggest that organizational strength may never really lose its salience, no matter how much democracies or parties mature.

The relevance of the research presented here to new democracies outside Europe is also evident. Literature on democracies in Africa and Latin America often addresses the question of party institutionalization (e.g., Basedau and Stroh 2008; Mainwaring 1998). Understanding which parties are more likely to succeed and survive, and consequently to define the characteristics of the emerging party systems as well as prospects for democratic stability, are, if not more than at least as urgent in those countries as they are in post-communist Europe. A crucial side note emerging from almost each chapter of this study is that organizational strength does not just separate ex-communist parties from their new democratic competitors but also helps understand differences within the latter group of parties. Thus, the story advanced in this book is not one of ex-communism versus post-communism. Rather, it is a story about how to succeed, as a party, especially in a tumultuous context of new democracies where few existing resources are available to any of the aspiring competitors. Most clearly, this book underlines the importance of agency in addition to just context in affecting the fate of parties – a lesson that is likely to be applicable anywhere.

Appendixes

Appendix 2.1. Data Sources

Variable	Source
Vote share	National Election Commissions
Membership	Personal communication with party staff, party archives,
Branches	general archives, national newspapers, and secondary
Staff	literature
Participation in local elections	National Election Commissions
Budget	Personal correspondence with parties, party archives, financial reports by parties, secondary literature
Leader centeredness	National Election Commissions, http://www.essex.ac.uk/elections/; Enyedi 2008.
Government membership	Keesing's World News Archive
Unemployment	National statistical offices, Global Development Network Growth Database
Number of lists	National Election Commissions
Turnout	National Election Commissions

Appendix 2.2. Descriptive Statistics: Party Organizational Strength

Dataset	Variable	N	Mean	SD	Min	Max
Cross-national	Participation in local elections	104	0.196	0.195	0	0.787
	Branches	84	0.327	0.293	0	1.090
	Members	104	0.003	0.004	0.00003	0.025
	Staff	63	0.829	0.820	0	2.786
Estonia	Participation in local elections	184	0.240	0.273	0	1
	Branches	154	0.219	0.221	0	0.870
	Members	136	0.005	0.005	0.0003	0.030
Czech Rep.	Participation in local elections	222	0.198	0.200	0	0.914
	Members	83	0.004	0.005	0.0002	0.018
Poland	Participation in local elections	835	0.318	0.260	0	0.978
Hungary	Participation in local elections (PR sample)	451	0.177	0.202	0	1
	Participation in local elections (SMD sample)	455	0.176	0.201	0	1

Note: The descriptive statistics are calculated based on cases included in Tables 2.5 and 2.10.

Appendix 4.1. Number of Parties Per Country and Legislative Term

Country	Legislative Term	Number of Observations
Czech Republic	1996–1998	7
	1998–2002	5
	2002–2006	5
	2006–2009	5
Estonia	1999–2003	7
	2003–2007	6
Hungary	1994–1998	6
	1998–2002	6
	2002–2006	4
	2006–2010	5
Poland	1997–2001	6
	2001–2005	7
	2005–2007	6
TOTAL		75

Appendix 4.2. Formulas for Calculating Various Measures of Party Unity

Regular Rice score is the absolute difference between "yes" and "no" votes for party i on vote j calculated as follows:

$$Rice_{ij} = \left| \%yes_{ij} - \%no_{ij} \right|$$

Agreement Index accounts for "yes," "no," and "abstain" votes and is calculated as follows:

$$Agreement\ Index_i = \frac{\max\{Y_i, N_i, A_i\} - \frac{1}{2}[(Y_i + N_i + A_i) - \max\{Y_i, N_i, A_i\}]}{(Y_i + N_i + A_i)}$$

where Y_i denotes the number of yes votes expressed by party i on a given vote; N_i the number of no votes; and A_i the number of abstain votes.

Weighted Rice score accounts for the closeness of votes and is calculated as follows:

$$Weighted\ Rice = \frac{\sum_{j=1}^{n} Rice_{ij} * weight_j}{\sum_{j=1}^{n} weight_j}$$

where n is the number of votes; $Rice_{ij}$ is calculated as indicated above; and the weight of any single vote is defined as:

$$weight_j = 1 - \left| \frac{\text{total "yes"}_j - \text{total "no"}_j}{\text{total votes}_j} \right|$$

Weighted Agreement Index uses a similar weighting to the Agreement Index.

Appendix 4.3. Descriptive Statistics: Party Unity

Variable	N	Mean	SD	Min	Max
Weighted Agreement Index	75	0.867	0.133	0.204	0.991
Participation in local elections	73	0.207	0.182	0.000	0.787
Local branches	63	0.352	0.286	0.017	1.090
Members	73	0.004	0.004	0	0.025
Staff	50	0.893	0.864	0.007	3.722
Centralized candidate selection	75	0.707	0.458	0	1
Party size (vote share)	75	0.161	0.119	0	0.461
Governing party	75	0.427	0.498	0	1
Size of governing majority	75	0.040	0.074	−0.130	0.223
Number of votes (in thousands)	75	8.024	4.253	1.844	15.682
Party budget (% GDP, in thousands)	75	0.036	0.041	0.0002	0.226

Appendix 4.4. Regression Analysis of Party Organizational Strength and Voting Unity in Parliament, Alternative Measures of the Dependent Variable

	Agreement Index				Weighted Rice			
	Local Elections	Members	Branches	Staff	Local Elections	Members	Branches	Staff
Participation in local elections	0.038 (0.027)				0.143** (0.066)			
Members		2.700* (1.497)				4.842*** (1.476)		
Local branches			0.062*** (0.019)				0.139** (0.067)	
Staff				-0.004 (0.009)				-0.014 (0.014)
Centralized candidate selection	0.012 (0.013)	0.008 (0.013)	0.011 (0.012)	0.010 (0.014)	0.036 (0.035)	-0.001 (0.018)	0.033 (0.037)	-0.011 (0.025)
Party size	-0.001 (0.046)	0.011 (0.044)	0.005 (0.042)	0.061 (0.039)	0.184** (0.074)	0.206*** (0.075)	0.178** (0.082)	0.220* (0.112)
Governing party	-0.007 (0.011)	-0.007 (0.012)	0.001 (0.011)	0.009 (0.011)	0.061** (0.024)	0.044*** (0.014)	0.074** (0.031)	0.045** (0.020)
Size of governing majority	-0.657*** (0.111)	-0.653*** (0.110)	-0.694*** (0.116)	-0.496*** (0.131)	-0.462** (0.208)	-0.399* (0.192)	-0.569*** (0.222)	-0.480** (0.220)
Number of votes	-0.002 (0.002)	-0.002 (0.002)	-0.002 (0.002)	-0.003 (0.002)	0.001 (0.004)	-0.004 (0.003)	-0.003 (0.004)	-0.004 (0.004)
Party budget	0.139 (0.133)	0.136 (0.139)	0.238* (0.147)	0.250 (0.193)	0.352 (0.318)	0.250 (0.242)	0.498 (0.352)	0.435* (0.245)
Constant	0.980*** (0.023)	0.989*** (0.022)	0.943*** (0.022)	0.967*** (0.027)	0.797*** (0.072)	0.882*** (0.028)	0.748*** (0.091)	0.872*** (0.064)
R^2	0.71	0.71	0.82	0.83	0.31	0.28	0.37	0.30
N	73	73	63	50	73	73	63	50

Note: Dependent variable is indicated in the column heading. Table entries are unstandardized regression coefficients with robust standard errors in parentheses. Country dummies are included but not reported. $* p \leq 0.1$, $** p \leq 0.05$, $*** p \leq 0.01$

Appendix 5.1. The Formula for Calculating Defection Rates

Let s_i and v_i be the total number of defections and the total number of votes cast (i.e., not including abstentions and absences) by the ith MP, respectively; P_i be MP i's party; x_{in} be MP i's choice during vote n (equal to 0 if MP i did not cast a vote during vote n); V_{pn} be the mode of the frequency distribution of party P_i votes during vote n (equal to 0 if the distribution is multimodal); A_n be an indicator function that is equal to 1 iff $x_n \neq V_{pn}$, $x_n \neq 0$, and $V_{pn} \neq 0$, and 0 otherwise. Let F_{pn} be a function that returns the fraction of party P_i membership present and voting during vote n; M_{pn} be an indicator function equal to 1 iff $F_{pn} \geq 0.5$, and 0 otherwise; and t be the total number of votes taken during a legislature. Then

$$s_i = \sum_{n=1}^{t} (A_n M_{pn})$$

and

$$d_i = s_i / v_i$$

is the *Defection rate* for the ith MP.

Appendix 5.2. Descriptive Statistics: Power Within Parties

Variable	Dataset	N	Mean	SD	Min	Max
Defection rate	Pooled	3931	0.02	0.03	0	1.00
	Czech R. 1996–1998	216	0.02	0.01	0	0.12
	Czech R. 1998–2002	182	0.03	0.01	0.01	0.08
	Czech R. 2002–2006	235	0.01	0.01	0	0.06
	Czech R. 2006–2009	208	0.01	0.01	0	0.06
	Estonia 1999–2003	80	0.01	0.01	0	0.05
	Estonia 2003–2007	106	0.01	0.02	0	0.17
	Hungary 1994–1998	365	0.06	0.04	0	0.23
	Hungary 1998–2002	324	0.02	0.02	0	0.31
	Hungary 2002–2006	368	0.01	0.01	0	0.04
	Hungary 2006–2010	366	0.01	0.01	0	0.06
	Poland 1997–2001	481	0.04	0.04	0	0.35
	Poland 2001–2005	311	0.02	0.01	0	0.10
	Poland 2005–2007	450	0.02	0.05	0	1.00
Defection rate (logged)	Pooled	3931	−4.15	0.92	−6.91	0.001
	Czech R. 1996–1998	216	−4.18	0.80	−6.91	−2.15
	Czech R. 1998–2002	182	−3.56	0.41	−5.00	−2.55
	Czech R. 2002–2006	235	−4.40	0.57	−6.91	−2.80
	Czech R. 2006–2009	208	−4.50	0.78	−6.91	−2.76
	Estonia 1999–2003	80	−4.47	0.69	−6.34	−2.97
	Estonia 2003–2007	106	−4.87	1.06	−6.91	−1.77

(continued)

Appendix 5.2 (*continued*)

Variable	Dataset	N	Mean	SD	Min	Max
	Hungary 1994–1998	365	−3.11	0.97	−6.91	−1.49
	Hungary 1998–2002	324	−4.13	0.85	−6.91	−1.16
	Hungary 2002–2006	368	−4.73	0.66	−6.91	−3.23
	Hungary 2006–2010	366	−4.78	0.71	−6.91	−2.73
	Poland 1997–2001	481	−3.41	0.66	−6.91	−1.05
	Poland 2001–2005	311	−4.44	0.78	−6.91	−2.26
	Poland 2005–2007	450	−4.20	0.74	−6.91	0.001
Subunit organizational strength	Pooled	3931	0.32	0.26	0	1
	Czech R. 1996–1998	216	0.21	0.18	0.01	0.79
	Czech R. 1998–2002	182	0.26	0.12	0.05	0.61
	Czech R. 2002–2006	235	0.34	0.19	0.03	0.81
	Czech R. 2006–2009	208	0.35	0.22	0.04	0.93
	Estonia 1999–2003	80	0.24	0.32	0	1
	Estonia 2003–2007	106	0.55	0.28	0.04	1
	Hungary 1994–1998	365	0.39	0.28	0.02	1
	Hungary 1998–2002	324	0.25	0.19	0.01	0.91
	Hungary 2002–2006	368	0.32	0.23	0.02	0.87
	Hungary 2006–2010	366	0.43	0.32	0	1
	Poland 1997–2001	448	0.25	0.33	0	1
	Poland 2001–2005	311	0.35	0.22	0	0.86
	Poland 2005–2007	450	0.26	0.34	0	1
Committee leadership position	Pooled	3931	0.29	0.45	0	1
	Czech R. 1996–1998	216	0.31	0.46	0	1
	Czech R. 1998–2002	182	0.32	0.47	0	1
	Czech R. 2002–2006	235	0.38	0.49	0	1
	Czech R. 2006–2009	208	0.52	0.50	0	1
	Estonia 1999–2003	80	0.25	0.44	0	1
	Estonia 2003–2007	106	0.25	0.44	0	1
	Hungary 1994–1998	365	0.18	0.38	0	1
	Hungary 1998–2002	324	0.26	0.44	0	1
	Hungary 2002–2006	368	0.35	0.48	0	1
	Hungary 2006–2010	366	0.17	0.38	0	1
	Poland 1997–2001	448	0.29	0.45	0	1
	Poland 2001–2005	311	0.31	0.46	0	1
	Poland 2005–2007	450	0.24	0.42	0	1

Appendix 5.3. Fractional Logit and Extended Beta Binomial Models of the Effect of Subunit Organizational Strength on Defections

	Fractional Logit		Extended Beta Binomial	
	Main Analysis	Additional Controls	Main Analysis	Additional Controls
Organizational strength	0.716***	0.737***	0.406***	0.414***
	(0.193)	(0.197)	(0.082)	(0.083)
Parliamentary term	0.111***	0.113***	0.077***	0.075***
	(0.016)	(0.015)	(0.010)	(0.011)
National politician	0.023	0.026	0.034	0.030
	(0.046)	(0.047)	(0.028)	(0.028)
Local politician		0.018		−0.033
		(0.063)		(0.026)
Number of competitors		0.008*		0.003
		(0.004)		(0.003)
Vote share		−0.009**		−0.005
		(0.005)		(0.004)
Constant	−4.097***	−3.896***	−3.704***	−3.705***
	(0.096)	(0.161)	(0.272)	(0.273)
Gamma constant			0.009	0.009
Log likelihood			−2358547	−2354911
AIC	0.261	0.262		
N	3931	3927	3696	3927

Note: Table entries are unstandardized regression coefficients with standard errors in parentheses. All models also include country, term, party, and district dummies. $^*p \leq 0.1$, $^{**}p \leq 0.05$, $^{***}p \leq 0.01$

Appendix 6.1. The Effect of Environmental Factors on Party Organizational Strength, Interaction Model

	Participation in Local Elections
Poor/rural voters	0.055*
	(0.037)
Environmental hostility	0.080*
	(0.051)
Poor/rural voters* environmental hostility	0.126*
	(0.078)
Campaign expenditure	0.003***
	(0.001)
Constant	0.056*
	(0.030)
R^2	0.57
N	55

Note: The dependent variable is "Participation in local elections." Table entries are unstandardized regression coefficients with standard errors in parentheses. Country dummies are included in the models but not reported. $^*p \leq 0.1$, $^{***}p \leq 0.01$

Appendix 6.2. Information on Party Leaders

This Appendix provides, by country, a summary table that lists all leaders of the main parties included in the leadership analysis in Chapter 6. The table provides basic information about each leader. The information included in the table ends with the year 2010; if a leader stayed in office beyond that year, the end year under the column "In office" is still recorded as 2010. The last column identifies whether a given leader was classified as a professional or amateur, given the definitions presented in Table 6.3. The coding is based on the narratives presented in Chapter 6. For parties not covered in the chapter, the coding is explained in the narratives following the table for the respective country. In addition to identifying the type of the leader, each narrative also briefly covers their behavior in office and highlights any leader effects on organizational strength. As such, it serves to complement the narratives presented as part of the text.

Czech Republic

Party	Leader	Born	In Office	Education	Main Positions Held before Becoming the Leader	Professional (0/1)*
ČSSD	Jiří Horák	1924	1990–1993	PhD, political science, Columbia Univ.	Active in the youth organization of ČSSD before 1948 Professor, Columbia Univ.	n/a
	Miloš Zeman	1944	1993–2001	Higher, economics, Univ. of Economics in Prague	Research jobs (prognostic modeling) at sports and agricultural organizations, and the Czech Academy of Sciences Elected to Federal Assembly 1990	1
	Vladimír Špidla	1951	2001–2004	Higher, history, Charles' Univ.	Various manual jobs before the regime change Leadership jobs in the Jindřichův Hradec District MP since 1996	0
	Stanislav Gross	1969	2004–2005	Higher, law, Charles' Univ.	Engine-driver trainee for the state railways company MP since 1992	n/a
	Bohuslav Sobotka (acting)	1971	2005–2006	Higher, political science, Masaryk Univ.	Member of Young Social Democrats MP since 1996 Minister of finance	n/a

Party	Leader	Born	In Office	Education	Main Positions Held before Becoming the Leader	Professional (o/i)*
	Jiří Paroubek	1952	2006–2010	Higher, tourism, Univ. of Economics	Manager/economist in catering business ČSSD party manager, other leadership positions City councilor and deputy mayor of Prague Minister of regional development Prime minister	i
KDU-ČSL	Josef Bartončík	1944	1989–1990	Doctorate, law	Member of ČSL since 1964	n/a
	Josef Lux	1956	1990–1998	Higher, agricultural engineering, Agricultural Univ. in Bern	Agricultural engineer in a collective farm MP since 1990	i
	Jan Kasal	1951	1998–2001	Higher, engineering, Prague Technical Univ.	Engineer MP since 1990	o
	Cyril Svoboda	1956	2001–2003	Higher, law, Charles' Univ.	Notary Legislative council of the Czech government	o
	Miroslav Kalousek	1960	2003–2006	Higher, Univ. of Chemical Technology, Prague	Head of an investment department in a manufacturing company Various positions in high-level civil service (e.g., consultant on economic transition, director of consultants, deputy minister in the Ministry of Defense) MP since 1998	i
	Jiří Čunek	1959	2006–2009	Secondary, car mechanic	Mechanic Head of safety in an armament company Mayor of Vsetín	o
	Cyril Svoboda	1956	2009–2010	Higher, law, Charles' Univ.	Notary Legislative Council of the Czech government	o
KSČM	Jiří Machalík		1990–1990			n/a
	Jiří Svoboda	1945	1990–1993	Higher, film directing, Academy of Performing Arts	Screenwriter Film director Academic appointments at the Academy of Performing Arts	o

(*continued*)

Czech Republic (*continued*)

Party	Leader	Born	In Office	Education	Main Positions Held before Becoming the Leader	Professional (0/1)*
	Miroslav Grebeníček	1947	1993–2005	Higher, philosophy, Masaryk Univ.	Univ. lecturer MP since 1990	1
	Vojtěch Filip	1955	2005–2010	Higher, law, Univ. of Brno	Corporate lawyer MP 1990–1992 Operated his own law firm since 1993	1
ODA	Pavel Bratinka	1946	1990–1992	Higher, physics	Manual jobs before the regime change MP since 1990	0
	Jan Kalvoda	1953	1992–1997	Higher, law	MP since 1990	0
	Michael Žantovský	1949	1997–1997	Higher, psychology, Charles' Univ.	Prague Psychiatric Research Institute Correspondent to Reuters Vaclav Havel's spokesperson Ambassador to the U.S.	0
	Jiří Skalický	1956	1997–1998	Higher, chemistry, Prague's College of Chemical Technology	Research and development assistant MP 1990–1992, 1996 Privatization minister Minister of environment	0
	Daniel Kroupa	1949	1998–2001	PhD, philosophy	Manual jobs Academic positions at Charles Univ. MP 1990–1992, and since 1996	0
	Michael Žantovský	1949	2001–2007	Higher, psychology, Charles' Univ.	Prague Psychiatric Research Institute Correspondent to Reuters Vaclav Havel's spokesperson Ambassador to the U.S.	0
ODS	Václav Klaus	1942	1991–2002	PhD, economics, Charles Univ., Czech Academy of Sciences	Researcher at the Czech Academy of Sciences Economist at the Czechoslovak State Bank Researcher at the Prognostic Institute of the Czech Academy of Sciences	1
	Mirek Topolánek	1956	2002–2010	Higher, mechanical engineering, Brno Univ. of Technology	Engineer (designer) Founder and CEO of an engineering company Senator since 1996	1

Party	Leader	Born	In Office	Education	Main Positions Held before Becoming the Leader	Professional (o/i)*
SPR-RSČ	Miroslav Sládek	1950	1990–2000	Higher, information and library sciences, Charles' Univ.	Informatics	o
US	Jan Ruml	1953	1998–1999	Secondary	Variety of manual jobs before the regime change Deputy interior minister; interior minister	o
	Karel Kühnl	1954	2000–2001	Higher, law, Charles' Univ.	Radio Free Europe Ambassador to the UK Minister of economy and trade	o
	Hana Marvanová	1962	2001–2002	Higher, law, Charles' Univ.	Lawyer MP since 1989	o
	Ivan Pilip	1963	2002–2003	Higher, Univ. of Economics	Lecturer at the Univ. of Economics Deputy interior minister Executive director and member of supervisory board of different companies Minister of education, youth and sports Minister of finance	o
	Petr Mareš	1953	2003–2004	PhD, philosophy, Charles' Univ.	Academia	o
	Pavel Němec	1971	2004–2006	Higher, law, Charles Univ.	Lawyer Entrepreneur MP since 1998 Minister of regional development	o
	Jan Hadrava	1955	2006–2007	Vocational, engineering	Textile engineer Mayor of Loket Senator 2000–2006	o
	Jan Černý	1959	2007–2010	Higher, veterinary, Veterinary Univ. in Brno	District veterinarian MP 1992–1998 Minister of regional development Local councilor in Kostelec Founder of his own veterinary practice Deputy mayor of Kostelec	o

* For ČSSD, ODA, ODS, and US, the classification of leaders as professionals (as opposed to amateurs) is based on the information provided in the text of Chapter 6. For other parties, the coding is based on the following information.

Communist Party of Moravia and Bohemia (KSČM) has been chaired by four different leaders during the timeframe under study: Jiří Machalík (1990), Jiří Svoboda (1990–1993), Miroslav Grebeníček (1993–2005), and Vojtěch Filip (since 2005). This group of leaders is relatively difficult to classify as amateurs or professionals. At first glance, they all appear relatively ideological in their relationship with their organization. However, this has probably been more of a strategic move to appeal to a relatively ideological membership base (Hanley 2001) than an indication of them being genuine ideologues. Furthermore, the ideological-looking leaders were all committed to maintaining and investing in the strong organization of the party.

Machalík was in office for a very short time, and his leadership style is therefore hard to determine. He was considered to be a hard-line conservative communist, but as most people in the party leadership at the time, he expressed a strong preference to use the party's organizational assets as a strategy of electoral survival (Advertiser 1990; BBC Summary of World Broadcasts 1990; Grzymala-Busse 2002a). In contrast, the successor to Machalík, Jiří Svoboda, was considered by most accounts a reformist who wanted to regenerate the communist party (Grzymala-Busse 2002a), and this was the goal toward which he spent most energy: trying to convince co-partisans to change the party name and its ideology to something less radical and more social-democracy oriented. Svoboda was not vocal about developing and maintaining party organization; rather, he called for dismantling the organization and relinquishing all assets that the party had received from the state (Pehe 1990). Indeed, observers have called him an "intellectual dreamer" (CTK 1993d), and his background in arts as a film director also suggests more of an amateur than a professional profile.

The longest-serving leader, and therefore presumably also the most influential for the party's long-term development, was Miroslav Grebeníček. Although his background and experience before becoming leader do not suggest managerialism or pragmatism – he was a university lecturer in history (Hanley 2001) – he certainly was not an ideologue for its own sake. Grebeníček was described as a pragmatist who left an impression in parliament and the media (i.e., outside the party) of being constructive and collaborative (CTK 2004a). At the same time, he was also skillful in appealing to hard-liners within the party by appearing ideological himself (CTK 2004a). Being ideological was for him a strategy of effectively managing internal and external party affairs. On balance, it is probably fair to classify him as a professional leader. As such, Grebeníček's commitment to party organization was unquestionable. Throughout his tenure, he stressed the need to maintain the party's organizational strength, saw members as the reliable source of votes (Grzymala-Busse 2002a), and praised the mass character and organizational structure of the party, which it had managed to retain despite fierce battle waged against it from outside (CTK 1996a). Even at the end of his tenure in the 2000s, he was convinced that the party's main asset was its large and experienced membership base (Handl 2005a). Grebeníček did not just talk about maintaining a strong organization, he also actively sought to cultivate and uphold contacts with the party's local structures; as Klaus in ODS and Zeman in ČSSD, he thereby acquired a loyal following within the organization (CTK 1999b; Czech News Agency 2004b).

The latest KSČM chairman, Vojtěch Filip, made a career as a corporate lawyer and had considerable political experience in the local level before being elected to the national political office. He has been characterized as a power-hungry pragmatist (Czech News Agency 2005b), who once again raised the question of party ideological modernization in order to make it an acceptable coalition partner. His opponents, at the same time, describe him as "a staunch communist demagogue" (Czech News Agency 2006b). Overall, he was certainly less concerned about ideas, principles, and ideologies, and possessed the necessary administrative skills and expertise to qualify as a professional leader. However, his attitude toward organizational development remains unclear. He may be a pragmatist in the sense of trying to get into government and be accepted by other parties – a goal for which organizational development is not as crucial. Furthermore, he took over the party helm at a time when organizational structures were already entrenched and functioning well, and while he made less use of the organization and more use of billboards during election campaigns (Czech News Agency 2005c), he also did not actively seek to dismantle or abandon the organization; rather, he is considered to hold a pragmatic continuity position (i.e., continue with party development internally, and pragmatically adjust to accommodate ČSSD and/or ODS externally, as necessary to advance the party's coalition potential) (Handl 2005b). Under his leadership, KSČM has remained a mass programmatic party with a disciplined membership base.

In sum, the leaders of KSČM exhibit somewhat different leadership styles, with Svoboda being more of an intellectual and ideologue, and the longest-time leader, Miroslav Grebeníček, representing a skillful pragmatist who had an instrumental concern for the party as a vehicle for electoral success and party survival. His successor Vojtěch Filip's position was harder to determine: although less actively investing in the organization, Filip is clearly a professional and pragmatist with the necessary expertise and administrative skills to sustain KSČM's organizational strength.

Christian Democratic Union (KDU-ČSL) leaders include Josef Bartončík (1989–1990), Josef Lux (1990–1998), Jan Kasal (1998–2001), Cyril Svoboda (2001–2003; 2009–2010), Miroslav Kalousek (2003–2006), and Jiří Čunek (2006–2009). The first leader, Bartončík, set as his goal the creation of a large party with widely developed structures and many sympathizers (Hanley 2008). Lux modified that organizational strategy somewhat, but the party remained strongly socially embedded (Enyedi and Linek 2008; Klima 1998). He was a farmer by education and profession before becoming the party leader.

This does not necessarily suggest that he possessed particular administrative skills and expertise, but it helped him realize the importance of a grassroots presence and the need to personally cultivate the support of local branches and rank-and-file members (CTK 1998f). Furthermore, Lux was credited with having exceptional political abilities and being one of the few politicians showing professionalism and real pragmatism within and outside the party (CTK 1997a). He can, therefore, be classified as a professional leader for current purposes.

After Lux resigned, no other strong and long-term leader has emerged. The two subsequent leaders – Kasal and Svoboda – seem to better fit the description of amateur rather than professional leaders. Neither of them had a managerial background. Furthermore, under Kasal's leadership, the professionalism of the party disappeared, and the party was perceived as "a group of country bumpkins" (CTK 2000). Svoboda, in turn, was a Prague intellectual considered to be highly personally ambitious (Czech News Agency 2002). It is therefore fitting that under Kasal, the party suffered a significant organizational decay with decreases in the thousands of members and disintegration of tens of local branches (Czech News Agency 1999). As for Svoboda, he was effectively not dealing with the party at all (CTK 2003e), although it is not clear that this can be attributed to his amateurism rather than to his position as a foreign minister. Miroslav Kalousek, in turn, appears more like a professional leader, at least according to his background. He had worked in high-level civil service as well as managerial jobs and might therefore have possessed some skills for an effective professional leader. However, contrary to the expectations of the leadership hypothesis, he did not behave like a professional with regard to building the party organization.[1] Rather than grow, the party only declined further under his leadership (Czech News Agency 2006c). The main effort of these three leaders was channeled to the party in government, not to the party on the ground.

In 2006, the party elected its most controversial chairman – Jiří Čunek – who also appeared more of an amateur than a professional. He lacked any managerial experience and has not been characterized as particularly pragmatic. Rather, characteristically of an amateur leader, Čunek never accepted his own mistakes, but blamed "some forces" that wanted to destroy him or his party (Czech News Agency 2008). Čunek's leadership style corresponded with organizational decline, although it is not clear that the correspondence occurred for the reasons envisioned by the leadership hypothesis. In line with the hypothesized mechanism, he was accused of not having a clear vision and ability to lead the party (CTK 2007). However, Čunek was also publicly accused of corruption and considered racist against Romas, so that the rest of the party

---

[1] Kalousek's leadership was also tainted from the beginning with accusations about involvement in various corruption scandals (Weiss 2003).

became exhausted from having to fight for Čunek's reputation (CTK 2007). It is, therefore, hard to say whether his amateur style would have mattered absent these additional scandals.

In sum, KDU leadership after Josef Lux has been characterized either by inability to effectively govern the party or by a lack of interest in doing so. Although no effort has been made to systematically dismantle the initially very strong party organization, almost no effort has also been made to actively sustain it, leading to a downward spiral in party organizational strength.[2] The dynamics in leadership style seem to, at least partially, account for the dynamics in organizational strength. The cases of Lux, Kasal, and Svoboda fit the expectations of the leadership hypothesis especially well. Kalousek's case contradicts it: despite being classified as a professional leader, he did not invest in the organization. Evidence from Čunek's case remains inconclusive, given the confounding scandals.

Republicans (SPR-RSČ) had only one leader throughout its existence: Miroslav Sládek. Sládek was widely recognized as an extremely unstable person with erratic behavior. For example, already in 1991 news outlets were reporting that Sládek was thought to have mental problems, as he was summoned to a psychiatric evaluation after he attacked everyone and everything at a party meeting (CTK 1992a).[3] In terms of the party organization, Sládek was not willing or able to build one (Deegan-Krause 2006), but, rather, insisted that the entire party be under his control. Some of the early defectors said that there was an atmosphere of fear in the party. For example, Sládek had demanded that all MPs sign a blank sheet of paper, which was one of the ways he could control them (CTK 1995b). This is hardly representative of a professional leader, a pragmatist, someone with administrative skills and expertise, and someone who is ambitious but humble. Sládek's behavior was mostly driven by his ideas and ideology. Not interested in organization, he prohibited party branches from holding a conference to discuss the party's future (Larsen 1995), singlehandedly composed party electoral lists and gave positions high on the list to his relatives or people close to him (CTK 1996b), led "billboard campaigns" rather than grassroots campaigns involving party activists (Horak 1998), expelled, en masse, members who disagreed with him, and eliminated branches that wanted to change the party organization (CTK 1998g). As Mudde (2007) notes, Sládek's erratic behavior and problematic personality goes a long way toward explaining the organizational weakness of his party.

---

[2] The organizational decline is sometimes also attributed to aging membership (Linek and Pecháček 2007), which is, of course, an additional exacerbating condition; however, as the narratives imply, there was no attempt by the post-Lux era leadership to maintain and develop the organization.

[3] There is actually no evidence that he was mentally ill and some attacks on him were inaccurate, but the broader description of him as unstable and erratic is generally shared.

Estonia

Party	Leader	Born	In Office	Education	Main Positions Held before Becoming the Leader	Professional (o/i)*
IL	Lagle Parek	1941	1988–1993	Secondary		n/a
	Tunne Kelam	1936	1993–1995	Higher, history, Univ. of Tartu	Researcher in the Estonian Central Archive Lecturer Librarian MP since 1993	n/a
	Toivo Jürgenson	1957	1995–1998	Higher, engineering, Tallinn Technical Univ.	Engineering Leadership position in the ESSR Planning Committee Leadership position in private sector MP since 1992 Minister of economic affairs	o
	Mart Laar	1960	1998–2002	MA, history, Univ. of Tartu	History teacher MP since 1992 Prime minister	o
	Tunne Kelam	1936	2002–2005	Higher, history, Univ. of Tartu	Researcher in the Estonian Central Archive Lecturer Librarian MP since 1993	n/a
	Tõnis Lukas	1962	2005–2006	MA, history, Univ. of Tartu	Teacher Lecturer Director of the Estonian National Museum MP since 1995 (with gaps) Mayor of Tartu Minister of education	n/a
	Mart Laar	1960	2007–2010	MA, history, Univ. of Tartu	History teacher MP since 1992 Prime minister	o
K	Edgar Savisaar	1950	1991–1995	Higher, history, Univ. of Tartu	Chair of the ESSR Planning Committee Academic director of a private consultation company Minister of economic affairs	i
	Andra Vei-demann	1955	1995–1996	Higher, history, Univ. of Tartu	Academy of Sciences, Institute of History Director of the Bureau on Religious Affairs, Ministry of Cultural Affairs MP since 1992	n/a

Party	Leader	Born	In Office	Education	Main Positions Held before Becoming the Leader	Professional (o/1)*
	Edgar Savisaar	1950	1996–2010			1
KE	Jaak Tamm	1950	1991–1992	Higher, Univ. of Tartu	Minister of industry	n/a
	Peeter Lorents		1992–1993	Higher, physics		n/a
	Tiit Vähi	1947	1993–1997	Higher, engineering, Tallinn Technical Univ.	Several top management positions in the Valga Trucking Company Minister of transportation	1
	Mart Siimann	1946	1997–1999	Higher, psychology, Univ. of Tartu	Univ. of Tartu Correspondent for, and later the director of, the Estonian State Television Managing director of Advertising Television Company MP since 1995	o
	Andrus Öövel	1957	1999–2000	MSc, law, global security, Univ. of Tartu, Cranfield Univ.	Administrative positions at the state structures of ESSR Chair of the Estonian Olympic Committee Chief of staff of the Estonian Home Guard Director of the Border Protection Office Minister of defense	1
	Märt Kubo	1944	2000–2002			n/a
RE	Siim Kallas	1948	1994–2004	Higher, finance, Univ. of Tartu	ESSR finance minister Director of the Estonian Central Board of Savings Banks Deputy editor of a major daily Chairman of the Central Association of Trade Unions President of the Bank of Estonia	1
	Andrus Ansip	1956	2004–2010	Higher, chemistry, Univ. of Tartu	Univ. of Tartu Leadership positions in the Estonian Communist Party Tartu District Committee Managerial positions in private sector Mayor of Tartu	1

(*continued*)

Estonia (*continued*)

Party	Leader	Born	In Office	Education	Main Positions Held before Becoming the Leader	Professional (o/1)*
ERL	Arnold Rüütel	1928	1994–2000	Candidacy, agriculture, Estonian Academy of Agriculture	Leadership positions in several collective farms Rector of the Estonian Academy of Agriculture Leadership positions in the Estonian Communist Party Chairman of the Supreme Soviet of the ESSR	1
	Villu Reiljan	1953	2000–2007	Higher, forestry, Estonian Academy of Agriculture	Director of several agricultural vocational schools Minister of Environment	1
	Jaanus Marrandi	1963	2007–2009	Higher, amelioration, Estonian Academy of Agriculture	Ameliorator Director of a collective farm MP since 1999 Minister of agriculture	1
RP	Rein Taagepera	1933	2001–2002	PhD, physics, Univ. of Delaware	Working in industry Professor of political science	1
	Juhan Parts	1966	2002–2005	Higher, law, Univ. of Tartu	Civil servant in the Ministry of Justice Auditor general	1
SDE	Marju Lauristin	1940	1990–1995	Candidacy, journalism, Univ. of Tartu, Moscow Univ.	Manual worker at a radio works factory Journalist at the Estonian Radio Univ. of Tartu, different academic appointments Delegate to the ESSR Supreme Soviet	o
	Eiki Nestor	1953	1995–1996	Higher, mechanical engineering, Tallinn Technical Univ.	Director of Keila Trucking Company Leadership position in trade unions MP since 1992	n/a
	Andres Tarand	1940	1996–2001	Candidacy, climatology, Univ. of Tartu	Univ. of Tartu, research Director of the botanical gardens Delegate of the ESSR Supreme Soviet MP since 1992	o
	Toomas Hendrik Ilves	1953	2001–2002	MA, psychology, Columbia Univ., Univ. of Pennsylvania	Radio Free Europe Ambassador to the U.S., Mexico, Canada Minister of foreign affairs	n/a

Party	Leader	Born	In Office	Education	Main Positions Held before Becoming the Leader	Professional (0/1)*
	Ivari Padar	1965	2002–2009	Higher, history, Univ. of Tartu	Carpenter Middle school teacher Vice-mayor Civil servant at the Ministry of Finance Minister of agricultural affairs	1
	Jüri Pihl	1954	2009–2010	Higher, law, Univ. of Tartu	Inspector in the Interior Ministry of the ESSR Various leadership positions in the local police structures of the ESSR Director general of the Estonian Security Police Prosecutor general Chancellor in the Ministry of Justice Minister of interior	1

* For IL, K, RE, and SDE, the classification of leaders as professionals (as opposed to amateurs) is based on the information provided in the text of Chapter 6. For other parties, the coding is based on the following information.

Res Publica (RP) is an interesting case because at the time of its foundation and main organizational development the party did not have a single leader. Rather, it was founded by a group of young enthusiasts who started looking for a suitable person to head the party after the major foundational work with regard to the party organization had already been done. The first leader of the party was Rein Taagepera, who served as an interim chairman for six months. For all practical purposes, he can be considered a nominal leader: he agreed to be "part of the team" but not manage things directly (Postimees 2001c). His "hands-off" approach was underlined, for example, by the fact that he did not contest any elections under the RP label and lived in California three of the six months that he was the nominal leader of the party. The second leader of the party was Juhan Parts (a person with a background of a professional leader, as indicated by his prior career in civil service and as auditor general), who was selected to serve at that post right before the 2003 parliamentary election as someone who would be attractive as a candidate for prime minister. It is likely that Parts had prior informal contacts with the group of young founders of RP, but he entered the scene when much of the foundational organization building had already been done. The group of enthusiasts whose leadership was important for turning the movement Res Publica into a party included Indrek Raudne, Urmas Reinsalu, Ken-Marti Vaher, Taavi Veskimägi, and their ideational as well as financial sponsor, a former banker, Olari Taal. This group of people was most directly responsible for the initial organizational strength of the party as well as its subsequent organizational failure. In terms of the theoretical frame about professionals versus amateurs, they probably more fit the description of the former: although they were in their twenties when they started with this party building, all of them held relatively high-level positions in civil service with Reinsalu, for example, having served as the director of the Office of the President. They also got advice from professionals such as Olari Taal. I have, therefore, coded the leadership of Rein Taagepera, which was actually dominated by the young founders as professional rather than amateur in nature.

As described in Chapter 3, the novelty and brand of RP was its organization. It came to the electoral arena not selling an ideology, but selling its organization (Ideon 2001; Postimees 2001a; Sildam 2001; Vaher 2001). When describing the existing political forces in Estonia, Taal referred to them as consisting of and representing a few dozen politicians; he wanted to see RP as different – a party with an extensive membership, strong and functioning structure, and open yet professional governance (Sildam 2001). Taal explained that RP was not about "doing" but about "being" (Ideon 2001). The other four agreed by arguing that they wanted to build RP into a mass party, one that consisted of a diverse set of members and had a widespread grassroots presence (Postimees 2001b; Vaher 2001). The party founders personally traveled across the country to meet with people, recruit members, and set up branches (Taagepera 2006). Juhan Parts also believed in the idea of building a strong party organization. Even after the 2003 electoral success, Parts reminded the party, "[W]e must not lose the connection between our rank-and-file members and the party elite"; he urged MPs to stay in touch with their branches and not abandon organizational development (PM Online 2004b). However, the young party founders did not follow this advice. Indeed, because all four had become members of parliament or served as ministers, their focus was now on governing and no longer on organization building. They justified the change of focus by the need for quick decision making while in government – something that a large and actively involved organization does not allow (Ernits 2004a).

Overall, thus, the RP case seems to suggest a significant role for the leadership (in terms of founders) in determining the level of organizational strength of a party. However, it also illustrates how preoccupation with governing can undermine party organizational strength even in the case of professional leaders: leaders may recognize the need to maintain organizational strength (as Parts did) but be unable to pursue it because of governing responsibilities and pressures (as expressed by the young activists).

People's Party (ERL) has had two main long-term leaders, Arnold Rüütel (1994–2000) and Villu Reiljan (2000–2007), and a few more recent short-term leaders including Jaanus Marrandi (2007–2009) and Karel Rüütli (2009–2010), Juhan Aare (2010) and Andrus Blok (2010). Both Rüütel and Reiljan held managerial positions in the agricultural sector prior to entering politics. Rüütel also served in significant positions in government under both the communist as well as post-communist regimes, and Reiljan had administrative experience as a director of an agricultural vocational school. The backgrounds of both leaders are in line with the profile of a professional party leader as defined here. In accord with this profile, both leaders greatly valued building an extensive and active party organization and saw such an organization as the "core purpose of their party" as well as a necessary vehicle for public office. Marrandi, too, had the background of a professional leader, having served in managerial- and high-level administrative positions under the previous as well as current regimes.

Rüütel talked about the importance of developing the party organization in his speeches to the party at major party meetings and congresses from the time the party was created (Paet 1998a). Although the party already had twice as many members as its rivals in the second half of the 1990s, Rüütel criticized the party for being too focused on finding partners to build electoral alliances and not looking for opportunities to develop the party internally and increase ties to local communities (Porila 1999). Rüütel acknowledged that "only daily, planned activities in local branches will bring us success" (Porila 1999). He also claimed, "The role of the leader is very important, but first and foremost, it is important that the organization as a whole is strong and the local branches are strong" (Rand 2009).

Reiljan similarly recognized the importance of building and maintaining strong organization on the ground. When Reiljan became the party leader in 2000, he delivered a speech at a party congress showing a picture of a shabby man that was supposed to depict the dismal state of ERL's organization at the time (recall that the party actually already had the largest membership and most extensive network of branches); he then explained how he planned to invest in strengthening the party organization, including doubling its membership, and ended his speech with a picture in which the shabby man had turned into a handsome athlete – the kind of strong and attractive party ERL was supposed to become under his leadership (Hagelberg 2000). Reiljan not only talked about the relevance of the organization, but also personally helped create such an organization. He was working hard at the grassroots level, talking to people, convincing them to support the party and become members, candidates, and supporters (Koch 2007; Kuimet 2007; Reiljan 2005). He was quick to win the hearts of people with his open and friendly style of communication and his endless jokes (Ammas 2004). Reiljan actively recruited local elites to become party members and candidates, a strategy that led to local politicians joining the party in great numbers and bringing their friends with them (Hüvato 2005).

In sum, the two most influential and long-term leaders of ERL were professionals, interested in building the party organization, and, especially in the case of Reiljan, personally helping build the organization. Indeed, throughout its existence, ERL probably has had the strongest organization of all Estonian parties (Koch 2007). In 2009, its membership exceeded 10,000, the highest of all parties in Estonia. In the mid-1990s, when many other parties did not even think about recruiting members, ERL was meticulously developing its organization (Kaldmaa 1997; Paet 1998a). According to its former general secretaries, the party also had the most extensive network of local offices, which were staffed with professionals and fully functional during as well as between elections.[4] The ERL case therefore provides direct support for the leadership hypothesis and illustrates that leaders, rather than being figureheads, had a direct role in the organization-building process. That said, the fact that ERL's electorate consisted mostly of a rural population might have motivated organization building either directly or indirectly by influencing the type of leaders that emerged.

The Coalition Party (KE) case is less clear about the role of the leaders in determining the organizational weakness. The main leader and founder of the party was Tiit Vähi, succeeded by Mart Siimann. For a short period of time, Andrus Öövel was the nominal leader of the party. Although a professional leader by his background – he had served in a host of managerial and administrative positions – he was argued to never have commanded any actual power (Ideon 2000b). Vähi, too, had the background of a manager during the previous regime and was generally considered to be very pragmatic and rationally calculating (Made 1997), someone who knows how to motivate people and is very decisive and persistent (Rozental 2008; Vähi 2006) – these are the characteristics of a professional leader as defined here. However, neither he nor his rival and successor, Siimann, nor the party leadership in general were interested in building party organization (Kubo 1997). The leaders created the party to get to power because the political system did not favor independents (Vöörmann 2001), but they did not realize the importance of building an organization to maintain access to power. The party was basically defined by those who held public office – these people held the main party leadership positions as well, and no attention was paid to rank and file (Karpa 1998; Tammer 1996b). Thus, although pragmatists in terms of pursuing short-term access to power, these leaders did not behave like professionals with regard to organization building (Kons 1998; Vöörmann 2001).

By the time Siimann took over, the party was already in decline. As opposed to Vähi and Öövel, Siimann was more of an intellectual: he had worked in academia and television (Siimann 2005), and lacked managerial experience. This predisposed him to an amateur style of leadership. Fitting with this style, his leadership was characterized by continued lack of sustained work on organization: nothing substantive in the party structure and organization changed. However, it is not clear whether this was because of Siimann's disinterest in building an organization. He himself argued that the organization remained deficient because the party concentrated on governing and had no time for the party on the ground (EPL 2001b). Also, by the time Siimann took over, KE's government was unpopular, and the party suffered from corruption scandals and internal rifts. It is therefore likely that any leader in Siimann's

---

[4] ERL Respondent 1, ERL Respondent 2, personal communications, August 6, 2007.

position would have had to focus on crisis management rather than organizatio building regardless of his or her leadership style or preferences. That said, Siimann also did not show much interest in developing a party organization in a different situation where such environmental conditions were absent. Specifically, after leaving the KE in 2001, he served as the leader of a party called With Reason and Heart (Mõistuse ja südamega) that he helped to create. There was no particular effort to build the organization of this new formation, and when it became clear that the newcomer would not survive its first election, Siimann deserted the party to become the leader of the Estonian Olympic Committee (EPL 2001a). By the end of Öövel's tenure, the party had essentially disintegrated; I therefore have included only the years 1991–2000 in the calculation of the party score of leadership style.

In sum, the KE case does not provide unequivocal support for the leadership hypothesis. Although Vähi's background was that of a pragmatic manager, he did not develop the party organization as predicted by the theory. Siimann's background and the outcome of weak party organization coincide in the expected manner, although the relevance of the environmental factors can also not be ruled out.

Hungary

Party	Leader	Born	In Office	Education	Main Positions Held before Becoming the Leader	Professional (o/1)*
Fidesz	Viktor Orbán	1963	1993–2000	Higher, law, Eötvös Univ.	Sociologist at the Management Training Institute of the Ministry of Agriculture and Food	1
	László Kövér	1959	2000–2001	Higher, law, Eötvös Univ.	Sociologist at the Management Training Institute of the Ministry of Agriculture and Food	Orban de facto leader
	Zoltán Pokorni	1962	2001–2002	Higher, history, Hungarian language and literature, Eötvös Univ.	High school teacher Minister of education	Orban de facto leader
	János Áder	1959	2002–2003	Higher, law, Eötvös Univ.		Orban de facto leader
	Viktor Orbán		2003–			1
FKgP	Ferenc József Nagy	1923	1990–1991	Higher, agriculture	Farmer, director of a collective farm	n/a
	József Torgyán	1932	1991–2002	Higher, law, Eötvös Univ.	Manual worker Lawyer MP since 1990	0
	Miklós Réti		2002–2003	Higher, medical	MP since 1990	n/a

(continued)

Hungary (*continued*)

Party	Leader	Born	In Office	Education	Main Positions Held before Becoming the Leader	Professional (o/1)*
KDNP	Sándor Keresztes	1919	1989–1990	PhD, law, political science, Univ. of Cluj Napoca/Royal Franz Ferdinand Univ. and Univ. of Pécs	Civil servant Head of the Új Ember Catholic publishing house	o
	László Surján	1941	1990–1994	Higher, medical, theology, Semmelweis Medical Univ., Kalazantum College of Theology	Pathologist Manual worker MP since 1990	o
	György Giczy	1953	1995–2001	PhD, theology, Roman Catholic Theological Academy in Budapest	Journalist MP since 1990	o
	Tivadar Bartók		2001–2002	Higher, medical, Semmelweis Medical Univ.	Doctor at the Hungarian National Ambulance Service	n/a
	László Varga	1910	2002–2003	Higher, law, Pázmány Péter Univ. (currently Eötvös Univ.)	Lawyer Radio Free Europe	n/a
	Zsolt Semjén	1962	2003–2010	PhD, theology, sociology (BA), Roman Catholic Theological Academy in Budapest, Eötvös Univ.	Representative in local government MP since 1994	n/a
MDF	Zoltán Bíró	1941	1989–1989	PhD, Hungarian language and literature, Eötvös Univ.	Manual jobs Teacher Civil servant at the Ministry of Culture Professor of literature	o
	József Antall	1932	1989–1993	Higher, humanities, Eötvös Univ.	Hungarian State Archives Teacher Researcher on history of medicine	o
	Lajos Für	1930	1994–1996	Higher, law, Kossuth Lajos Univ.	Primary school teacher Research fellow, Hungarian Museum of Agriculture Minister of Defense	o

Party	Leader	Born	In Office	Education	Main Positions Held before Becoming the Leader	Professional (o/1)*
	Sándor Lezsák	1949	1996–1999	Higher, history, Hungarian language and literature, Juhász Gyula College	Manual laborer Elementary school teacher Poet MP since 1994	o
	Ibolya Dávid	1954	1999–2010	Doctor of law, Univ. of Pécs	Lawyer MP since 1990	o
MIÉP	István Csurka	1934	1993–2010	Higher, arts, College of Theatre and Film	Author, playwright, journalist MP since 1990	o
MSzP	Rezső Nyers	1923	1989–1990	Higher, economics, Karl Marx Univ. of Economic Sciences of Budapest Univ. (Corvinus Univ. today) & Kossuth Academy	Typographer Assembly delegate Minister responsible for the food industry Minister of finance Member of Politburo	1
	Gyula Horn	1932	1990–1998	Higher, economics, Don-Rostov College	Civil servant, Ministry of Finance Deputy minister of foreign affairs	1
	László Kovács	1939	1998–2004	Higher, foreign trade, Karl Marx Univ. of Economic Sciences (Corvinus Univ. today)	Technician Various leadership positions in the Communist Party Deputy foreign minister State secretary at the Ministry of Foreign Affairs	1
	István Hiller	1964	2004–2007	PhD, history, Latin, Eötvös Univ.	Academia MP since 2002	o
	Ferenc Gyurcsány	1961	2007–2009	Higher, pedagogy, economics, Janus Pannonius Univ.	Leadership positions at the Organization of Young Communists Leadership positions in private sector Minister of sports, youth and children	1
	Ildikó Lendvai	1946	2009–2010	Higher, pedagogy, philosophy, Eötvös Univ.	Teacher Leadership positions in the Communist Party on cultural matters MP since 1994	n/a

(continued)

Hungary (*continued*)

Party	Leader	Born	In Office	Education	Main Positions Held before Becoming the Leader	Professional (o/1)*
SzDSz	János Kis	1943	1990–1991	Higher, philosophy, Eötvös Univ.	Researcher Freelance translator Professor of political science	o
	Péter Tölgyessy	1957	1991–1992	Higher, law, Eötvös Univ.	Researcher MP since 1991	o
	Iván Pető	1946	1992–1997	PhD, history, Eötvös Univ.	Hungarian Central Archives MP since 1990	o
	Gábor Kuncze	1950	1997–1998	Higher, geotechnical engineering, economics, Ybl Miklós Technical College in Budapest; Karl Marx Univ. of Economic Sciences (Corvinus Univ. today)	Technician Deputy director of an economic enterprise MP since 1990	1
	Bálint Magyar	1952	1998–2000	PhD, history, sociology, Eötvös Univ.	Researcher Minister of culture and education	o
	Gábor Demszky	1952	2000–2001	Higher, law, sociology, Eötvös Univ.	Taxi driver Librarian Journalist Mayor of Budapest	o
	Gábor Kuncze		2001–2007			1
	János Kóka	1972	2007–2008	Higher, medical, Semmelweis Medical Univ.	Civil servant, Ministry of Economy and Transport	1
	Gábor Fodor	1962	2008–2009	Higher, law, Eötvös Univ.	Assistant professor Minister of education Minister of environmental protection	o
	Attila Retkes	1972	2009–2010	Music (BA), economics (MBA, PhD), Liszt Ferenc Univ. of Music, Corvinus Univ., Newport International Univ.	Radio DJ Journalist, editor, producer	n/a

* For Fidesz, KDNP, MDF, and MSzP, the classification of leaders as professionals (as opposed to amateurs) is based on the information provided in the text of Chapter 6. For other parties, the coding is based on the following information.

Independent Smallholders' Alliance (FKgP) was plagued by low managerial capacity although its organization was initially sizeable because it was mostly inherited from the pre-communist era. None of its leaders had substantial managerial background. The party's longest-serving and most influential leader, József Torgyán, a lawyer by profession, was an extremely authoritarian leader (Machos 1999) interested in his own personal greatness – another characteristic that suggests his amateur style of leadership. Indeed, Torgyán treated the party like his own property (Hetek 1998b) and made changes to the party constitution to lengthen his term and otherwise consolidate his power (Sebestyén and Szlazsánszky 2001). He paid little attention to local organizations and other party structures as long as his own leadership remained untouched (Hetek 1998a). Torgyán's great personal ambition, authoritarian leadership style, unruly behavior, and extremist statements led to major party splits (BBC Summary of World Broadcasts 1992; Bozóki 1992). The dominance of Torgyán as leader also hampered organizational development, especially in terms of creating an effective central office (Bélafi 2003) and the party was managed in an ad hoc manner, as one of the subsequent leaders of the party claimed.[5] The leader of the FKgP, thus, rather than just being a bystander clearly had an effect on the state of its organization: organizational weakness followed from Torgyán's nonprofessional leadership style as manifested in his great personal ambition and authoritarianism.

Hungarian Justice and Life Party (MIÉP) can be considered organizationally weak, which most likely originated from its extreme leader-centeredness, as is characteristic of radical right-wing parties (Mudde 2007). Its only leader, István Csurka, considered the party his personal property (HVG 2006) and resisted any changes to the party structures, claiming that things were already "right" (Tamás 2002). This authoritarian style and his nonmanagerial background point more in the direction of amateur than professional leader. Csurka's leadership style made many local politicians as well as prominent people leave the party (HVG 2006; Szlazsánszky 2003), a general decline in membership (Kenyeres 2001; Kisgyőri 2007), and considerable disorganization of the party. It was generally acknowledged that Csurka's leadership style was the biggest obstacle to the survival of MIÉP (Kisgyőri 2007).

The Alliance of Free Democrats (SzDSz), like many other opposition parties in Eastern Europe, started out as an intellectual movement or "independent social organization" (Balázs and Enyedi 1996, 44). Many of its subsequent leaders came from among the founding members of that movement and remained intellectually oriented and ideological (i.e., amateur rather than professional leaders as defined here). The first leader, János Kis (1990–1991), is the best example of this: he was primarily a philosopher rather than a politician (Lőke 2005). Balázs and Enyedi (1996) document how under his leadership the party remained very much an intellectual club with a disorganized party

---

[5] FKgP Respondent 2, personal communication, June 15, 2007.

headquarters and structurally weak organization. In fact, Kis realized that his amateur style of leadership was not appropriate for a political party and decided to become a full-time scholar instead (Lőke 2005). His successor, Péter Tölgyessy (1991–1992), also a founding member of SzDSz, although quite ideological (he attempted to steer the party in the direction of conservatism) actually recognized the importance of building party structures and local presence (Balázs and Enyedi 1996). However, his party presidency was too short and his leadership qualities too poor for him to accomplish anything on this front (Balázs and Enyedi 1996). After 1992, power within the party returned to the more intellectually minded elite under the leadership of Iván Pető (1992–1997) – a history PhD with a prior career of working in the National Archives. He mostly focused on the programmatic development, and "party organization and the development of organizational activities received less attention" (Balázs and Enyedi 1996, 53).

Pető's leadership was followed by that of Gábor Kuncze, who was the party president twice: 1997–1998 and 2001–2007. Kuncze was a prominent politician, one of the most popular ones in the country, even before becoming the president of the party. In contrast to other leaders of SzDSz, he had some prior managerial experience and his leadership style was often described as "pragmatic" (Ágh 1998; Racz and Kukorelli 1995), both of which fit the description of a professional leader. Indeed, Kuncze was ready to sacrifice the party's programmatic identity and goals for the purposes of becoming and remaining a governing party. However, contrary to the theoretical expectations laid out here, investing in party organization was not part of that pragmatism. During his leadership, the local organizations of the party started to wither (Zádori 2007). Local organizations complained that communication with the center was bad and they were excluded from all decision making (Hajdú and Szobota 2007). In hindsight, Kuncze recognized that the decline in the organizational strength of the party was at least partially responsible for its declining electoral performance.[6]

Before Kuncze's second term, the party was ruled for a short period of time by two founding members of the intellectual club predating SzDSz (Bozóki 2003): Bálint Magyar (1998–2000) and Gábor Demszky (2000–2001). The election of both of these leaders was the triumph of the ideological rather than the pragmatic wing of the party: both focused their efforts on revitalizing the ideological debates within the party, and Demszky even tried to create a "third force" in the Hungarian politics otherwise dominated by a bipolar competition between Fidesz and MSzP (Index 2001). Their focus on ideology follows logically from their backgrounds as intellectuals.

The leaders following Kuncze's second term were heading a party that was already in deep decline. János Kóka (2007–2008), an outsider who had joined

[6] SzDSz Respondent 1, personal communication, June 13, 2007.

the party only a year before becoming the leader, was Kuncze's protégé, had worked in managerial positions in the private sector for eight years, and had also served as the minister of economics (Hajdú 2006). This professional background corresponded with his declared goal to double the party's support by way of strengthening and rebuilding local party organizations that the earlier leadership had neglected (Hajdú and Szobota 2007). However, due to short time in office and his status as an outsider, Kóka was unable to materialize his goal. In a year, the power in the party was again in the hands of the original founding elites with the leadership of Gábor Fodor. The focus returned to values and ideology, and Fodor was accused of letting the organizational structure of the party fall apart entirely (HVG 2009).

With the exception of Kuncze, the SzDSz case confirms the expectation that leadership style is associated with organizational strength. The case of Kuncze, however, demonstrates that pragmatic, nonideological leaders interested primarily in party success and office rather than policy do not always turn to building party organization to reach their goal. Kuncze explicitly accepted the status of SzDSz as a small party (Tóth and Török 2002) and played elite-level pragmatic politics to keep the party in the governing coalition to serve his ends.

Poland

Party	Leader	Born	Years in Office	Education	Main Positions Held before Becoming the Leader	Professional (0/1)*
LPR	Marek Kotlinowski	1956	2001–2006	Higher, law, Jagiellonian Univ.	Specialist working on the historic conservation of Krakow Lawyer at the Wieliczka salt mine Legal adviser in Krakow Telecommunications Enterprise Personal law practice	0
	Roman Giertych	1971	2006–2007	MA, law and history, Adam Mickiewicz Univ. in Poznań	Lawyer MP since 2001	0
	Sylwester Chruszcz	1972	2007–2008	Higher, engineering, Technical Univ. of Szczecin	In vojvodship council since 2002 Member of European Parliament since 2004	n/a
	Miroslaw Orzechowski	1957	2008–2010	Higher, theology, film, journalism	Author, producer, journalist MP 2006–2007	n/a

(*continued*)

Poland (*continued*)

Party	Leader	Born	Years in Office	Education	Main Positions Held before Becoming the Leader	Professional (0/1)*
PiS	Lech Kaczynski	1949	2001–2003	PhD, law, Univ. of Gdansk	Researcher at the Univ. of Gdansk Professor at the Univ. of Gdansk and Cardinal Stefan Wyszyński Univ. in Warsaw Solidarity activist; worked for Lech Walesa in the 1980s Senator Minister of state MP President of the Supreme Chamber of Control Minister of justice	1
	Jaroslaw Kaczynski	1949	2003–2010	PhD, law, Warsaw Univ.	Researcher, lecturer, Warsaw Univ. Manager of publishing company Silver Minister of state Senator MP since 1993 for various different parties	0
PD (UD, UW)	Tadeusz Mazowiecki	1927	1991–1995	Secondary (attended Warsaw Univ. but did not graduate)	Member of Catholic PAX Association Editor of a Catholic weekly Member of the Sejm under previous regime Editor-in-chief of Solidarity weekly Prime minister	0
	Leszek Balcerowicz	1947	1995–2000	PhD, economics, Warsaw School of Economics	Economist at the Institute of Marxism-Leninism Economics advisor to Solidarity Deputy prime minister, minister of finance	1
	Bronisław Geremek	1932	2000–2001	PhD, history, Polish Academy of Sciences	Historian, associate professor at the Polish Academy of Sciences MP since 1989 Minister of foreign affairs	0

Party	Leader	Born	Years in Office	Education	Main Positions Held before Becoming the Leader	Professional (o/l)*
	Wladysław Frasyniuk	1954	2001–2006	Secondary, transportation, Technical Automotive Wroclaw	Worked in transportation business Solidarity activist MP since 1991	n/a
	Janusz Onyszkiewicz	1937	2006–2009	Higher, mathematics, Warsaw Univ.	Mathematician Solidarity spokesperson MP since 1989 Minister of defense	n/a
PO	Andrzej Olechowski (coleader)	1947	2001–2002	PhD, economics, Central School of Planning and Statistics in Warsaw	Economist, United Nations Conference on Trade and Development; World Bank Civil servant at the Ministry of Foreign Economic Cooperation Deputy president of the Polish National Bank Finance minister Foreign minister	l
	Donald Tusk (coleader)	1957	2001–2002	MA, history, Univ. of Gdansk	Journalist Physical worker Leader of KLD Vice-president of UW MP, senator	o
	Maciej Plazynski (coleader)	1958	2001–2002	Higher, law, Univ. of Gdansk	One of the leaders of student Solidarity Governor of Gdansk vojvodship MP since 1997	l
	Maciej Plazynski		2002–2003			l
	Donald Tusk		2003–2010			o
PSL	Roman Bartoszcze	1946	1990–1991	Higher, mining, School of Mining		o
	Waldemar Pawlak	1959	1991–1997	Higher, engineering, Warsaw Univ. of Technology	Teacher Member of Sejm for United Peoples' Party MP since 1989	l
	Jarosław Kalinowski	1962	1997–2004	Higher, zootechnics, School of Life Sciences	Mayor of Somianka MP since 1993	l
	Janusz Wojciechowski	1954	2004–2005	Higher, law, Univ. of Lodz	Judge MP 1993–2009	n/a
	Waldemar Pawlak		2005–2010			l

(continued)

Poland (*continued*)

Party	Leader	Born	Years in Office	Education	Main Positions Held before Becoming the Leader	Professional (o/I)*
SLD	Aleskander Kwaśniewski	1954	1990–1995	Higher, economics, Univ. of Gdansk	Activist in the communist student movement Minister of youth affairs Chairman of the Committee for Youth and Physical Culture Member of Mieczysław Rakowski government	I
	Józef Oleksy	1946	1996–1997	PhD, economics, School of Planning and Statistics in Warsaw	Served in the Bureau of the Socialist Union of Polish Students Various positions in the Communist party (labor, audit) Government minister MP since 1989	I
	Leszek Miller	1946	1997–2004	Secondary, power engineering	Engineer in a textile plant Communist Party activist MP since 1991	I
	Krzysztof Janik	1950	2004–2004	PhD, political science, Univ. of Silesia	Activist and later vice president of the Central Committee of the Communist Party MP 1993–2005 Minister of internal affairs and administration	n/a
	Józef Oleksy		2004–2005			I
	Wojciech Olejniczak	1974	2005–2008	PhD, agricultural economics, Warsaw Agricultural Univ.	MP since 2001	o
	Grzegorz Napieralski	1974	2008–2010	MA, political science, Szczecin Univ.	Worked in graphics and production management City council of Szczecin	I
SRP	Andrzej Lepper	1954	1992–2010	Primary	Farmer	o
AWS	Marian Krzaklewski	1950	1996–1999	PhD, computer science, metallurgy, Silesian Univ. of Technology	Department of Systematic Control of Complex Sciences in Gliwice Researcher at the Silesian Univ. of Technology President of Solidarity	I

Party	Leader	Born	Years in Office	Education	Main Positions Held before Becoming the Leader	Professional (0/1)*
	Jerzy Karol Buzek	1940	1999–2001	PhD, chemical engineering, Silesian Univ. of Technology	Institute of Chemical Engineering Polish Academy of Sciences in Gliwice Academic appointments at the Silesian Technical Univ. and the Technical Univ. of Opole	n/a
	Mieczysław Janowski	1947	2001–2002	PhD, engineering, Rzeszów Univ. of Technology	Design specialist Lecturer at the Rzeszów Univ. of Technology Local councilor	n/a
	Krzysztof Piesiewicz	1945	2002–2004	Higher, law, Warsaw Univ.	Lawyer Co-author of scripts for films by Krzysztof Kieslowski Senator for PC and AWS	n/a
UP	Ryszard Bugaj	1944	1992–1997	PhD, economics, Warsaw Univ.	Assistant professor of economics, Polish Academy of Sciences MP since 1989	o
	Marek Pol	1953	1998–2004	Higher, mechanics, Poznan Univ.	Agricultural Automobile Factory MP since 1989 Minister of industry and commerce	o
	Izabela Jaruga-Nowacka	1950	2004–2006	Higher, ethnography, Warsaw Univ.	Ethnographer, Polish Academy of Sciences MP since 1993	n/a
	Waldemar Witkowski	1953	2006–2010	Post-graduate, electrical engineering, education, Poznan Univ.	Univ. lecturer CEO of a large housing cooperative	n/a

* For PD, PSL, SLD, and UP, the classification of leaders as professionals (as opposed to amateurs) is based on the information provided in the text of Chapter 6. For other parties, the coding is based on the following information.

The **Solidarity Election Action (AWS)** was a coalition of right-wing parties dominated by the Solidarity trade union and its political representation, RS AWS. Marian Krzaklewski was the leader of all three entities: the coalition, trade union, and its political representation. In 1999, the position of the RS AWS leader was given to Jerzy Buzek. After its electoral failure and before the party fully disintegrated, it had two additional leaders: Mieczysław Janowski (2001–2002) and Krzysztof Piesiewicz (2002–2004).

Krzaklewski's leadership style can more easily be classified as professional than amateur given the fact that he possessed long-term experience as a high-level administrator, having been the leader of the Solidarity trade union since 1991 – an organization of about 160,000 members that Krzaklewski helped build up (Polish News Bulletin 1991c). His pragmatism and skills were further exemplified by the fact that he was the person who kept the AWS coalition together in 1997 with an iron fist (Szczerbiak 2004), which represents his ambition to lead the right wing to electoral success. However, his political ambitions may have been as much, or even more, personal than partisan – he had personal aspirations to become the president. For this personal reason, he avoided active involvement in managing the party in government after the 1997 electoral victory, and before the 2000 presidential election he was reluctant to engineer any changes within the party, including developing the organization (Polish News Bulletin 2000a), out of fear of losing control of the party (Matraszek 2005). Although Krzaklewski's iron-fist style of leadership managed to guarantee AWS unity for the crucial 1997 election, he was unable to fully unite the right-wing forces comprising AWS and build a strong and unified nationwide organization. From the very beginning, Krzaklewski "did not encourage grassroots initiatives" within AWS (Mac 1996), and kept the coalition as an elite-level project. Although a handful of parties belonging to AWS had some organizational presence, "'couch parties', products of party splits, [were] firmly in majority" (Mac 1996). Furthermore, in addition to experience as a union leader, Krzaklewski was also strongly ideological and principled (Dudek 2008; Perlez 1997), and spent most of his energy on ideological and programmatic disputes over the direction of AWS rather than on building its organizational structures. After AWS's election victory, he became more focused on his personal political ambitions to become president, and his failure to win the presidency significantly undermined his position as the leader of the right. Overall, then, although Krzaklewski exhibited characteristics of a professional leader, especially in terms of his background, experience, and skills, as an AWS leader he did not behave like one and failed to build a strong single organization for the right-wing coalition. This case, therefore, fails to support the theoretical expectation about the effect of leadership style on organizational development.

The Law and Justice (PiS) was essentially the project of the twin brothers Jarosław and Lech Kaczyński. Both brothers were active in the Solidarity movement and the creators as well as leaders of Civic Alliance (PC) – a party, like so many other post-Solidarity formations, that did not rush with building an organization. As P. Lewis (1994, 792) describes it, the PC was reluctant "to develop in traditional party lines," "was not concerned with recruiting members and was of the opinion that the time of mass political parties was over." Indeed, they did not even have a good sense of their membership because no one bothered to keep track (Rogala 1990). The party did, however, establish a national structure with regional organizations. Still, PC was a relatively short-lived entity: having been created in 1990, "the party had become virtually defunct as a political force by the end of 1992" (P. Lewis 1994, 795). Jarosław was described as highly ideological, even radical at the time, with his radicalism causing discontent within the party (Polish News Bulletin 1993a). All of this points in the direction of an amateur style. However, Jarosław had also served as the head of the presidential chancellery under Walesa in the early 1990s, suggesting that he certainly was not a stranger to administrative experience. Still, on balance, it is probably fair to argue that his background before the creation of the PiS allows classifying him as an amateur leader.

Lech Kaczyński, although also active in the PC, served as the leader of the Supreme Audit Office (the top independent state audit body responsible for safeguarding public spending) at the same time – a position from which he was dismissed because of accusations of corruption and mismanagement. Both brothers were also active in AWS, with Lech serving as the justice minister under AWS government. In contrast to Jarosław, Lech can, therefore, be classified as a professional leader.

Lech Kaczyński was the first leader of PiS and held the position from 2001 until 2003, when Jarosław succeeded him. Despite one being classified as a professional, the behavior of both brothers as leaders of PiS has been relatively amateur, especially early in the party's history. After the creation of the party, the brothers capitalized on political elite – well-known people mostly from the crumbling AWS – and did not see party organization as the core purpose of the party; as common among the anti-communist opposition, they saw politics more as a debate about ideology and program than about practical action (Polish News Bulletin 2002b). The brothers decided that the party was to be small and selective, and considered a large organization a liability rather than an asset, a factor that would drag the party to its doom (Polish News Bulletin 2002d). This attitude changed only under Jarosław's leadership, after the realization that reelection as well as election victory at other levels of government (regional and local) depended crucially on the organizational reach of the party (BBC Summary of World Broadcasts 2002c; Polish News Bulletin 2002d).

Civic Platform (PO) leadership shared this initial skepticism about the relevance of party organization. Similar to the Kaczyński brothers, the main leaders of this party – Donald Tusk (coleader in 2001–2002, leader since 2003) Andrzej Olechowski (coleader in 2001–2002), and Maciej Płażyński (coleader in 2001–2002, leader in 2002–2003) – were all seasoned politicians in post-communist Poland. Tusk was the member and leader of Liberal Democratic Congress (KLD) – a party that later became part of UW. For a period, he was also the leader of UW. In his prior career, he behaved as more of an amateur than professional: he prioritized ideas and principles over pragmatism. For example, unlike professional leaders, he did not admit his party's (KLD) own mistakes, leading to its electoral failures, but blamed the "society" who was not ready for his party (PAP 1993b).

Olechowski was active in the Nonpartisan Bloc for Support of Reforms (BBWR) and worked as economic advisor to President Walesa. In 1995, he created his own party called 100 Movement. Contrary to Tusk, he showed the traits of a pragmatic professional leader: he did not just create 100 Movement, but spent 100 days setting up 150 founding committees all over the country. Even the motto of the party included the word "pragmatism," and Olechowski saw the party organization as being based on local efforts and members (Polish News Bulletin 1995d). The party remained small, however, and became part of AWS. Finally, Płażyński also had professional background – he served as the provincial governor of Gdansk and belonged to the leadership of AWS. As characteristic of pragmatic leaders, he was not concerned with ideological purity but rationality in behavior and decision making (Polish News Bulletin 2000b). He realized the importance of organization building and actually left AWS in 2000, referring to the fact that he had a different vision about building an organization than that pursued by AWS (Polish News Bulletin 2000c). For calculating the leadership-style score for the entire party, the level of professionalism for the coleadership of Olechowski, Płażyński, and Tusk is coded 2/3 given that the former two were professionals and the latter was identified as an amateur.

Of the three PO leaders, Tusk was undoubtedly the most influential. Despite the fact that two of the original three leaders showed characteristics of professional leaders, the party initially did not invest in building an organization (BBC Monitoring Europe 2001). Even in 2003, Płażyński accused Tusk of creating an elite party – reason enough for him to leave the party altogether (BBC Summary of World Broadcasts 2003). In 2004, Tusk decided to change the party strategy from focusing on the elites and ideology to building an organization. The change was motivated by the realization that this was necessary in order to remain competitive in the increasingly crowded electoral market (Polish News Bulletin 2004b). Tusk personally campaigned in about 100 localities in the 2005 local government elections (PAP 2006a) and as the party ratings were steadily increasing, he interpreted the new "mass party" strategy as the right one (PAP 2006b). Grassroots connections remained important for Tusk even when the party was in government – the party conducted numerous local meetings, about 1,000 in total, to stay in touch with its voters and win new supporters (PAP 2009).

League of Polish Families (LPR) and Self-Defense (SRP) both had leaders mostly interested in personal ambition and/or ideology rather than building party organization. The SRP leader Andrzej Lepper was clearly creating a leader-centered authoritarian party and was driven by personal ambition rather than the success of the party organization; he was amateur in his leadership style and highly ideological (Mazur 2002; Packer 2003; Polish News Bulletin 2001c, 2002c, 2003a, 2003b). LPR leaders were also characterized by amateur style and/or personal ambition. The party had two main leaders: Marek Kotlinowski (2001–2006) and Roman Giertych (2006–2007). The subsequent leaders – Sylwester Chruszcz (2007–2008) and Mirosław Orzechowski (since 2008) – were basically heading an already-defunct party. During the tenure of Kotlinowski and Giertych, much of the actual power within the party belonged to Father Tadeusz Rydzyk, the director of Radio Maryja and creator of LPR. Rydzyk was highly ideological, demanded personal loyalty, and had no instrumental concern for the party (BBC Summary of World Broadcasts 2002b). Although Kotlinowski was characterized as a quiet man with no leadership ambition (BBC Summary of World Broadcasts 2002a), Roman Giertych was very ambitious and had already gained prominence and influence within the party under Kotlinowski's leadership. Giertych's ambition was directed toward personal gain rather than toward building a sustainable organization (Polish News Bulletin 2004d). Party campaigns were media-centered and expensive rather than grassroots oriented. As explained in the earlier case study, this led to the disappearance of the party as soon as it performed poorly in elections.

The examples of SRP and LPR suggest that leadership style may matter for whether a party ends up with a strong organization or not: both parties were dominated by amateur leaders and had relatively weak party organizations. The examples of PiS and PO are less straightforward. At least some of their leaders had professional backgrounds but amateur attitudes and behavior, which corresponded with weak party organizations initially. However, the leaders of both parties changed their attitude and behavior when facing rigorous electoral competition. It was the leaders' initiative to start building party organizations, but their background was not predictive of this change of heart. This illustrates how factors other than innate characteristics can influence the decisions that leaders take with regard to organizational development. In this case, the other factors were environmental developments and pressure from competition.

References

Abney, Ronni, James Adams, Michael Clark, Malcolm Easton, Lawrence Ezrow, Spyros Kosmidis, and Anja Neundorf. 2013. "When Does Valence Matter? Heightened Valence Effects for Governing Parties during Election Campaigns." *Party Politics* 19(1): 61–82.

Aczél, Endre. 2001. "Hatezer leütés az MSZP-ről." *NOL*, April 30. http://nol.hu/archivum/archiv-17785.

Adams, James, Samuel Merrill, and Bernard Grofman. 2005. *A Unified Theory of Party Competition*. Cambridge: Cambridge University Press.

Advertiser. 1990. "Reds Stay Quiet amid Czech Poll Rhetoric." June 9.

Ágh, Attila. 1991. "A felemás fordulat éve." In *Magyarország politikai évkönyve 1990-ről*, eds. Péter Sándor and László Vass. Budapest: Demokrácia Kutatások Magyar Központja Alapítvány. CD-Rom.

Ágh, Attila. 1995. "The Experiences of the First Democratic Parliaments in East Central Europe." *Communist and Post-Communist Studies* 28(2): 203–214.

Ágh, Attila. 1997. "Defeat and Success as Promoters of Party Change: The Hungarian Socialist Party after Two Abrupt Changes." *Party Politics* 3(3): 427–444.

Ágh, Attila. 1998. "The Year of Early Consolidation." In *Magyarország politikai évkönyve 1997-ről*, eds. Péter Sándor and László Vass. Budapest: Demokrácia Kutatások Magyar Központja Alapítvány. CD-Rom.

Ágh, Attila. 2000. "Party Formation Process and the 1998 Elections in Hungary: Defeat as Promoter of Change for the HSP." *East European Politics & Societies* 14: 288–315.

Ágh, Attila. 2002. "The Dual Challenge and the Reform of the Hungarian Socialist Party." *Communist and Post-Communist Studies* 35(3): 269–288.

Ahlquist, John S. and Margaret Levi. 2011. "Leadership: What It Means, What It Does, and What We Want to Know About It." *Annual Review of Political Science* 14: 1–24.

Alaküla, Allan. 1995. "Isamaa ja ERSP uus maine." *Postimees*, December 1.

Alaküla, Allan. 1996. "Välja visatakse ainult tugevatest parteidest." *Postimees*, September 14.

Aldrich, John. 1995. *Why Parties?* Chicago: University of Chicago Press.

Ames, Barry. 2001. *The Deadlock of Democracy in Brazil*. Ann Arbor: University of Michigan Press.

Ammas, Anneli. 2004. "Villu anektoodid ehk maapoliitiku kavalantsulik pale." *EPL*, October 9.

Amorim Neto, Octavio and Fabiano Santos. 2001. "The Executive Connection: Presidentially Defined Factions and Party Discipline in Brazil." *Party Politics* 7(2): 213–34.

Andrews, Edmund L. 2001. "Former Communist Who Led Left to Victory in Poland." *New York Times*, September 24.

Ansolabehere, Stephen and James M. Snyder. 2000. "Valence Politics and Equilibrium in Spatial Election Models." *Public Choice* 103: 327–336.

Appleton, Andrew M. and Daniel S. Ward. 1994. "Measuring Party Organization in the United States." *Party Politics* 1(1): 113–131.

Ashworth, Scott and Ethan Bueno de Mesquita. 2008. "Electoral Selection, Strategic Challenger Entry, and the Incumbency Advantage." *Journal of Politics* 70(4): 1006–1025.

Astley, Graham W. and Paramjit S. Sachdeva. 1984. "Structural Sources of Intraorganizational Power: A Theoretical Synthesis." *Academy of Management Review* 9(1): 104–113.

Bakke, Elisabeth and Nick Sitter. 2005. "Patterns of Stability: Party Competition and Strategy in Central Europe since 1989." *Party Politics* 11(2): 243–263.

Balázs, Magdolina and Zsolt Enyedi. 1996. "Hungarian Case Studies: The Alliance of Free Democrats and Alliance of Young Democrats." In *Party Structure and Organization in East-Central Europe*, ed. P. G. Lewis. Cheltenham: Edward Elgar. Pp. 43–65.

Balbat, Maris. 2004. "Tarkus ei tähenda süüdistamist, vaid mõistmist." *Elukiri*, September 21.

Bartolini, Stefano. 2000. *The Political Mobilization of the European Left, 1860–1980: The Class Cleavage*. Cambridge: Cambridge University Press.

Basedau, Matthias and Alexander Stroh. 2008. "Measuring Party Institutionalization in Developed Countries: A New Research Instrument Applied to 28 African Political Parties." GIGA Working Paper No. 69.

Bass, Bernard M. 1985. *Leadership and Performance Beyond Expectations*. New York: Free Press.

Battiata, Mary. 1991. "Prague Finance Minister: Economist with Fan Club." *The Washington Post*, April 18.

BBC Monitoring Europe. 1998. "Poland: Government Coalition Junior Partner Claims to Be Largest Party." March 1.

BBC Monitoring Europe. 1999. "Poland: Left Party Congress Ends on Upbeat Note." December 19.

BBC Monitoring Europe. 2001. "Poland: New Political Initiative Not to Form Own Local Government Structures." January 23.

BBC Monitoring Europe. 2005. "Polish Weekly Says Ruling Party's New Leaders Mean 'Trouble' for Other Parties." June 1.

BBC Summary of World Broadcasts. 1990. "Czech Communist Party Assesses Election Result." June 20.

BBC Summary of World Broadcasts. 1992. "Smallholders in Leadership Deadlock after Claims of Putsch against Torgyan." June 16.

BBC Summary of World Broadcasts. 1994a. "Communist Party Chief Pleased with Results." November 22.

BBC Summary of World Broadcasts. 1994b. "Klaus: Goal for 1995 Is to Expand Party Membership Base." December 20.

BBC Summary of World Broadcasts. 1998a. "Labour Union Must Stay Sovereign, Leadership Candidate Says." February 26.

BBC Summary of World Broadcasts. 1998b. "Coalition Partner Discusses 'Lower Than Expected' Election Result." October 20.

BBC Summary of World Broadcasts. 2000. "Left-Wing Leaders Sign Electoral Alliance." December 19.

BBC Summary of World Broadcasts. 2002a. "Polish Newspaper Outlines Background to Potential Split in Right-Wing Party." April 23.

BBC Summary of World Broadcasts. 2002b. "Polish Daily Reports New Conflict in Right-Wing Party." May 13.

BBC Summary of World Broadcasts. 2002c. "Polish Centre-Right Party Elects New Caucus Leader." December 19.

BBC Summary of World Broadcasts. 2003. "Former Leader of Polish Centre Party Resigns Membership." May 30.

BBC Summary of World Broadcasts. 2004. "New Leader of Polish Agrarian Party to Seek Centre Position, Wide Coalitions." March 16.

Beck, Nathaniel, Jonathan N. Katz, and Richard Tucker. 1998. "Taking Time Seriously: Time-Series-Cross-Section Analysis with a Binary Dependent Variable." *American Journal of Political Science* 42(4): 1260–1288.

Bélafi, Antal, 2003. *A Kisgazdapárt újjászervezésének programja.* Budapest: Független Kisgazda-, Földmunkás és Polgári Párt. http://fkgp.hu/modules.php?name=Sections &op=viewarticle&artid=3.

Benoit, Kenneth and Michael Laver. 2006. *Party Policy in Modern Democracies.* London: Routledge.

Benkő, Péter. 2002. "A Független Kisgazdapárt." In *Magyarország politikai évkönyve 2001-ről,* eds. Péter Sándor and László Vass. Budapest: Demokrácia Kutatások Magyar Központja Alapítvány. CD-Rom.

Bielasiak, Jack. 1997. "Substance and Process in the Development of Party Systems in East Central Europe." *Communist and Post-Communist Studies* 30(1): 23–44.

Bielasiak, Jack. 2002. "The Institutionalization of Electoral and Party Systems in Post-communist States." *Comparative Politics* 34(2): 189–210.

Bihari, Mihály. 1991. "Rendszerváltás és hatalomváltás Magyarországon (1989–1990)." In *Magyarország politikai évkönyve 1990-ről,* eds. Péter Sándor and László Vass. Budapest: Demokrácia Kutatások Magyar Központja Alapítvány.

Birch, Sarah. 2003. *Electoral Systems and Political Transformation in Post-Communist Europe.* New York: Palgrave Macmillan.

Black, Jerome H. 1984. "Revising the Effects of Canvassing Behaviour." *Canadian Journal of Political Science* 17(2): 361–374.

Blahoz, Josef. 1994. "Political Parties in the Czech and Slovak Federal Republics: First Steps toward the Rebirth of Democracy." In *How Political Parties Work: Perspectives from Within,* ed. Kay Lawson. Westport: Praeger. Pp. 229–248.

Blais, André, Elisabeth Gidengil, Agnieszka Dobrzynska, Neal Nevitte, and Richard Nadeau. 2003. "Does the Local Candidate Matter?" *Canadian Journal of Political Science* 36: 657–664.

Boix, Carles. 2007. "The Emergence of Parties and Party Systems." In *The Oxford Handbook of Comparative Politics*, eds. Carles Boix and Susan Stokes. Oxford: Oxford University Press. Pp. 499–521.

Borger, Julian. 1993. "Smooth Talker's Rule May Be Very Brief." *Guardian*, September 21.

Bos, Stefan. 2009. "Czech Government Collapses after Losing No-Confidence Vote." GlobalSecurity.org, March 25. http://www.globalsecurity.org/space/library/news/2009/space-090325-voa01.htm.

Bowler, Shaun and David M. Farrell. 1993. "Legislator Shirking and Voter Monitoring: Impacts of European Parliament Electoral Systems upon Legislator/Voter Relationships." *Journal of Common Market Studies* 31(1): 45–69.

Bowler, Shaun and David M. Farrell. 1996. "Constituency Campaigning in Parliamentary Systems with Preferential Voting: Is There a Paradox?" *Electoral Studies* 15(4): 461–476.

Bowler, Shaun, David M. Farrell, and Richard S. Katz. 1999. "Party Cohesion, Party Discipline, and Parliaments." In *Party Discipline and Parliamentary Government*, eds. Shaun Bowler, David M. Farrell, and Richard S. Katz. Columbus: Ohio State University Press. Pp. 3–22.

Bozóki, András. 1992. "A magyar pártok 1991-ben." In *Magyarország politikai évkönyve 1991-ről*, eds. Péter Sándor and László Vass. Budapest: Demokrácia Kutatások Magyar Központja Alapítvány.

Bozóki, András. 2003. *Politikai pluralizmus Magyarországon, 1987–2002*. Budapest: Századvég.

Bozóki, András and Bill Lomax. 1996. "The Revenge of History: The Portuguese, Spanish and Hungarian Transitions – Some Comparisons." In *Stabilising Fragile Democracies: Comparing New Party Systems in Southern and Eastern Europe*, eds. Geoffrey Pridham and Paul G. Lewis. London: Routledge. Pp. 186–205.

Bozóki, András and Eszter Simon. 2006. "Formal Institutions and Informal Politics in Hungary." In *Formal Institutions and Informal Politics in Central and Eastern Europe. Hungary, Poland, Russia, and Ukraine*, ed. Gerd Meyer. Opladen and Farmington Hills: Barbara Budrich Publishers. Pp. 145–194.

Brooks, Clem. 2006. "Voters, Satisficing, and Policymaking: Recent Directions in the Study of Electoral Politics." *Annual Review of Sociology* 32: 191–211.

Brusco, Valeria, Marcelo Nazareno, and Susan Carol Stokes. 2004. "Vote Buying in Argentina." *Latin American Research Review* 39(2): 66–88.

Buch Jensen, Roger. 1999. "Local Party Organisations in Denmark: Crisis or Adaptation?" in *Local Parties in Political and Organisational Perspective*, eds. Martin Saiz and Hans Geser. Oxford: Westview Press. Pp. 258–261.

Bueno de Mesquita, Bruce, Alastair Smith, Randolph M. Siverson, and James D. Morrow. 2003. *The Logic of Political Survival*. Cambridge: MIT Press.

Buras, Piotr. 2005. "Polish Social Democracy, Policy Transfer and Programmatic Change." *Journal of Communist Studies and Transition Politics* 21(1): 84–104.

Butler, David and Neil Kavanagh. 1974. *British General Election of February 1974*. London: Macmillan.

Bynander, Frederik and Paul 't Hart. 2007. "The Politics of Party Leader Survival and Succession: Australia in Comparative Succession." *Australian Journal of Political Science* 42(1): 47–72.

Cain, Bruce, John Ferejohn, and Morris Fiorina. 1987. *The Personal Vote: Constituency Service and Electoral Independence*. Cambridge: Harvard University Press.

Cantu, Francisco and Scott W. Desposato. 2009. "The New Federalism of Mexico's Party System." University of California, San Diego. Unpublished manuscript.

Carey, John M. 2007. "Political Institutions, Competing Principals, and Party Unity in Legislative Voting." *American Journal of Political Science* 51(1): 92–107.

Carey, John M. 2009. *Legislative Voting and Accountability*. Cambridge: Cambridge University Press.

Carey, John M. and Matthew Soberg Shugart. 1995. "Incentives to Cultivate a Personal Vote: A Rank Ordering of Electoral Formulas." *Electoral Studies* 14(4): 417–439.

Carrubba, Clifford J., Matthew Gabel, Lacey Murrah, Ryan Clough, Elizabeth Montgomery, and Rebecca Schambach. 2006. "Off the Record: Unrecorded Legislative Votes, Selection Bias and Roll-Call Vote Analysis." *British Journal of Political Science* 36: 691–704.

Carty, R. Kenneth. 1991. *Canadian Political Parties in the Constituencies*. Toronto: Dundrun Press.

Carty, R. Kenneth and Munroe Eagles. 1999. "Do Local Campaigns Matter? Campaign Spending the Local Canvass and Party Support in Canada." *Electoral Studies* 18: 69–87.

Chandra, Kanchan. 2004. *Why Ethnic Parties Succeed: Patronage and Ethnic Head Counts in India*. Cambridge: Cambridge University Press.

Cheibub, Jose Antonio, Argelina Figueiredo, and Fernando Limongi. 2009. "Political Parties and Governors as Determinants of Legislative Behavior in Brazil's Chamber of Deputies, 1988–2006." *Latin American Politics and Society* 51(1): 1–30.

Chhibber, Pradeep K. 1999. *Democracy without Associations: Transformation of the Party System and Social Cleavages in India*. Ann Arbor: University of Michigan Press.

Clark, Alistair. 2004. "The Continued Relevance of Local Parties in Representative Democracies." *Politics* 24(1): 35–45.

Clark, Michael. 2009. "Valence and Electoral Outcomes in Western Europe, 1976–1998." *Electoral Studies* 28(1): 111–122.

Clark, Peter B. and James Q. Wilson. 1961. "Incentive Systems: A Theory of Organizations." *Administrative Science Quarterly* 6(2): 129–166.

Clark, Terry D., Egle Verseckaite, and Alvidas Lukosaitis. 2006. "The Role of Committee Systems in Post-Communist Legislatures: A Case Study of the Lithuanian Seimas." *Europe-Asia Studies* 58(5): 731–750.

Clarke, Soule John W. and James W. 1970. "Amateurs and Professionals: A Study of Delegates to the 1968 Democratic National Convention." *American Journal of Political Science* 64(4): 888–898.

Coleman, John J. 1996. "Party Organizational Strength and Public Support for Parties." *American Journal of Political Science* 40(3): 805–824.

Collins, Jim. 2001. *Good to Great*. New York: HarperCollins.

Cook, Karen and Richard Emerson. 1978. "Power, Equity, and Commitment in Exchange Networks." *American Sociological Review* 43: 721–739.

Cook, Karen, Richard Emerson, Mary Gillmore, and Toshio Yamagishi. 1983. "The Distribution of Power in Exchange Networks: Theory and Experimental Results." *American Journal of Sociology* 89(2): 275–305.

Coppedge, Michael. 1994. *Strong Parties and Lame Ducks: Presidential Patriarchy and Factionalism in Venezuela.* Stanford: Stanford University Press.

Cotter, Cornelius P., James L. Gibson, John F. Bibby, and Robert J. Huckshorn. 1984. *Party Organizations in American Politics.* New York: Praeger.

Courtney, John C. 1995. *Do Conventions Matter? Choosing National Party Leaders in Canada.* Montreal: McGill-Queens University Press.

Cox, Gary. 1997. *Making Votes Count.* Cambridge: Cambridge University Press.

Cox, Gary W. and Matthew McCubbins. 1993. *Legislative Leviathan: Party Government in the House.* Berkeley: University of California Press.

Crisp, Brian F., Maria C. Escobar-Lemmon, Bradford S. Jones, Mark P. Jones, and Michelle M. Taylor-Robinson. 2004. "Vote-Seeking Incentives and Legislative Representation in Six Presidential Democracies." *Journal of Politics* 66(3): 823–846.

Crisp, Brian F. and Rachel E. Ingall. 2002. "Institutional Engineering and the Nature of Representation: Mapping the Effects of Electoral Reform in Colombia."*American Journal of Political Science* 46(4): 733–748.

Cross, William P. and Andre Blais. 2012. *Politics at the Center: The Selection and Removal of Party Leaders in the Anglo Parliamentary Democracies.* Oxford: Oxford University Press.

Crotty, William. 1971. "Party Effort and Its Impact on the Vote." *American Political Science Review* 65(2): 439–450.

Crozier, Michael. 1964. *The Bureaucratic Phenomenon.* Chicago: University of Chicago Press.

Csizmadia, Ervin. 2005. "Pártok, verseny és alkalmazkodás. Egy változáselmélet alapvonalai." *Politikatudományi Szemle* 14: 5–50.

Csizmadia, Ervin. 2006a. "Akaratkampány." *Hetek* 10(12), March 24. http://www.hetek.hu/belfold/200603/akaratkampany.

Csizmadia, Ervin. 2006b. "Miniszterelnökök és politkai környezet." *Politikatudományi Szemle* 4(4): 5–40.

CTK National News Wire. 1992a. "Party Facing Split, Leader's Psychic Condition Questioned." February 12.

CTK National News Wire. 1992b. "After One Year of Existence, Rightist Party Is the Strongest." February 27.

CTK National News Wire. 1992c. "We Are not Czech Separatists: ODA, the Non-Revolutionary Right." April 22.

CTK National News Wire. 1992d. "Czech Communist Party Leader Stabbed in His Apartment." December 5.

CTK National News Wire. 1993a. "Head of Social Democrats Feels Discriminated, Wants Back to USA." January 26.

CTK National News Wire. 1993b. "Social Democrats before Congress as Seen by Rank-and-File Member." February 17.

CTK National News Wire. 1993c. "New CSSD Chairman Represents Radical Current." March 1.

CTK National News Wire. 1993d. "Svoboda's Resignation Shows Communist Party Cannot Be Reformed." March 10.

CTK National News Wire. 1993e. "Communists Keep Name, Change Chairman." June 27.

CTK National News Wire. 1993f. "Strongest Czech Party to Hold Conference." November 25.

CTK National News Wire. 1994a. "New Right-Wing Party Not Registered." March 2.

CTK National News Wire. 1994b. "Number of CSSD Election Candidates Grows Three Times." November 2.

CTK National News Wire. 1994c. "ODS Conference Made Life More Complicated for Klaus." December 21.

CTK National News Wire. 1995a. "ODA'S Experience from Local Elections 'Almost Banal' Kalvoda." March 4.

CTK National News Wire. 1995b. "Sladek Reigns with Terror among Republicans." August 11.

CTK National News Wire. 1995c. "KSCM Promises Mass Meetings in Election Campaign." September 2.

CTK National News Wire. 1995d. "Elections Top of Agenda." December 9.

CTK National News Wire. 1996a. "Communists Surviving 'Fierce Battle.'" May 11.

CTK National News Wire. 1996b. "Some SPR-RSC Members Intend to Leave Party." June 4.

CTK National News Wire. 1997a. "KDU-CSL Owes Its Rise to Lux's Cool Mind, Consensual Policy-Pehe" February 24.

CTK National News Wire. 1997b. "Zeman Warns of Mutiny Within CSSD." October 2.

CTK National News Wire. 1997c. "MP Hofhanzl Afraid of ODA's Collapse." October 15.

CTK National News Wire. 1997d. "CSSD Leadership Seeking to Triple Party Membership Base." October 10.

CTK National News Wire. 1998a. "ODA Was Politically Dead When I Became Chairman – Skalicky." April 2.

CTK National News Wire. 1998b. "Freedom Union Hasn't Managed to Create Convincing Profile." April 18.

CTK National News Wire. 1998c. "KSCM – Party with Most Disciplined Members and Voters." May 14.

CTK National News Wire. 1998d. "Lidove Noviny Analyzes Freedom Union Troubles." May 28.

CTK National News Wire. 1998e. "Freedom Union Losing Momentum after a Promising Start." June 6.

CTK National News Wire. 1998f. "Lux Not Afraid of Intra-Party Plot." July 17.

CTK National News Wire. 1998g. "Republican Leadership Start Purge." July 29.

CTK National News Wire. 1998h. "Zeman Wants to Make Replacements in CSSD Local Leaderships." September 7.

CTK National News Wire. 1999a. "KSCM's Prospects Rosy, but Should Not Be Overestimated." May 5.

CTK National News Wire. 1999b. "Profiles of Newly Elected KSCM Deputy Chairpersons." December 5.

CTK National News Wire. 2000. "Dissatisfaction with Zeman Growing among Social Democrats." October 5.

CTK National News Wire. 2001. "It Is Not Enough to Preach Values, New Political Style." June 23.

CTK National News Wire. 2002a. "Communists Are Ignored by other Parties but Show Stable Support." March 22.

CTK National News Wire. 2002b. "No Changes to Freedom Union after Unsuccessful Elections." November 8.

CTK National News Wire. 2002c. "Spidlas Chairmanship Weakening amid Intra-CSSD Battle." December 10.

CTK National News Wire. 2003a. "Freedom Union-DEU Resigned to Its Fate." January 23.

CTK National News Wire. 2003b. "ODS Organisations Happy with New Leadership." February 18.

CTK National News Wire. 2003c. "Klaus Wins Thanks to Communists." March 1.

CTK National News Wire. 2003d. "Presidential Elections Unveil Disputes in Czech Ruling Party." March 3.

CTK National News Wire. 2003e. "KDU-CSL at Crossroads after Weekend Conference." November 10.

CTK National News Wire. 2004a. "Miroslav Grebenicek Head of Communist for almost 11 Years." May 12.

CTK National News Wire. 2004b. "Spidla Govt Ends after Two Years, Was CSSD Head for Three Years." June 26.

CTK National News Wire. 2004c. "ODS Candidates to Use 14 Blue Buses In Election Campaign." October 4.

CTK National News Wire. 2004d. "Gross Surprises by Resolute Words, CSSD Leftists Unprepared." December 6.

CTK National News Wire. 2005. "US-DEU to Hold Conference in Autumn, Could Exchange Leadership." June 19.

CTK National News Wire. 2007. "Czech KDU Exhausted from Struggle for Cunek, Has no Vision." June 21.

CTK National News Wire. 2008a. "Czech Social Democrats Expel MP Who Voted to Reelect Incumbent President." March 3.

CTK National News Wire. 2008b. "ODS's Schwippel Sixth Czech MP to Leave Deputy Group since Polls." September 17.

CTK National News Wire. 2008c. "Rakovnická ODS Tlustého nevyloučila, vedení se nevzdává." September 22.

CTK National News Wire. 2009a. "O osudu Tlustého a Schwippela v ODS se bude jednat příští týden." March 24.

CTK National News Wire. 2009b. "Czech Coalition to Expel MPs for Voting to Sack Cabinet." March 26.

CTK National News Wire. 2009c. "Rada ODS žádá o vyloučení Tlustého a Schwippela." March 26.

CTK National News Wire. 2009d. "Schwippel v ODS zůstává. Zatím." March 31.

Curry, Jane Leftwich. 2003. "Poland's Ex-Communists: From Pariahs to Establishment Party." In *The Left Transformed in Post-Communist Societies*, eds. Jane Leftwich Curry, and Joan Barth Urban. New York: Rowman and Littlefield. Pp. 19–60.

Curry, Jane Leftwich and Joan Barth Urban. 2003. *The Left Transformed in Post-Communist Societies*. New York: Rowman and Littlefield.

Curry, Tom. 2008. "Why Obama Won and What His Win Gets Him." msnbc.com. January 26. http://www.msnbc.msn.com/id/22859254/ns/politics-decision_08/t/why-obama-won-what-his-win-gets-him/#.UO-Lr7b8Pco.

Cutright, Phillips. 1963. "Measuring the Impact of Local Party Activity on the General Election Vote." *Public Opinion Quarterly* 27(3): 372–386.

Czech News Agency. 1999. "KDU-CSL Recording Decrease of Members." May 21.

Czech News Agency. 2000. "Kasal Repeals Rebels' Attack." March 20.

Czech News Agency. 2002. "KDU-CSL May Change from 'Quiet Force' to Razor-Sharp Party." January 25.

Czech News Agency. 2003. "CSSD in Chaos, Unpredictable without Zema's Firm Authority." February 21.

Czech News Agency. 2004a. "Communists Might Become 'Leading Force' of Czech Left." February 10.

Czech News Agency. 2004b. "Most District Organisations Want Grebenicek as KSCM Head." March 8.

Czech News Agency. 2005a. "Outgoing CSSD Head Gross Leaves High Politics after 15 Years." September 24.

Czech News Agency. 2005b. "Communist Party Is Quietly Changing." October 20.

Czech News Agency. 2005c. "Communists to Spend 22 Million Crowns on 2006 Election Campaign." November 19.

Czech News Agency. 2006a. "Disappointed KSCM Considering Changes in Leadership." June 3.

Czech News Agency. 2006b. "Vojtech Filip Leads Communists to Election for First Time." June 4.

Czech News Agency. 2006c. "KDU-CSL Should Seek Ways to Prevent Its Further Decline." June 7.

Czech News Agency. 2006d. "CSSD Wants to Change Party's Image, Increase Membership." August 31.

Czech News Agency. 2006e. "CSSD Presidium Chooses Havlicek for Party Chief Manager." September 8.

Czech News Agency. 2006f. "Paroubek Admits CSSD May Stay in Opposition for Years." September 9.

Czech News Agency. 2006g. "Basic Data about Civic Democrats." November 14.

Czech News Agency. 2008. "Czech KDU-CSL Leader Says Some Forces Want to Destroy His Party." January 7.

Czech News Agency. 2009a. "Populism Prevails in Czech CSSD Under Duo Paroubek-Rath." February 6.

Czech News Agency. 2009b. "Paroubek Rules Czech Social Democrats without Any Challenger." March 17.

Dahlberg, Matz and Eva Johansson. 2002. "On the Vote-Purchasing Behavior of Incumbent Governments." *American Political Science Review* 96(1): 27–40.

Davis, James W. 1998. *Leadership Selection in Six Western Democracies*. Westport: Greenwood Press.

Debreczeni, József. 1998. *A miniszterelnök. Antall József és a rendszerváltozás.* Budapest: Osiris.

Debreczeni, József. 2006. *Az új miniszterelnök.* Budapest: Osaris Kiadó.

Deegan-Krause, Kevin. 2006. *Elected Affinities: Democracy and Party Competition in Slovakia and the Czech Republic*. Stanford: Stanford University Press.

Denver, David T. and Gordon Hands. 1997. *Modern Constituency Electioneering: Local Campaigning in the 1992 General Election*. London: Frank Cass.

Deschouwer, Kris. 1994. "The Decline of Consociationalism and the Reluctant Modernization of Belgian Mass Parties." In *How Parties Organize: Change and Adaptation in Party Organizations in Western Democracies*, eds. Richard S. Katz and Peter Mair. London: Sage. Pp. 80–108.

Desposato, Scott W. 2004. "The Impact of Federalism on National Party Cohesion in Brazil." *Legislative Studies Quarterly* 29(2): 259–285.

Desposato, Scott W. 2005. "Correcting for Small Group Inflation of Roll-Call Cohesion Scores." *British Journal of Political Science* 35: 731–744.

Desposato, Scott W. 2006. "The Impact of Electoral Rules on Legislative Parties: Lessons from the Brazilian Senate and Chamber of Deputies." *Journal of Politics* 68(4): 1018–1030.

Deutsch, Tamás and László Gyarmati. 1999. "A jövő választása." In *Magyarország politikai évkönyve 2000-ről*, eds. Péter Sándor and László Vass. Budapest: Demokrácia Kutatások Magyar Központja Alapítvány. CD-Rom.

Diamond, Larry, and Juan J. Linz. 1989. "Introduction: Politics, Society, and Democracy in Latin America." In *Democracy in Developing Countries*, eds. Diamond, Larry, Juan J. Linz, and Seymour Martin Lipset. Boulder, CO: Lynne Rienner and London: Adamantine Press. Pp. 1–58.

Diermeier, Daniel and Timothy J. Feddersen. 1998. "Cohesion in Legislatures and the Vote of Confidence Procedure." *American Political Science Review* 92(3): 611–621.

Dix, Robert H. 1992. "Democratization and the Institutionalization of Latin American Political Parties." *Comparative Political Studies* 24(4): 488–511.

Drabikowska, Agnieszka. 2003. "Skandal w MSWiA." *Gazeta Wyborcza*, July 4.

Dudek, Antoni. 2008. *Historia polityczna Polski 1989–2005*. Krakow: Arcana.

Duverger, Maurice. 1954. *Political Parties: Their Organization and Activity in the Modern State*. London: Methuen.

Eldersveld, Samuel J. 1956. "Experimental Propaganda Techniques and Voting Behavior." *American Political Science Review* 50(1): 154–165.

Eldersveld, Samuel J. 1986. "The Party Activist in Detroit and Los Angeles: A Longitudinal View, 1956–1980." In *Political Parties in Local Areas*, ed. William Crotty. Knoxville: University of Tennessee Press. Pp. 89–119.

Elster, John, Claus Offe, and Ulrich K. Preuss. 1998. *Institutional Design in Post-Communist Societies*. Cambridge: Cambridge University Press.

Emerson, Richard M. 1962. "Power-Dependence Relations." *American Sociological Review* 27(1): 31–40.

Enyedi, Zsolt. 2005. "The Role of Agency in Cleavage Formation." *European Journal of Political Research* 44(1): 1–25.

Enyedi, Zsolt. 2006. "Accounting for Organisation and Financing: A Comparison of Four Hungarian Parties." *Europe-Asia Studies* 58(7): 1101–1117.

Enyedi, Zsolt. 2008. "Dataset of Hungarian Political Parties." Budapest: Central European University.

Enyedi, Zsolt and Lukáš Linek. 2008. "Searching for the Right Organization: Ideology and Party Structure in East-Central Europe." *Party Politics* 14(4): 455–477.

EPL. 2001a. "Siimanni harakiri." November 7.

EPL. 2001b. "Miks Koonderakond kokku varises?" November 19.

EPL. 2001c. "Noored mässajad asutavad erakonna." December 8.

Epperly, Brad. 2011. "Institutions and Legacies: Electoral Volatility in the Postcommunist World." *Comparative Political Studies* 44(7): 829–853.

Ernits, Peeter. 2004a. "Ülo Vooglaid: Res Publical puudub kompass." *Postimees*, February 27.

Ernits, Peeter. 2004b. "Äraostmatute juhtimisel on Res Publica jõudnud kurnavasse kodusõtta." *Postimees*, June 21.

EU Business. 2008. "Poland, Slovakia, Embrace EU's Lisbon Treaty." April 10.

Evans, Geoffrey. 2006. "The Social Bases of Political Divisions in Post-Communist Eastern Europe." *Annual Review of Sociology* 32: 245–270.

Evans, Geoffrey and Stephen Whitefield. 1993. "Identifying the Bases of Party Competition in Eastern Europe." *British Journal of Political Science* 23: 521–548.

Evans, Geoffrey and Stephen Whitefield. 1995. "Social and Ideological Cleavage Formation in Post-Communist Hungary." *Europe-Asia Studies* 47(7): 1177–1204.

Evans, Geoffrey and Stephen Whitefield. 1998. "The Structuring of Political Cleavages in Post-Communist Societies: The Case of the Czech Republic and Slovakia." *Political Studies* 46(1): 115–139.

Ezrow, Lawrence. 2008. "Parties' Policy Programmes and the Dog that Didn't Bark: No Evidence that Proportional Systems Promote Extreme Party Positioning." *British Journal of Political Science* 38(3): 479–497.

Fenno, Richard F. 1973. *Congressmen in Committees*. Boston: Brown.

Ferejohn, John. 1974. *Pork Barrel Politics*. Palo Alto: Stanford University Press.

Fiorina, Morris P., Samuel J. Abrams, and Jeremy Pope. 2005. *Culture War?* New York: Longman.

Fligstein, Neil. 1987. "The Intraorganizational Power Struggle: Rise of Finance Personnel to Top Leadership in Large Corporations, 1919–1979." *American Sociological Review* 52(1): 44–58.

Földvári, Katalin. 2001. "Őszinte a Fidesz konzervativizmusa." *Hetek* 5(19), May 12. http://www.hetek.hu/interju/200105/oszinte_a_fidesz_konzervativizmusa.

Fowler, Brigid. 2004. "Concentrated Orange: Fidesz and the Remaking of the Hungarian Centre-Right, 1994–2002." *Journal of Communist Studies and Transition Politics* 20(3): 80–114.

Fowler, James H. and Michael Laver. "A Tournament of Party Decision Rules." *Journal of Conflict Resolution* 52(1): 68–92.

Frendreis, John P., James L. Gibson, and Laura L Vertz. 1990. "The Electoral Relevance of Local Party Organizations." *American Political Science Review* 84(1): 225–235.

Gajewski, Jaroslaw. 2003. "Polish Peasant Party Politicians Call on Chairman Kalinowski to Resign." *World News Connection*, September 15.

Gallagher, Michael. 1985. "Social Backgrounds and Local Orientations of Members of the Irish Dail." *Legislative Studies Quarterly* 10: 373–394.

Gavra, Gábor. 2004. "Lezáruló tisztogatás a Fideszben: Minden szinten szinte mind megy." *MaNcs* 16(13), March 25. http://www.mancs.hu/index.php?gcPage=/public/hirek/hir.php&id=9941.

Gazeta.pl. 2011. "Partie w Polsce. Historia." September 14. http://wybory.gazeta
.pl/wyboryparlamentarne/1,118273,10278431,Partie_w_Polsce__Historia__
INFOGRAFIKA_.html.

Gazeta Wyborcza. 2004. "Kulisy afery Orlenu – raport Giertycha." December 13.

Gazsó Ferenc and István Stumpf. 1997. "Pártok és szavazóbázisok." In *Magyarország politikai évkönyve 1996-ról*, eds. Péter Sándor and László Vass. Budapest: Demokrácia Kutatások Magyar Központja Alapítvány. CD-Rom.

George, Alexander L. and Timothy J. McKeown. 1985. "Case Studies and Theories of Organizational Decision Making." In *Advances in Information Processing in Organizations*, eds. Robert F. Coulam and Richard A. Smith. Greenwich: JAI Press. Pp. 21–58.

Gerber, Alan S. and Donald P. Green. 2000. "The Effects of Canvassing, Telephone Calls, and Direct Mail on Voter Turnout." *American Political Science Review* 94(3): 653–663.

Geser, Hans. 1999. "The Local Party as an Object of Interdisciplinary Comparative Study: Some Steps Toward Theoretical Integration." In *Local Parties in Political and Organizational Perspective*, eds. Martin Saiz and Hans Geser. Boulder, CO: Westview Press. Pp. 3–43.

Giannetti, Daniela and Michael Laver. 2001. "Party System Dynamics and the Making and Breaking of Italian Governments." *Electoral Studies* 20(4): 529–553.

Gibson, James L., Cornelius P. Cotter, and John F. Bibby. 1983. "Assessing Party Organizational Strength." *American Journal of Political Science* 27(2): 193–222.

Gibson, James L., Cornelius P. Cotter, John F. Bibby, and Robert J. Huckshorn. 1985. "Whither the Political Parties?: A Cross-Sectional and Longitudinal Analysis of the Strength of Party Organizations." *American Journal of Political Science* 29(1): 139–160.

Gibson, James L., John B. Frendreis, and Laura L. Vertz. 1989. "Party Dynamics in the 1980s: Change in County Party Organizational Strength, 1980–1984." *American Journal of Political Science* 33(1): 67–90.

Gilardi, Fabrizio. 2010. "Who Learns from What in Policy Diffusion Process?" *American Journal of Political Science* 54(3): 650–666.

Giró-Szász, András, Dávid Héjj, Tamás Kern, and Gábor Schultz. 2008. "A Fidesz-MPP 2007-es helyzete." In *Magyarország politikai évkönyve 2007-ről*, eds. Péter Sándor and László Vass. Budapest: Demokrácia Kutatások Magyar Központja Alapítvány. CD-Rom.

Giró-Szász, András, Dávid Héjj and Roland Kisgyőri. 2007. "A Fidesz-MPSZ változása 2006-ban." In *Magyarország politikai évkönyve 2006-ról*, eds. Péter Sándor and László Vass. Budapest: Demokrácia Kutatások Magyar Központja Alapítvány. CD-Rom.

Golosov, Grigorii V. 1998. "Who Survives?: Party Origins, Organizational Development, and Electoral Performance in Post-Communist Russia." *Political Studies* 46:511–543.

Golosov, Grigorii V. 2004. *Political Parties in the Regions of Russia: Democracy Unclaimed*. Boulder: Lynne Rienner.

Greenhouse, Steven. 1990. "Upheaval in the East: Poland." *New York Times*, January 30.

Groseclose, Timothy J. 2001. "A Model of Candidate Location: When One Candidate Has a Valence Advantage." *American Journal of Political Science* 45(4): 862–886.

Grzymala-Busse, Anna M. 2002a. *Redeeming the Communist Past: The Regeneration of Communist Parties in East Central Europe.* Cambridge: Cambridge University Press.

Grzymala-Busse, Anna M. 2002b. "The Effects of Communist Party Transformation on the Institutionalization of Party Systems." In András Bozóki and John Ishiyama (Eds.) *Communist Successor Parties a Decade After: Reform or Transmutation?* New York: M.E. Sharpe.

Grzymala-Busse, Anna M. 2007. *Rebuilding Leviathan.* Cambridge: Cambridge University Press.

Gunther, Richard and Jonathan Hopkin. 2002. "A Crisis of Institutionalization: The Collapse of the UCD in Spain." In *Political Parties: Old Concepts and New Challenges,* eds. Richard Gunther, José Ramon Montero, and Juan J. Linz. Oxford: Oxford University Press. Pp. 191–232.

Gunther, Richard, Jose Ramon Montero, and Juan J. Linz, eds. 2002. *Political Parties: Old Concepts and New Challenges.* Oxford: Oxford University Press.

Hadjiiski, Magdalena. 2001. "The Failure of the Participatory Democracy in the Czech Republic." *West European Politics* 24(3): 43–64.

Hagelberg, Tõnu. 2000. "Suure keskpartei sünd." *Maaleht,* June 15.

Hajdú, Sándor. 2006. "Nagyobb gázzal." *Hetek* 10(1), January 6. http://www.hetek .hu/belfold/200601/nagyobb_gazzal.

Hajdú, Sándor and Zoltán Szobota. 2007. "Bebetonozott érdekek." *Hetek* 11(12), March 23. http://www.hetek.hu/fokusz/200703/bebetonozott_erdekek.

Handl, Vladimir. 2005a. "Choosing Between China and Europe? Virtual Inspiration and Policy Transfer in the Programmatic Development of the Czech Communist Party." *Journal of Communist Studies and Transition Politics* 21(1): 123–141.

Handl, Vladimír. 2005b. "The Development and the Prospects of the Czech Left: The Role of the Communist Party." Friedrich Ebert Stiftung Working Paper 12/2005.

Hanley, Sean. 2001. "Towards Breakthrough or Breakdown?: The Consolidation of KSČM as a Neo-Communist Successor Party in the Czech Republic." *Journal of Communist Studies and Transition Politics* 17(3): 96–116.

Hanley, Sean. 2003. "Are the Exceptions Really the Rule?: Questioning the Application of 'Electoral-Professional' Type Models of Party Organization in East Central Europe." In *Pan-European Perspectives on Party Politics,* eds. Paul Lewis and Paul Webb. Leiden: Brill. Pp. 151–77.

Hanley, Sean. 2004. "Blue Velvet: The Rise and Decline of the New Czech Right." *Journal of Communist Studies and Transition Politics* 20(3): 28–54.

Hanley, Sean. 2008. *The New Right in the New Europe: Czech Transformation and Right-Wing Politics, 1989–2006.* London: Routledge.

Hannan, Michael T. and John Freeman. 1984. "Structural Inertia and Organizational Change." *American Sociological Review* 49(2): 149–164.

Harmel, Robert and Kenneth Janda. 1982. *Parties and Their Environment: Limits to Reform?* London and New York: Longman.

Harmel, Robert and Kenneth Janda. 1994. "An Integrated Theory of Party Goals and Party Change." *Journal of Theoretical Politics* 6(3): 259–287.

Haspel, Moshe, Thomas D. Remington, and Steven Smith. 1998. "Electoral Institutions and Party Cohesion in the Russian Duma." *Journal of Politics* 60: 417–439.

Hazan, Reuven Y. 1999. "Constituency Interests without Constituencies: The Geographical Impact of Candidate Selection on Party Organization and Legislative Behavior in the 14th Israeli Knesset, 1996–1999." *Political Geography* 18: 791–811.

Hazan, Reuven Y. 2003. "Does Cohesion Equal Discipline?: Towards a Conceptual Delineation." *Journal of Legislative Studies* 9(4): 1–11.

Herrnson, Paul S. 1986. "Do Parties Make a Difference?: The Role of Party Organizations in Congressional Elections." *Journal of Politics* 48(3): 589–615.

Herron, Erik. 2002. "Electoral Influences on Legislative Behavior in Mixed-Member Systems: Evidence from the Ukraine's Verkhovna Rada." *Legislative Studies Quarterly* 27: 361–381.

Hetek. 1998a. "Hajsza a cédulákért." March 14. http://www.hetek.hu/hatter/199803/hajsza_a_cedulakert.

Hetek. 1998b. "Torgyánt nem lehet kihagyni." May 16. http://www.hetek.hu/belfold/199805/torgyant_nem_lehet_kihagyni.

Hetek. 1998c. "Tovább marakodnak a kereszténydemokraták." September 5. http://www.hetek.hu/belfold/199809/tovabb_marakodnak_a_keresztenydemokratak.

Hickson, D. J., C. R. Hinings, C. A. Lee, R. E. Schneck, and T. M. Pennings. 1971. "A Strategic Contingencies' Theory of Intraorganizational Power." *Administrative Science Quarterly* 16(2): 216–229.

Hiiesalu, Hanna, Lauri Naber, Alvar Nõukas, Tõnis Poom, and Karl-Erik Tender. 2002. "Mõõdukad." Department of Political Science, University of Tartu. http://www.ut.ee/teaduskond/Sotsiaal/Politoloogia/2002KOVanalyys/Moodukad.pdf.

Hinings, C. R., David J. Hickson, Johannes M. Pennings, and R. E. Schneck. 1974. "Structural Conditions of Intraorganizational Power." *Administrative Science Quarterly* 19(1): 22–44.

Hix, Simon. 2004. "Electoral Institutions and Legislative Behavior: Explaining Voting Defection in the European Parliament." *World Politics* 56(2): 194–223.

Hix, Simon, Abdul Noury, and Gerard Roland. 2005. "Power to the Parties: Cohesion and Competition in the European Parliament, 1979–2001." *British Journal of Political Science* 35(2): 209–234.

Hoffstetter, C. Richard. 1971. "The Amateur Politician: A Problem in a Construct Validation." *Midwest Journal of Political Science* 15(1): 34–50.

Holbrook, Thomas M. and Charles M. Tidmarch. 1993. "The Effects of Leadership Positions on Votes for Incumbents in State Legislative Elections." *Political Research Quarterly* 46(4): 897–909.

Horak, Martin. 1998. "Republicans Lick Their Wounds in Private." *Prague Post*, July 1.

Horn, Gyula. 1999. *Azok a 90-es évek*... Budapest: Kossuth.

House, Robert J. 1977. "A 1976 Theory of Charismatic Leadership." In *Leadership: The Cutting Edge*, eds. James G. Hunt and Lars L. Larson. Carbondale: Southern Illinois University Press. Pp. 189–204.

Huang, Mel. 1999. "A Deflating Election Experience." *Central European Review*, October 20.

Huckfeldt, Robert and John Sprague. 1992. "Political Parties and Electoral Mobilization: Political Structure, Social Structure, and the Party Canvass." *American Political Science Review* 86(1): 70–86.

Huckshorn, Robert J., James L. Gibson, Cornelius P. Cotter, and John F. Bibby. 1986. "Party Integration and Party Organizational Strength." *Journal of Politics* 48(4): 976–991.

Humphreys, Macartan, William A. Masters, and Martin E. Sandbu. 2006. "The Role of Leaders in Democratic Deliberations: Results from a Field Experiment in São Tomé and Príncipe." *World Politics* 58(4): 583–622.

Hungary Around the Clock. 2008. "Two Socialist MPs to Defy Party Whip Over Health Care Bill." *Hungary Around the Clock*, February 6.

Hüvato, Mari-Liis. 2005. "Rahavliit tugevdab Tartumaal positsioone." *Postimees*, September 26.

HVG. 2004a. "Hiller István lesz az MSZP új elnöke?" June 17. http://hvg.hu/itthon/00000000057B3EF.

HVG. 2004b. "Pártelnökválasztás: esélyek nyugtalansága." July 22. http://hvg.hu/itthon/00000000058E112.

HVG. 2005. "A Fidesz sms-ben kér tanácsot a választóktól." February 5. http://hvg.hu/itthon/20050205fideszsms.

HVG. 2006. "Országos listás pártok." March 22. http://hvg.hu/hvgfriss/2006.12/200612HVGFriss12206.

HVG. 2009. "Pető: 'Retkes hülyeségeket beszél." July 14. http://hvg.hu/itthon/20090714_szdsz_peto_retkes_fodor_demszky.

Ideon, Argo. 1999a. "Reformierakond jätkab Siim Kallase käe all." *Postimees*, May 17.

Ideon, Argo. 1999b. "Keskerakondlased hakkavad oma valijaid üles kirjtuama." *Postimees*, October 6.

Ideon, Argo. 1999c. "Rahvaerakond Mõõdukad lubab seista töövõtjate ja maainimeste huvide eest." *Postimees*, November 29.

Ideon, Argo. 2000a. "Keskerakond hääletas kongressil muutused maha." *Postimees*, February 21.

Ideon, Argo. 2000b. "Koonderakond valib lõpu ja üritamise vahel." *Postimees*, March 21.

Ideon, Argo. 2000c. "Keskerakond värbab tuhatkond liiget." *Postimees*, May 16.

Ideon, Argo. 2001. "Olari Taal: Res Publica juht saab peaministriks." *Postimees*, December 10.

Ideon, Argo. 2002. "Parteide kampaaniategemise võhm sõltub rahast, ajast ja inimestest." *Postimees*, September 9.

Ideon, Argo. 2009a. "Keskerakond lööb võistlejaid valimiste põhjaliku eeltööga." *Postimees*, October 10.

Ideon, Argo. 2009b. "Savisaar ja vene valijate hääled." *Postimees*, October 27.

Ilonszki, Gabriella. 1994. "Parliament and Parliamentarians in Hungary: A Comparative Perspective." In *The First Steps*, eds. Attila Agh and Sandor Kurtan. Budapest: Center for Democratic Studies. Pp. 237–251.

Ilonszki, Gabriella. 1999. "Legislative Recruitment: Personnel and Institutional Development in Hungary, 1990–1994." In *Elections to the Hungarian National Assembly*

1994: Analysis, Documents and Data, eds. Gábor Toká and Zsolt Enyedi. Berlin: Sigma. Pp. 82–107.

Index. 2001. "'A Fidesz és az MSZP egymást erősíti.'" January 30. http://index.hu/belfold/demszkyo130/.

Index. 2004. "Kovácstalanság." *Index.hu*, October 18. http://index.hu/velemeny/jegyzet/kovacso41017/.

Innes, Abby. 2002. "Party Competition in Postcommunist Europe: The Great Electoral Lottery." *Comparative Politics* 35(1): 85–104.

Ishiyama, John T. 2001. "Party Organization and the Political Success of the Communist Parties." *Social Science Quarterly* 82(4): 844–864.

Iversen, Torben. 1994. "Political Leadership and Representation in West European Democracies: A Test of Three Models of Voting." *American Journal of Political Science* 38(1): 45–74.

Jakl, Rene. 1998. "ODS Heals from Scandals as Right Rivals Fail to Thrill." *Prague Post*, June 3.

Jakus, Ibolya. 2005. "A vizsgálat lezárult. Párthétvége az államfőválasztás után." *HVG*, June 15. http://hvg.hu/hvgfriss/2005.24/200524HVGFriss2.

Janda, Kenneth. 1980. *Political Parties: A Cross-National Survey*. New York: The Free Press.

Janda, Kenneth. 1983. "Cross-National Measures of Party Organizations and Organizational Theory." *European Journal of Political Research* 11: 319–332.

Janda, Kenneth. 1993. "Comparative Political Parties: Research and Theory." In *Political Science: The State of the Discipline II*, ed. Ada W. Finifter. Washington, DC: APSA. Pp. 163–191.

Janda, Kenneth and Tyler Colman. 1998. "Effects of Party Organization on Performance during the 'Golden Age' of Parties." *Political Studies* 46: 611–632.

Janicki, Mariusz. 1994. "Pawlak and His Party." *Polish News Bulletin*, November 17.

Jarne, Aivar. 1996a. "Savisaare soolo." *Postimees*, March 1.

Jarne, Aivra. 1996b. "Keskerakonna reanimatsioon." *Postimees*, April 2.

Jason, Leonard A., Thomas Rose, Joseph R. Ferrari, and Russ Barone. 1984. "Personal versus Impersonal Methods for Recruiting Blood Donations." *Journal of Social Psychology* 123: 139–140.

Jędrzejczyk, Agnieszka. 2003. "Rok z Rywinem." *Gazeta Wyborcza*, November 30.

John, Peter and Martin Saiz. 1999. "Local Political Parties in Comparative Perspective." In *Local Parties in Political and Organizational Perspective*, eds. Martin and Hans Geser Saiz. Boulder: Westview Press. Pp. 44–76.

Johnston, Ron and Charles Pattie. 2006. *Putting Voters In Their Place*. Oxford: Oxford University Press.

Juhász, Attila, and Péter Krekó. 2008. "A vezéreken túl is van politikai élet. Gyurcsány Ferenc és Orbán Viktor 2007-ben." In *Magyarország politikai évkönyve 2007-ről*, eds. Péter Sándor and László Vass. Budapest: Demokrácia Kutatások Magyar Központja Alapítvány. CD-Rom.

Juhász, Attila and Krisztián Szabados. 2006. "A populizmus éve." In *Magyarország politikai évkönyve 2005-ről*, eds. Péter Sándor and László Vass. Budapest: Demokrácia Kutatások Magyar Központja Alapítvány. CD-Rom.

Juhász, Gábor. 2001. *Pártpénzügyek*. Budapest: Aula.

Kagge, Rasmus. 2005. "Analüütikud ennustavad Res Publicale mõõnast pääsu." *Postimees*, June 6.

Kaldmaa, Urmas. 1997. "Arnold Rüütel ja Andres Varik valiti tagasi." *Postimees*, January 2.

Kalmre, Vahur. 1996. "Keskerakond murendab Eesti demokraatiat." *Postimees*, March 15.

Kalukin, Rafal. 2008. "Napieralski – Man of the People." *Gazeta Wyborcza*, June 7–8.

Kalyvas, Stathis. 1998. "From Pulpit to Party: Party Formation and the Christian Democratic Phenomenon." *Comparative Politics* 31(2): 293–312.

Kam, Christopher. 2009. *Party Discipline and Parliamentary Politics.* Cambridge: Cambridge University Press.

Kancelaria Sejmu. 1999. *Sejm Rzeczypospolitej Polskiej. III Kadencja. Przewodnik.* Warsaw: Wydanictwo Sejmove.

Kancelaria Sejmu. 2002. *Sejm Rzeczypospolitej Polskiej. IV Kadencja. Przewodnik.* Warsaw: Wydanictwo Sejmove.

Kancelaria Sejmu. 2006. *Sejm Rzeczypospolitej Polskiej. V Kadencja. Przewodnik.* Warsaw: Wydanictwo Sejmove.

Kangur, Riho. 2004. "Kandidaatide selekteerimise protsess Eesti erakondades." BA Thesis, University of Tartu.

Karpa, Kärt. 1998. "Tiit Vähi tahab tagasi võimule." *EPL*, July 27.

Katz, Daniel and Samuel J. Eldersveld. 1961. "The Impact of Local Party Activity upon the Electorate." *Public Opinion Quarterly* 25(1): 1–24.

Katz, Jonathan and Gary King. 1999. "A Statistical Model for Multiparty Electoral Data." *American Political Science Review* 93(1): 15–32.

Katz, Richard S. 1980. *A Theory of Parties and Electoral Systems.* Baltimore: Johns Hopkins University Press.

Katz, Richard and Lucanio Bardi. 1980. "Preference Voting and Turnover in Italian Parliamentary Elections." *American Journal of Political Science* 24(1): 97–114.

Katz, Richard S. and Peter Mair, eds. 1994. *How Parties Organize: Change and Adaptation in Party Organizations in Western Democracies.* London: Sage.

Katz, Richard S. and Peter Mair. 1995. "Changing Models of Party Organization and Party Democracy: The Emergence of the Cartel Party." *Party Politics* 1(1): 5–28.

Katz, Richard S. and Peter Mair. 2009. "The Cartel Party Thesis: A Restatement." *Perspective on Politics* 7(4): 753–766.

Kauba, Tõnu. 2001. "Tee rahva soovidest poliitikute tegudeni." *Postimees*, October 12.

Keck, Margaret. 1992. *The Workers' Party and Democratization in Brazil.* New Haven: Yale University Press.

Kedar, Orit. 2005. "When Moderate Voters Prefer Extreme Parties: Policy Balancing in Parliamentary Elections." *American Political Science Review* 99(2): 185–199.

Keefer, Philip and Stuti Khemani. 2009. "When Do Legislators Pass on Pork?: The Role of Political Parties in Determining Legislator Effort." *American Political Science Review* 103(1): 99–112.

Keesing's World News Archive. http://www.keesings.com/home.

Kenig, Ofer. 2009. "Democratization of Party Leadership Selection: Do Wider Selectorates Produce More Competitive Contests?" *Electoral Studies* 28(2): 240–247.

Kenyeres, Zoltán. 2001. "Hatalomra készül a MIÉP." *Hetek* 5(36), September 8. http://www.hetek.hu/belfold/200109/hatalomra_keszul_a_miep.

Kéri, László. 1995. "A többpártrendszer – a második választás után." In *Parlamenti választások, 1994*, eds. Antal Bőhm and György Szoboslai. Budapest: MTA PTI, Budapest. Pp. 70–84.

King, Gary, James Honaker, Anne Joseph, and Kenneth Scheve. 2001. "Analyzing Incomplete Political Science Data: An Alternative Algorithm for Multiple Imputation." *American Political Science Review* 95(1): 49–69.

Kirkpatrick, Jeane J. 1976. *The New Presidential Elite*. New York: Sage.

Kisgyőri, Roland. 2007. "Akik nem adták fel – kis pártok küzdelme a túlélésért." In *Magyarország politikai évkönyve 2006-ról*, eds. Péter Sándor and László Vass. Budapest: Demokrácia Kutatások Magyar Központja Alapítvány. CD-Rom.

Kiss, Csilla. 2002. "From Liberalism to Conservatism: The Federation of Young Democrats in Post-Communist Hungary." *East European Politics and Societies* 16: 739–763.

Kitschelt, Herbert. 1989. "The Internal Politics of Parties: The Law of Curvilinear Disparity Revisited." *Political Studies* 37: 400–421.

Kitschelt, Herbert. 1994. *The Transformation of European Social Democracy*. Cambridge: Cambridge University Press.

Kitschelt, Herbert. 2000. "Linkages Between Citizens and Politicians in Democratic Politics." *Comparative Political Studies* 33(6/7): 845–879.

Kitschelt, Herbert, Zdenka Mansfeldova, Radoslaw Markowski, and Gabor Toka. 1999. *Post-Communist Party Systems: Competition, Representation, and Inter-Party Cooperation*. Cambridge: Cambridge University Press.

Kitschelt, Herbert and Anthony J. McGann. 1995. *The Radical Right in Western Europe: A Comparative Analysis*. Ann Arbor: University of Michigan Press.

Klima, Michal. 1998. "Consolidation and Stabilization of the Party System in the Czech Republic." *Political Studies* 46(3): 492–510.

Klingemann, Hans-Dieter, Andrea Volkens, Judith Bara, Ian Budge, and Michael McDonald. 2006. *Mapping Policy Preferences II: Estimates for Parties, Electors, and Governments in Eastern Europe, the European Union and the OECD, 1990–2003*. Oxford: Oxford University Press.

Koch, Tuuli. 2006. "Res Publica Riigikogu read hõrenevad veelgi." *Postimees*, February 21.

Koch, Tuuli. 2007. "Kopsaka kaasavaraga pruut – Rahvaliit." *Postimees*, November 30.

Koch, Tuuli. 2008. "Meelis Atonen: Reformierakond pole vahel populismist kaugel." *Postimees*, January, 26.

Koni, Laur. 2000. "Koonderakonda ähvaradab likvideerimine." *EPL*, August 25.

Kons, Tõnis. 1998. "Koonderakond krambis." *EPL*, September 27.

Kopeček, Lubomír. 2005. "Comparison of Left Parties in Central Europe: Some Causes of Different Successfulness." In *Trajectories of the Left, Social Democratic and (Ex)Communist Parties in Contemporary Europe: Between Past and Future*, ed. Lubomír Kopecek. Brno: CDK a ISPO. Pp. 109–117.

Kopeček, Lubomír and Pavel Pšeja. 2008. "Czech Social Democracy and Its 'Cohabitation' with the Communist Party: The Story of a Neglected Affair." *Communist and Post-Communist Studies* 41(3): 317–338.

Kopecky, Petr. 1995. "Developing Party Organizations in East-Central Europe." *Party Politics* 1(4): 515–534.

Kopecky, Petr. 2000. "The Limits of Whips and Watchdogs: Parliamentary Parties in the Czech Republic." In *Parliamentary Party Groups in European Democracies*, eds. Knut Heidar and Ruud Koole. London: Routledge. Pp. 177–194.

Kopecky, Petr. 2006. "Political Parties and the State in Post-Communist Europe: The Nature of Symbiosis." *Journal of Communist Studies and Transition Politics* 22(3): 251–273.

Kopecky, Petr. 2007. *Political Parties and the State in Post-Communist Europe*. London: Routledge.

Kopecky, Petr. 2008. "Political Parties and the State in Post-Communist Europe: The Nature of Symbiosis." In *Political Parties and the State In Post-communist Europe*, ed. Petr Kopecky. London: Routledge. Pp. 1–22.

Körösényi, András. 2006. "Gyurcsány-vezér. A magyar politika 'prezidencialódása.'" In *Magyarország politikai évkönyve 2005-ről*, eds. Péter Sándor and László Vass. Budapest: Demokrácia Kutatások Magyar Központja Alapítvány. CD-Rom.

Kostelecky, Tomas. 2002. *Political Parties after Communism*. Baltimore: Johns Hopkins University Press.

Kowalczyk, Krzysztof. 2004. "Prawo i Sprawiedliwość." In *Polskie partie i ugrupowania parlamentarne*, eds. Jerzy Sielski and Krzysztof Kowalczyk. Toruń: Adam Marshall.

Krysiak, Piotr. 2007. "Sprzątanie po Kwaśniewskim." *Wprost*, November 3.

Kubiak, Hieronim. 2007. "Poland's Democratic Left Alliance: Beyond Postcommunist Success." In *When Parties Prosper: The Uses of Electoral Success*, eds. Kay Lawson and Peter H. Merkl. London: Lynne Rienner. Pp. 61–87.

Kubo, Märt. 1997. "Erakonnad ei kao kuhugi." *Postimees*, June 9.

Kuenzi, Michelle and Gina Lambright. 2001. "Party System Institutionalization in 30 African Countries." *Party Politics* 1(3): 21–44.

Kuenzi, Michelle and Gina Lambright. 2005. "Party Systems and Democratic Consolidation in Africa's Electoral Regimes." *Party Politics* 4(11): 423–446.

Kuimet, Peeter. 2007. "Lahkuv Villu Reiljan: 'Jäime ellu, kuigi meid taheti hävitada!'" *Postimees*, March 6.

Kunicova, Jana and Thomas Frederick Remington. 2008. "Mandates, Parties, and Dissent: Effect of Electoral Rules on Parliamentary Party Cohesion in the Russian State Duma, 1994–2003." *Party Politics* 14(5): 555–574.

Kurski, Jaroslaw, Agata Nowakowska, and Dominika Wielowieyska. 1993. "Poland's Major Political Parties: An Overview." *Polish News Bulletin*, June 11.

Laar, Mart. 2005. "Mart Laar: Peaminister 21.10.1992–08.11.1994; 25.03.1999–08.01.2002." Public lecture delivered at Nord University, Tallinn, Estonia, April 27.

Lánczi, András. 2002. "Milyen a Fidesz 2001 év végén?" In *Magyarország politikai évkönyve 2001-ről*, eds. Péter Sándor and László Vass. Budapest: Demokrácia Kutatások Magyar Központja Alapítvány. CD-Rom.

Lánczi, Tamás. 2005. "Why Fidesz Lost: A Successful Government and Unsuccessful Party." In *Why We Lost*, eds. Peter Učeň and Jan Erik Surochak. Bratislava: International Republican Institute. Pp. 31–50.

Larsen, Ross. 1995. "Republican Party Splits Apart." *Prague Post*, August 16.

Lauristin, Marju. 2010. *Punane ja sinine*. Tallinn: Eesti Ajalehed.

Laver, Michael. 1998. "Models of government formation." *Annual Review of Political Science* 1: 1–25.

Laver, Michael and Norman Schofield. 1998. *Multiparty Government*. Ann Arbor: University of Michigan Press.

Laver, Michael and Kenneth A. Shepsle. 1990. "Government Coalitions and Intraparty Politics." *British Journal of Political Science* 20(4): 489–507.

Lawson, Kay, Andrea Römmele, and Georgi Karasimeonov. 1999. *Cleavages, Parties, and Voters*. Westport: Praeger.

LeBas, Adrianne. 2011. *From Protest to Parties: Party-Building and Democratization in Africa*. Oxford: Oxford University Press.

LeDuc, Lawrence. 2001. "Democratizing Party Leadership Selection." *Party Politics* 7(3): 323–341.

Lengyel, László. 2004. "Kétezer-három." In *Magyarország politikai évkönyve 2003-ról*, eds. Péter Sándor and László Vass. Budapest: Demokrácia Kutatások Magyar Központja Alapítvány. CD-Rom.

Lengyel, László. 2009. "Nehéz döntések előtt a Fidesz." *HVG*, September 1. http://hvg. hu/velemeny/20090831_fidesz_orban_hatalom.

Lenz, R.T. 1980. "Environment, Strategy, Organization Structure and Performance: Patterns in One Industry." *Strategic Management Journal* 1(3): 209–226.

Levitsky, Steven. 2003. *Transforming Labor-Based Parties in Latin America*. Cambridge: Cambridge University Press.

Levitsky, Steven and Maxwell A. Cameron. 2003. Democracy without Parties?: Political Parties and Regime Change in Fujimori's Peru. *Latin American Politics and Society* 45(3): 1–33.

Lewis, Jeffrey B. and Gary King. 1999. "No Evidence on Directional versus Proximity Voting." *Political Analysis* 8(1): 21–33.

Lewis, Paul G. 1994. "Political Institutionalisation and Party Development in Post-Communist Poland." *Europe-Asia Studies* 46(5): 779–799.

Lewis, Paul G. 1996. *Party Structure and Organization in East-Central Europe*. Aldershot: Edward Elgar.

Lewis, Paul G. 2000. *Political Parties in Post-Communist Eastern Europe*. London: Routledge.

Lewis, Paul G. 2001. "Introduction: Democratization and Political Change in Post-Communist Eastern Europe." In *Party Development and Democratic Change in Post-Communist Europe*, ed. Paul G. Lewis. London: Frank Cass. Pp. 1–15.

Lewis, Paul G., Bill Lomax, and Gordon Wightman. 1994. "The Emergence of Multi-Party Systems in East-Central Europe: A Comparative Analysis." In *Democratization in Eastern Europe*, eds. Geoffrey Pridham and Tatu Vanhanen. London: Routledge. Pp. 151–190.

Lieberman, Evan S. 2005. "Nested Analysis as a Mixed-Method Strategy for Comparative Research." *American Political Science Review* 99(1): 435–452.

Linek, Lukáš and Zsolt Enyedi. 2008. "Searching for the Right Organization: Ideology and Party Structure in East-Central Europe." *Party Politics* 14(4): 455–477.

Linek, Lukáš and Štěpán Pecháček. 2007. "Low Membership in Czech Political Parties: Party Strategy or Structural Determinants?" *Journal of Communist Studies and Transition Politics* 23(2): 259–275.

Lipset, Seymour Martin. 1994. "The Social Requisites of Democracy Revisited." *American Sociological Review* 59(1): 1–22.

Lipset, Seymour Martin and Stein Rokkan. 1967. *Party Systems and Voter Alignments.* Toronto: Free Press.

Lister, Richard. 2008. "Why Barack Obama Won." *BBC News*, November, 5.

Löffler, Tibor. 2006. "'Nem vagyok Fidesz-ellenes.'" In *Magyarország politikai évkönyve 2005-ről*, eds. Péter Sándor and László Vass. Budapest: Demokrácia Kutatások Magyar Központja Alapítvány. CD-Rom.

Lőke, András. 2005. "'A politikai osztály nem maffiaként működik.' Interjú Kis Jánossal." June 1, *HVG*. http://hvg.hu/hvgfriss/2005.22/200522HVGFriss113.

Lomax, Bill. 1999. "The 1998 Elections in Hungary: Third Time Lucky for the Young Democrats." *Journal of Communist Studies and Transition Politics* 15(2): 111–125.

Lowenberg, Gerhard and Samuel C. Patterson. 1979. *Comparing Legislatures.* Boston: Little Brown.

Luebbert, Gregory. 1986. *Comparative Democracy: Policymaking and Governing Coalitions in Europe and Israel.* New York: Columbia University Press.

Lukas, Tõnis. 1995. "Erakonnad on elu loomulik osa." *Postimees*, December 12.

Luther, Kurt Richard and Ferdinand Müller-Rommel. 2002. *Political Parties in the New Europe: Political and Analytical Challenges.* Oxford: Oxford University Press.

Lyne, Mona M. 2008. "Proffering Pork: How Party Leaders Build Party Reputations in Brazil." *American Journal of Political Science* 52(2): 290–303.

Mac, Jerzy Slawomir. 1996. "Solidarity Election Action: What Odds?" *Polish News Bulletin*, August 8.

Machos, Csilla. 1999. "A magyar pártok alapszabályai és szervezeti típusai." *Politikatudományi Szemle* 1: 23–45.

Machos, Csilla. 2000. *A Magyar Parlamenti Pártok Szervezeti Felépítése (1990–1999).* Budapest: Rejtjel Kiadó.

Made, Vahur. 1996. "Keskerakond muutuste ees." *Postimees*, January 11.

Made, Vahur. 1997. "Ekspeaminister Vähi enampakkumisel." *Postimees*, August 3.

Mahr, Alison and John Nagle. 1995. "Resurrection of the Successor Parties and Democratization in East-Central Europe." *Communist and Post-Communist Studies* 28(4): 393–409.

Mainville, Michael. 2001. "ODA Leader Sees Humor in Politics." *Prague Post*, July 11.

Mainwaring, Scott. 1998. "Party Systems in the Third Wave." *Journal of Democracy* 9(3): 67–81.

Mainwaring, Scott. 1999. *Rethinking Party Systems in the Third Wave of Democratization: The Case of Brazil.* Stanford: Stanford University Press.

Mainwaring, Scott and Timothy R. Scully. 1995. *Building Democratic Institutions: Party Systems in Latin America.* Stanford: Stanford University Press.

Mair, Peter. 1997. *Party System Change.* Oxford: Oxford University Press.

Majcherek, Janusz A. 2000. "Democratic Left Alliance: An Easy Victory May Spoil the Victors." *Rzeczpospolita*, April 3.

Markus, György G. 1999. "Cleavages and Parties in Hungary after 1989." In *Cleavages, Parties, and Voters*, eds. Kay Lawson, Andrea Römmele, and Georgi Karasimeonov. Westport: Praeger. Pp. 141–158.

Marsh, Michael. 1987. "Electoral Evaluations of Candidates in Irish General Elections 1948–1982." *Irish Political Studies* 2(1): 65–76.

Marvick, Dwaine. 1986. "Stability and Change in the Views of Los Angeles Party Activists, 1968–1980." In *Political Parties in Local Areas*, ed. William Crotty. Knoxville: University of Tennessee Press. Pp. 121–155.

Matraszek, Marek. 2002. "Practically Bedfellows." *Warsaw Business Journal*, March 4.

Matraszek, Marek. 2005. "Victories, Defeats, Reconfigurations and Reinventions of the Polish Right." In *Why We Lost*, eds. Peter Učeň and Jan Erik Surotchak. Bratislava: International Republican Institute. Pp. 87–100.

Mattheus, Ülo. 2004a. "Keskerakonna juhatus hakkab arutama mässajate küsimust." *Postimees*, March 26.

Mattheus, Ülo. 2004b. "Tõnisson: Keskerakonda on saabunud vaikiv ajastu." *Postimees*, April 14.

Mattson, Toomas and Toomas Sildam. 2004. "'Mässulised' nõuavad Keskerakonna demokratiseerimist." *Postimees*, April 3.

Matušková, Anna. 2007. "Poland: The Victory of 'Social Oriented' over 'Liberal Oriented' Poland." In *Visegrad Votes*, eds. Pavel Šaradin and Eva Bradová. Olomouc: Palacký University. Pp. 59–88.

May, John D. 1973. "Opinion Structure of Political Parties: The Special Law of Curvilinear Disparity." *Political Studies* 21(2): 135–151.

Mayhew, David. 1974. *Congress: The Electoral Connection*. New Haven, CT: Yale University Press.

Mazur, Boguslaw. 2002. "Heil Lepper!" *Wprost*, May 23.

McGuire, James W. 1997. *Peronism without Peron: Unions, Parties, and Democracy in Argentina*. Stanford: Stanford University Press.

McMenamin, Iain and Anna Gwiazda. 2011. "Three Roads to Institutionalisation: Vote-, Office- and Policy-Seeking Explanations of Party Switching in Poland." *European Journal of Political Research* DOI: 10.1111/j.1475-6765.2010.01985.x.

Meleshevich, Andrey A. 2007. *Party Systems in Post-Soviet Countries: A Comparative Study of Political Institutionalization in the Baltic States, Russia, and Ukraine*. New York: Palgrave Macmillan.

Meseguer, Covadonga. 2005. "Policy Learning, Policy Diffusion, and the Making of a New Order." *Annals of the American Academy of Political and Social Science* 598(1): 67–82.

Michels, Robert. 1966. *Political Parties*. New York: Free Press.

Mickiewicz, Ellen and Andrei Richter. 1996. "Television, Campaigning, and Elections in the Soviet Union and Post-Soviet Russia." In *Politics, Media, and Modern Democracy*, eds. David L. Swanson and Paolo Mancini. Westport: Praeger. Pp. 107–128.

Mikkel, Evald. 1999. "1999. aasta Riigikogu valimised ja kandidaadid." In *Riigikogu valimised 1999*, ed. Rein Toomla. Tartu: Tartu University Press. Pp. 84–133.

Millard, Frances. 2003. "Elections in Poland 2001: Electoral Manipulation and Party Upheaval." *Communist and Post-Communist Studies* 36: 69–86.

Millard, Frances. 2007. "The 2005 Parliamentary and Presidential Elections in Poland." *Electoral Studies* 26(1): 196–231.

Millard, Frances. 2009. "Poland: Parties without a Party System, 1991–2008." *Politics & Polity* 37(4): 781–798.

Mohai, V. Lajos. 2006. "Gyurcsány de facto átvette az MSZP-t." *HVG*, October 21. http://hvg.hu/gyurcsany/20061021gyurcsi.

Montero, Jose Ramon and Richard Gunther. 2002. "Introduction: Reviewing and Reassessing Parties." In *Political Parties: Old Concepts and New Challenges*, eds. Richard Gunther, Jose Ramon Montero, and Juan Linz. Oxford: Oxford University Press. Pp. 1–38.

Montgomery, Kathleen A. 1996. "Crafting Representation in a New Democracy: The Case of Hungary." PhD dissertation, Emory University.

Montgomery, Kathleen A. 1999. "Electoral Effects on Party Behavior and Development: Evidence from the Hungarian National Assembly." *Party Politics* 5(4): 507–523.

Morgenstern, Scott. 2004. *Patterns of Legislative Politics*. Cambridge: Cambridge University Press.

Morgenstern, Scott and Stephen M. Swindle. 2005. "Are Politics Local?: An Analysis of Voting Patterns in 23 Democracies." *Comparative Political Studies* 38(2): 143–170.

Morlang, Diana. 2003. "Hungary: Socialists Building Capitalism." In *The Left Transformed in Post-Communist Societies*, eds. Jane Leftwich Curry and Joan Barth Urban. New York: Rowman & Littlefield. Pp. 61–99.

Moser, Robert G. 2001. *Unexpected Outcomes: Electoral Systems, Political Parties, and Representation in Russia*. Pittsburgh: Pittsburgh University Press.

Mõttus, Aaro (ed.). 2004. *Riigikogu VII, VIII, ja IX koosseis. Statistikat ja kommentaare*. Tallinn: Riigikogu Kantselei.

Mozaffar Shaheen and Hames R. Scarritt. 2005. "The Puzzle of African Party Systems." *Party Politics* 11(4): 399–421.

Mrozinski, Michel. 2004. "Poland's Ruling Left Faced with Unprecedented Crisis." *Agence France Presse*, February 13.

MTI. 1992. "Surjan to Remain as CDPP President." August 30.

MTI. 1994a. "Democratic Forum Press Conference on Elections." May 13.

MTI. 1994b. "Lajos Fur Is Re-elected As HDF Chairman." September 10.

MTI. 1995. "Democratic Forum Ends 9th National Conference." May 28.

MTI. 1996. "Divided HDF Preparing for National Meeting." February 28.

MTI. 2003. "Fidesz: Orbán vállalja az elnökjelöltséget." *HVG*, February 28. http://hvg.hu/nonbase/000000000483E9D.

Mudde, Cas. 2007. *Populist Radical Right Parties in Europe*. Cambridge: Cambridge University Press.

Nagle, John and Alison Mahr. 1999. *Democracy and Democratization: Post-Communist Europe in Comparative Perspective*. London: Sage.

Nagyné, G. and Ágnes Maczó. 1995. "A Független Kisgazdapárt kampánya." In *Magyarország politikai évkönyve 1994-ről*, eds. Péter Sándor and László Vass. Budapest: Demokrácia Kutatások Magyar Központja Alapítvány. CD-Rom.

Nalewajko, Ewa and Włodzimierz Wesołowski. 2007. "Five Terms of the Polish Parliament, 1989–2005." *Journal of Legislative Studies* 13(1): 59–82.

Nannestad, Peter and Martin Paldam. 2002. "The Cost of Ruling: A Foundation Stone for Two Theories." In *Economic Voting*, eds. Hans Dorussen and Michell Taylor. London: Routledge. Pp. 17–44.

Navracsics, Tibor. 2005. "Egy európai néppárt születése. A Fidesz – Magyar Polgári Szövetség 2004-ben." In *Magyarország politikai évkönyve 2004-ről*, eds. Péter Sándor and László Vass. Budapest: Demokrácia Kutatások Magyar Központja Alapítvány. CD-Rom.

Népszava online. 2004. "Szétválasztaná az MSZP a párt- és állami tisztségeket." July 15. http://www.nepszava.hu/articles/article.php?id=18215.

Nicholson, Norman K. 1972. "The Factional Model and the Study of Politics." *Comparative Political Studies* 5(1): 50–61.

Nooruddin, Irfan and Pradeep Chhibber. 2008. "Unstable Politics: Fiscal Space and Electoral Volatility in the Indian States." *Comparative Political Studies* 41(8): 1069–1081.

Norris, Pippa and Joni Lovenduski. 1995. *Political Recruitment: Gender, Race, and Class in the British Parliament*. Cambridge: Cambridge University Press.

Odres, Elo. 2004. "Aasta tegija: Oodatud täht Anrus Ansip." *Kroonika*, December 30.

Olczyk, Eliza. 2003a. "The SLD Before a Face Lifting." *World News Connection*, June 25.

Olczyk, Eliza. 2003b. "A Titular Social Democracy." *World News Connection*, October 2.

Olczyk, Eliza. 2003c. "Labor of Union Star." *World News Connection*, October 14.

Olczyk, Eliza. 2008. "Left Wing at Crossroads (for Last Time?)" *Rzeczpospolita*, January 23.

Olson, David M. 1998. "Party Formation and Party System Consolidation in the New Democracies of Central Europe." *Political Studies* 46: 432–464.

Org, Rein. 1996. "Miks sotsiaaldemokraadid ei soovi mõõukateks hakata?" *Postimees*, January 23.

Osser, Bernard. 2001. "Poland's Leszek Miller, a Communist Apparatchik Turned Social Democrat." *Agency Free Press*, September 21.

Ost, D. 1995. "Labor, Class and Democracy: Shaping Political Antagonisms in Post-Communist Society." In *Markets, States, and Democracy: The Political Economy of Post-Communist Transformation*, ed. B. Crawford. Boulder: Westview Press. Pp. 177–203.

Otepalu, Olavi. 2008. "Poliitilist edukust mõjutavad tegurid Riigikogu kandidaatide selekteerimise protsessis." MA thesis, University of Tartu.

Ottas, Aita. 1996. "Koonderakond peab Tartu soma nimekirjaks 'Tartu 2000.'" *Postimees*, August 15.

Owens, John E. 2003. "Explaining Party Cohesion and Discipline in Democratic Legislatures: Purposiveness and Contests." *Journal of Legislative Studies* 9(4): 12–40.

Pacek, Alexander C. 1994. "Macroeconomic Conditions and Electoral Politics in East Central Europe." *American Journal of Political Science* 38(3): 723–744.

Packer, Tomos. 2003. "Polish Radical Party Leader Asserts Authority in Party Purge." *World Markets Analysis*, July 24.

Paet, Urmas. 1997. "Mart Laar hea meelega Isamaliitu ei juhiks." *Postimees*, November 20.

Paet, Urmas. 1998a. "Maarahava Erakond ootab ühinemist." *Postimees*, February 8.

Paet, Urmas. 1998b. "Ants Leemets usub Mart Siimanni jätkamisse." *Postimees*, July 29.

Paet, Urmas. 1998c. "Andres Tarandile terendub valimisvõit." *Postimees*, September 16.

Paet, Urmas. 1998d. "Noormõõdukad peavad erakonna sisevõitlust." *Postimees*, October 14.

Paet, Urmas. 1999. "Reformierakonnas võitsid noorendajad." *Postimees*, May 18.

Palmquist, Bradley. 1999. "Analysis of Proportions Data." Paper presented at the Annual Meeting of the Political Methodology Society, College Station, TX, July 15–19.

Panebianco, Angelo. 1988. *Political Parties: Organization and Power*. Cambridge: Cambridge University Press.

PAP News Wire. 1991. "PSL Leader Wants to Cleanse Party of Pro-Communists." March 23.

PAP News Wire. 1992. "Waldemar Pawlak Says Peasant Party is Growing Strong." November 17.

PAP News Wire. 1993a. "PSL Wants to Be Rooted in Society before Entering Political Game." April 18.

PAP News Wire. 1993b. "Tusk Says Liberal Democratic Congress – Party of the Future." September 29.

PAP News Wire. 1996. "Union of Labour to Defend Its Identity." February 25.

PAP News Wire. 1998. "Social Alliance Wants Map of Election Districts Earlier." August 12.

PAP News Wire. 2001. "Leader of Troubled Centre Party Urges Defectors to Return." January 23.

PAP News Wire. 2006a. "PO Leader: I Will Run for Re-Election in May." March 1.

PAP News Wire. 2006b. "Tusk: Civic Platform Strategy Is Good." April 21.

PAP News Wire. 2009. "PO launches rural campaign." November 16.

Papke, Leslie E. and Jeffrey Wooldridge. 1996. "Econometric Methods for Fractional Response Variables with an Application to 401(k) Plan Participation Rates." *Journal of Applied Econometrics* 11(6): 619–632.

Papp, László Tamás. 2009. "Belpolitikai szezonzárás Gyurcsány után, Orbán előtt." *HVG*. July 2. hvg.hu/velemeny/20090702_papp_laszlo_tamas_gyurcsany_orban.

Parve, Ralf R. 2002. "Nädal Toompeal." *Kesknädal*, October 30.

Patora, Tomasz and Marcin Stelmasiak. 2004. "Poseł Pęczak za ciemnymi szybami, Nawigacja, telewizorek i zasłony." *Gazeta Wyborcza*, November 14.

Pattie, C. J. and R. J. Johnston. 2003. "Local Battles in a National Landslide: Constituency Campaign at the 2001 British General Election." *Political Geography* 22(4): 381–414.

Pattie, Charles, Paul Whiteley, Ron Johnston, and Patrick Seyd. 1994. "Measuring Local Campaign Effects: Labour Party Constituency Campaigning at the 1987 General Election." *Political Studies* 42(3): 469–479.

Pečinka, Bohumil. 2003. "Co se dělo na kongresu ODS?" *Revue Politika* 1. http://www.revuepolitika.cz/2003/1.

Pehe, Jiri. 1990. "Changes in the Communist Party." *Radio Free Europe/Radio Liberty Report on Eastern Europe*, November 30.

Perkins, Doug. 1996. "Structure and Choice: The Role of Organizations, Patronage and the Media in Party Formation." *Party Politics* 2(3): 355–375.

Perlez, Jane. 1993. "Polish Cabinet Falls over Tight Budget." *New York Times*, May 29.

Perlez, Jane. 1997. "Man in the News: Marian Krzaklewski, Architect of Solidarity's Victory." *New York Times*, September 23.

Peters, B. Guy. 1998. *Comparative Politics: Theory and Method*. New York: New York University Press.

Pfeffer, Jeffrey. 1994. *Managing with Power: Politics and Influence in Organizations.* Cambridge: Harvard Business School Press.

Pfeffer, Jeffrey. 1997. *New Directions for Organization Theory.* Oxford: Oxford University Press.

Pfeffer, Jeffrey and Gerald R. Salancik. 2003. *The External Control of Organizations: A Resource Dependence Perspective.* Palo Alto: Stanford University Press.

Pitkin, James. 2001. "New US Leader Looks Forward." *Prague Post*, July 18.

PM Online. 2003. "Keskerakonna uus peasekretär on Kadri Must." *Postimees*, December 10.

PM Online. 2004a. "Kreitzbergi ja Tõnissoni ähvardab väljaheitmine." March 27.

PM Online. 2004b. "Parts arvustas Res Publica tipp-poliitikute eemaldumist erakonnast." *Postimees*, April 10.

PM Online. 2004c. "Sinikraed hääletasid sotsid võidule." June 16.

Pogonyi, Lajos. 2002. "Socialist Leader on Party's Public Messages, Media Control." *Nepszabadsag*, May 10.

Poguntke, Thomas. 2002. "Party Organizational Linkage: Parties without Firm Social Roots?" In *Political Parties in the New Europe*, eds. Kurt Richard Luther and Ferdinand Müller-Rommel. Oxford: Oxford University Press. Pp. 43–62.

Polish News Bulletin. 1991a. "Impasse in PSL Continues." April 4.

Polish News Bulletin. 1991b. "Roman Bartoszcze in Trouble." June 3.

Polish News Bulletin. 1991c. "Krzaklewski Elected Solidarity Chairman." February 25.

Polish News Bulletin. 1992a. "Prime Minister Waldemar Pawlak in the Eyes of other Politicians." June 9.

Polish News Bulletin. 1992b. "Parties Count on Their Members." July 16.

Polish News Bulletin. 1993a. "PC Congress in Sosnowiec." April 26.

Polish News Bulletin. 1993b. "Ryszard Bugaj: The Balcerowicz of the Left." October 8.

Polish News Bulletin. 1993c. "Democratic Union: Out of Sync." October 25.

Polish News Bulletin. 1995a. "Who is Jozef?" February 9.

Polish News Bulletin. 1995b. "Freedom Union Elects Chairman." April 3.

Polish News Bulletin. 1995c. "Interview with Freedom Union Leader Leszek Balcerowicz." April 20.

Polish News Bulletin. 1995d. "Olechowski to Set Up New Party." July 21.

Polish News Bulletin. 1995e. "An Effective Alternative: Interview with UW Chairman Leszek Balcerowicz." December 14.

Polish News Bulletin. 1996a. "What's Going On in the SLD?" March 15.

Polish News Bulletin. 1996b. "Middle Distance Strategy: Interview with Leszek Balcerowicz, Chairman of Freedom Union (UW)." July 18.

Polish News Bulletin. 1997a. "UW National Council Meets." January 13.

Polish News Bulletin. 1997b. "Ziolkowska Blames Bugaj for UP Failure." October 7.

Polish News Bulletin. 1997c. "The Losers: UP, PSL, ROP." October 9.

Polish News Bulletin. 1997d. "Miller Elected SdRP Chairman." December 8.

Polish News Bulletin. 1998. "SLD Headed Towards Political Party." October 19.

Polish News Bulletin. 2000a. "Krzaklewski's Stalling on Presidency Question Erodes His Position as AWS Party Leader." April 10.

Polish News Bulletin. 2000b. "Will Plazynski Step into Krzaklewski's Shoes?" October 19.

Polish News Bulletin. 2000c. "Plazynski Quits RS AWS." December 21.

Polish News Bulletin. 2001a. "Miller versus Kwasniewski – SLD's Homogeneity at Stake?" July 2.

Polish News Bulletin. 2001b. "Polish Voters Divided between SLD Supporters and the Confused Rest." August 23.

Polish News Bulletin. 2001c. "Lepper's Team." October 25.

Polish News Bulletin. 2001d. "Waiting on the Platform." November 8.

Polish News Bulletin. 2001e. "SLD Council Meeting Reveals Inward Frictions." December 10.

Polish News Bulletin. 2002a. "Kalinowski Fights for Political Life as Mutineers Gather." March 7.

Polish News Bulletin. 2002b. "Centre-Right Lays Out Tough Party Structures." May 9.

Polish News Bulletin. 2002c. "The Andrzej Lepper Show Even Bigger than the World Cup." June 13.

Polish News Bulletin. 2002d. "PiS to Become a Larger Party." December 31.

Polish News Bulletin. 2003a. "Dictatorship of Andrzej Lepper More Deputies Leave Samoobrona." July 24.

Polish News Bulletin. 2003b. "Populist Leader Melts His Own Grouping." August 11.

Polish News Bulletin. 2004a. "Sinking Ship The SLD's Fortunes Seem to Have Reached Rock-Bottom? But Is the Party Capable of Bouncing Back?" February 26.

Polish News Bulletin. 2004b. "Going to War PO Throws Gauntlet at Self-Defence in Effort to Become a Mass Party." March 11.

Polish News Bulletin. 2004c. "Polish Left Lands in the Kindergarten of Democracy." May 20.

Polish News Bulletin. 2004d. "Ruthless, Pragmatic, Effective for Giertych and the LPR, the Only Way Seems to Be Up." October 21.

Polish News Bulletin. 2007a. "Former President's Return to Politics to Send Tremors through Left Wing of Domestic Political Scene." April 5.

Polish News Bulletin. 2007b. "Leszek Miller's Transfer or What Politics Has in Common with Football." September 27.

Polish News Bulletin. 2009. "PO Light Years Ahead of Pack in Strategic Thinking." March 26.

Pomper, Gerard M. 1990. "Party Organization and Electoral Success." *Polity* 23(2): 187–206.

Porila, Mart. 1999. "Maaparteid loovad endale laia põhja." *Maaleht*, July 1.

Postimees. 2000. "Aeg Hamletit mängida." March 21.

Postimees. 2001a. "Värsket verd poliitikasse." July 11.

Postimees. 2001b. "Res Publica lubab luau uut tüüpi erakonna." August 31.

Postimees. 2001c. "Res Publica esimeheks kandideerib Rein Taagepera." November 28.

Postimees. 2002a. "Reformierakonnal on 2500 liiget." May 22.

Postimees. 2002b. "Res Publica reha." November 23.

Postimees. 2003. "Reformierakonna peasekretär vahetub." April 14.

Postimees. 2004. "Juhtkiri: Suure juhi vari." March 25.

Postimees. 2006a. "Reformierakond sihib Riigikogu valimistel 27 kohta." April 29.

Postimees. 2006b. "Keskerakond saab täna 15-aastaseks." October 12.

Postimees. 2009a. "Keskerakond läheb bussiga maale valimisreklaami tegema." May 6.

Postimees. 2009b. "Enn Soosaar: Savisaar suudab, mida teised ei suuda, ei oska, ei jaksa." October 20.

Pridham, Geoffrey. 1995. "Political Parties and Their Strategies in the Transition from Authoritarian Rule: The Comparative Perspective." In *Party Formation in East–Central Europe: Post-Communist Politics in Czechoslovakia, Hungary, Poland, and Bulgaria*, ed. Gordon Wightman. Aldershot: Edward Elgar. Pp. 1–28.

Primo, David M. and James M. Snyder. 2010. "Party Strength, the Personal Vote, and Government Spending." *American Journal of Political Science* 54(2): 354–370.

Przweorski, Adam and Henry Teune. 1979. *The Logic of Comparative Social Inquiry*. New York: John Wiley & Sons.

Putnam, Robert D. 1976. *The Comparative Study of Political Elites*. Englewood Cliffs, NJ: Prentice-Hall.

Raciborski, Jacek. 1999. "How the Voters Respond: Poland." In *Cleavages, Parties, and Voters*, eds. Kay Lawson, Andrea Römmele, and Georgi Karasimeonov. Westport, CT: Praeger. Pp. 239–260.

Racz, Barnabas. 1993. "The Socialist-Left Opposition in Post-Communist Hungary." *Europe-Asia Studies* 45(4): 647–670.

Racz, Barnabas. 2000. "The Hungarian Socialists in Opposition: Stagnation or Renaissance." *Europe-Asia Studies* 52(2): 319–347.

Racz, Barnabas and Istvàn Kukorelli. 1995. "The "Second-Generation" Post-Communist Elections in Hungary in 1994." *Europe-Asia Studies* 47(2): 251–279.

Rand, Erik. 2009. "Arnold Rüütel: esimees on oluline, kuid organisatsiooni tegevus tähtsam." *EPL*, November 17.

Raudvere, Rein. 2008. "Rahvarinne viis vene tankide hirmu." *Maaleht*, April 17.

Raun, Mati. 2001. "Ema sünnitas isa." *Postimees*, December 17.

Raunio, Tapio. 2005. "Finland: One Hundred Years of Quietude." In *The Politics of Electoral Systems*, eds. Michael Gallagher and Paul Mitchell. Oxford: Oxford University Press. Pp. 473–489.

Reams, Margaret A. and Brooks H. Ray. 1993. "The Effects of Three Prompting Methods on Recycling Participation Rates: A Field Study." *Journal of Environmental Systems* 22(4): 371–379.

Reiljan, Villu. 2005. Interview with Erki Berens in KUKU radio program "Kukul külas." July 3, 2005.

Reinap, Aivar. 2006. "Online-intervjuu: küsimustele vastas Toomas Hendrik Ilves." *PM Online*, September 12.

Reinap, Aivar and Tuuli Koch. 2006. "Toompea raisakotkad Res Publica riismetel." *Postimees*, March 4.

Remmer, Karen. 2007. "The political economy of patronage: expenditure patterns in the Argentine provinces, 1983–2003." *Journal of Politics* 69(2): 363–377.

Rice, Stuart A. 1925. "The Behavior of Legislative Groups." *Political Science Quarterly* 40(1): 60–72.

Ripp, Zoltán. 2008. "Reformok és viták éve: az MSZP 2007-ben." In *Magyarország politikai évkönyve 2007-ről*, eds. Péter Sándor and László Vass. Budapest: Demokrácia Kutatások Magyar Központja Alapítvány. CD-Rom.

Roberts, Kenneth M. and Erik Wibbels. 1999. "Party Systems and Electoral Volatility in Latin America: A Test of Economic, Institutional, and Structural Explanations." *American Political Science Review* 93(3): 575–590.

Rogala, Jan. 1990. "On Central Alliance." *Polish News Bulletin*, August 2.

Rogers, William H. 1993. "Regression Standard Errors in Clustered Samples." *Stata Technical Bulletin* 13: 19–23.

Römmele, Andrea. 1999. "Cleavage Structures and Party Systems in East and Central Europe." In *Cleavages, Parties, and Voters*, eds. Kay Lawson, Andrea Römmele, and Georgi Karasimeonov. Westport, CT: Praeger. Pp. 3–18.

Rosas, Guillermo and Joy Langston. 2011. "Gubernatorial Effects on the Voting Behavior of National Legislators." *Journal of Politics* 73(2): 477–493.

Rosas, Guillermo and Yael Shomer. 2008. "Models of Nonresponse in Legislative Politics." *Legislative Studies Quarterly* 33(4): 573–601.

Rose, Richard. 1995. "Mobilizing Demobilized Voters in Post-Communist Societies." *Party Politics* 1(4): 549–563.

Rose, Richard, and William Mishler. 1998. "Negative and Positive Party Identification in Post-Communist Countries." *Electoral Studies* 17(2): 217–234.

Rose, Richard and Neil Munro. 2003. *Elections and Parties in New European Democracies*. Washington DC: CQ Press.

Rosenstone, Steven J. and John Mark Hansen. 1993. *Mobilization, Participation, and Democracy in America*. London: Longman.

Rozental, Väinu. 2008. "Tiit Vähi: Jõuline pragmaatik." *Äripäev*, September 12.

Ruusing, Helle (ed.). 2007. "Tulemuse määrab valimistevaheline töö." *Riigikogu Toimetised* 15. http://www.riigikogu.ee/rito/index.php?id=10856.

Rzeczpospolita. 2004. "Kulisy afery Orlenu." December 14.

Rzeczpospolita. 2005. "Aleksander łaskawy." December 2.

Saarlane. 2000. "Kallas tunnistas oma partei populaarsuse langust." May 9.

Saarts, Tõnis. 2004. "Mis suunas liigub Eesti ühiskond?" *Õpetajate leht*, June 4.

Sabbat-Swidlicka, Anna. 1990. "After the Peasants' Unity Congress: A New Political Constellation?" *RFE/RL Report on Eastern Europe*, May 25.

Saiz, Martin and Hans Geser. 1999. *Local Parties in Political and Organizational Perspective*. Boulder, CO: Westview Press.

Salancik, Gerald R. and Jeffrey Pfeffer. 1974. "The Bases and Use of Power in Organizational Decision Making: The Case of a University." *Administrative Science Quarterly* 19: 224–253.

Šaradín, Pavel. 2007. "The Influence of the Strong Bi-Polarization." In *Visegrad Votes: Parliamentary elections 2005–2006*, eds. Pavel Šaradín and Eva Bradová. Olomouc: Palacky University. Pp. 13–37.

Sartori, Giovanni. 1976. *Parties and Party Systems: A Framework for Analysis*. Cambridge: Cambridge University Press.

Savisaar, Edgar. 2002. "Eesti Keskerakonna valimiseelsetest positsioonidest." *Kesknädal*, August 28.

Saxonberg, Steven. 1999. "Václav Klaus: The Rise and Fall and Re-Emergence of a Charismatic Leader." *East European Politics & Societies* 13(2): 391–418.

Scarrow, Susan E. 1994. "The 'Paradox of Enrollment': Assessing the Costs and Benefits of Party Membership." *European Journal of Political Research* 25(1): 41–60.

Scarrow, Susan E. 1996. *Parties and Their Members: Organising for Victory in Britain and Germany*. Oxford: Oxford University Press.

Scarrow, Susan E. 1999. "Parties and the Expansion of Direct Democracy: Who Benefits?" *Party Politics* 5(3): 341–362.

Scarrow, Susan E. 2000. "Parties without Members? Party Organization in a Changing Electoral Environment." In *Parties without Partisans*, eds. Russell J. Dalton and Martin P. Wattenberg. Oxford: Oxford University Press.

Scarrow, Susan E., Paul Webb, and David M. Farrell. 2002. "From Social Integration to Electoral Contestation: The Changing Distribution of Power within Political Parties." In *Parties without Partisans*, eds. Russell J. Dalton and Martin P. Wattenberg. Oxford: Oxford University Press. Pp. 79–101.

Schlesinger, Joseph A. 1984. "On the Theory of Party Organization." *Journal of Politics* 46(2): 369–400.

Schofield, Norman and Gary Miller. 2003. "Activists and Partisan Realignment in the US." *American Political Science Review* 97(2): 245–260.

Schofield, Norman and Itai Sened. 2006. *Multiparty Democracy: Parties, Elections and Legislative Politics in Multiparty Systems*. Cambridge: Cambridge University Press.

Scott, Richard W. 2004. "Reflection on the Half-Century of Organizational Sociology." *Annual Review of Sociology* 30: 1–21.

Sebestyén, István. 2007. "Egy másik Fidesz." *Hetek* 11(14), April 6. http://www.hetek .hu/belfold/200704/egy_masik_fidesz.

Sebestyén, István and Ferenc Szlazsánszky. 2001. "Feldarabolt párt." *Hetek* 5(19), May 12. http://www.hetek.hu/belfold/200105/feldarabolt_part.

Seisselberg, Jörg. 1996. "Conditions of Success and Political Problems of a 'Media-Mediated Personality-Party': The Case of Forza Italia." *West European Politics* 19(4): 715–743.

Sepp, Evelyn. 2011. "Evelyn Sepp: KE valimisnimekirjast." Evelyn Sepa Sisering, Blog, January 17. http://sisering.blogspot.com/2011/01/evelyn-sepp-ke-valimisnimekirjast .html.

Seyd, Patrick and Paul Whiteley. 1992. *Labour's Grass Roots: The Politics of Party Membership*. Oxford: Oxford University Press.

Shabad, Goldie and Kazimierz M. Slomczynski. 2004. "The Emergence of Career Politicians in Post-Communist Democracies: Poland and the Czech Republic." *Legislative Studies Quarterly* 27(3): 333–359.

Shamir, Boas, Robert J. House, and Michale B. Arthur. 1993. "The Motivational Effects of Charismatic Leadership: A Self-Concept Based Theory." *Organization Science* 4(4): 577–594.

Shefter, Martin. 1994. *Political Parties and the State*. Princeton: Princeton University Press.

Shin, Michael. 2001. "The Politization of Place in Italy." *Political Geography* 20: 331–352.

Shippan, Charles R. and Craig Volden. 2008. The Mechanisms of Policy Diffusion." *American Journal of Political Science* 52(4): 840–857.

Shomer, Yael. 2009. "Candidate Selection Procedures, Seniority, and Vote-Seeking Behavior." *Comparative Political Studies* 42(7): 945–970.

Shugart, Matthew Søberg, Melody Ellis Valdini, and Kati Suominen. 2005. "Looking for Locals: Voter Information Demands and Personal Vote-Earning Attributes of Legislators under Proportional Representation." *American Journal of Political Science* 49(2): 437–449.

Sieberer, Ulrich. 2006. "Party Unity in Parliamentary Democracies: A Comparative Analysis." *Journal of Legislative Studies* 12(2): 150–178.

Siimann, Mart. 2005. "Mart Siimann: Peaminister 17.03.1997–25.03.1999." Public lecture delivered at Nord University, Tallinn, Estonia, May 24.

Sikk, Allan. 2005. "How Unstable? Volatility and the Genuinely New Parties in Eastern Europe." *European Journal of Political Research* 44: 391–412.

Sikk, Allan (ed.). 2007. *Riigikogu X koosseis. Statistikat ja ülevaateid.* Tallinn: Riigikogu Kantselei.

Sildam, Toomas. 2001. "Taal: poliitika pole kellegi monopol." *Postimees*, July 11.

Simson, Priit. 2002. "Keskerakond alustas valimiskampaaniat." *Postimees*, August 17.

Skjæveland, Asbjørn. 2001. "Party Cohesion in the Danish Parliament." *Journal of Legislative Studies* 7(1): 35–56.

Skórzyński, Jana. 2003. *System Rywina czyli druga strona III Rzeczpospolitej.* Warsaw: Świat Książki.

Smith, Ben and Jonathan Martin. 2008. "Why Obama Won." *Politico*, November 5.

Smith, Steven S. and Thomas F. Remington. 2001. *The Politics of Institutional Choice: The Formation of the Russian State Duma.* Princeton: Princeton University Press.

Smolar, Aleksander. 1998. "Poland's Emerging Party System." *Journal of Democracy* 9(2): 122–133.

Šmutov, Martin. 2006. "Sotsiaaldemokraadid alustasid märtsivalimiste kampaaniat." *Postimees*, September 26.

Sorauf, Frank J. and Scott A. Wilson. 1990. "Campaigns and Money: A Changing Role for the Political Parties?" In *The Parties Respond: Changes in the American Party System*, ed. L. Sandy Maisel. Boulder: Westview Press. Pp. 187–203.

Soule, John W. and James W. Clarke. 1970. "Amateurs and Professionals: A Study of Delegates to the 1968 Democratic National Convention." *American Political Science Review* 64(3): 888–898.

Spirova, Maria. 2007. *Political Parties in Post-Communist Societies: Formation, Persistence, and Change.* London: Palgrave Macmillan.

Spurek, Sylwia. 2002. Kobiety. Partie. Wybory. Łódź: Centrum Praw Kobiet.

Stark, David Charles and Lászlo Bruszt. 1998. *Post-Socialist Pathways and Property in East Central Europe.* Cambridge: Cambridge University Press.

Stegmaier, Mary and Klara Vlachová. 2009. "The Endurance of the Czech Communist Party." *Politics and Policy* 37(4): 799–820.

Stokes, Donald E. 1963. "Spatial Models of Party Competition." *American Political Science Review* 57(2): 368–377.

Stokes, Donald E. 1992. "Valence Politics." In *Electoral Politics*, ed. Dennis Kavanagh. Oxford: Clarendon Press. Pp. 141–164.

Stokes, Susan C. 2005. "Perverse Accountability: A Formal Model of Machine Politics with Evidence from Argentina." *American Political Science Review* 99(3): 315–325.

Stone, Walter D. and Alan I. Abramowitz. 1983. "Winning May Not Be Everything, But It's more than We Thought: Presidential Party Activists in 1980." *American Political Science Review* 77(4): 945–956.

Stoner-Weiss, Kathryn. 2001. "The Limited Reach of Russia's Party System: Under-Institutionalization in Dual Transitions." *Politics and Society* 29(3): 385–414.

Stránský, Jan Martin. 2004. "The Problem with Václav Klaus." *The New Presence* 1: 7–10.

Stratmann, Thomas and Martin Baur. 2002. "Plurality Rule, Proportional Representation, and the German Bundestag: How Incentives to Pork-Barrel Differ across Electoral Systems." *American Journal of Political Science* 46(3): 506–514.

Stroehlein, Andrew. 1998. "Klaus, One Year after the Fall." *Central Europe Review*, November 30.

Strom, Kaare. 1990. "A Behavioral Theory of Competitive Political Parties." *American Journal of Political Science* 34(2): 565–598.

Szabados, Krisztián and Péter Krekó. 2007. "Mi van még a csúcson túl? Hiller István politikusi portréja." *NOL*, November 26. http://www.nol.hu/archivum/archiv-471525.

Szabó, Tamás. 1995. "MDF – egy végre nem hajtott kampány." In *Magyarország politikai évkönyve 1994-ről*, eds. Péter Sándor and László Vass. Budapest: Demokrácia Kutatások Magyar Központja Alapítvány. CD-Rom.

Szarvas, László. 1998. "Sok mozgás közben helybenjárás – pártfarkciók '97." In *Magyarország politikai évkönyve 1997-ről*, eds. Péter Sándor and László Vass. Budapest: Demokrácia Kutatások Magyar Központja Alapítvány. CD-Rom.

Szczerbiak, Aleks. 1999a. "Testing Party Models in East-Central Europe: Local Party Organization in Postcommunist Poland." *Party Politics* 5(4): 525–537.

Szczerbiak, Aleks. 1999b. "The Impact of the 1998 Local Elections on the Emerging Polish Party System." *Journal of Communist Studies and Transition Politics* 15(3): 80–100.

Szczerbiak, Aleks. 2001a. "Party Structure and Organizational Development in Post-Communist Poland." *Journal of Communist Studies and Transition Politics* 17(2): 94–130.

Szczerbiak, Aleks. 2001b. "The Polish Peasant Party: A Mass Party in Postcommunist Eastern Europe?" *East European Politics & Societies* 15: 554–588.

Szczerbiak, Aleks. 2001c. "The 'Professionalization' of Party Campaigning in Post-Communist Poland." In *Party Development and Democratic Party Change in Post-Communist Europe*, ed. P. G. Lewis. London: Frank Cass. Pp. 78–92.

Szczerbiak, Aleks. 2001d. *Poles Together? The Emergence and Development of Political Parties in Postcommunist Poland*. Budapest: Central European University Press.

Szczerbiak, Aleks. 2004. "The Polish Centre-Right's (Last?) Best Hope: The Rise and Fall of Solidarity Electoral Action." *Journal of Communist Studies and Transition Politics* 20(3): 55–79.

Szekeres, Imre. 1995. "Magyar Szocialista Párt." In *Magyarország politikai évkönyve 1994-ről*, eds. Péter Sándor and László Vass. Budapest: Demokrácia Kutatások Magyar Központja Alapítvány. CD-Rom.

Szekeres, Imre and Péter Szeredi. 1999. "Látkép csata után." In *Magyarország politikai évkönyve 2000-ről*, eds. Péter Sándor and László Vass. Budapest: Demokrácia Kutatások Magyar Központja Alapítvány. CD-Rom.

Szlazsánszky, Ferenc. 2003. "Az Európai Parliament egy sóhivatal." *Hetek* 7(45), November 7. http://epa.oszk.hu/00800/00804/00297/44348.html.

Szobota, Zoltán. 2000. "Van-e liberálkonzervativizmus." *Hetek* 4(38), September 16. http://www.hetek.hu/riport/200009/van_e_liberalkonzervativizmus.

't Hart, Paul and John Uhr. (eds.). 2011. *How Power Changes Hands: Transition and Succession in Government*. Basingstoke: Palgrave Macmillan.

Taagepera, Rein. 2006. "Meteoric Trajectory: The Res Publica Party in Estonia." *Democratization* 13(1): 78–94.

Tallo, Ivar. 1996. "Daam roosas kleidis." *Postimees*, April 9.

Talving, Heikki. 1998a. "Isamaliit otsib oma ridadesse uusi inimesi." *Postimees*, August 16.

Talving, Heikki. 1998b. "Isamaliit taotleb valimisedu Mart Laari juhtimisel." *Postimees*, October 25.

Tamás, Tibor. 2002. "Grespik: a MIÉP gondjait Papolczy távozása sem oldaná meg." *NOL*, December 30. http://nol.hu/archivum/archiv-92670.

Tamási Orosz, János. 2006. "Nem gondoljuk azt, hogy mi vagyunk a kenyér I." *MKDSZ*, February 23. http://mkdsz.hu/content/view/647/202/.

Tamm, Merike. 2009. "Michal seadis Reformierakonna eesm'rgiks 10000 liiget." *Postimees*, December 12.

Tammer, Enno. 1995a. "Isamaliit on teel oppositisiooni." *Postimees*, December 7.

Tammer, Enno. 1995b. "Sotsid seisavad valiku ees." *Postimees*, December 18.

Tammer, Enno. 1996a. "Keskerakonna esimees loodab veel kongressile." *Postimees*, March 16.

Tammer, Enno. 1996b. "Koonderakond vahetab peasekretäri." *Postimees*, March 27.

Tammer, Enno. 1996c. "Andres Tarand parteistus." *Postimees*, May 7.

Tammer, Enno. 1997. "Valimisliidud poliitilisel vaekausil." *Postimees*, January 16.

Tan, Alexander C. 2000. *Members, Organization, Performance: An Empirical Analysis of the Impact of Party Membership Size*. Aldershot: Ashgate.

Tänavsuu, Hille. 2004. "Uurijad ennustavad Reformierkonnale edu." *Pärnu Postimees*, November 23.

Tarand, Andres. 1999a. "Kaks pead või üks pea." *Postimees*, May 22.

Tarand, Andres. 1999b. "Ebaõnn ei löö rööpaist välja." *Postimees*, October 28.

Tarand, Andres. 2002. "Vara veel hingekella lüüa." *Põhjarannik*, November 9.

Tarand, Kaarel. 1997. "Selgrootute partei." *Luup* 16(47), August 4.

TASR News Agency. 2001. "Slovak Premier Drafts Amendments to Approved Territorial Reform." TASR News Agency, July 23.

Tavits, Margit. 2005. "The Development of Stable Party Support: Electoral Dynamics in Post-Communist Europe." *American Journal of Political Science* 49: 283–298.

Tavits, Margit. 2008a. "Party Systems in the Making: The Emergence and Success of New Parties in New Democracies." *British Journal of Political Science* 38(1): 113–133.

Tavits, Margit. 2008b. "On the Linkage between Electoral Volatility and Party System Instability in Central and Eastern Europe." *European Journal of Political Research* 47(5): 537–555.

Tavits, Margit. 2009a. "The Making of Mavericks: Local Loyalties and Party Defections." *Comparative Political Studies* 42(6): 793–815.

Tavits, Margit. 2009b. "Party Organizations and Electoral Performance in Post-Communist Europe." Paper presented at the Annual Meeting of the American Political Science Association, Toronto, September 3–6.

Tavits, Margit. 2009c. "Geographically Targeted Spending: Exploring the Electoral Strategies of Incumbent Governments." *European Political Science Review* 1(1): 103–123.

Tavits, Margit. 2009d. *Presidents with Prime Ministers: Do Direct Elections Matter?* Oxford: Oxford University Press.

Tavits, Margit. 2010. "The Effect of Local Ties on Electoral Success and Parliamentary Behavior: The Case of Estonia." *Party Politics* 16(2): 215–235.

Tavits, Margit. 2012. "Party Organizational Strength and Party Unity in Post-Communist Europe." *European Political Science Review* 4(3): 409–431.

Tavits, Margit and Taavi Annus. 2006. "Learning to Make Votes Count: The Role of Democratic Experience." *Electoral Studies* 25(1): 72–90.

Tavits, Margit and Natalia Letki. 2009. "When Left Is Right: Party Ideology and Policy in Post-Communist Europe." *American Political Science Review* 103(4): 555–569.

Thames, Frank C. 2005. "A House Divided: Party Strength and the Mandate Divide in Hungary, Russia and Ukraine." *Comparative Political Studies* 38(3): 282–303.

Tjosvold, Dean and Barbara Wisse (eds.). 2009. *Power and Interdependence in Organizations.* Cambridge: Cambridge University Press.

Toka, Gabor. 1998. "Party Appeals and Voter Loyalty in New Democracies." *Political Studies* 46: 589–610.

Tomz, Michael, Joshua A. Tucker, and Jason Wittenberg. 2002. "An Easy and Accurate Regression Model for Multiparty Electoral Data." *Political Analysis* 10(1): 66–83.

Toole, James. 2003. "Straddling the East-West Divide: Party Organisation and Communist Legacies in East Central Europe." *Europe-Asia Studies* 55(1): 101–118.

Toomla, Rein. 1999. *Eesti Erakonnad.* Tallinn: Estonian Encyclopedia Press.

Tootsen, Toivo. 1998. *Keskerakond kohalikes omavalitsustes.* Tallinn: TEA Press.

Tóth, Csaba and Gábor Török. 2002. "SZDSZ: stagnálás vagy stabilizálódás." In *Magyarország politikai évkönyve 2001-ről,* eds. Péter Sándor and László Vass. Budapest: Demokrácia Kutatások Magyar Központja Alapítvány. CD-Rom

Třeštík, Michael, (ed.). 2005. *Kdo je kdo. Osobnosti české současnosti.* Prague: Agentura Kdo je kdo.

Tucker, Joshua A. 2006. *Regional Economic Voting: Russia, Poland, Hungary, Slovakia, and the Czech Republic, 1990–1999.* Cambridge: Cambridge University Press.

Turay, Abdul. 2009. "Savisaar – Eesti seksikaim mees." *Postimees,* September 2.

Tworzecki, Hubert. 2003. *Learning to Choose: Electoral Politics in East-Central Europe.* Stanford: Stanford University Press.

Ülavere, Raimo. 2007. "Ühe erakonna lõpuagoonia." *Postimees,* October 10.

Urbanek, Mariusz. 2002. "Human Resources Boss." *World News Connection,* November 16.

Vachudová, Milada Anna. 1993. "Divisions in the Czech Communist Party." *RFE/RL Report*, September 17.

Vahe, Urmas. 2011. "Kas Evelin Sepp kõrgest poliitmängust väljas?" *Õhtuleht*, January 18.

Vaher, Ken-Marti. 2001. "Uus erakond otsib terviklahendusi." *Postimees*, September 28.

Vähi, Tiit. 2006. "Tiit Vähi: Peaminister 30.01.1992–21.10.1992; 17.04.1995–06.11.1995; 06.11.1995–12.1996; 12.1996–17.03.1997." Public lecture delivered at Nord University, Tallinn, Estonia, March 29.

Valner, Sulev. 2003. "Ivari Padar: Olen nõus olema mudavasakpoolne." *Maaleht*, February 13.

Van Biezen, Ingrid. 2003. *Political Parties in New Democracies: Party Organization in Southern and East-Central Europe*. New York: Palgrave.

Van Buuren, Stef and Karin Groothuis-Oudshoorn. 2011. "MICE: Multivariate Imputation by Chained Equations in R." *Journal of Statistical Software* 45(3): 1–67.

Van der Brug, Wouter and Anthony Mughan. 2007. "Charisma, Leader Effects and Support for Right-Wing Populist Parties." *Party Politics* 13(1): 29–51.

Varga, Domokos György. 1996. "A Bokros éve." In *Magyarország politikai évkönyve 1995-ről*, eds. Péter Sándor and László Vass. Budapest: Demokrácia Kutatások Magyar Központja Alapítvány. CD-Rom.

Veidemann, Andra. 1996. "Keskerakonnale mõeldes." *Postimees*, March 28.

Vidos, Tibor. 1994. "The Gentlemanly Way to Do Insider Party Politics." *Budapest Business Journal*, September 16.

Villem, Andrus. 1996. "KMÜ satelliiterakonnad kohalike valimiste eel." *Postimees*, May 27.

Villem, Andrus. 1998. "Ellujäämistahe ja enesehävitustung." *Postimees*, October 12.

Volkens, Andrea, Onawa Lacewell, Sven Regel, Henrike Schultze, and Annika Werner. 2010. *The Manifesto Data Collection. Manifesto Project (MRG/CMP/MARPOR)*. Berlin: Wissenschaftszentrum Berlin für Sozialforschung (WZB).

Vöörmann, Mai. 2001. "Koonderakond on surnud!" *Postimees*, August 6.

Waller, Michael. 1995. "Adaptation of the Former Communist Parties of East-Central Europe: A Case of Social-Democratization?" *Party Politics* 1(4): 473–490.

Ward, Ian. 2003. "'Localizing the National' The Rediscovery and Reshaping of Local Campaign in Australia." *Party Politics* 9(5): 583–600.

Ware, Alan. 1992. "Activist–Leader Relations and the Structure of Political Parties: 'Exchange' Models and Vote-Seeking Behaviour in Parties." *British Journal of Political Science* 22(1): 71–92.

Waterbury, Myra A. 2006. "Internal Exclusion, External Inclusion: Diaspora Politics and Party-Building Strategies in Post-Communist Hungary." *East European Politics & Societies* 20: 483–515.

Webb, Paul D. 1995. "Are British Political Parties in Decline?" *Party Politics* 1(3): 299–322.

Weiss, Martin. 2003. "The KDU-CSL S Josef Lux Redux." *Prague Business Journal*, December 1.

Wellhofer, E. Spencer. 1979. "The Effectiveness of Party Organization: A Cross-National, Time Series Analysis." *European Journal of Political Research* 7(2): 205–244.

Whiteley, Paul F., Patrick Seyd and Jeremy Richardson. 1994. *True Blues: The Politics of Conservative Party Membership*. Oxford: Oxford University Press.

Whiteley, Paul F. and Patrick Seyd. 1994. "Local Party Campaigning and Electoral Mobilization in Britain." *Journal of Politics* 56(1): 242–252.

Widfeldt, Anders. 1999. *Linking Parties with People? Party Membership in Sweden 1960–1997*. Aldershot: Ashgate.

Wildavsky, Aaron. 1965. "The Goldwater Phenomenon: Purists, Politicians and the Two-Party System." *Review of Politics* 27(3): 386–413.

Wilson, James Q. 1962. *The Amateur Democrat*. Chicago: University of Chicago Press.

Wolinetz, Steven B. 1990. "The Transformation of West European Party Systems." In *The West European Party System*, ed. Peter Mair. Oxford: Oxford University Press. Pp. 218–231.

Wooldridge, Jeffrey. 2002. *Introductory Econometrics*. Mason: Cengage Learning.

World News Connection. 2002. "Senator Topolanek Explains Bid to Succeed Vaclav Klaus as Leader of Czech ODS." November 15.

Wyman, Matthew, Stephen White, Bill Miller, and Paul Heywood. 1995. "The Place of 'Party' in Post-Communist Europe." *Party Politics* 1(4): 535–548.

Zádori, Zsolt. 2007. "Kuncze után, de nem szabadon." January 19. http://hvg.hu/itthon/20070119_kuncze_koka_fodor_szdsz.

Zaluska, Wojciech. 1995. "Balcerowicz Wants Party Discipline." *Polish News Bulletin*, May 4.

Zaluska, Wojciech. 2008. "Napieralski Learns During Lunches." *Gazeta Wyborcza*, August 1.

Ziblatt, Daniel F. 1998. "The Adaptation of Ex-Communist Parties to Post-Communist East Central Europe: A Comparative Study of the East German and Hungarian Ex-Communist Parties." *Communist and Post-Communist Studies* 31(2): 119–137.

Zielinski, Jakub. 2002. "Translating Social Cleavages into Party Systems: The Significance of New Democracies." *World Politics* 54(2): 184–211.

Zielinski, Jakub, Kazimierz M. Slomczynski, and Goldie Shabad. 2005. "Electoral Control in New Democracies: The Perverse Incentives of Fluid Party Systems." *World Politics* 57(3): 365–395.

Zubek, Radoslaw. 2008. "Parties, Rules and Government Legislative Control in Central Europe: The Case of Poland." *Communist and Post-Communist Studies* 41(2): 147–161.

Zubek, Voytek. 1995. "The Phoenix Out of the Ashes: The Rise to Power of Poland's Post-Communist SdRP." *Communist and Post-Communist Studies* 28(3): 275–306.

Index